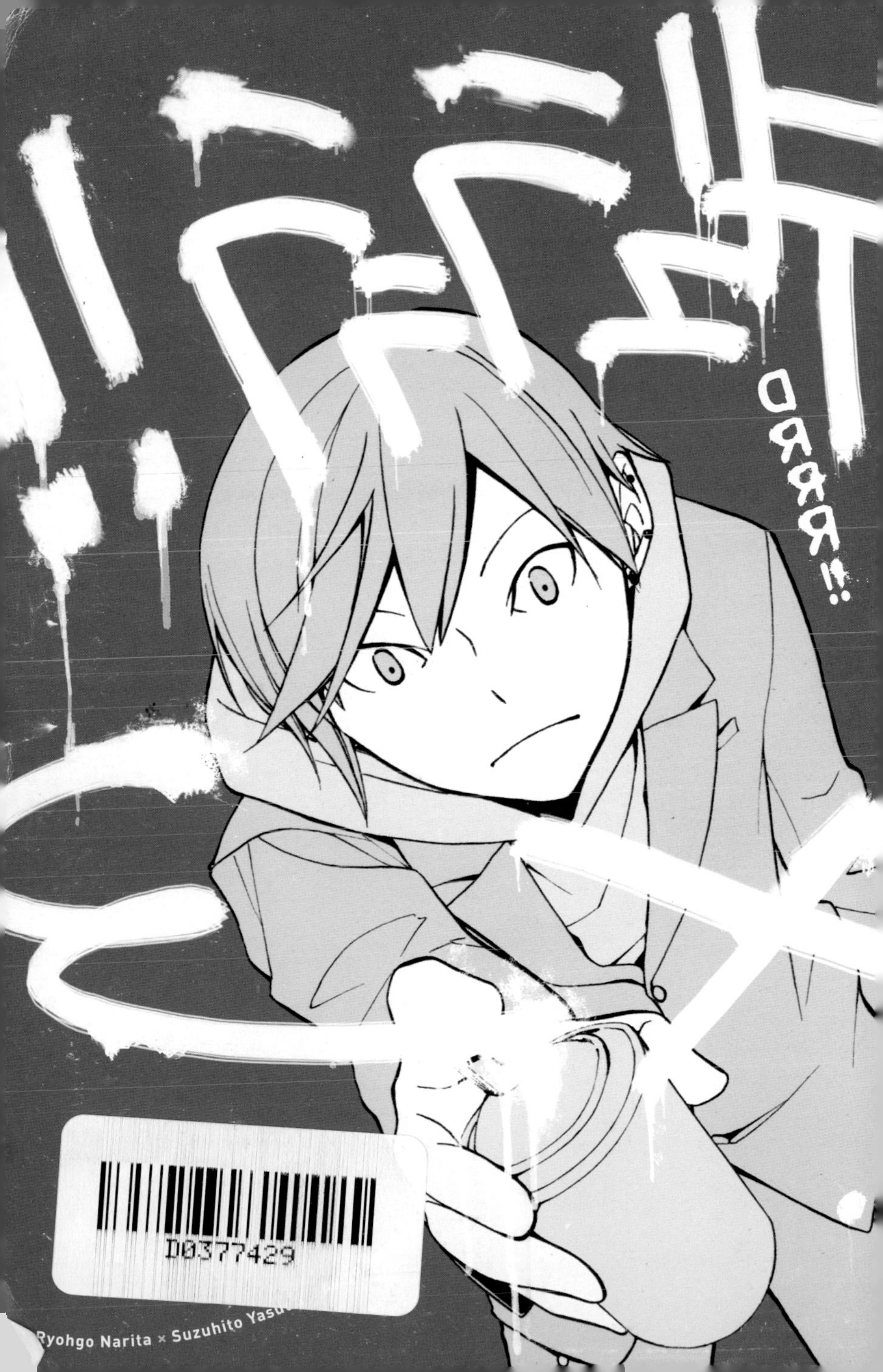
DRRRR!!
Ryohgo Narita × Suzuhito Yasu

Contents

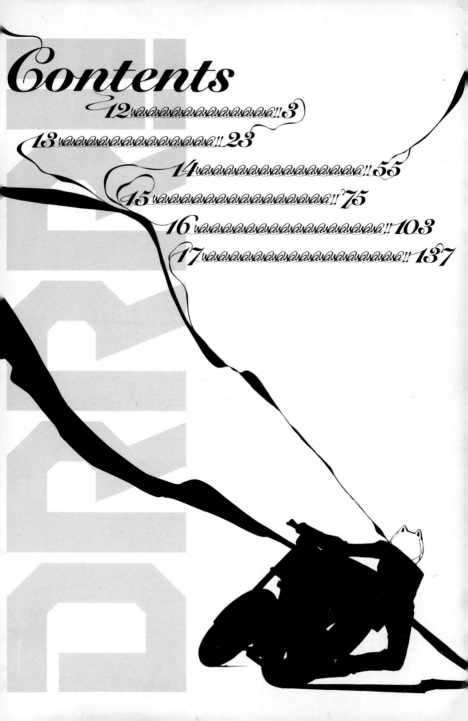

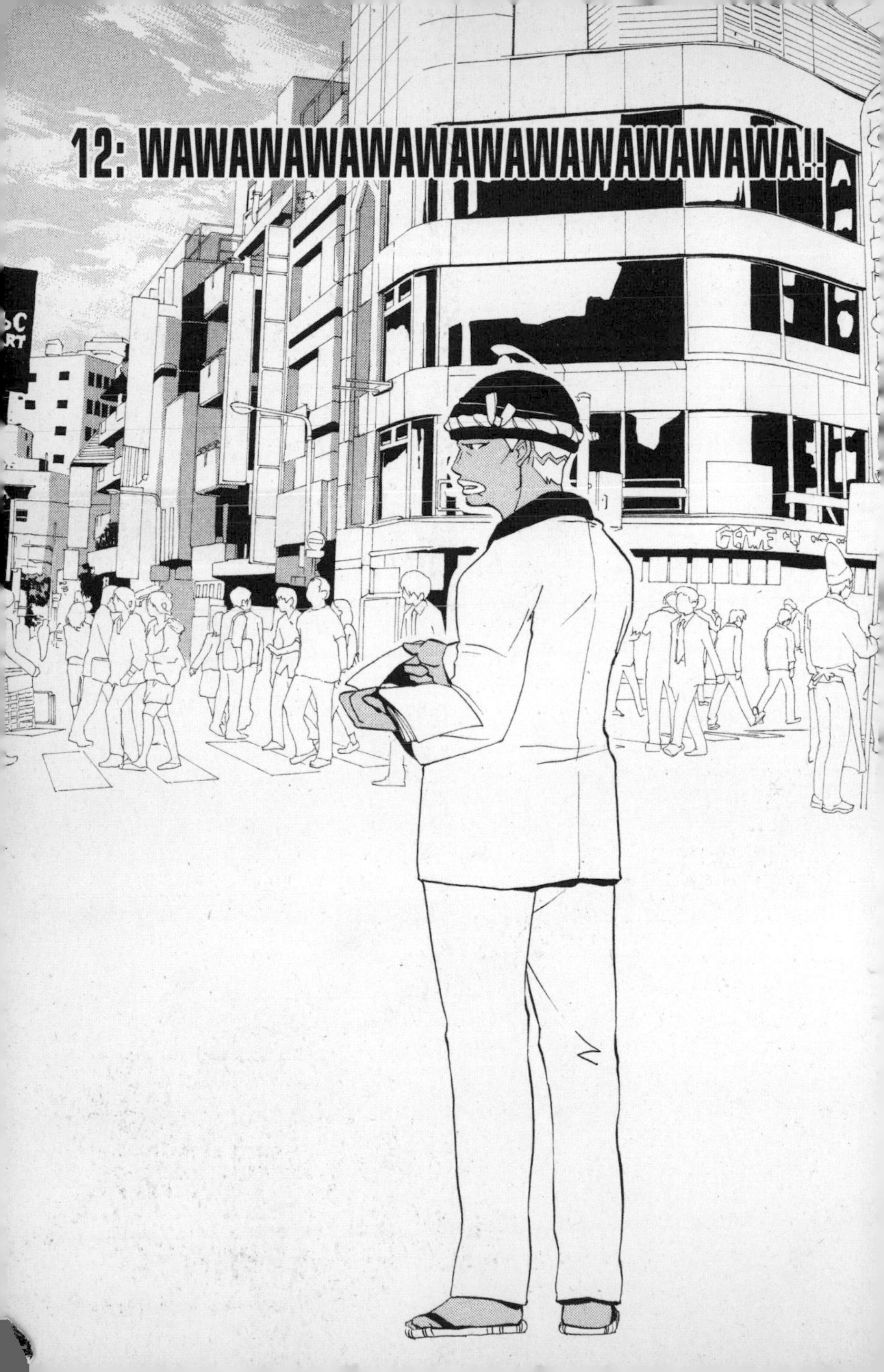
12: WAWAWAWAWAWAWAWAWAWAWAWA!!
GAME

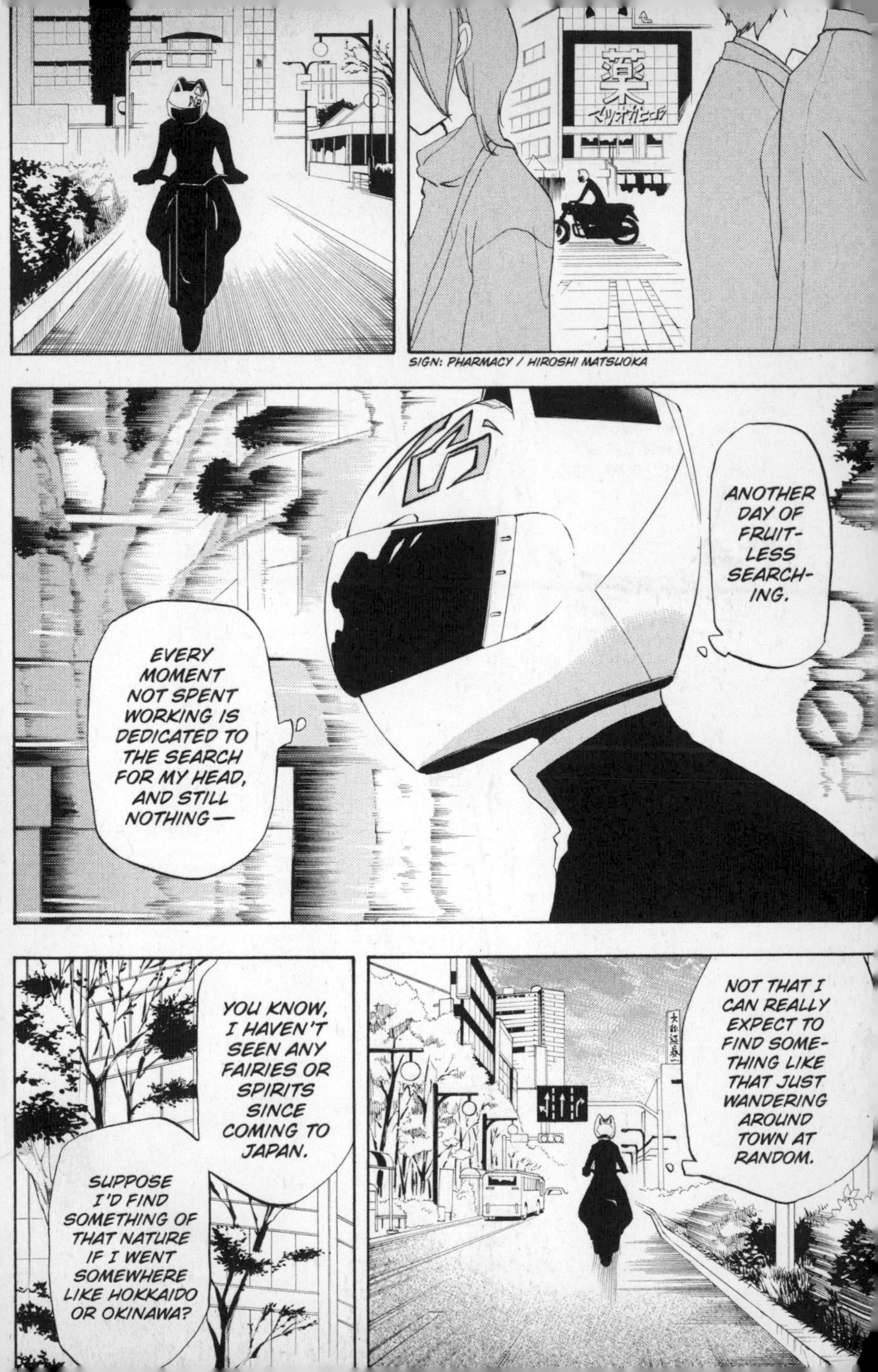
SIGN: PHARMACY / HIROSHI MATSUOKA
ANOTHER DAY OF FRUIT-LESS SEARCH-ING.
EVERY MOMENT NOT SPENT WORKING IS DEDICATED TO THE SEARCH FOR MY HEAD, AND STILL NOTHING—
NOT THAT I CAN REALLY EXPECT TO FIND SOME-THING LIKE THAT JUST WANDERING AROUND TOWN AT RANDOM.
YOU KNOW, I HAVEN'T SEEN ANY FAIRIES OR SPIRITS SINCE COMING TO JAPAN.
SUPPOSE I'D FIND SOMETHING OF THAT NATURE IF I WENT SOMEWHERE LIKE HOKKAIDO OR OKINAWA?

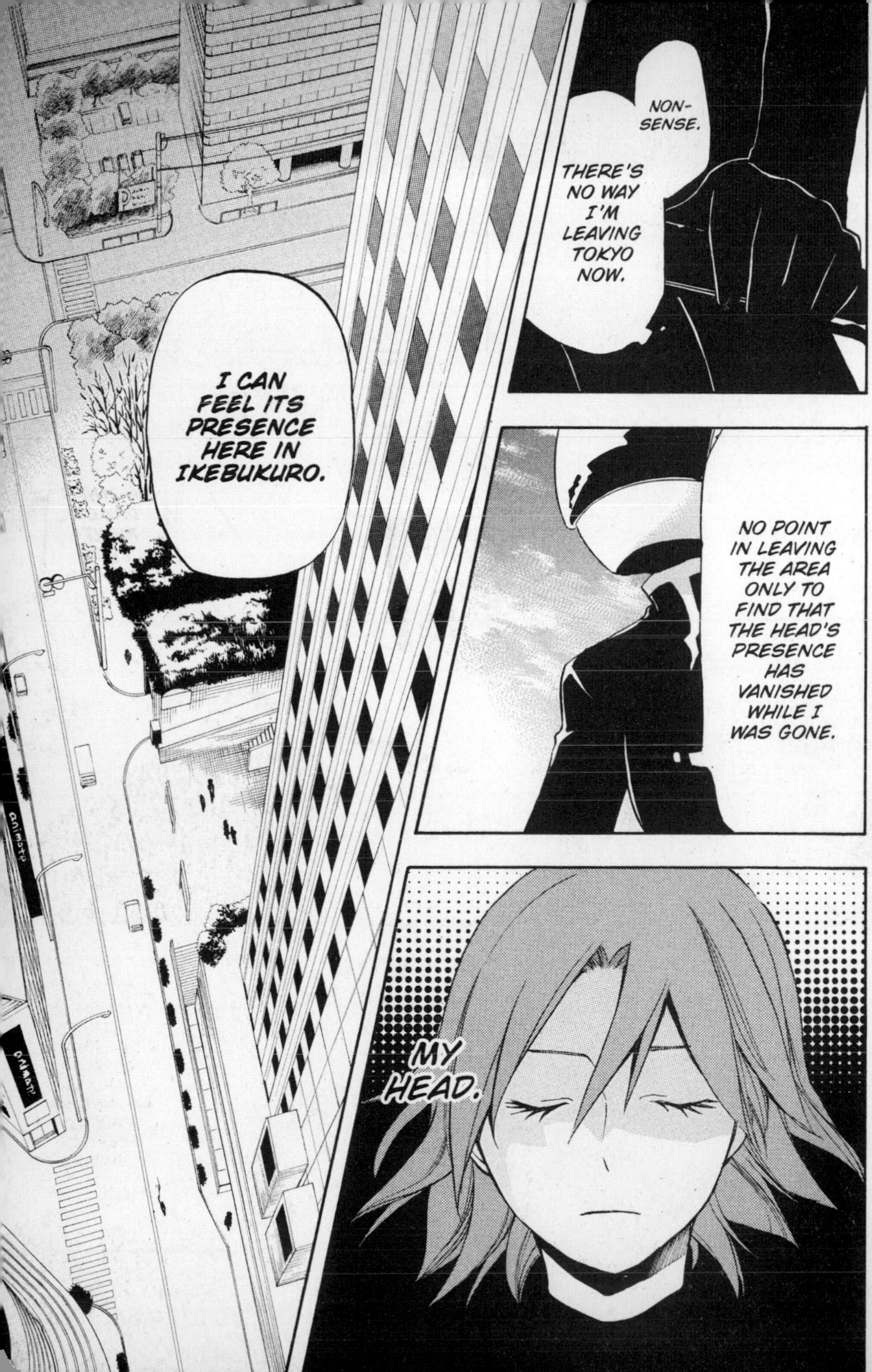
NON-SENSE.
THERE'S NO WAY I'M LEAVING TOKYO NOW.
NO POINT IN LEAVING THE AREA ONLY TO FIND THAT THE HEAD'S PRESENCE HAS VANISHED WHILE I WAS GONE.
MY HEAD.
I CAN FEEL ITS PRESENCE HERE IN IKEBUKURO.

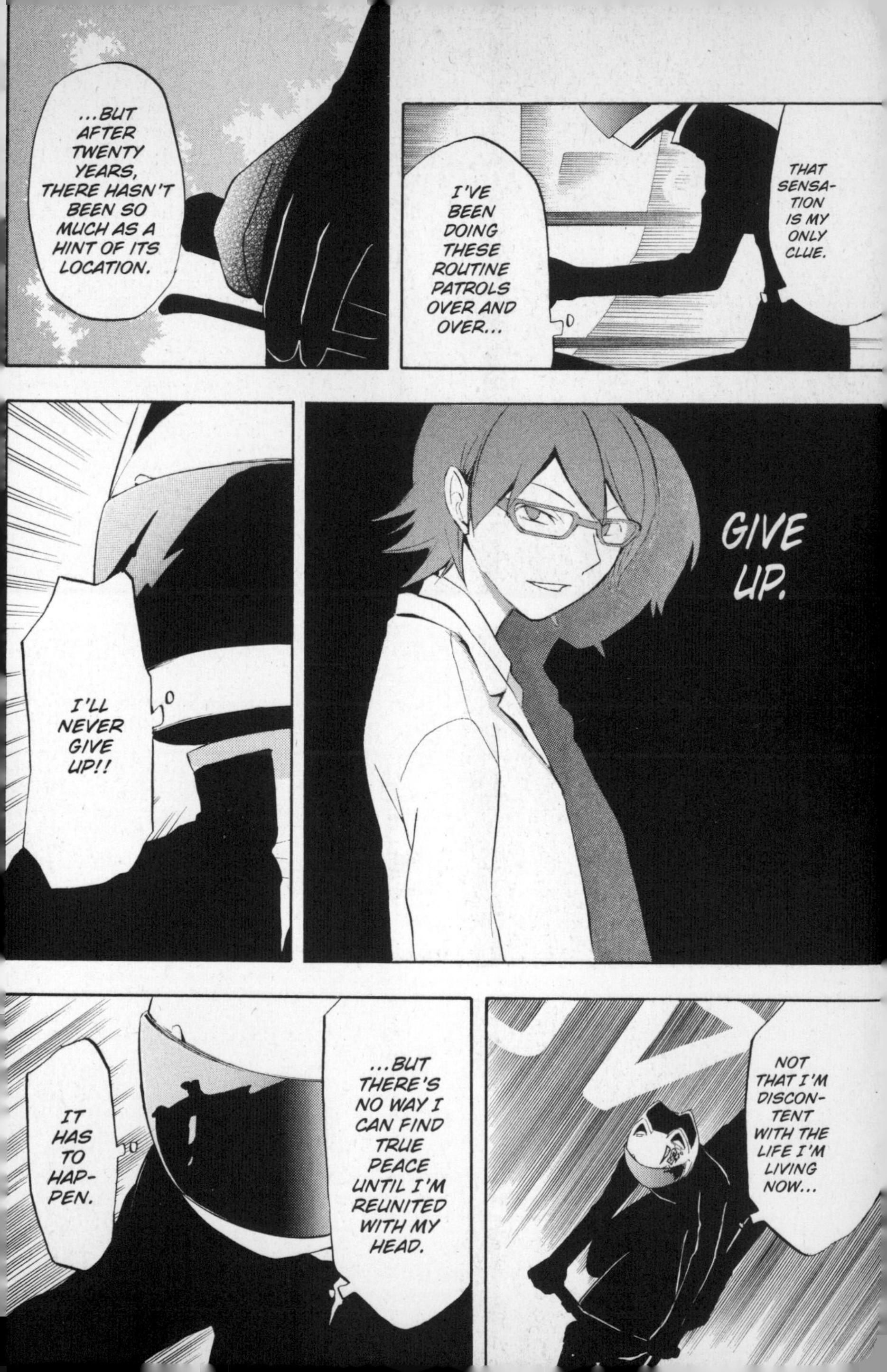
THAT SENSA-TION IS MY ONLY CLUE.
I'VE BEEN DOING THESE ROUTINE PATROLS OVER AND OVER...
...BUT AFTER TWENTY YEARS, THERE HASN'T BEEN SO MUCH AS A HINT OF ITS LOCATION.
GIVE UP.
I'LL NEVER GIVE UP!!
NOT THAT I'M DISCON-TENT WITH THE LIFE I'M LIVING NOW...
...BUT THERE'S NO WAY I CAN FIND TRUE PEACE UNTIL I'M REUNITED WITH MY HEAD.
IT HAS TO HAP-PEN.

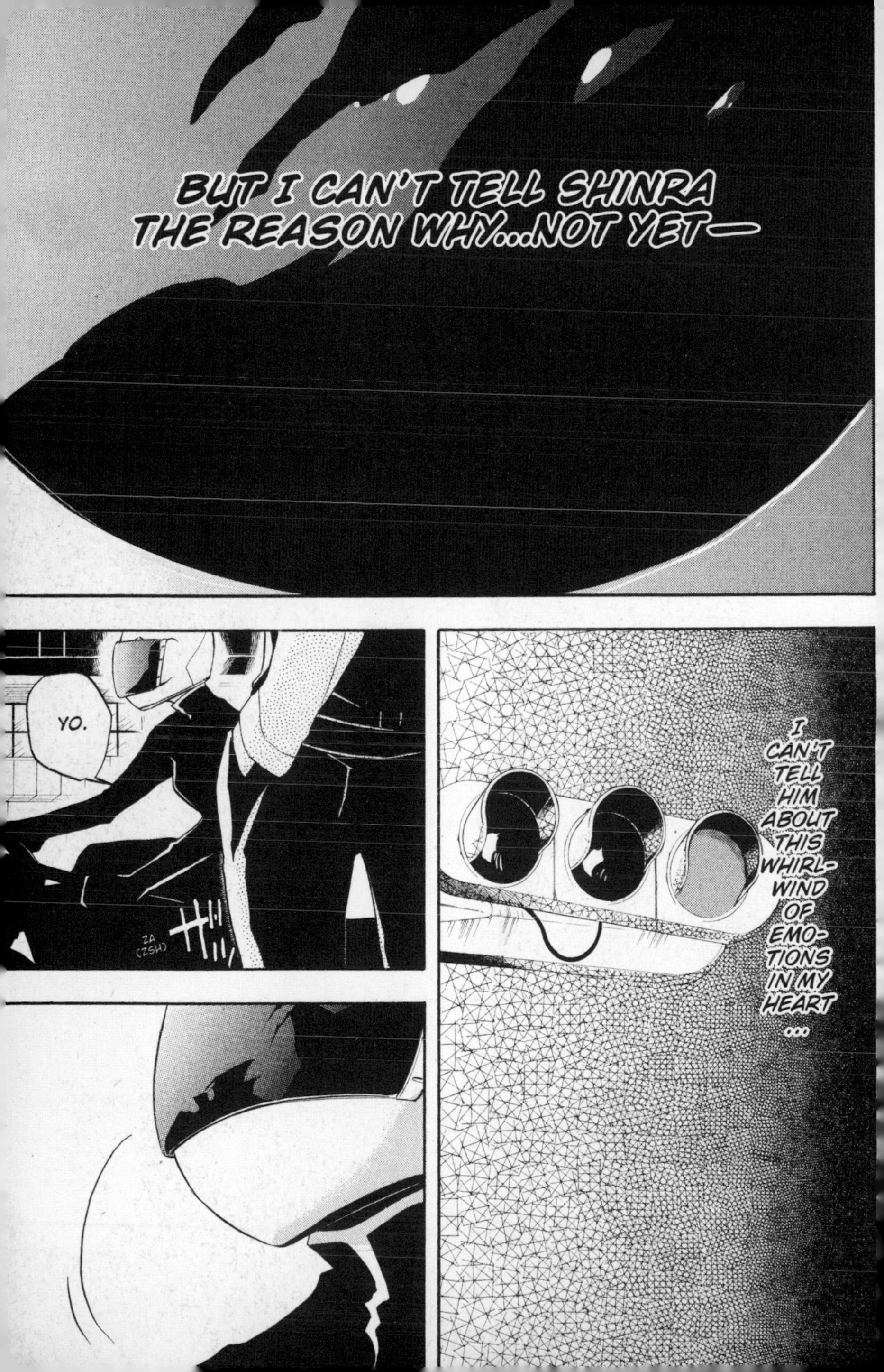
BUT I CAN'T TELL SHINRA THE REASON WHY...NOT YET—
I CAN'T TELL HIM ABOUT THIS WHIRLWIND OF EMOTIONS IN MY HEART...
YO.
ZA (ZSH)

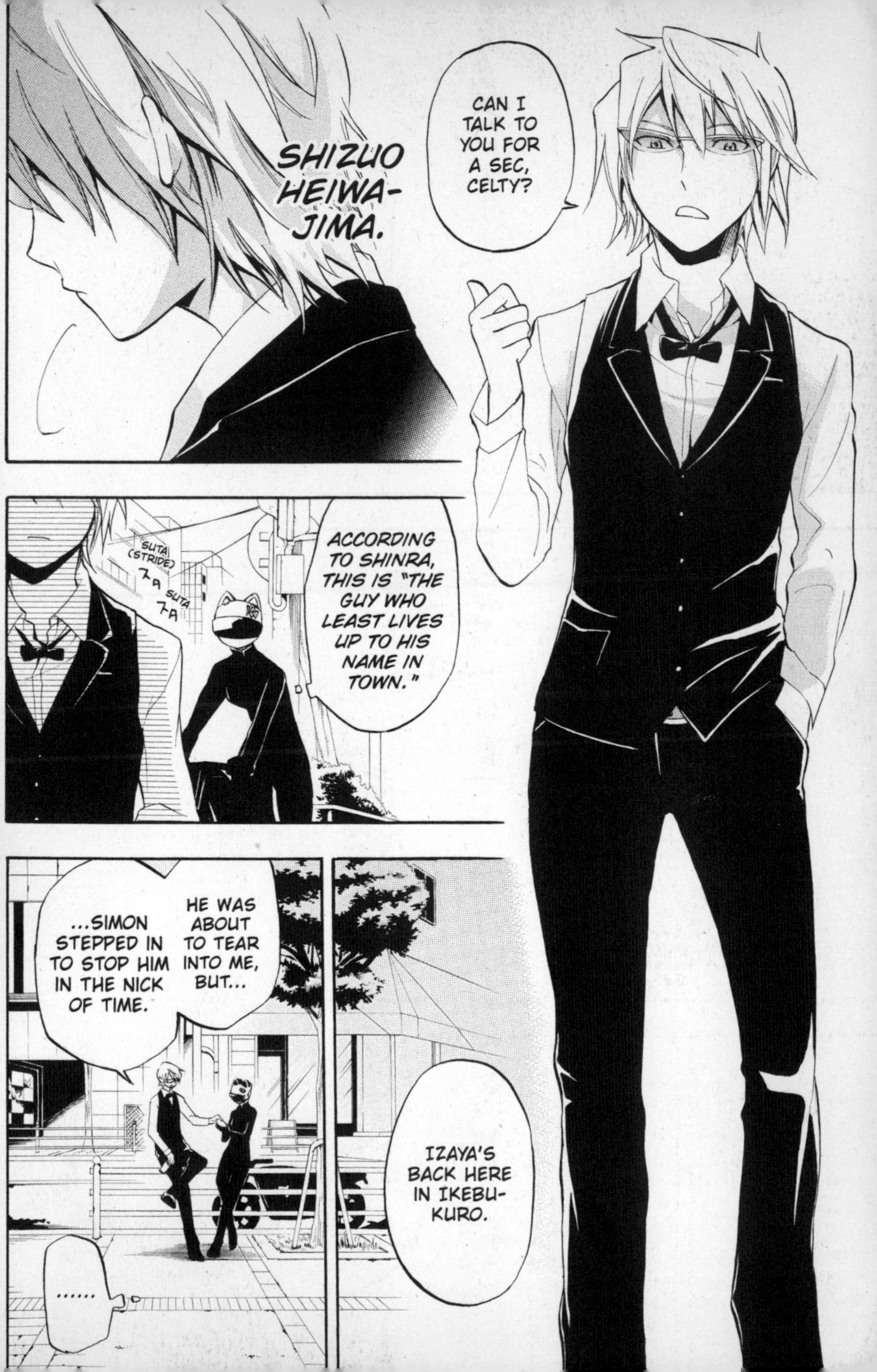
CAN I TALK TO YOU FOR A SEC, CELTY?
IZAYA'S BACK HERE IN IKEBUKURO.
SHIZUO HEIWA-JIMA.
SUTA (STRIDE)
SUTA
ACCORDING TO SHINRA, THIS IS "THE GUY WHO LEAST LIVES UP TO HIS NAME IN TOWN."
HE WAS ABOUT TO TEAR INTO ME, BUT...
...SIMON STEPPED IN TO STOP HIM IN THE NICK OF TIME.
......

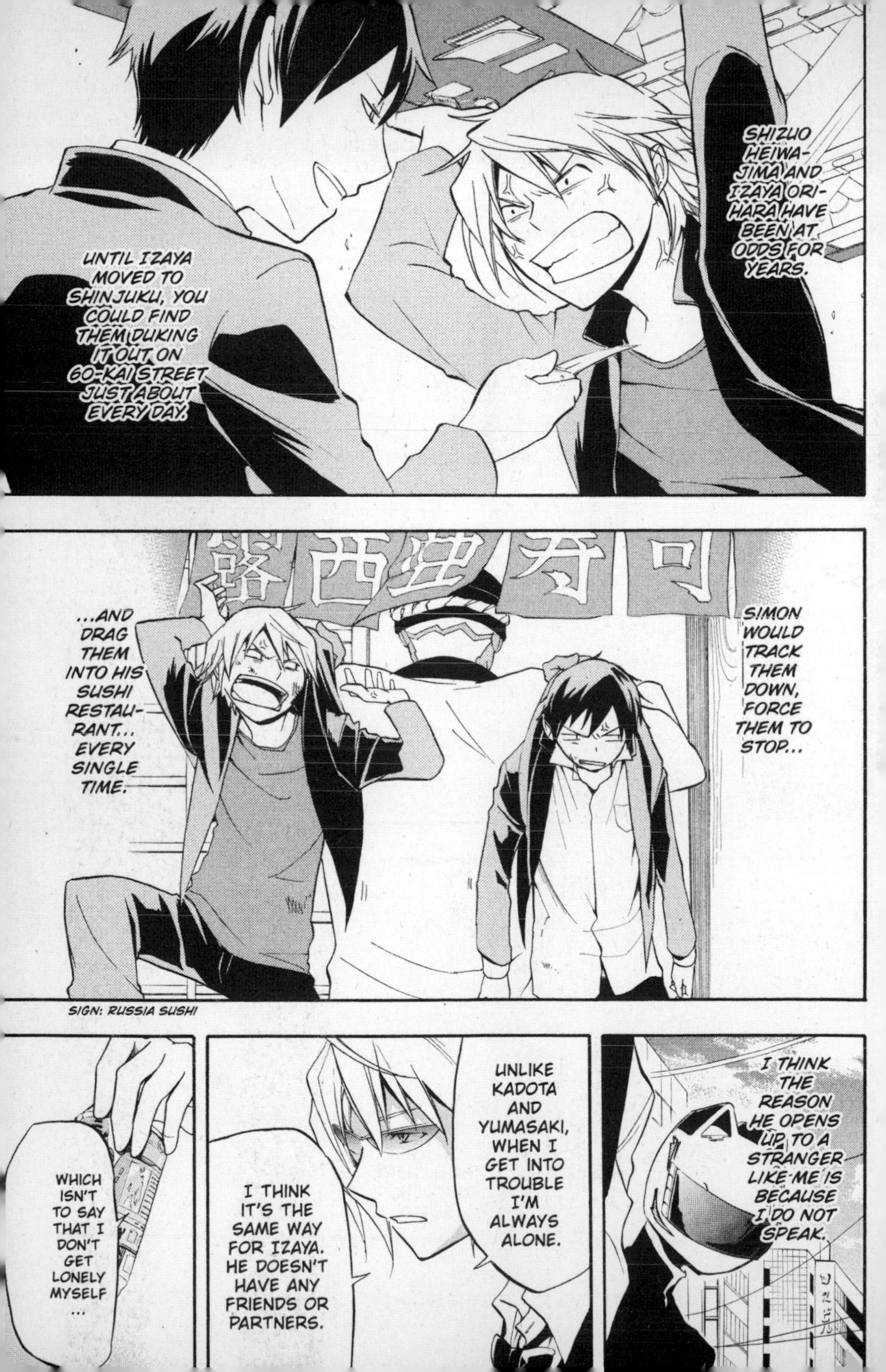
SHIZUO HEIWAJIMA AND IZAYA ORIHARA HAVE BEEN AT ODDS FOR YEARS.
UNTIL IZAYA MOVED TO SHINJUKU, YOU COULD FIND THEM DUKING IT OUT ON 60-KAI STREET JUST ABOUT EVERY DAY.
SIMON WOULD TRACK THEM DOWN, FORCE THEM TO STOP...
...AND DRAG THEM INTO HIS SUSHI RESTAURANT... EVERY SINGLE TIME.
SIGN: RUSSIA SUSHI
I THINK THE REASON HE OPENS UP TO A STRANGER LIKE ME IS BECAUSE I DO NOT SPEAK.
UNLIKE KADOTA AND YUMASAKI, WHEN I GET INTO TROUBLE I'M ALWAYS ALONE.
I THINK IT'S THE SAME WAY FOR IZAYA. HE DOESN'T HAVE ANY FRIENDS OR PARTNERS.
WHICH ISN'T TO SAY THAT I DON'T GET LONELY MYSELF...

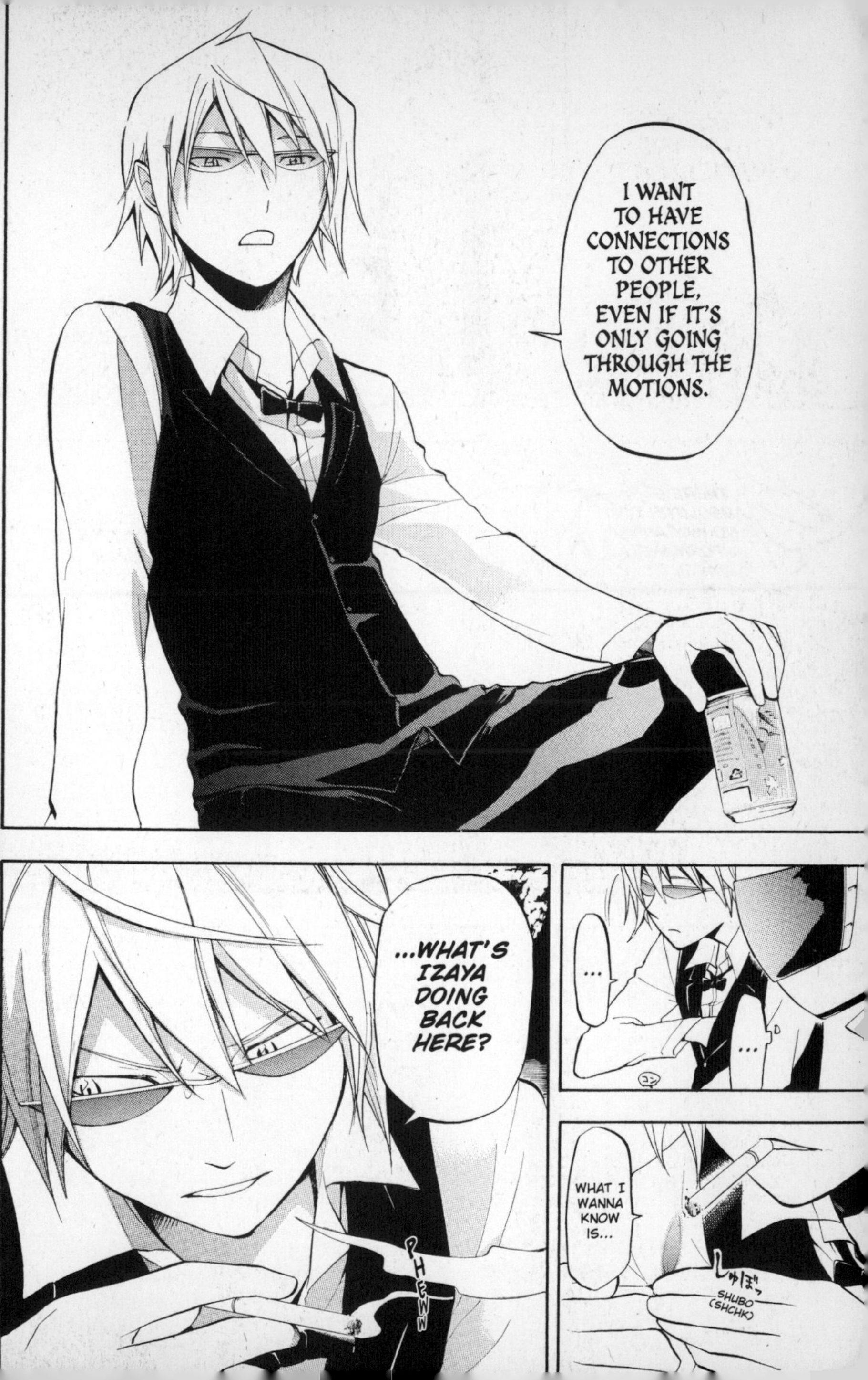
I WANT TO HAVE CONNECTIONS TO OTHER PEOPLE, EVEN IF IT'S ONLY GOING THROUGH THE MOTIONS.
...
...
コン
WHAT I WANNA KNOW IS...
しゅぼっ
SHUBO (SHCHK)
...WHAT'S IZAYA DOING BACK HERE?
PHEWW

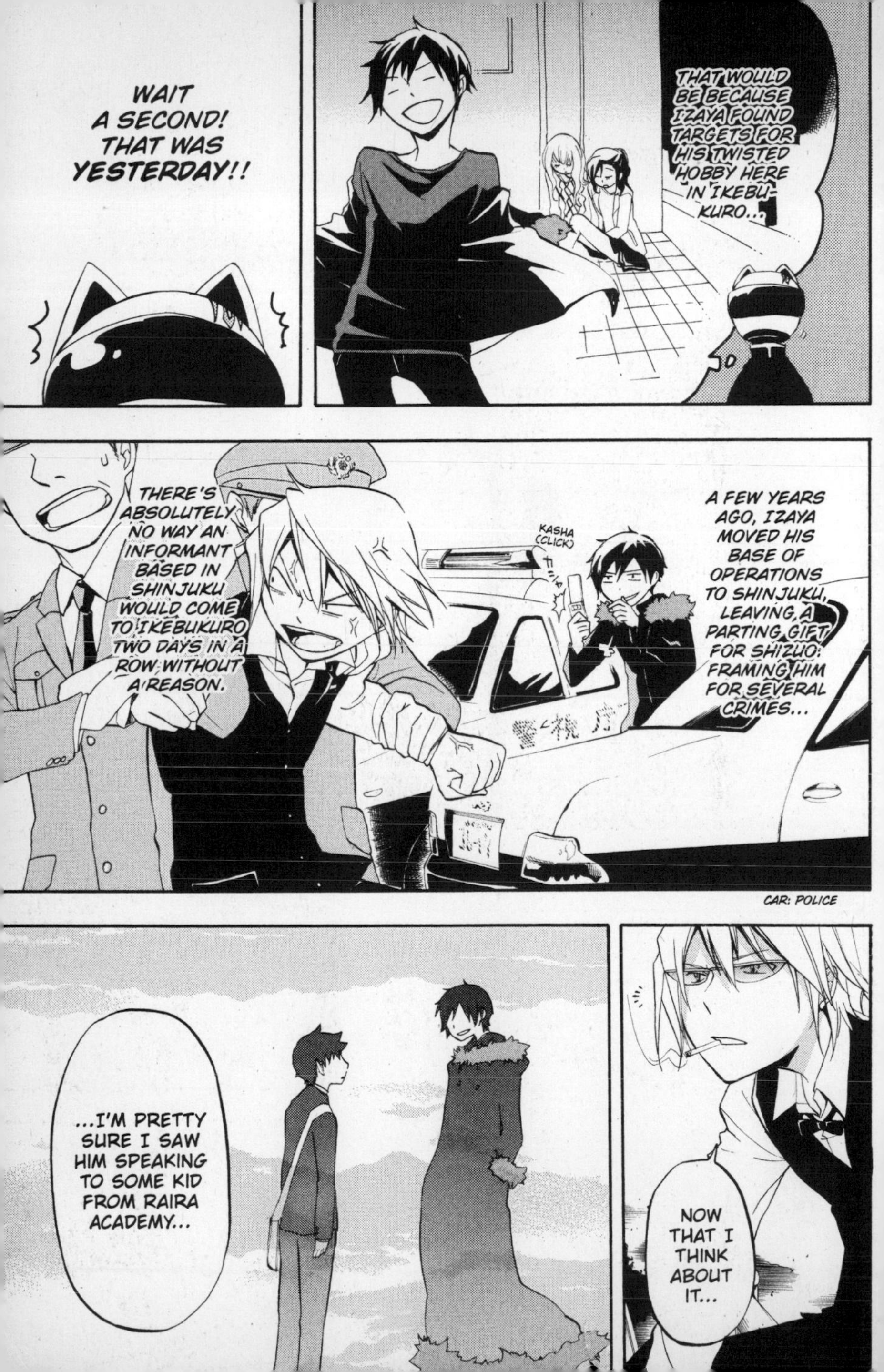
THAT WOULD BE BECAUSE IZAYA FOUND TARGETS FOR HIS TWISTED HOBBY HERE IN IKEBU-KURO...
WAIT A SECOND! THAT WAS YESTERDAY!!
A FEW YEARS AGO, IZAYA MOVED HIS BASE OF OPERATIONS TO SHINJUKU, LEAVING A PARTING GIFT FOR SHIZUO: FRAMING HIM FOR SEVERAL CRIMES...
KASHA (CLICK)
THERE'S ABSOLUTELY NO WAY AN INFORMANT BASED IN SHINJUKU WOULD COME TO IKEBUKURO TWO DAYS IN A ROW WITHOUT A REASON.
CAR: POLICE
NOW THAT I THINK ABOUT IT...
...I'M PRETTY SURE I SAW HIM SPEAKING TO SOME KID FROM RAIRA ACADEMY...

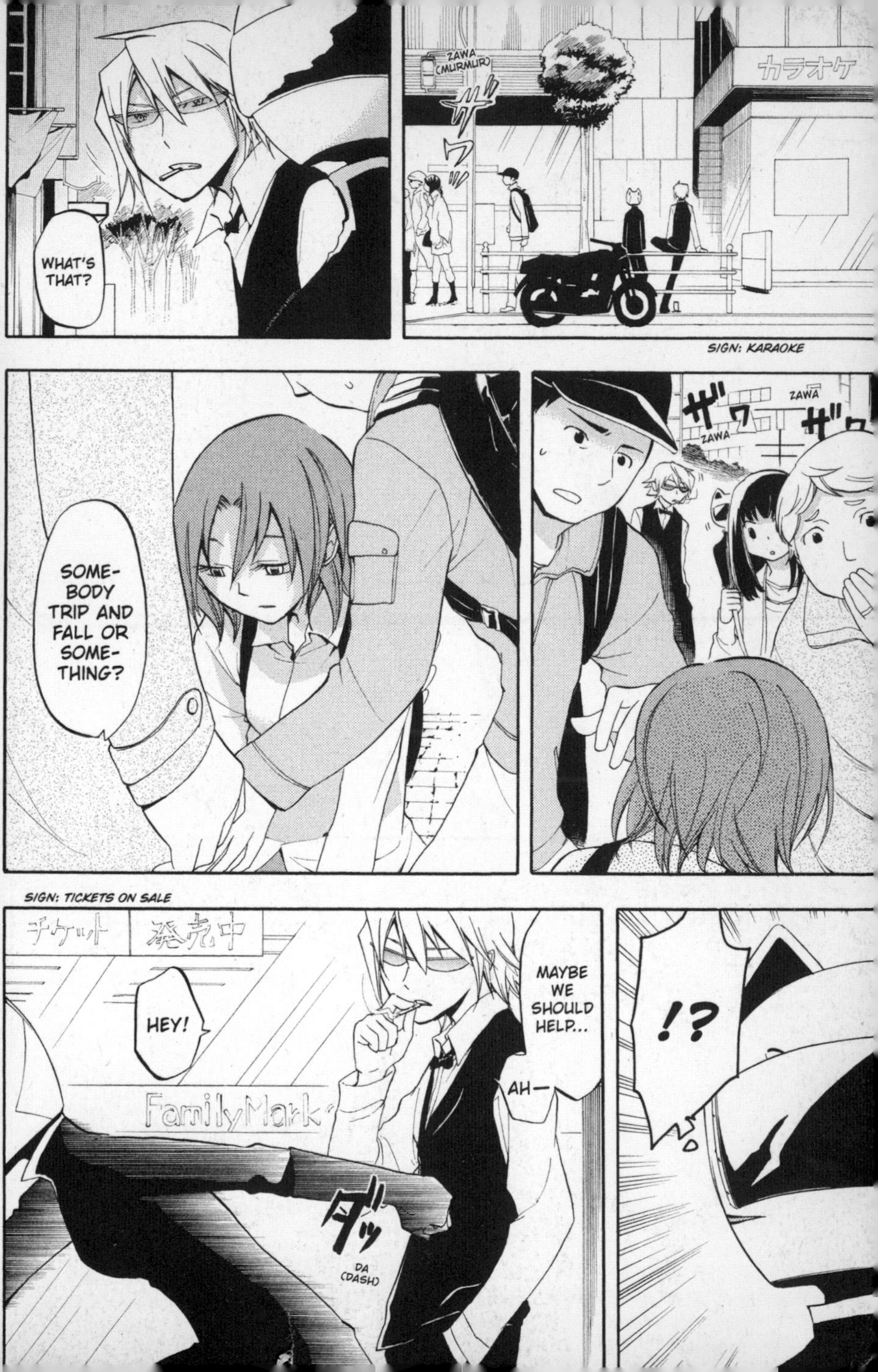
ZAWA (MURMUR)
SIGN: KARAOKE
WHAT'S THAT?
ZAWA
ZAWA
SOME-BODY TRIP AND FALL OR SOME-THING?
!?
SIGN: TICKETS ON SALE
MAYBE WE SHOULD HELP...
HEY!
AH—
FamilyMark
DA (DASH)

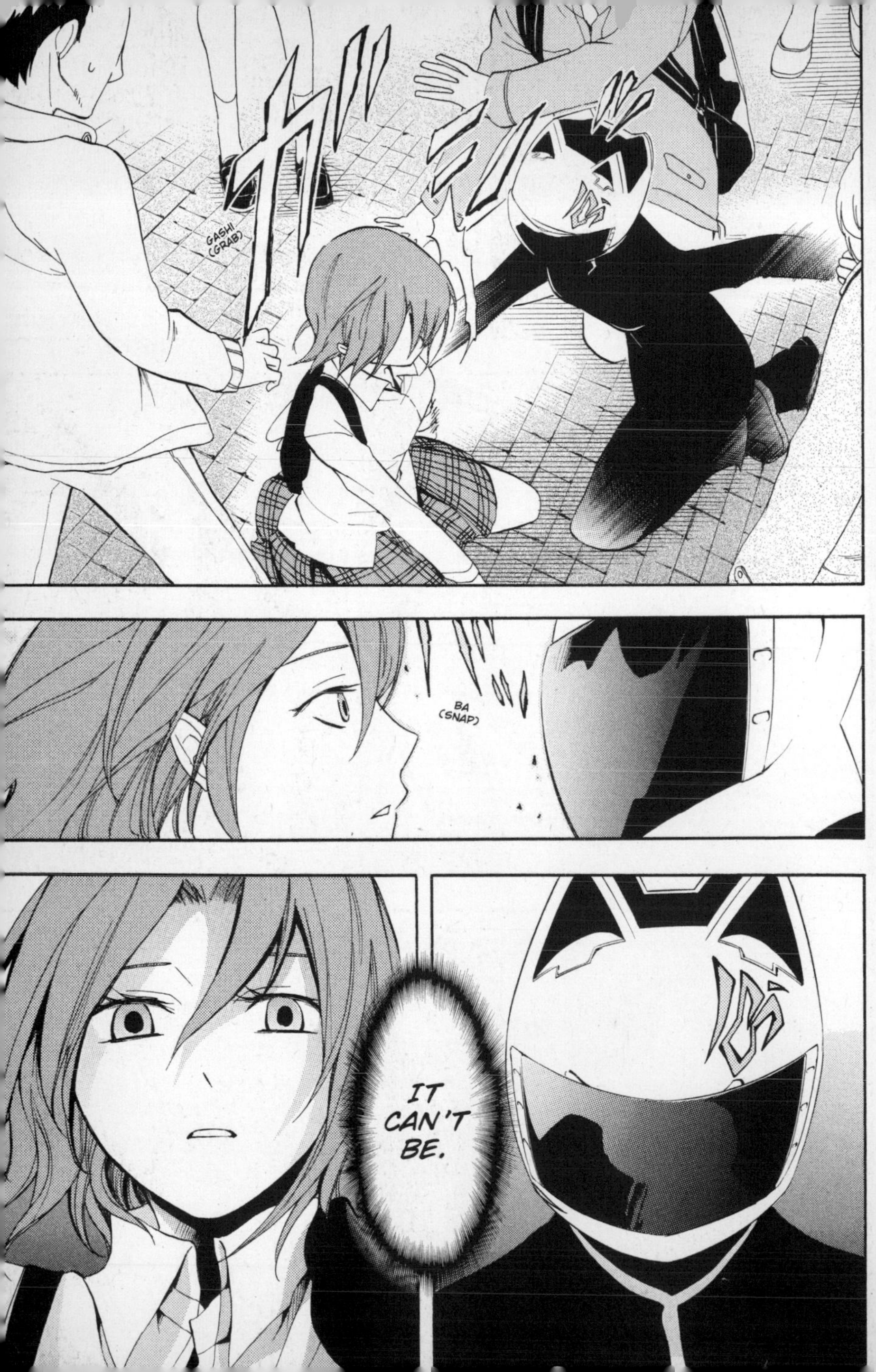
GASHI (GRAB)
BA (SNAP)
IT CAN'T BE.

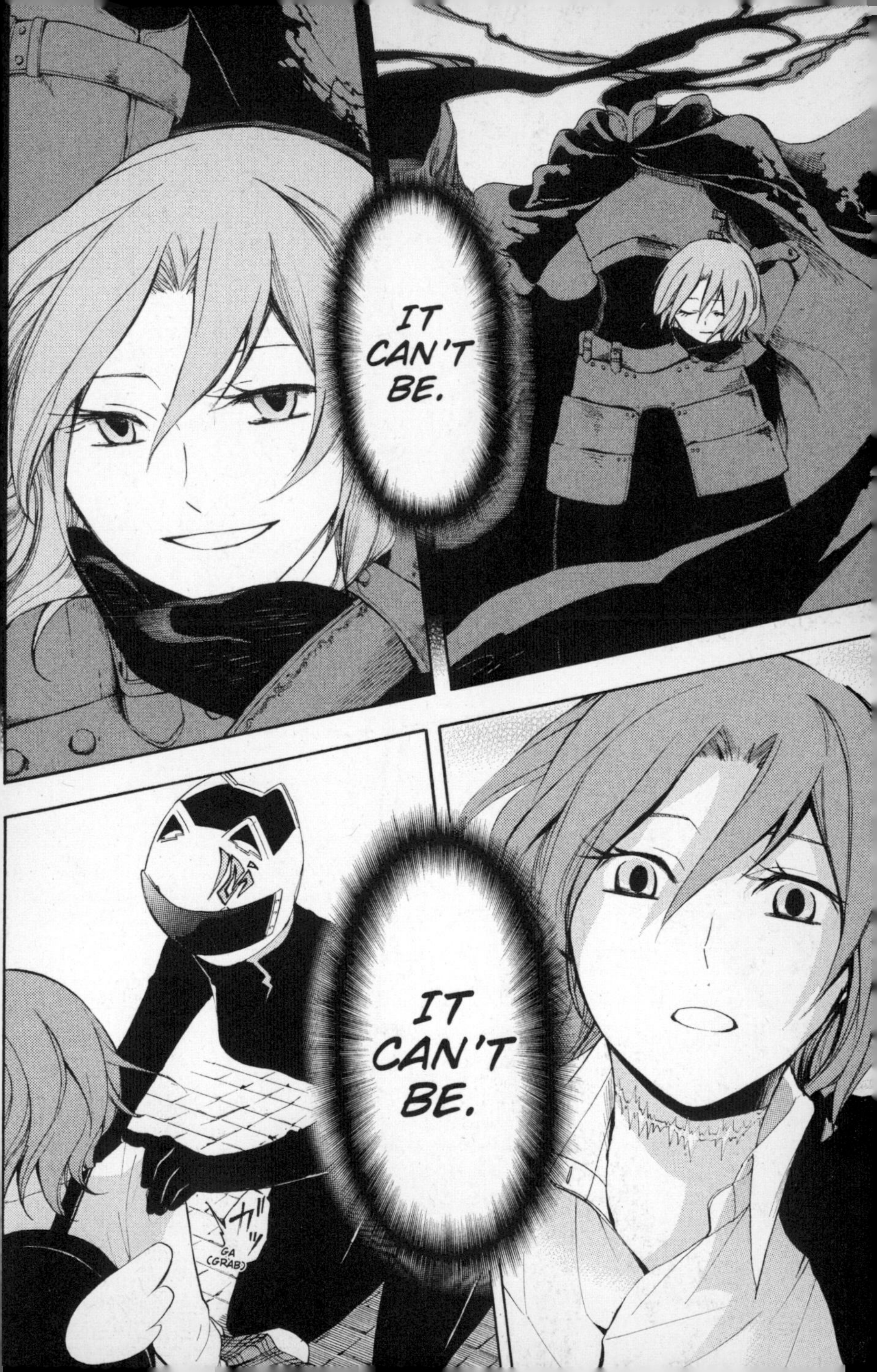
IT CAN'T BE.
IT CAN'T BE.
GA
(GRAB)

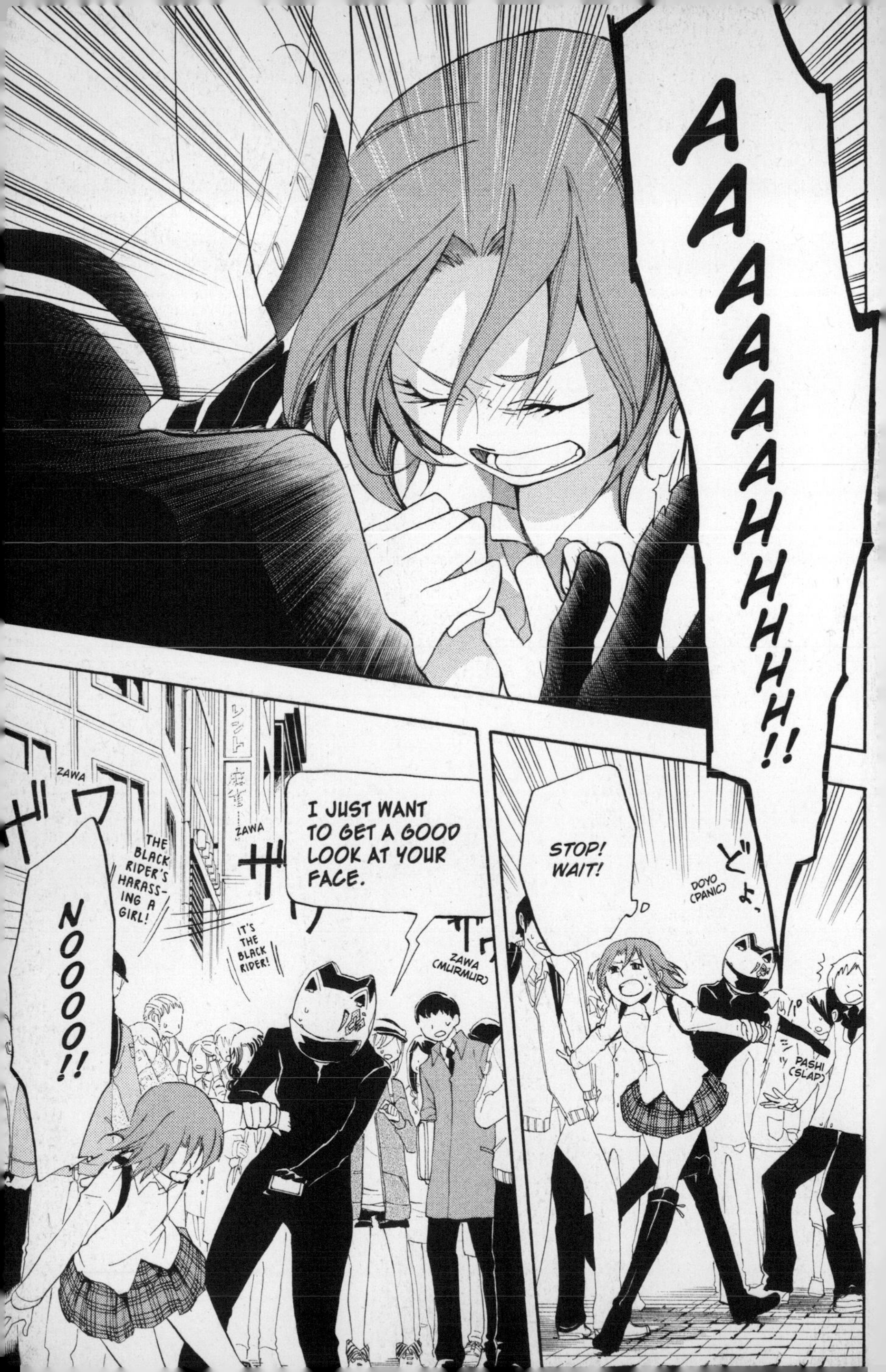
AAAAAAHHHHHH!!
STOP! WAIT!
DOYO (PANIC)
PASHI (SLAP)
I JUST WANT TO GET A GOOD LOOK AT YOUR FACE.
ZAWA
ZAWA
THE BLACK RIDER'S HARASSING A GIRL!
IT'S THE BLACK RIDER!
ZAWA (MURMUR)
NOOOOOO!!

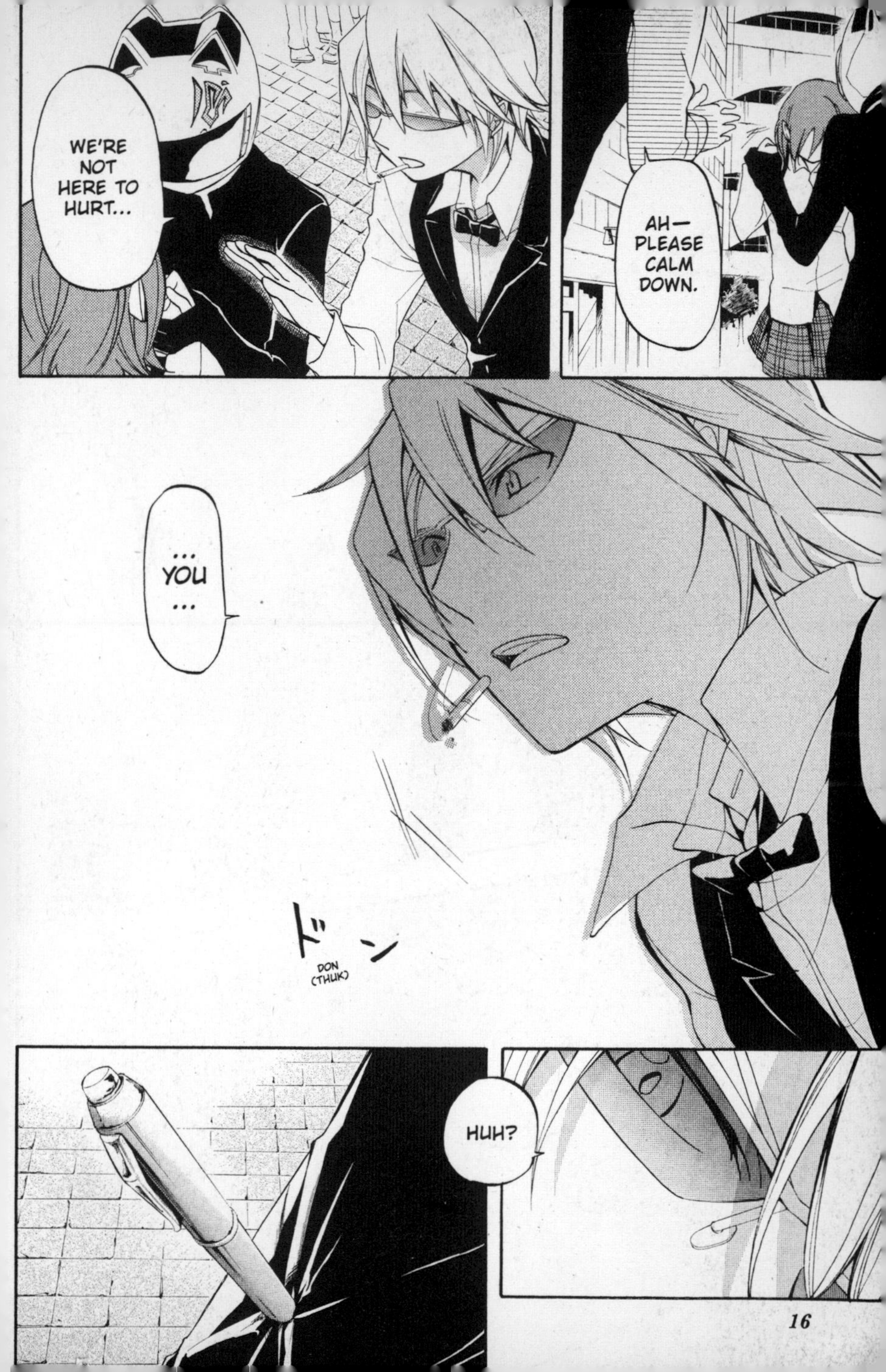
AH—PLEASE CALM DOWN.
WE'RE NOT HERE TO HURT...
... YOU ...
ドン
DON (THUK)
HUH?

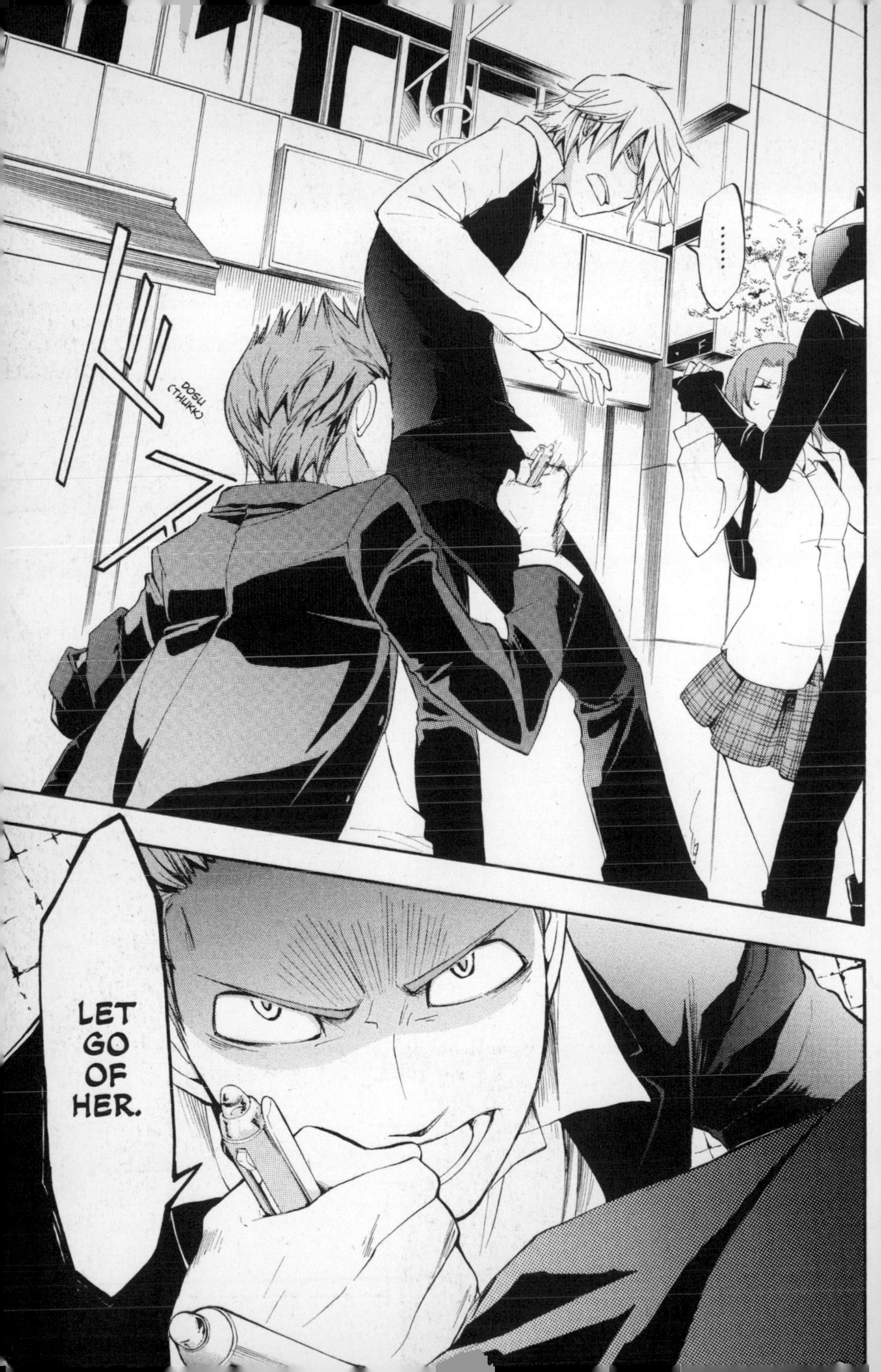
......
DOSU (THUKK)
LET GO OF HER.

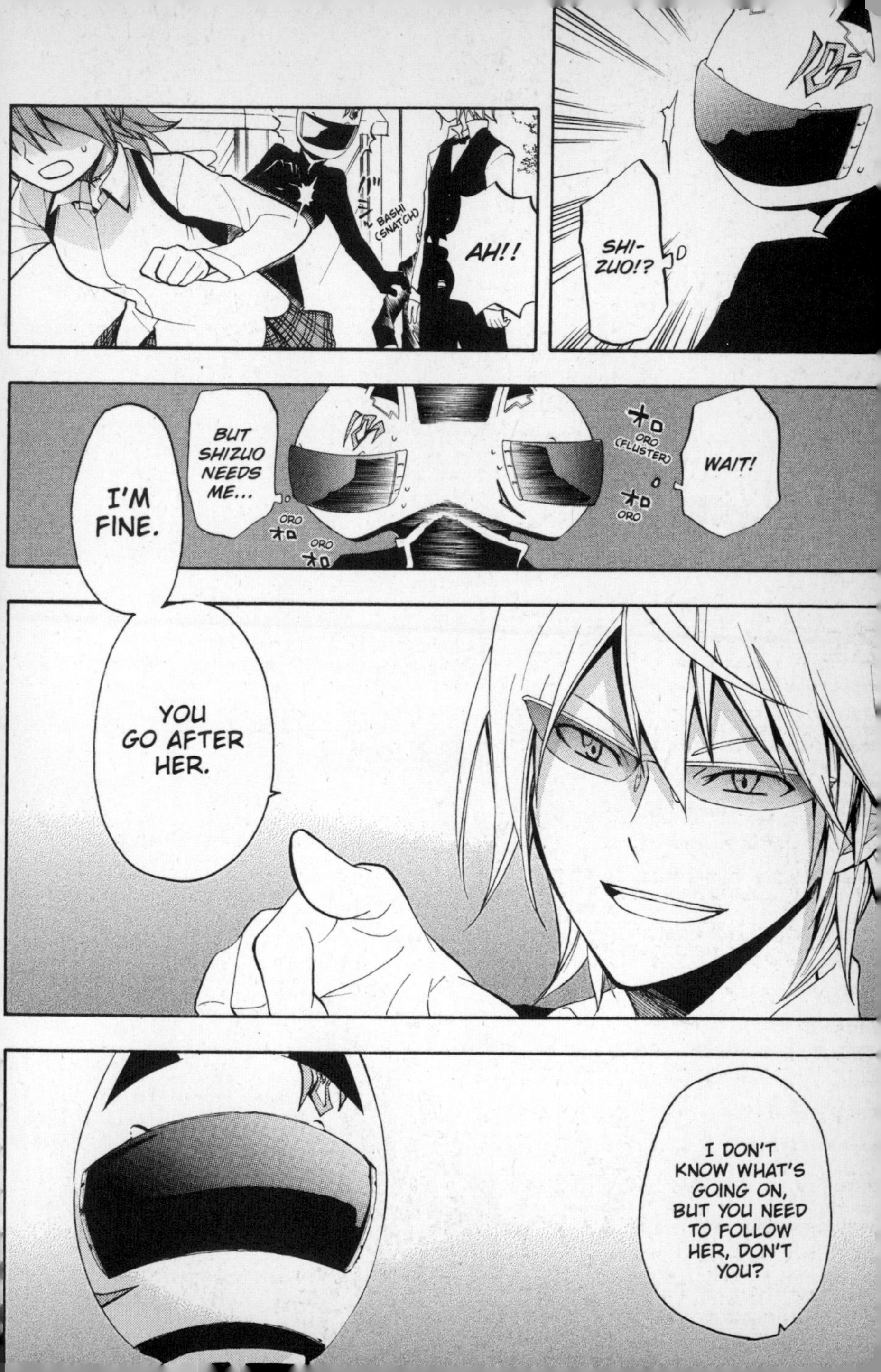
SHI-
ZUO!?
BASHI (SNATCH)
AH!!
WAIT!
オロ ORO (FLUSTER)
オロ ORO
BUT SHIZUO NEEDS ME...
オロ ORO
オロ ORO
I'M FINE.
YOU GO AFTER HER.
I DON'T KNOW WHAT'S GOING ON, BUT YOU NEED TO FOLLOW HER, DON'T YOU?

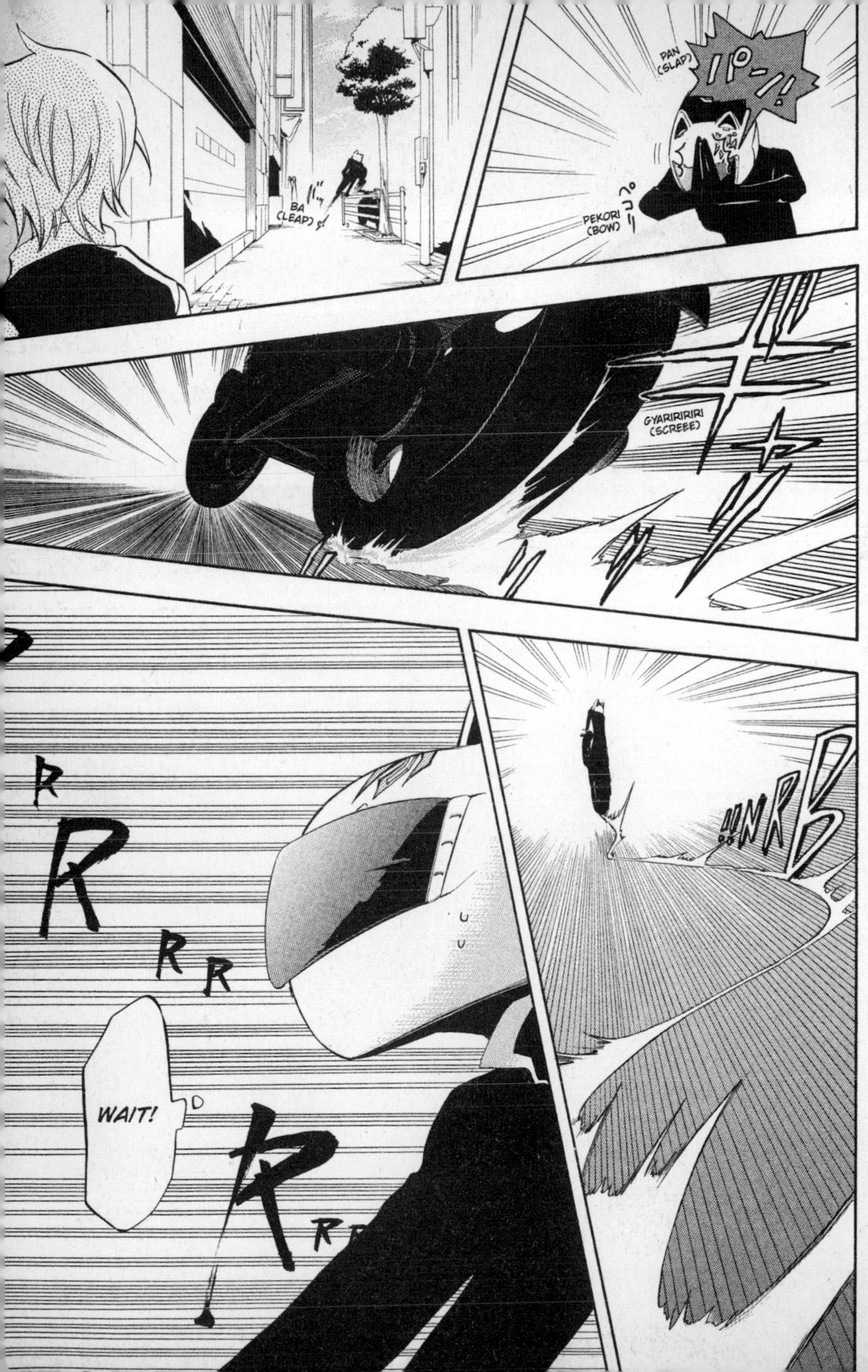
PAN (SLAP)
PEKORI (BOW)
BA (LEAP)
GYARIRIRIRI (SCREEE)
WAIT!

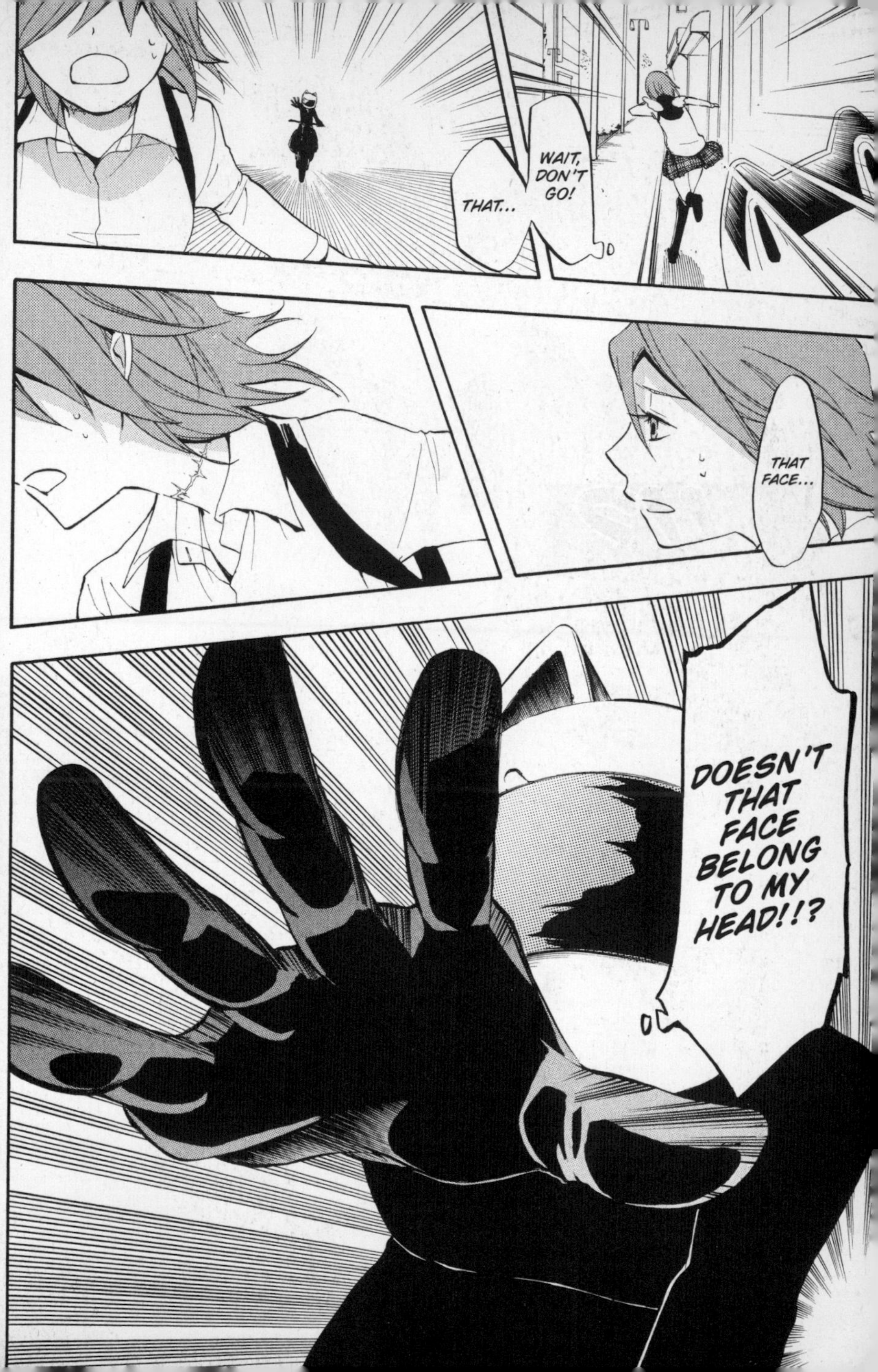
WAIT, DON'T GO!
THAT...
THAT FACE...
DOESN'T THAT FACE BELONG TO MY HEAD!!?

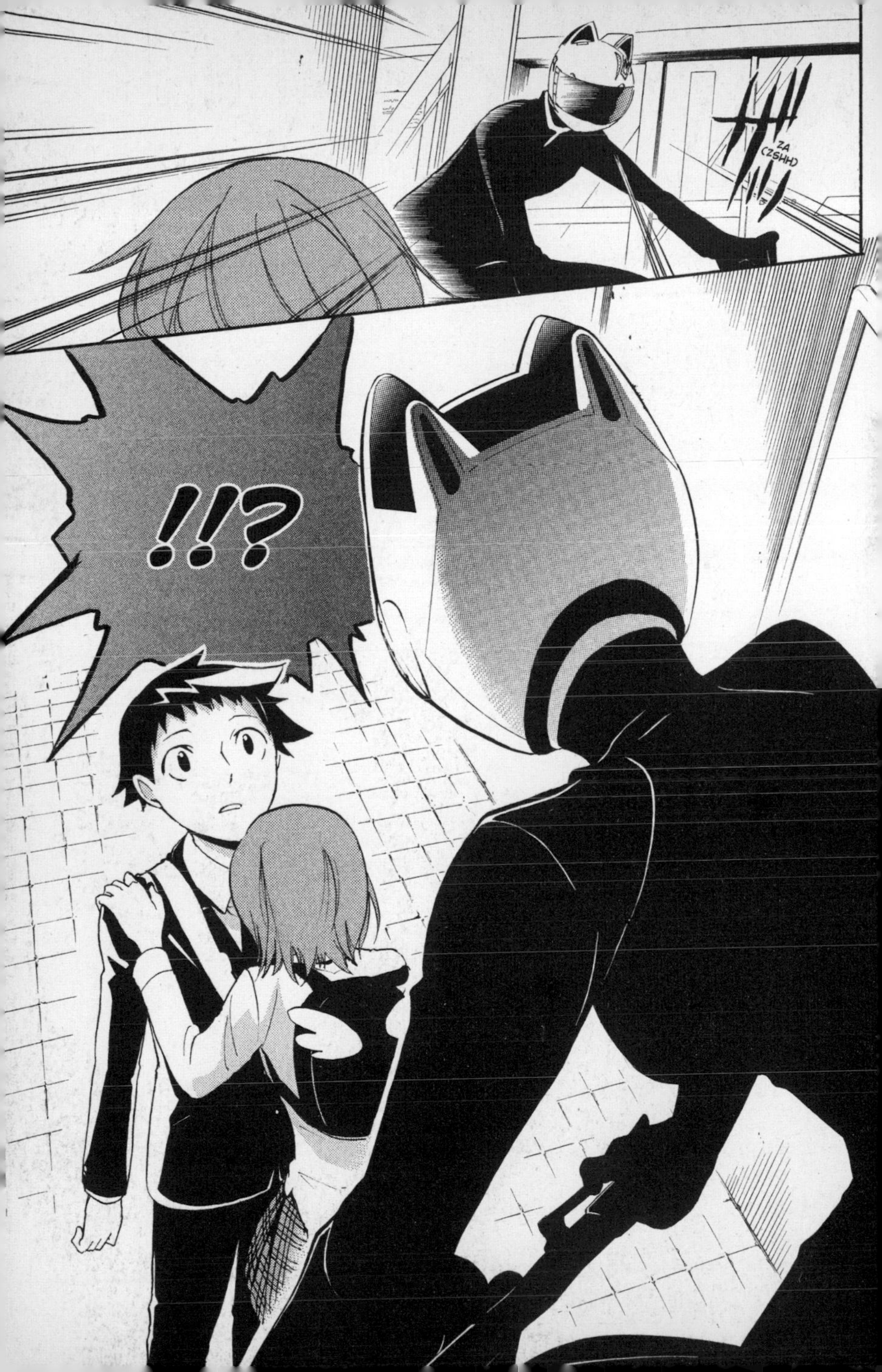
ZA
(ZSHH)
!!?

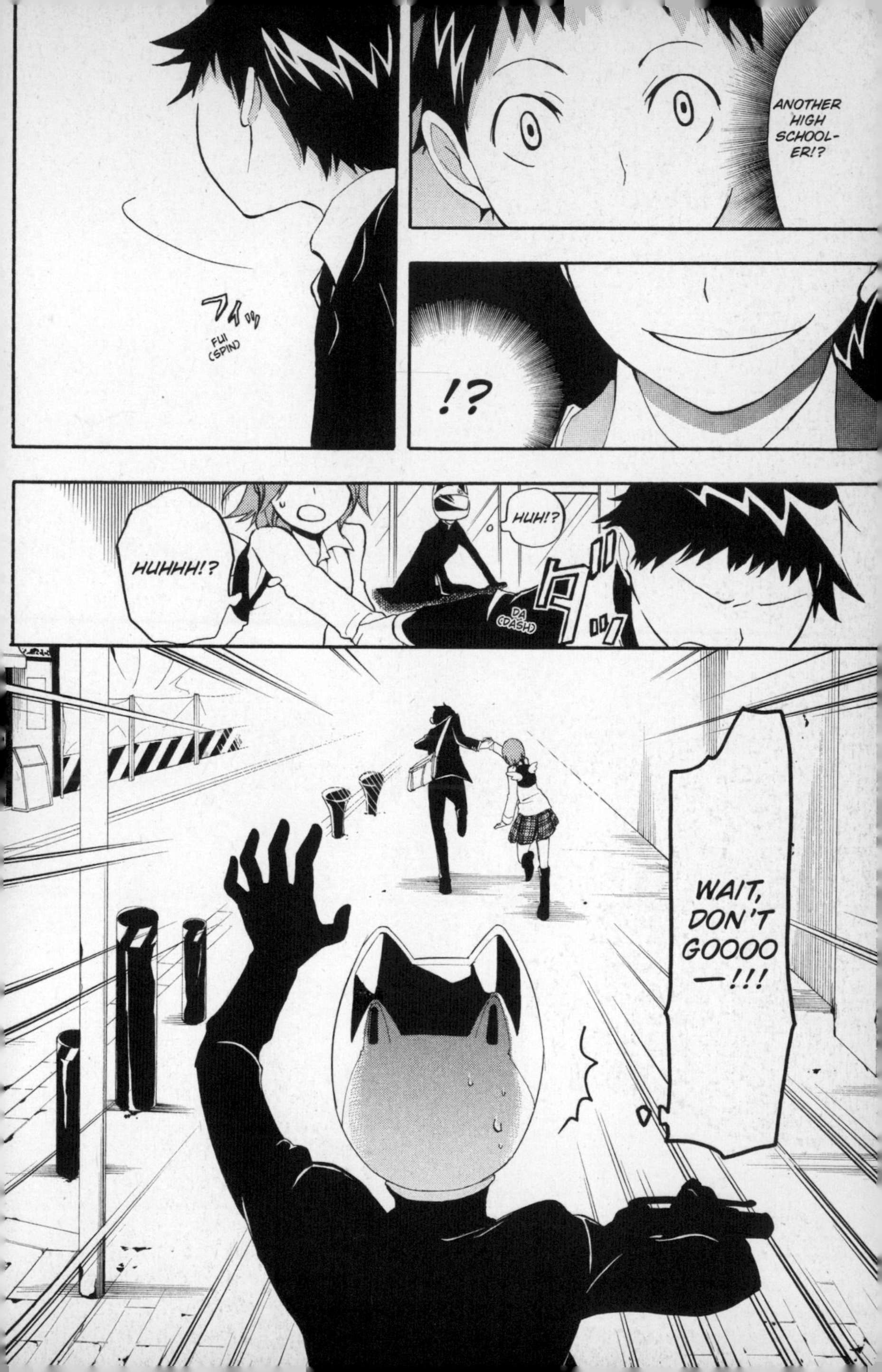
ANOTHER HIGH SCHOOLER!?
!?
フイッ
FUI (SPIN)
HUH!?
ダッ
DA (DASH)
HUHHH!?
WAIT, DON'T GOOOO—!!!

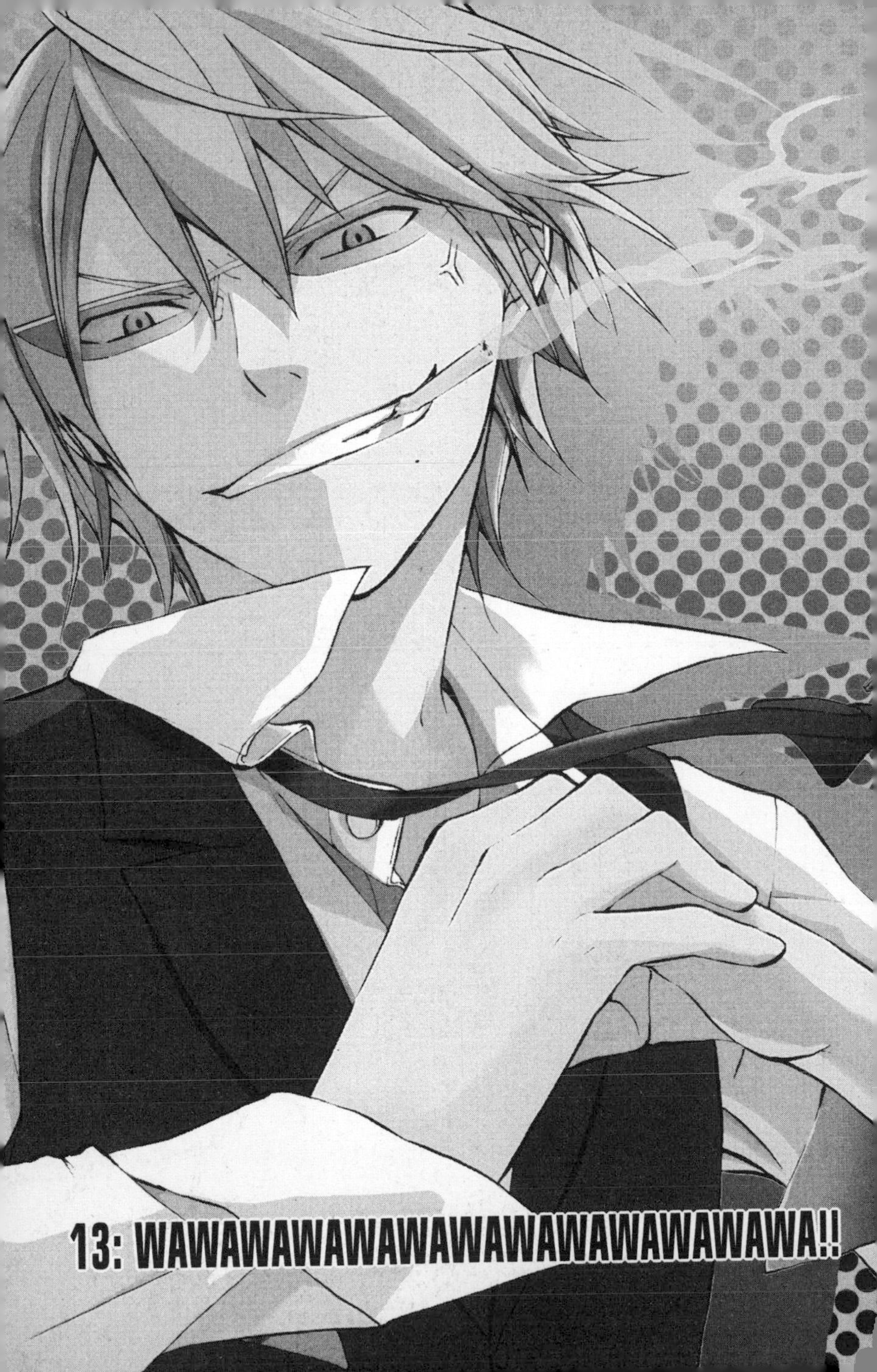
13: WAWAWAWAWAWAWAWAWAWAWAWAWAWA!!

DRRR!!

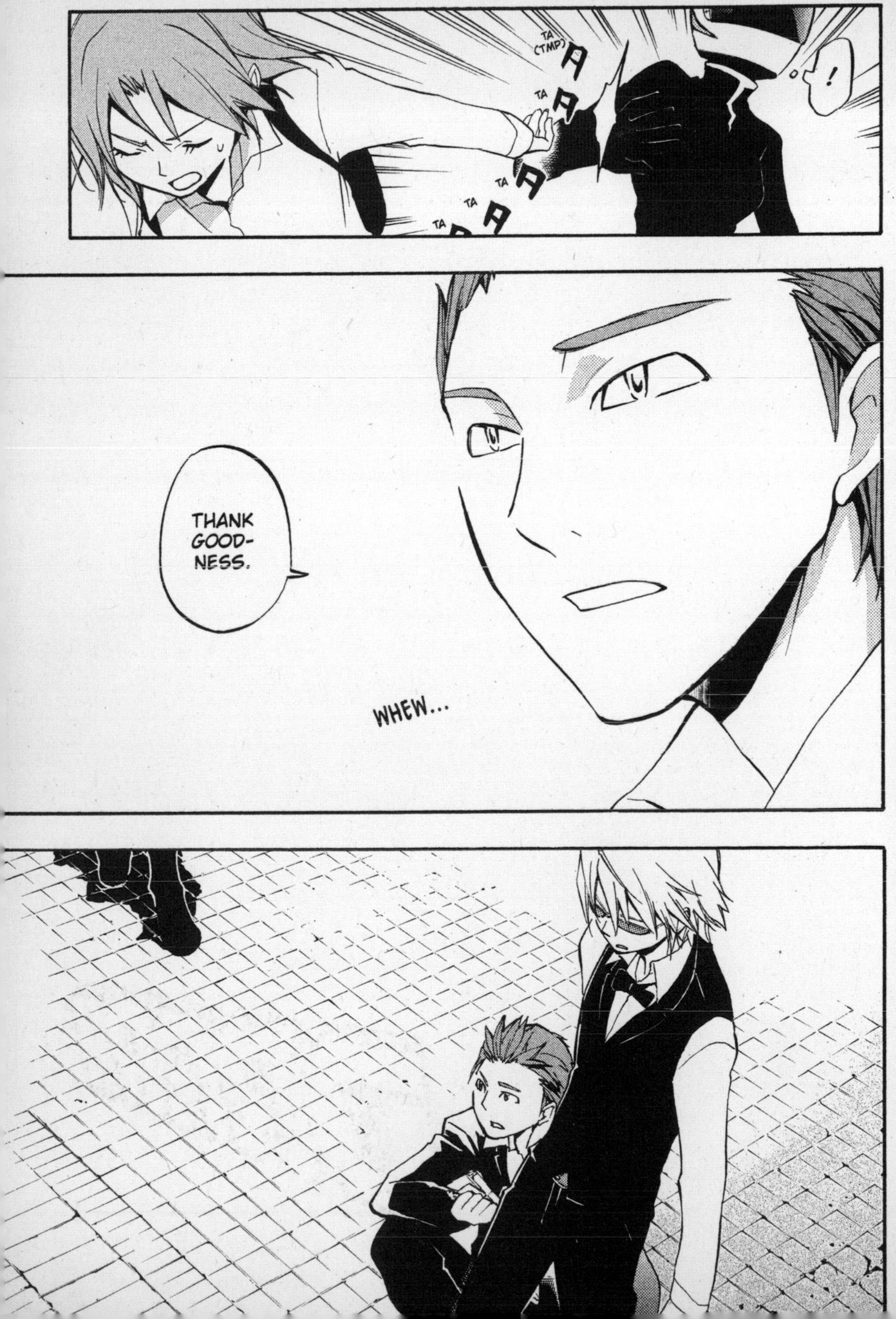
!
TA (TMP)
TA
TA
TA
TA
THANK GOOD-NESS.
WHEW...

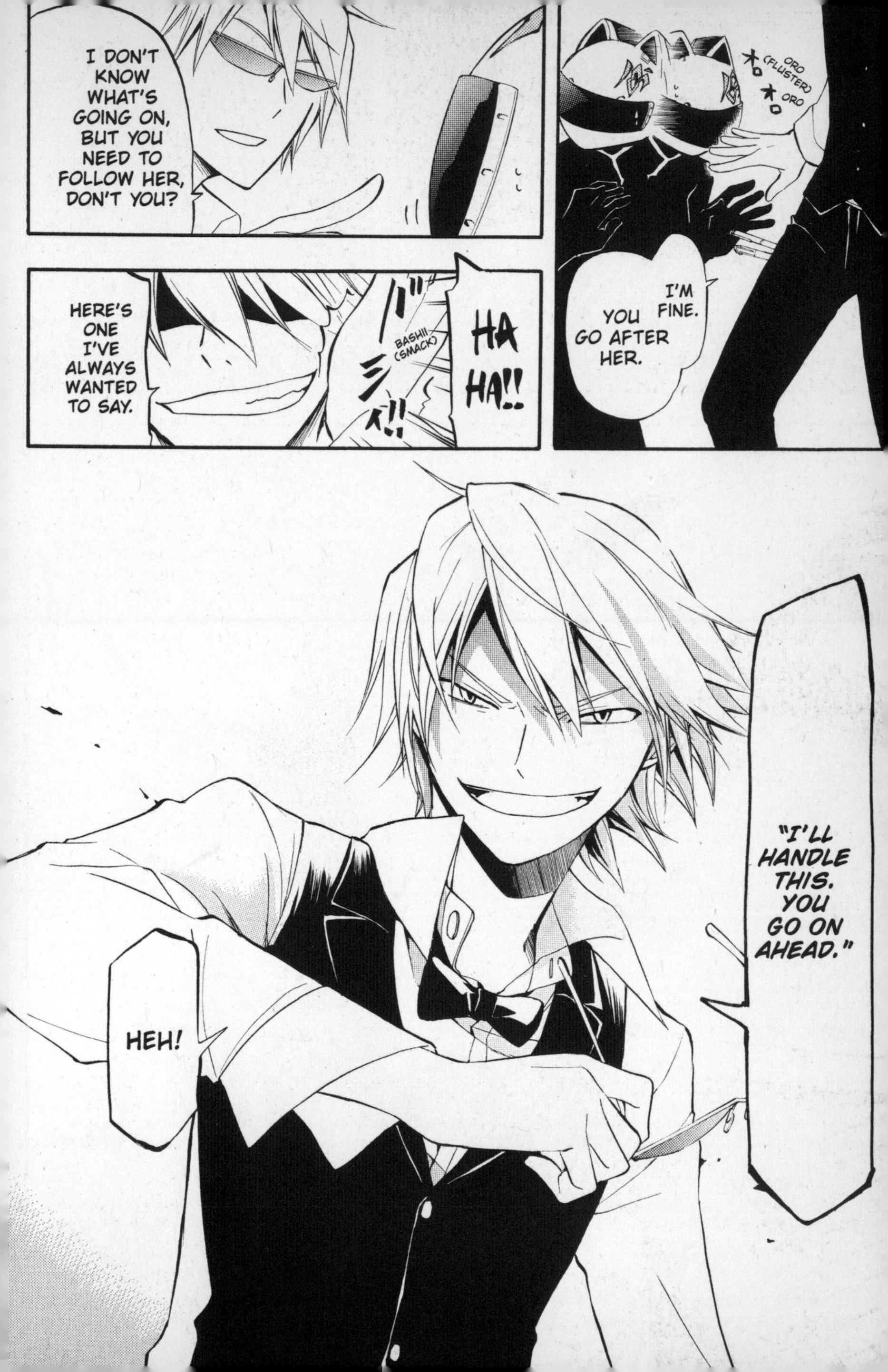

ORO (FLUSTER) ORO
I'M FINE. YOU GO AFTER HER.
I DON'T KNOW WHAT'S GOING ON, BUT YOU NEED TO FOLLOW HER, DON'T YOU?
HA HA!!
BASHII (SMACK)
HERE'S ONE I'VE ALWAYS WANTED TO SAY.
"I'LL HANDLE THIS. YOU GO ON AHEAD."
HEH!

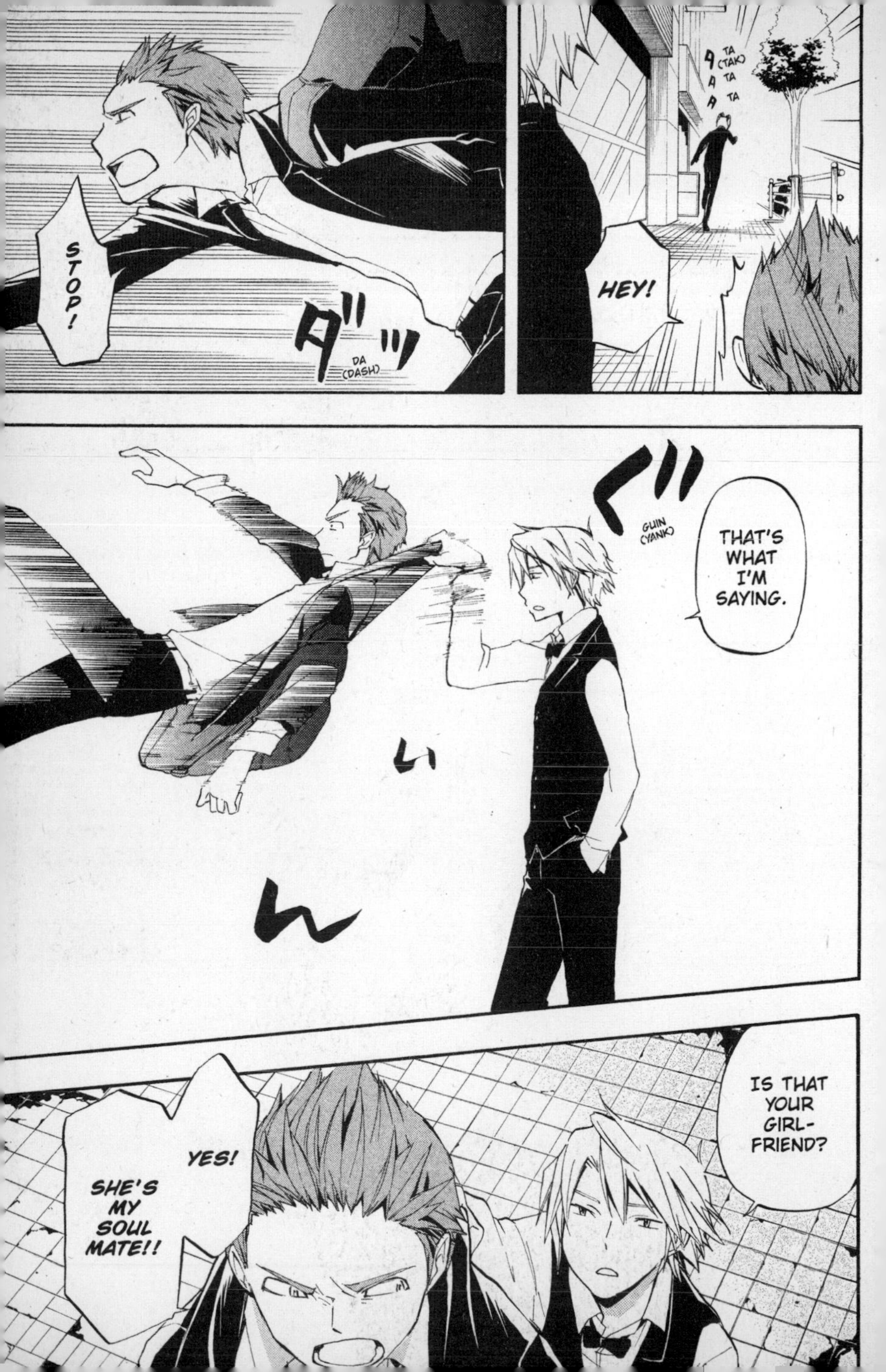

TA (TAK)
TA
TA
HEY!
STOP!
DA (DASH)
GUIN (YANK)
THAT'S WHAT I'M SAYING.
IS THAT YOUR GIRL-FRIEND?
YES!
SHE'S MY SOUL MATE!!

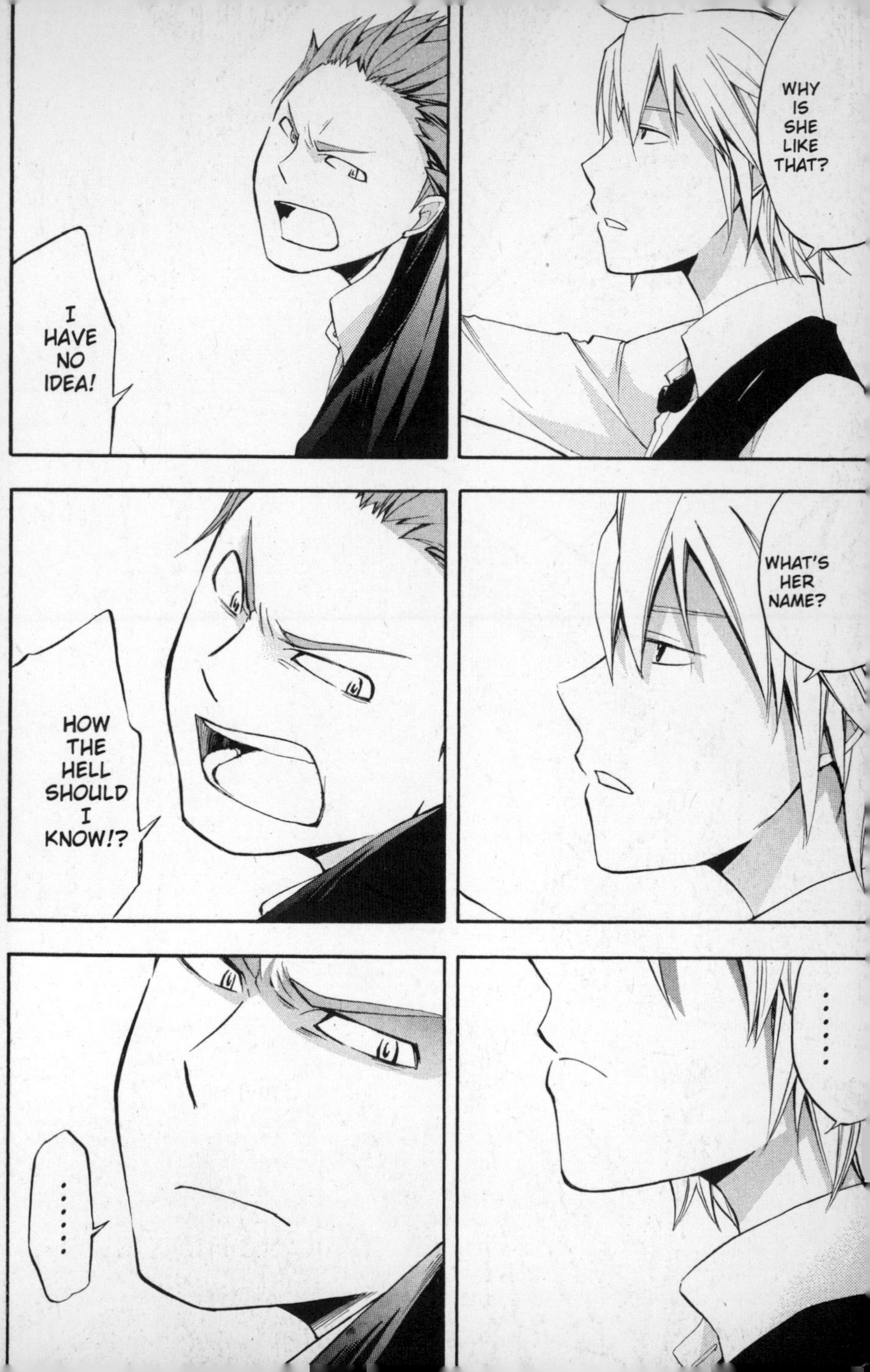
WHY IS SHE LIKE THAT?
I HAVE NO IDEA!
WHAT'S HER NAME?
HOW THE HELL SHOULD I KNOW!?
......
......

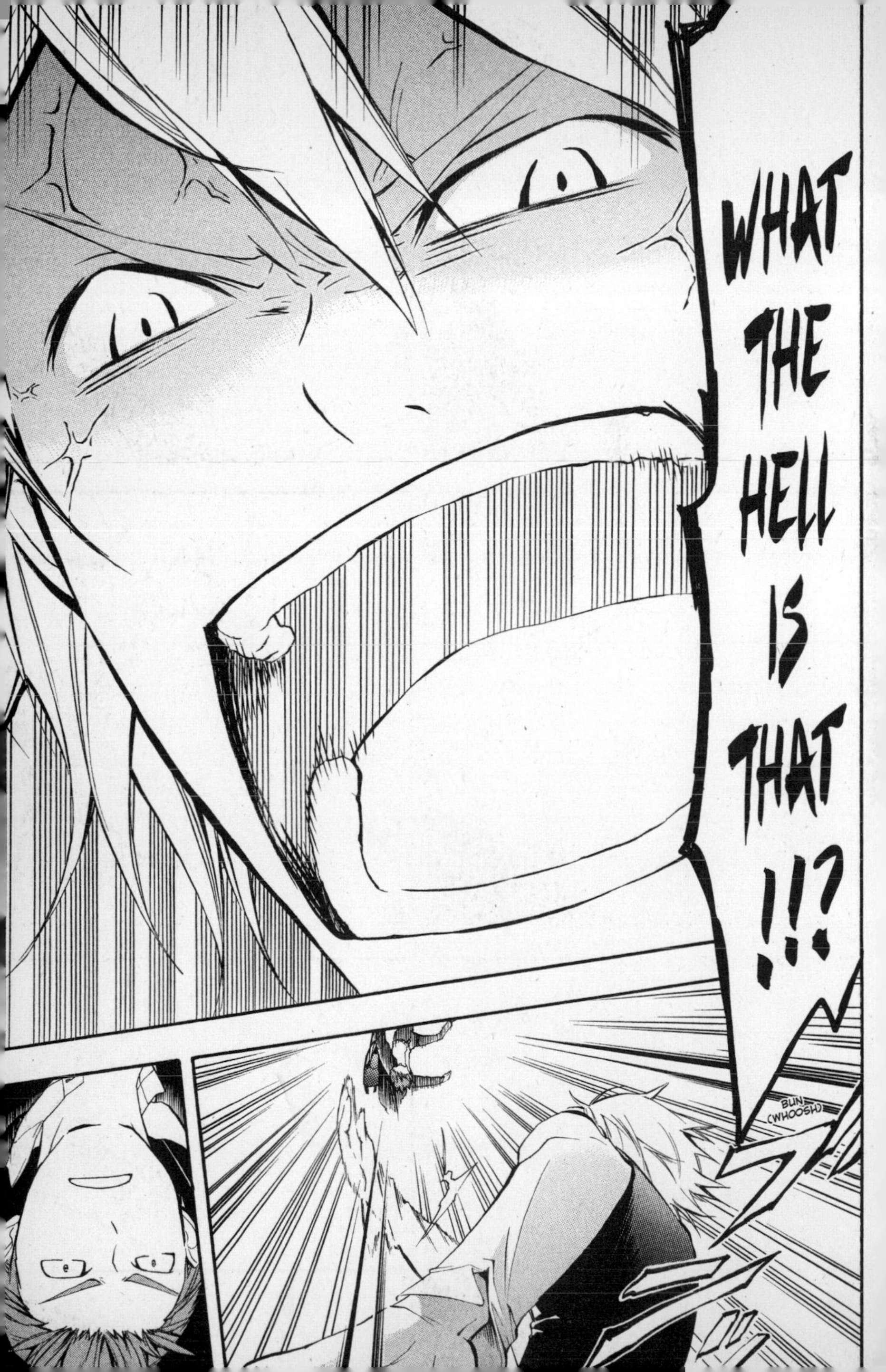
WHAT THE HELL IS THAT !!?
BUN (WHOOSH)

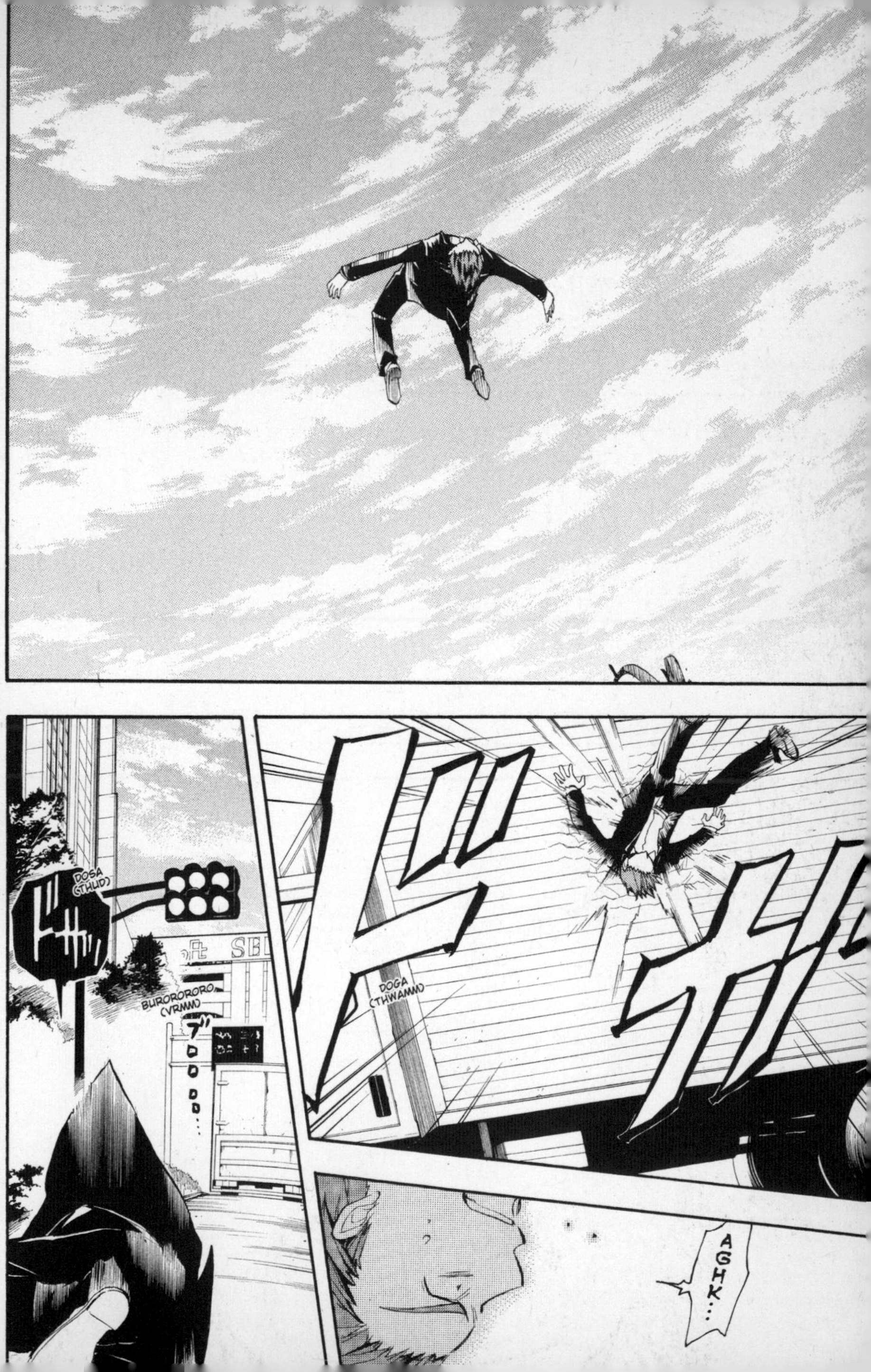
DOGA
(THWAMM)
AGHK...
DOSA
(THUD)
BURORORO
(VRMM)

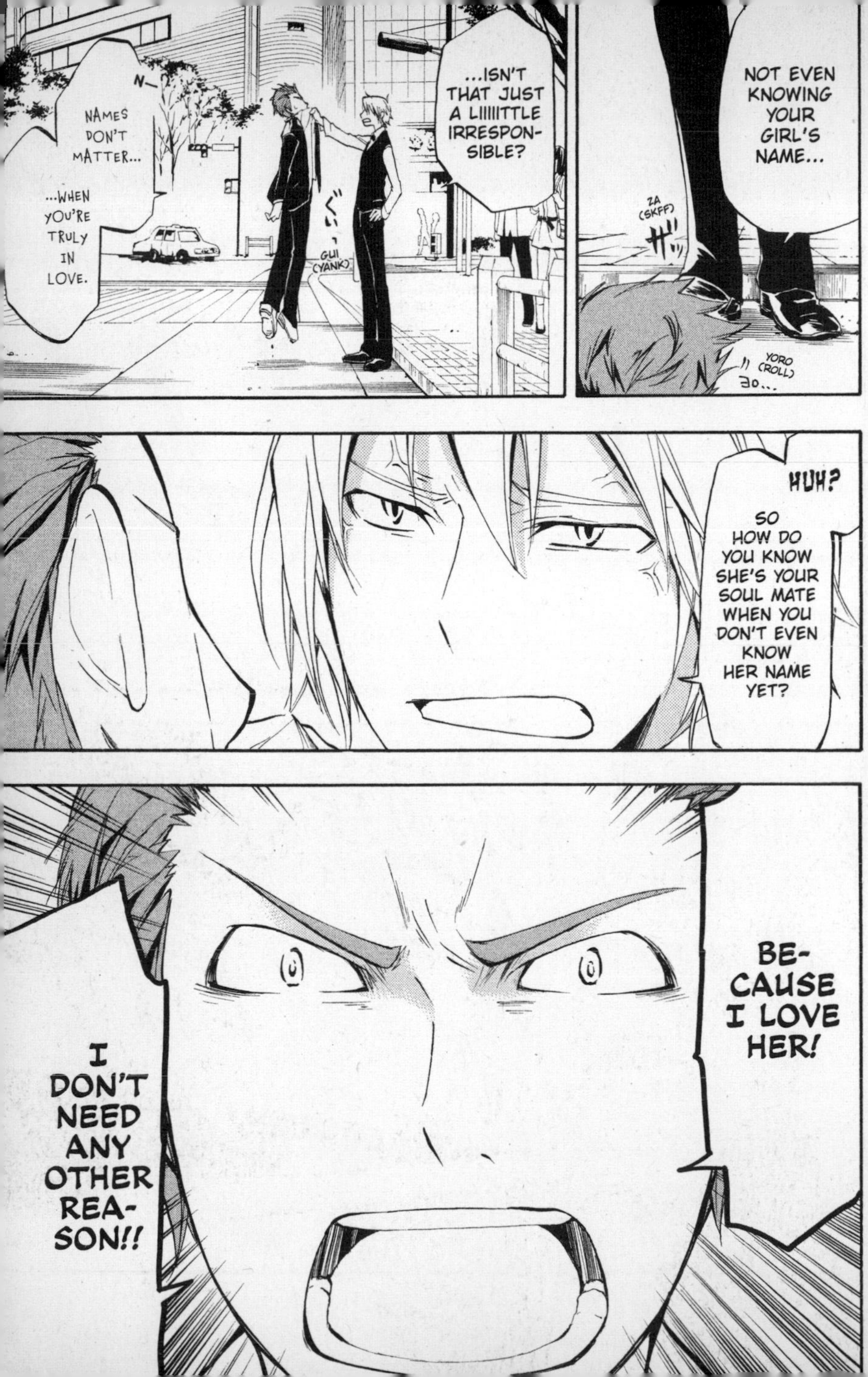
NOT EVEN KNOWING YOUR GIRL'S NAME...
ZA (SKFF)
ザッ
YORO (ROLL)
ヨロ...
...ISN'T THAT JUST A LIIIIITTLE IRRESPONSIBLE?
ぐいっ
GUI (YANK)
N—
NAMES DON'T MATTER...
...WHEN YOU'RE TRULY IN LOVE.
HUH?
SO HOW DO YOU KNOW SHE'S YOUR SOUL MATE WHEN YOU DON'T EVEN KNOW HER NAME YET?
BE-CAUSE I LOVE HER!
I DON'T NEED ANY OTHER REA-SON!!

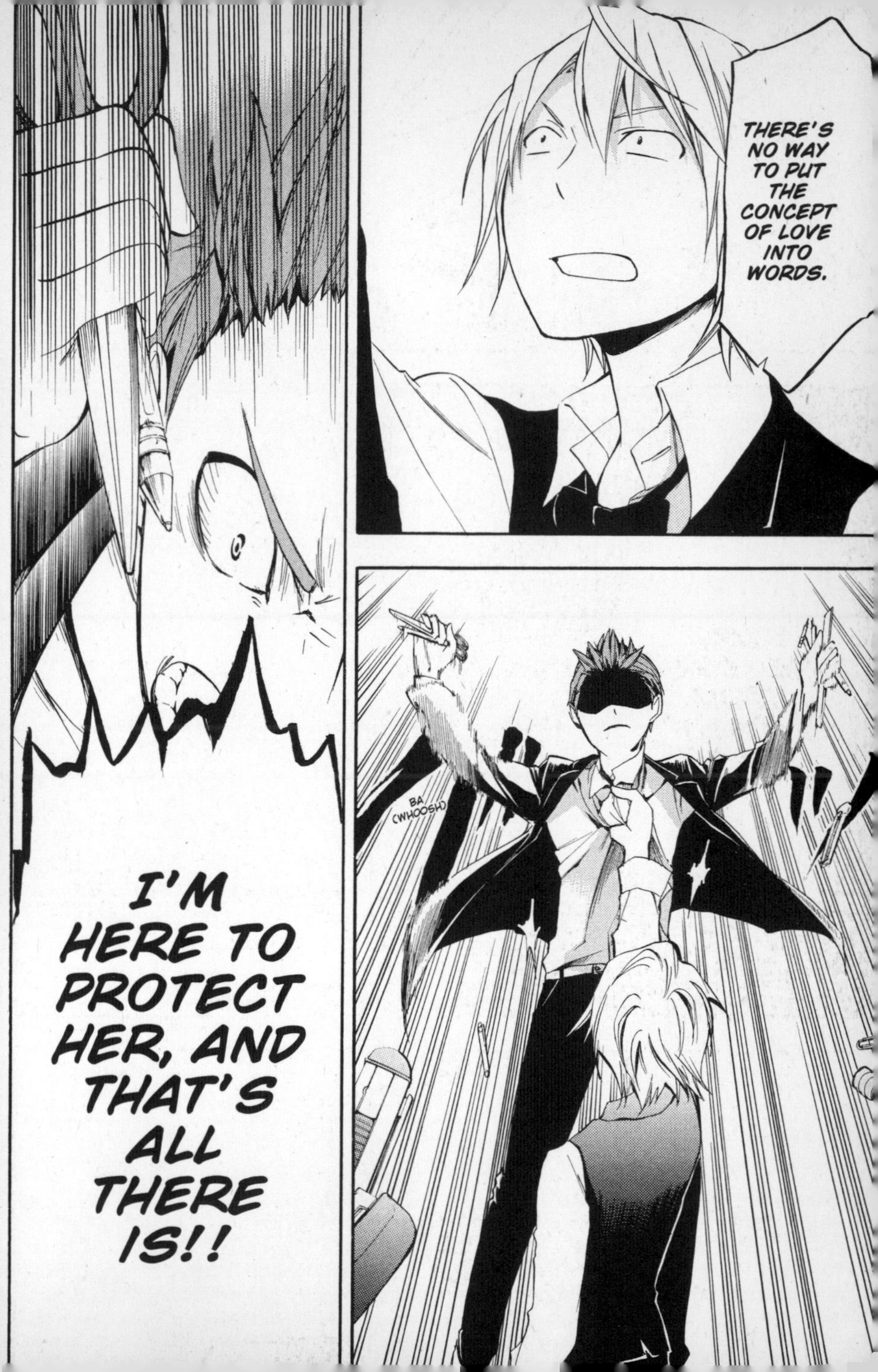
THERE'S NO WAY TO PUT THE CONCEPT OF LOVE INTO WORDS.
BA (WHOOSH)
I'M HERE TO PROTECT HER, AND THAT'S ALL THERE IS!!

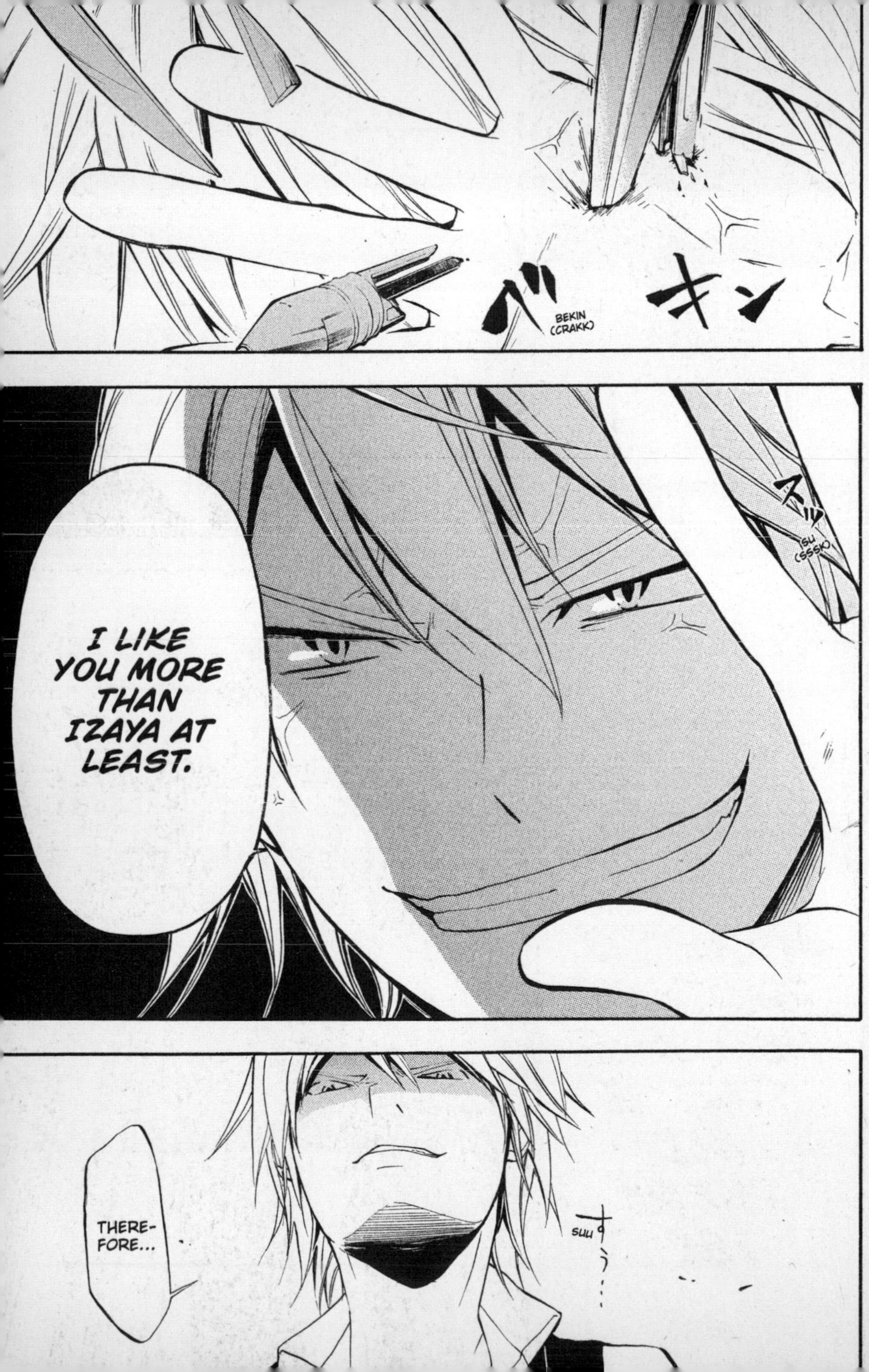
ベキン
BEKIN (CRAKK)
スッ
SU (SSSK)
I LIKE YOU MORE THAN IZAYA AT LEAST.
すう…
SUU
THERE-FORE...

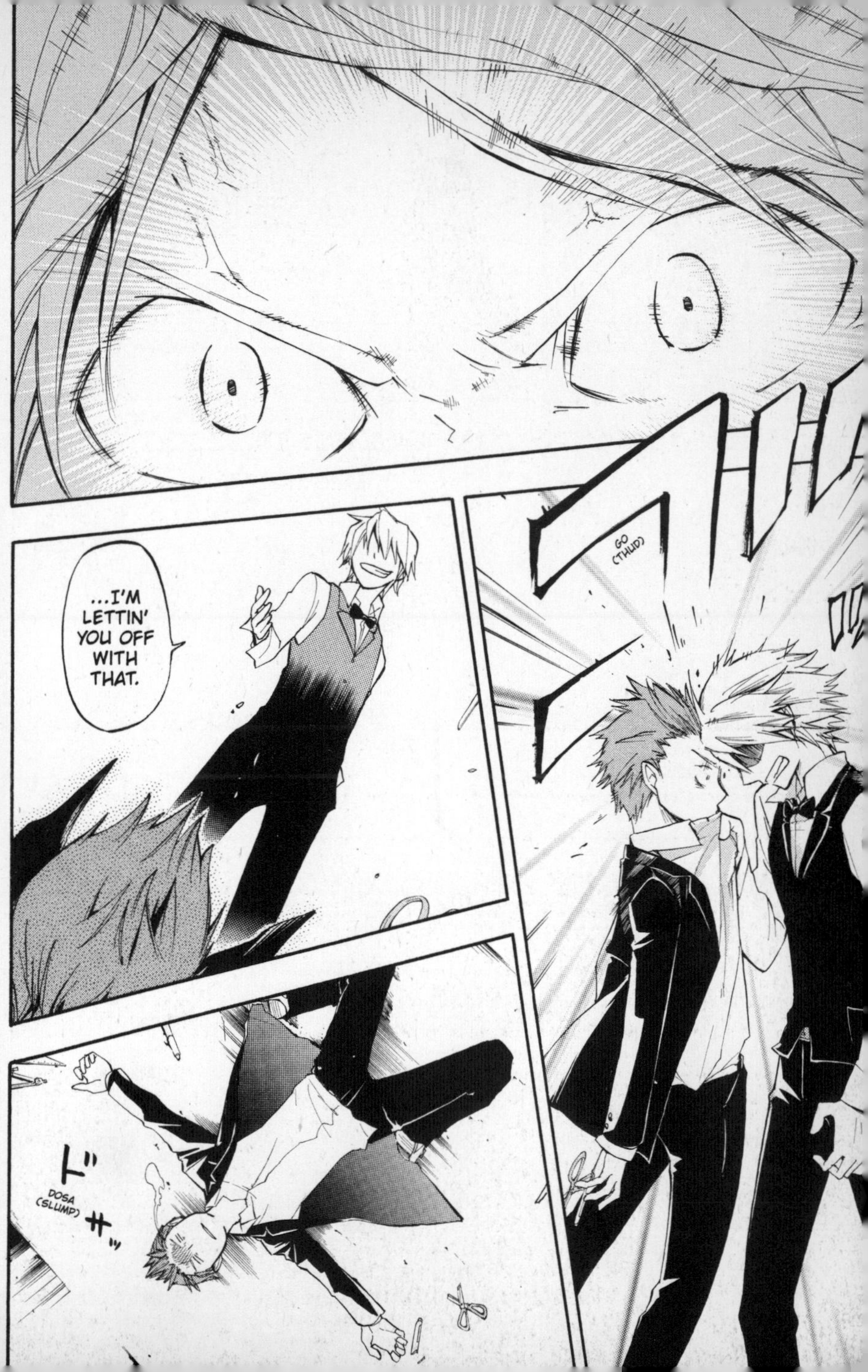
GO (THUD)
...I'M LETTIN' YOU OFF WITH THAT.
ドサッ
DOSA (SLUMP)

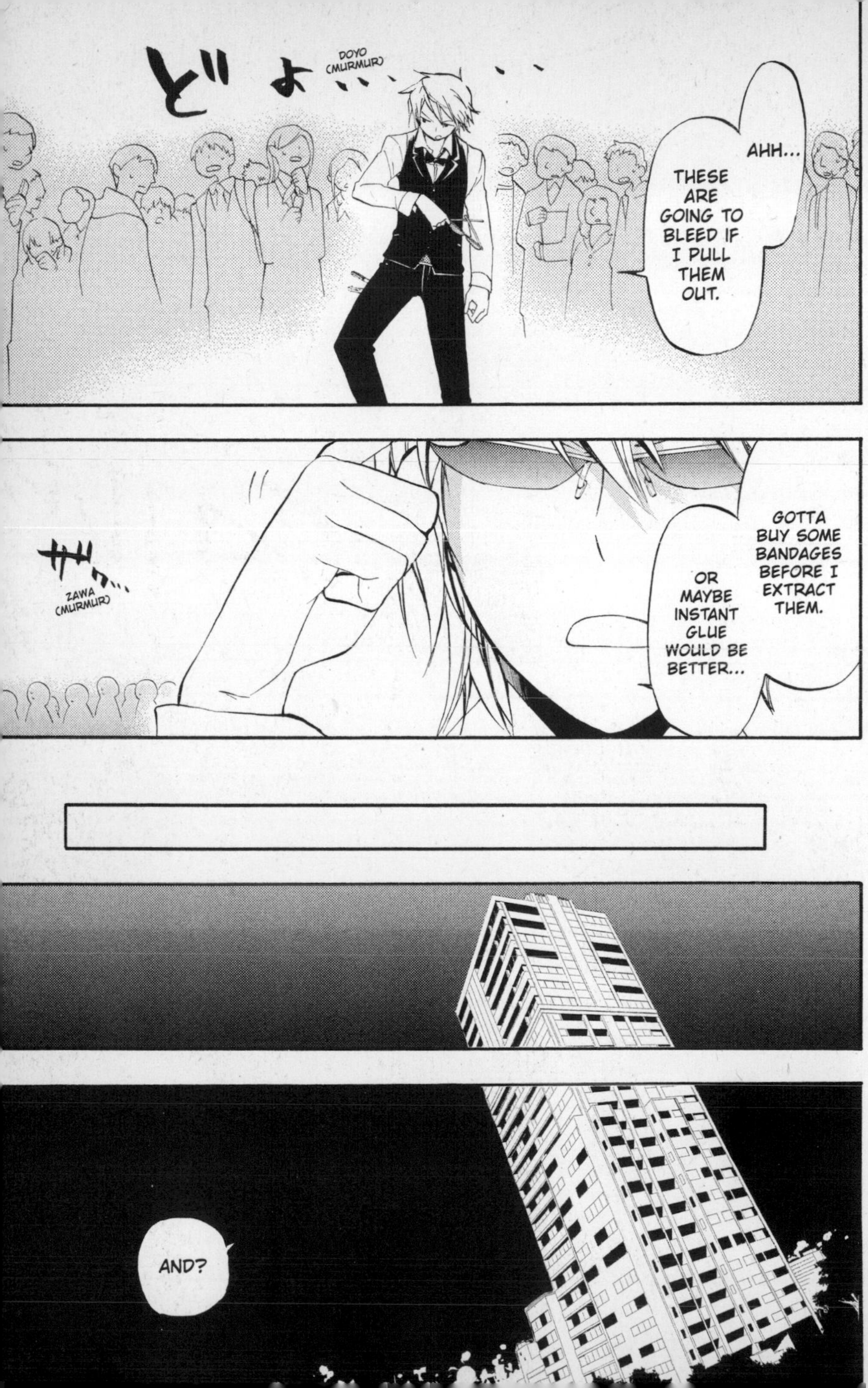
AHH... THESE ARE GOING TO BLEED IF I PULL THEM OUT.
どよ...
DOYO (MURMUR)
GOTTA BUY SOME BANDAGES BEFORE I EXTRACT THEM.
OR MAYBE INSTANT GLUE WOULD BE BETTER...
ザワ...
ZAWA (MURMUR)
AND?

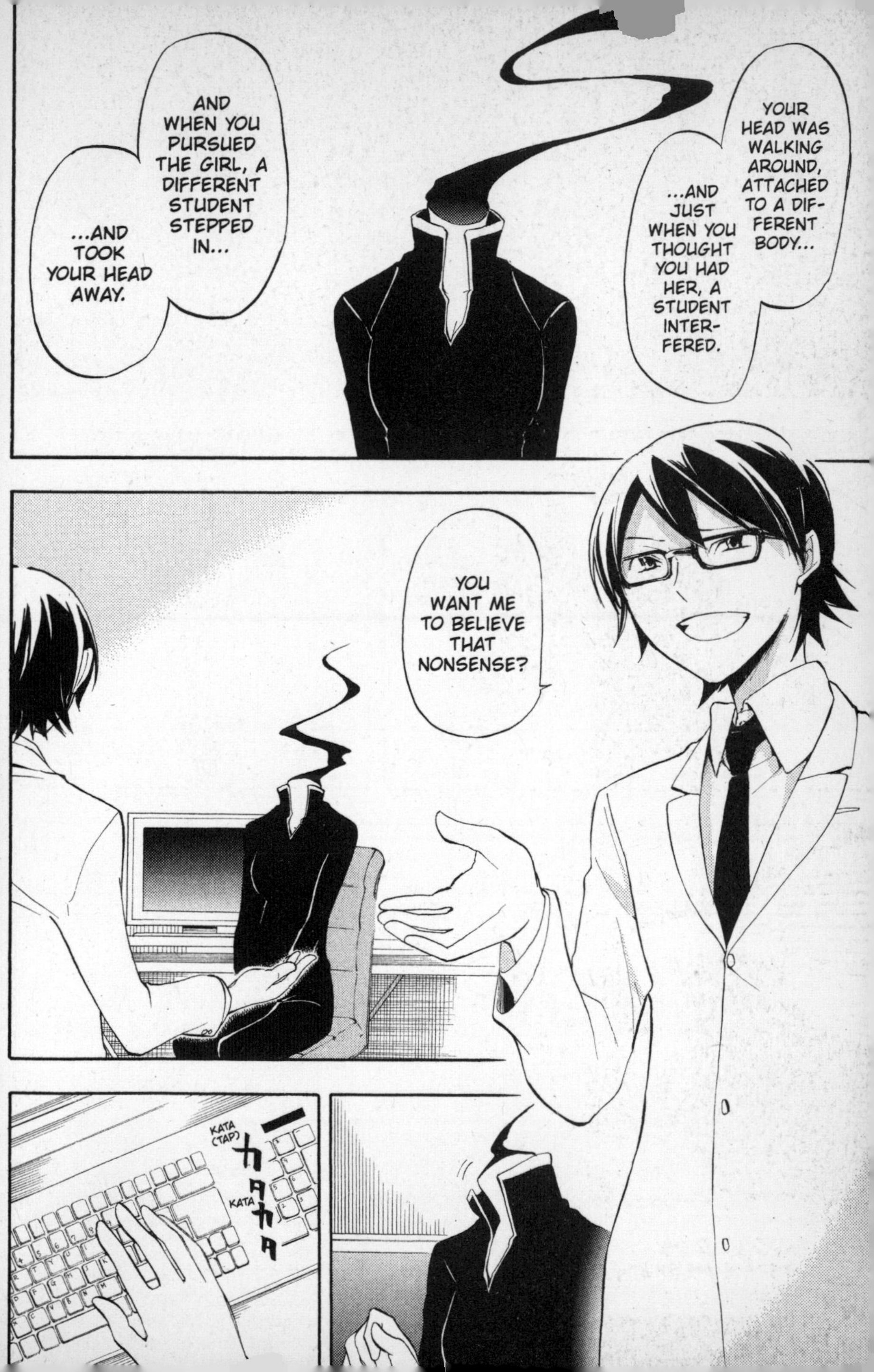
YOUR HEAD WAS WALKING AROUND, ATTACHED TO A DIFFERENT BODY...
...AND JUST WHEN YOU THOUGHT YOU HAD HER, A STUDENT INTERFERED.
AND WHEN YOU PURSUED THE GIRL, A DIFFERENT STUDENT STEPPED IN...
...AND TOOK YOUR HEAD AWAY.
YOU WANT ME TO BELIEVE THAT NONSENSE?
KATA (TAP)
KATA

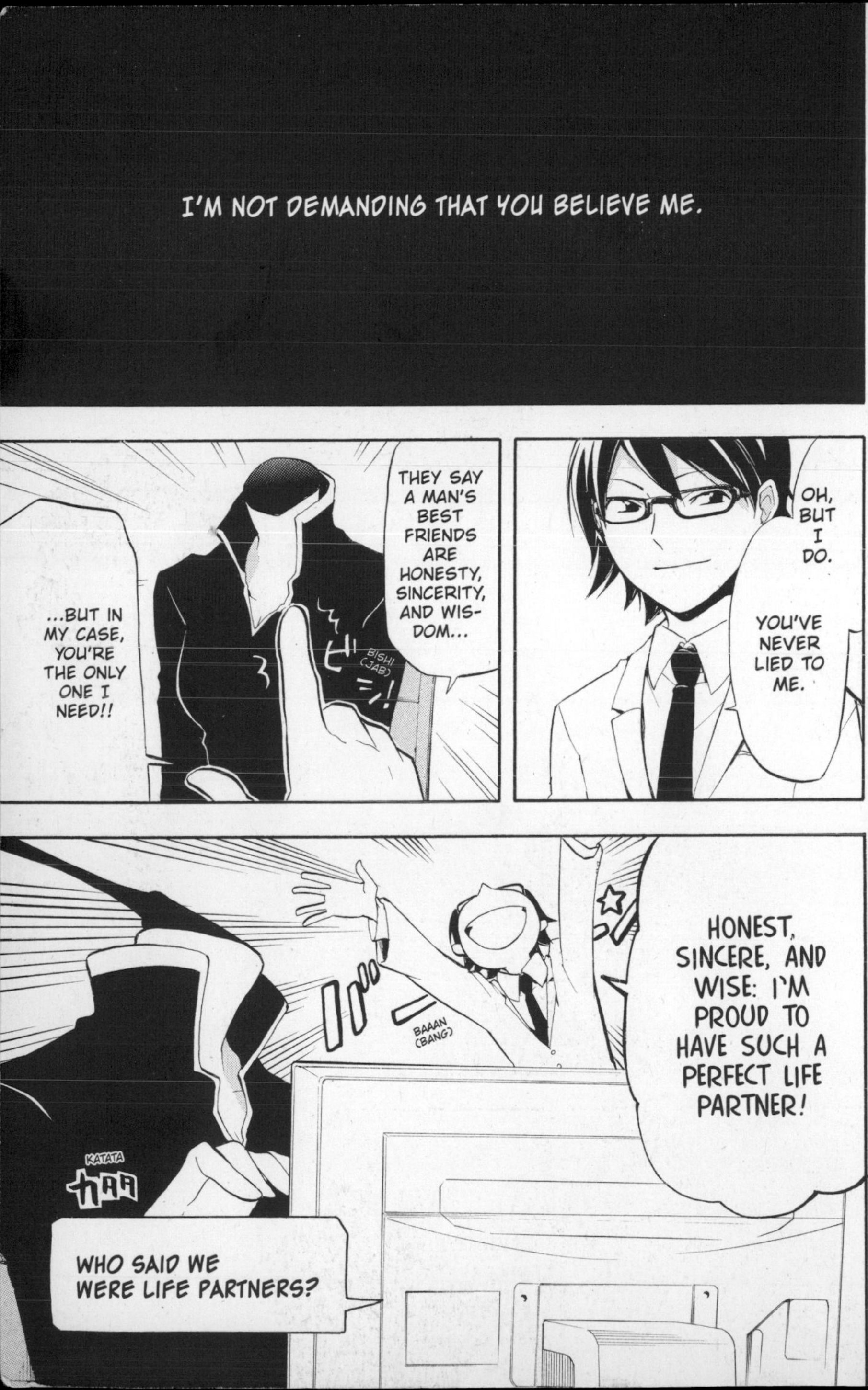
I'M NOT DEMANDING THAT YOU BELIEVE ME.
OH, BUT I DO.
YOU'VE NEVER LIED TO ME.
THEY SAY A MAN'S BEST FRIENDS ARE HONESTY, SINCERITY, AND WISDOM...
BISHI (JAB)
...BUT IN MY CASE, YOU'RE THE ONLY ONE I NEED!!
HONEST, SINCERE, AND WISE: I'M PROUD TO HAVE SUCH A PERFECT LIFE PARTNER!
BAAAN (BANG)
KATATA
WHO SAID WE WERE LIFE PARTNERS?

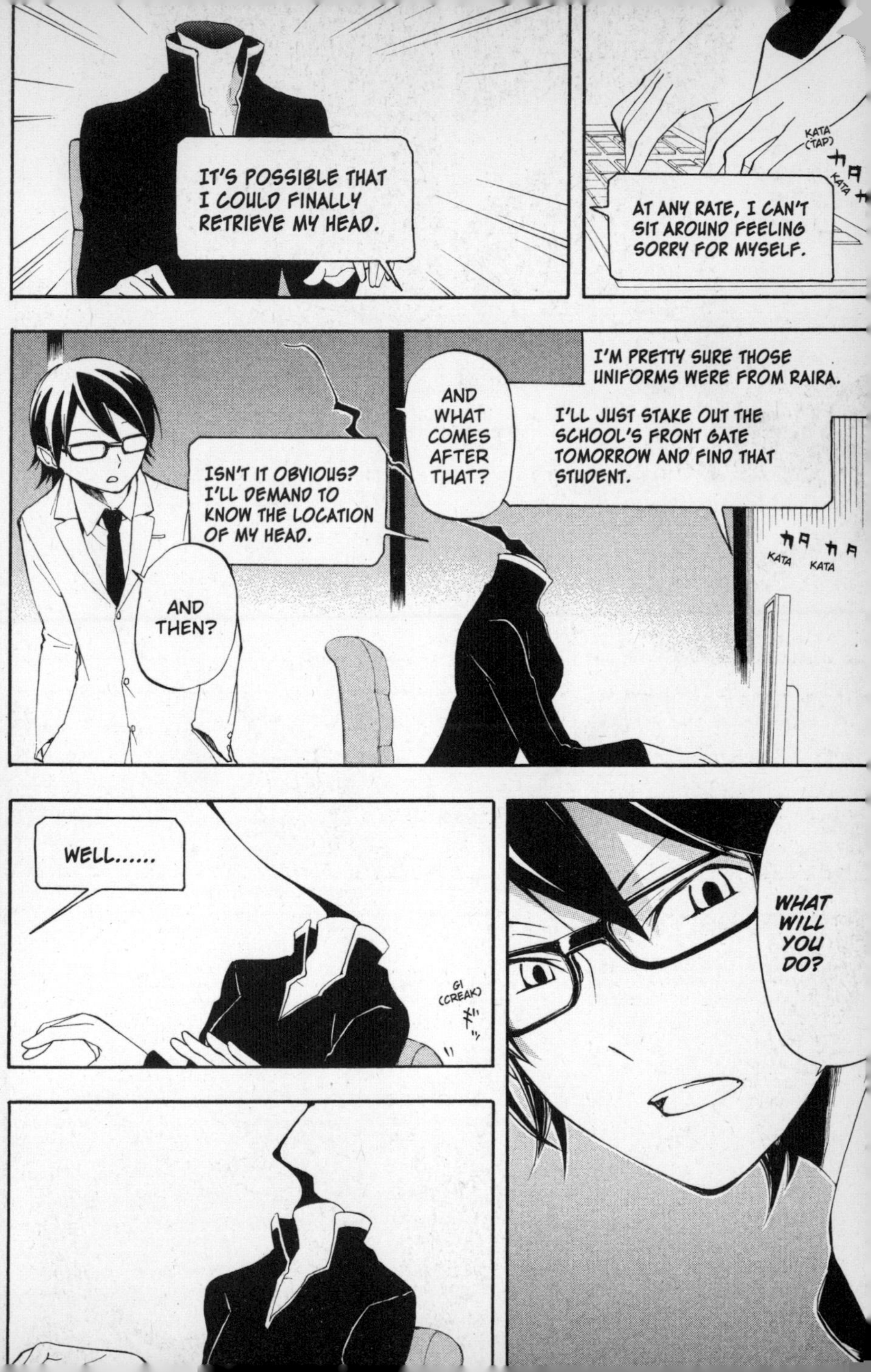
KATA (TAP)
カタ
KATA
AT ANY RATE, I CAN'T SIT AROUND FEELING SORRY FOR MYSELF.
IT'S POSSIBLE THAT I COULD FINALLY RETRIEVE MY HEAD.
I'M PRETTY SURE THOSE UNIFORMS WERE FROM RAIRA.
I'LL JUST STAKE OUT THE SCHOOL'S FRONT GATE TOMORROW AND FIND THAT STUDENT.
カタ KATA
カタ KATA
AND WHAT COMES AFTER THAT?
ISN'T IT OBVIOUS? I'LL DEMAND TO KNOW THE LOCATION OF MY HEAD.
AND THEN?
WHAT WILL YOU DO?
WELL......
GI (CREAK)

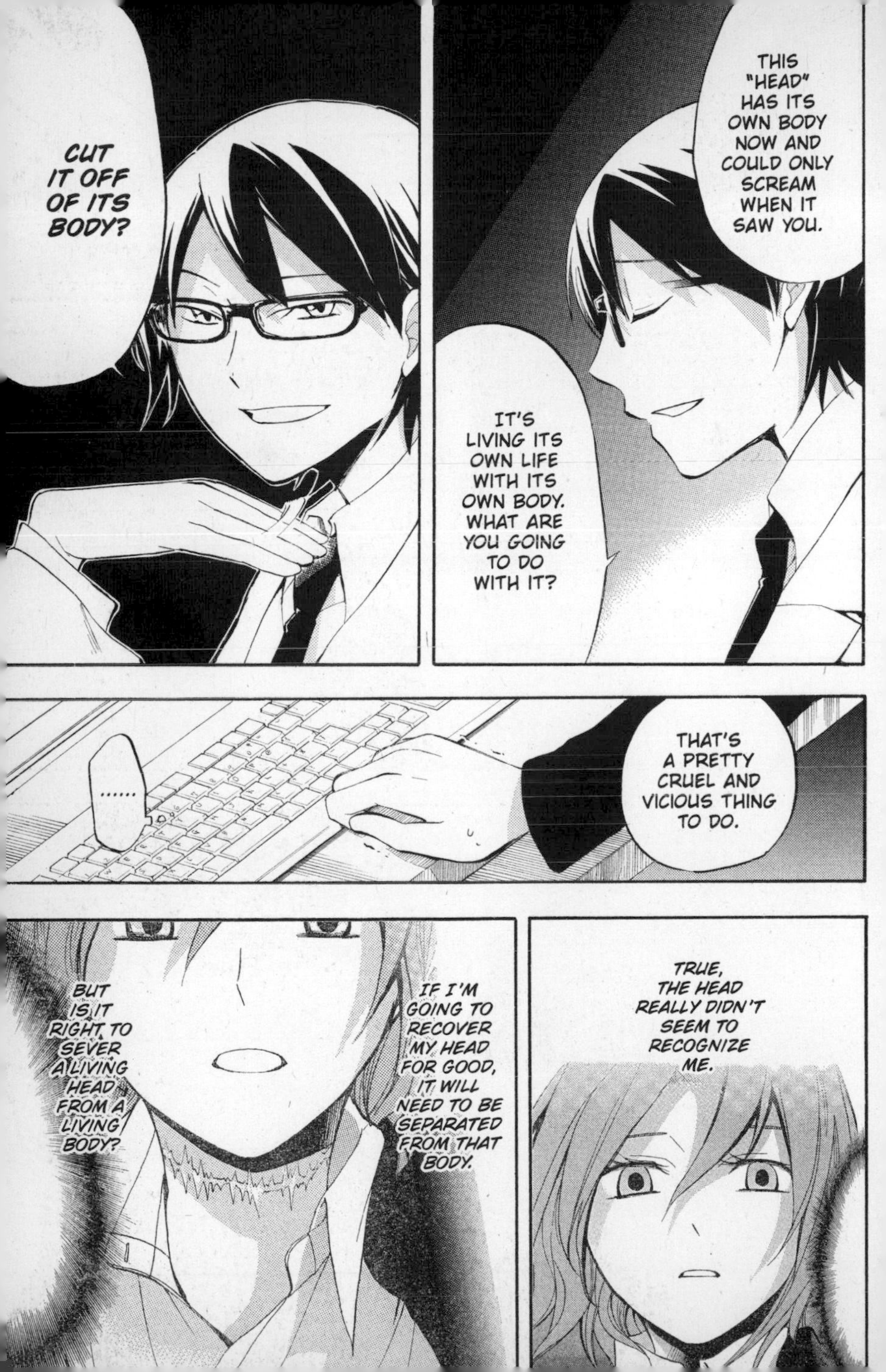
THIS "HEAD" HAS ITS OWN BODY NOW AND COULD ONLY SCREAM WHEN IT SAW YOU.
IT'S LIVING ITS OWN LIFE WITH ITS OWN BODY. WHAT ARE YOU GOING TO DO WITH IT?
CUT IT OFF OF ITS BODY?
THAT'S A PRETTY CRUEL AND VICIOUS THING TO DO.
......
TRUE, THE HEAD REALLY DIDN'T SEEM TO RECOGNIZE ME.
IF I'M GOING TO RECOVER MY HEAD FOR GOOD, IT WILL NEED TO BE SEPARATED FROM THAT BODY.
BUT IS IT RIGHT TO SEVER A LIVING HEAD FROM A LIVING BODY?

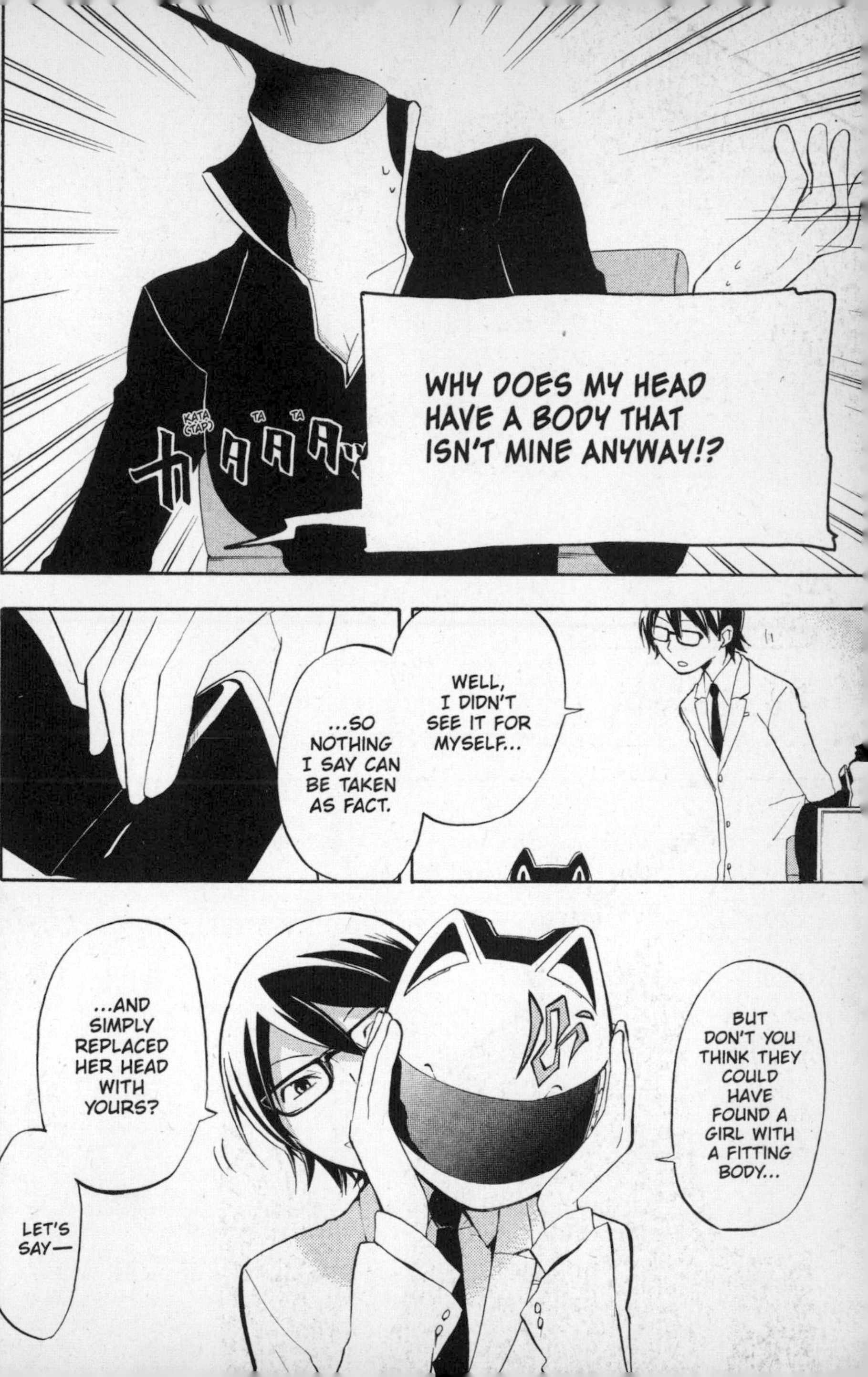

KATA (TAP) TA TA
WHY DOES MY HEAD HAVE A BODY THAT ISN'T MINE ANYWAY!?
WELL, I DIDN'T SEE IT FOR MYSELF...
...SO NOTHING I SAY CAN BE TAKEN AS FACT.
BUT DON'T YOU THINK THEY COULD HAVE FOUND A GIRL WITH A FITTING BODY...
...AND SIMPLY REPLACED HER HEAD WITH YOURS?
LET'S SAY—

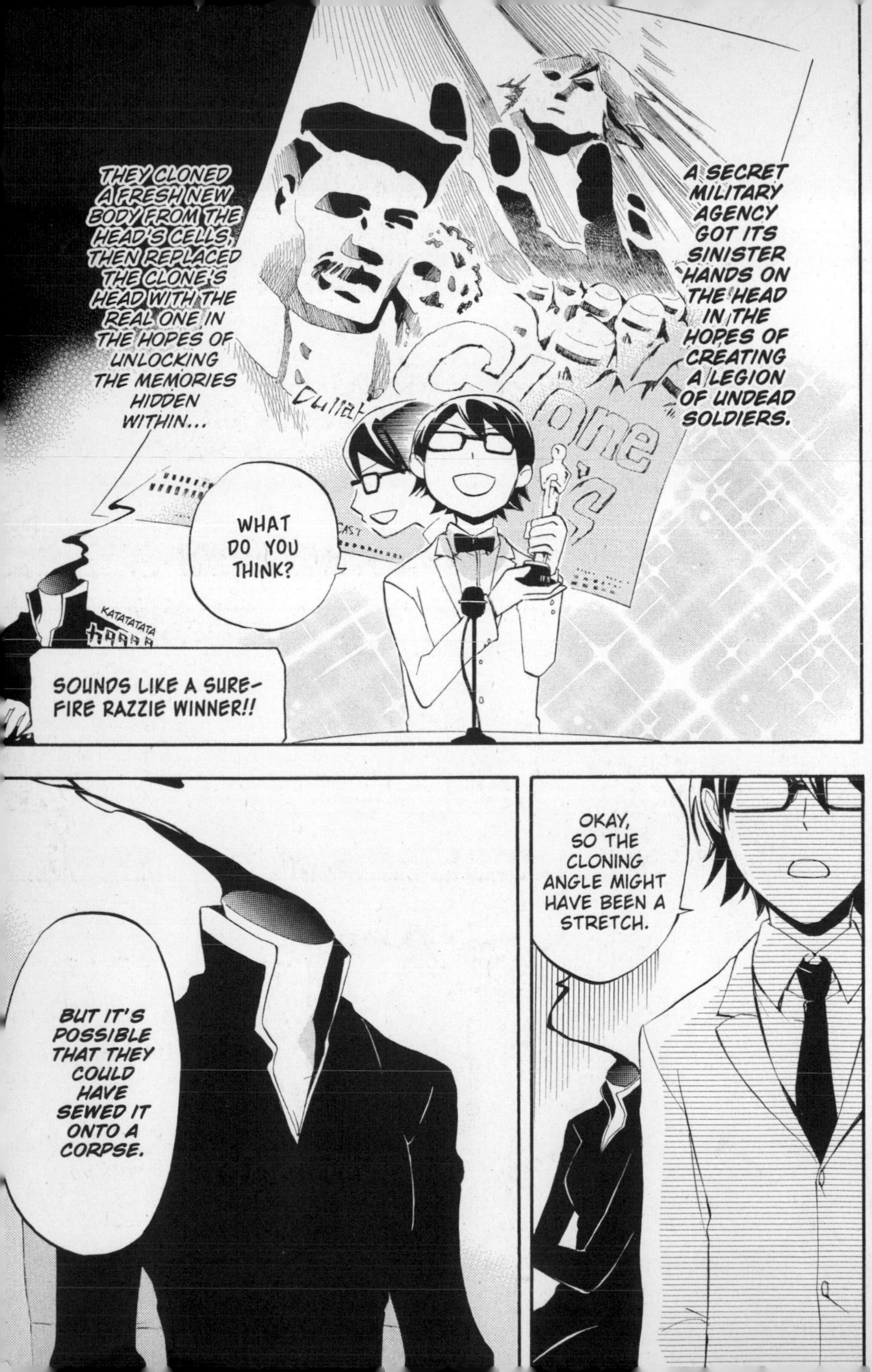
A SECRET MILITARY AGENCY GOT ITS SINISTER HANDS ON THE HEAD IN THE HOPES OF CREATING A LEGION OF UNDEAD SOLDIERS.
THEY CLONED A FRESH NEW BODY FROM THE HEAD'S CELLS, THEN REPLACED THE CLONE'S HEAD WITH THE REAL ONE IN THE HOPES OF UNLOCKING THE MEMORIES HIDDEN WITHIN...
WHAT DO YOU THINK?
KATATATATA
SOUNDS LIKE A SURE-FIRE RAZZIE WINNER!!
OKAY, SO THE CLONING ANGLE MIGHT HAVE BEEN A STRETCH.
BUT IT'S POSSIBLE THAT THEY COULD HAVE SEWED IT ONTO A CORPSE.

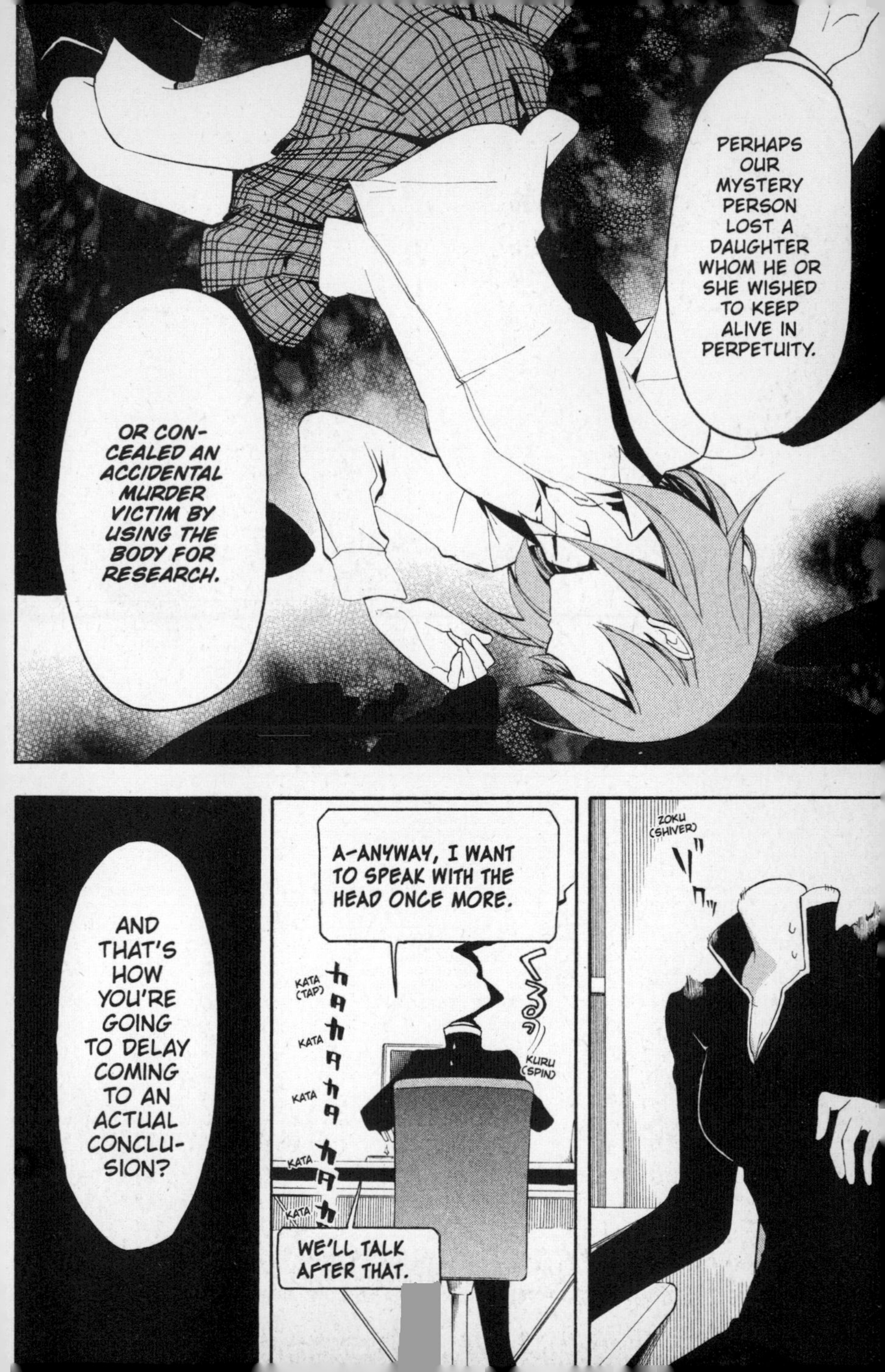
PERHAPS OUR MYSTERY PERSON LOST A DAUGHTER WHOM HE OR SHE WISHED TO KEEP ALIVE IN PERPETUITY.
OR CONCEALED AN ACCIDENTAL MURDER VICTIM BY USING THE BODY FOR RESEARCH.
ZOKU (SHIVER)
A-ANYWAY, I WANT TO SPEAK WITH THE HEAD ONCE MORE.
KURU (SPIN)
KATA (TAP)
KATA
KATA
KATA
KATA
WE'LL TALK AFTER THAT.
AND THAT'S HOW YOU'RE GOING TO DELAY COMING TO AN ACTUAL CONCLUSION?

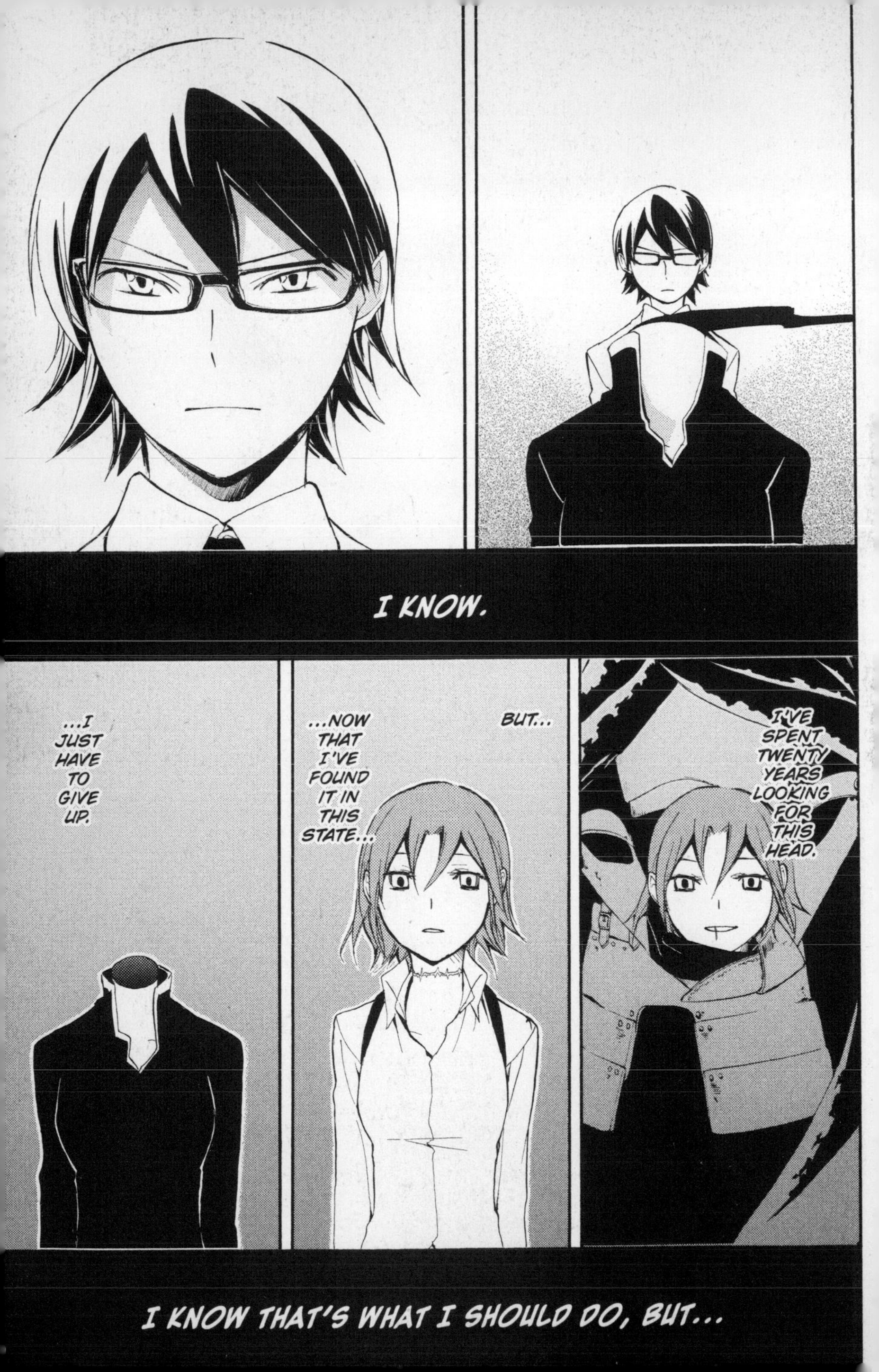
I KNOW.
I'VE SPENT TWENTY YEARS LOOKING FOR THIS HEAD.
BUT...
...NOW THAT I'VE FOUND IT IN THIS STATE...
...I JUST HAVE TO GIVE UP.
I KNOW THAT'S WHAT I SHOULD DO, BUT...

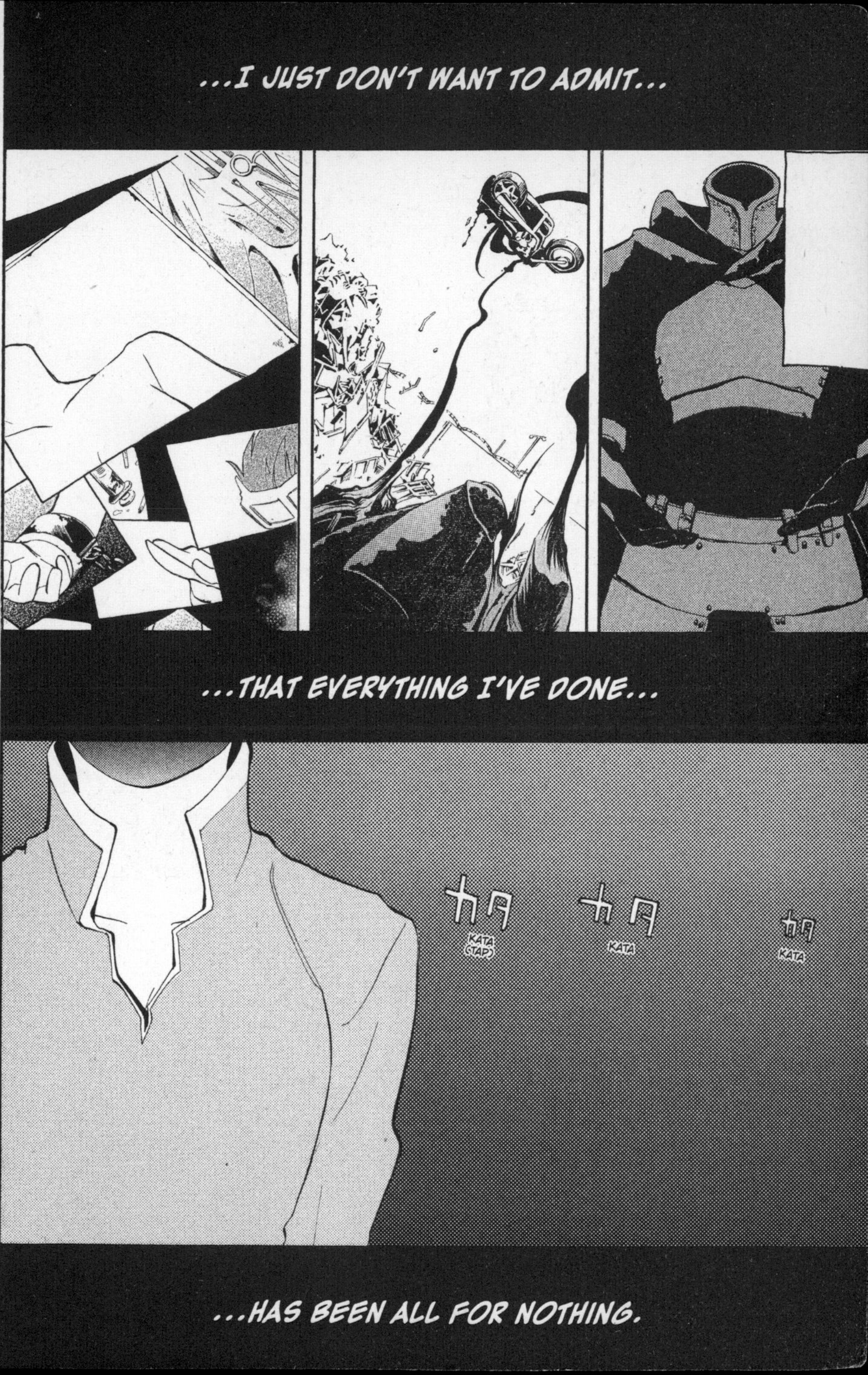
...I JUST DON'T WANT TO ADMIT...
...THAT EVERYTHING I'VE DONE...
カタ KATA
カタ KATA
カタ KATA (TAP)
...HAS BEEN ALL FOR NOTHING.

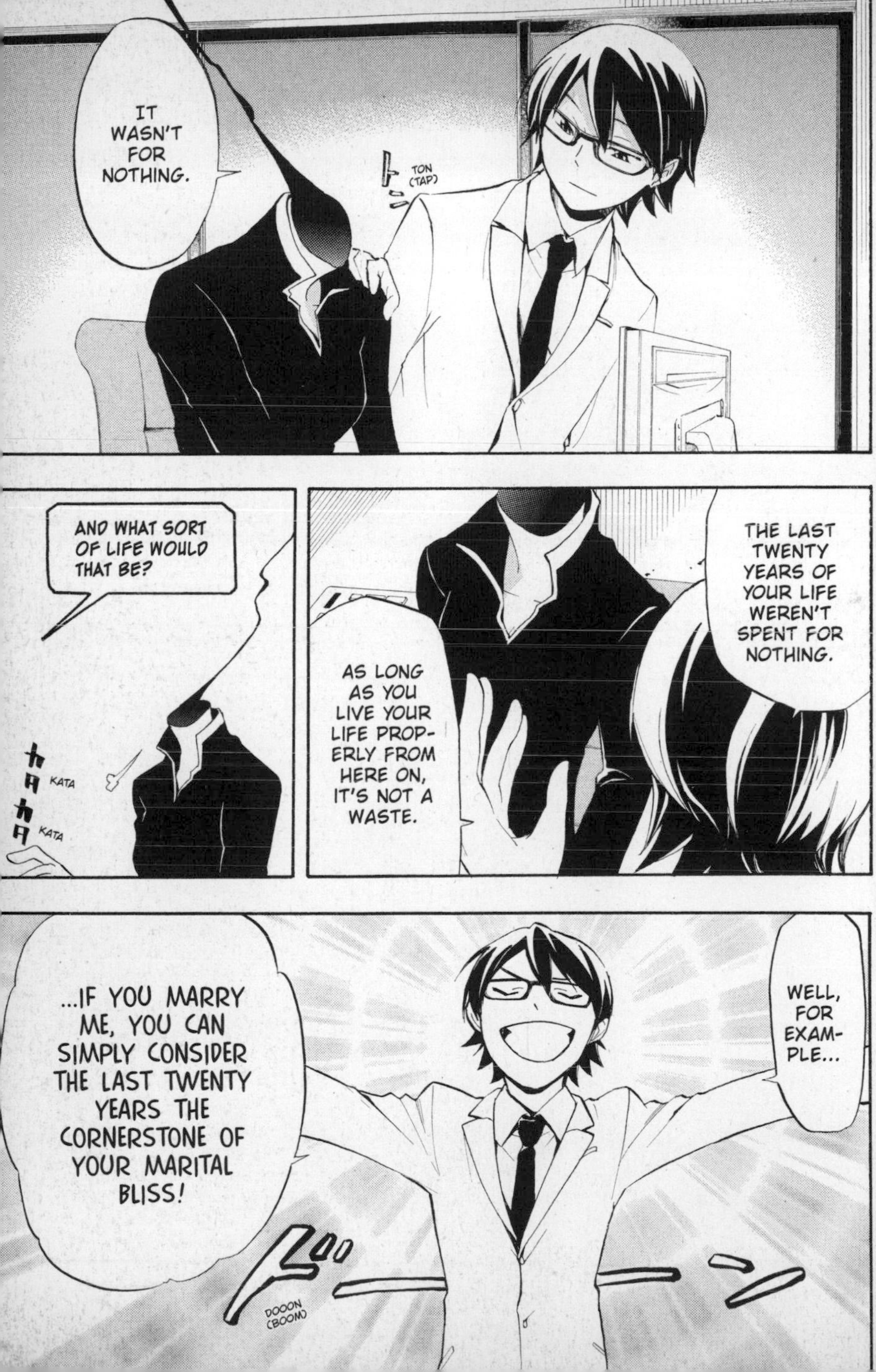
IT WASN'T FOR NOTHING.
TON (TAP)
THE LAST TWENTY YEARS OF YOUR LIFE WEREN'T SPENT FOR NOTHING.
AS LONG AS YOU LIVE YOUR LIFE PROPERLY FROM HERE ON, IT'S NOT A WASTE.
AND WHAT SORT OF LIFE WOULD THAT BE?
KATA
KATA
WELL, FOR EXAMPLE...
...IF YOU MARRY ME, YOU CAN SIMPLY CONSIDER THE LAST TWENTY YEARS THE CORNERSTONE OF YOUR MARITAL BLISS!
DOOON (BOOM)

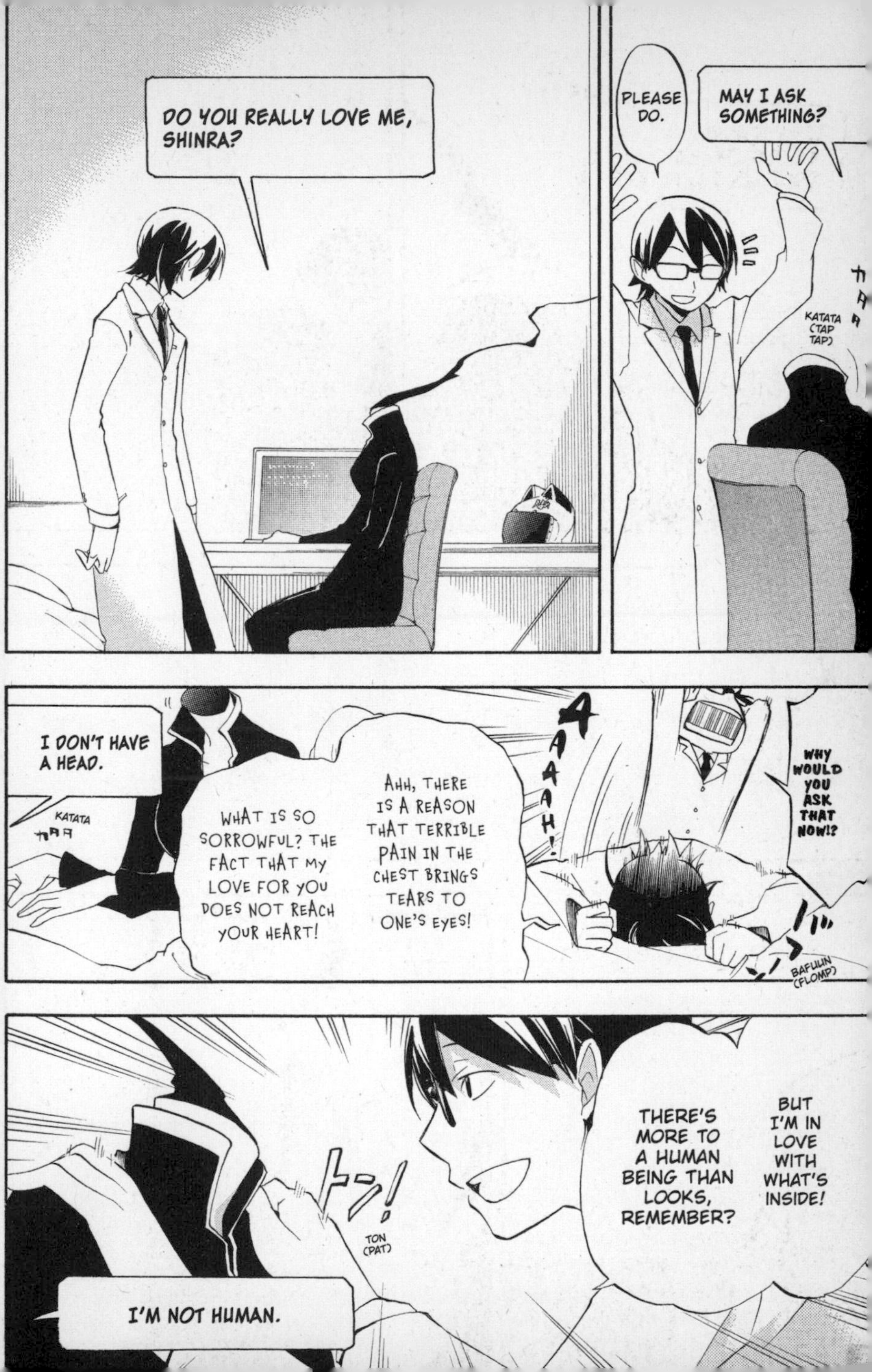
MAY I ASK SOMETHING?
PLEASE DO.
KATATA (TAP TAP)
DO YOU REALLY LOVE ME, SHINRA?
AAAAH!
WHY WOULD YOU ASK THAT NOW!?
BAFUUN (FLOMP)
AHH, THERE IS A REASON THAT TERRIBLE PAIN IN THE CHEST BRINGS TEARS TO ONE'S EYES!
WHAT IS SO SORROWFUL? THE FACT THAT MY LOVE FOR YOU DOES NOT REACH YOUR HEART!
I DON'T HAVE A HEAD.
KATATA
BUT I'M IN LOVE WITH WHAT'S INSIDE!
THERE'S MORE TO A HUMAN BEING THAN LOOKS, REMEMBER?
TON (PAT)
I'M NOT HUMAN.

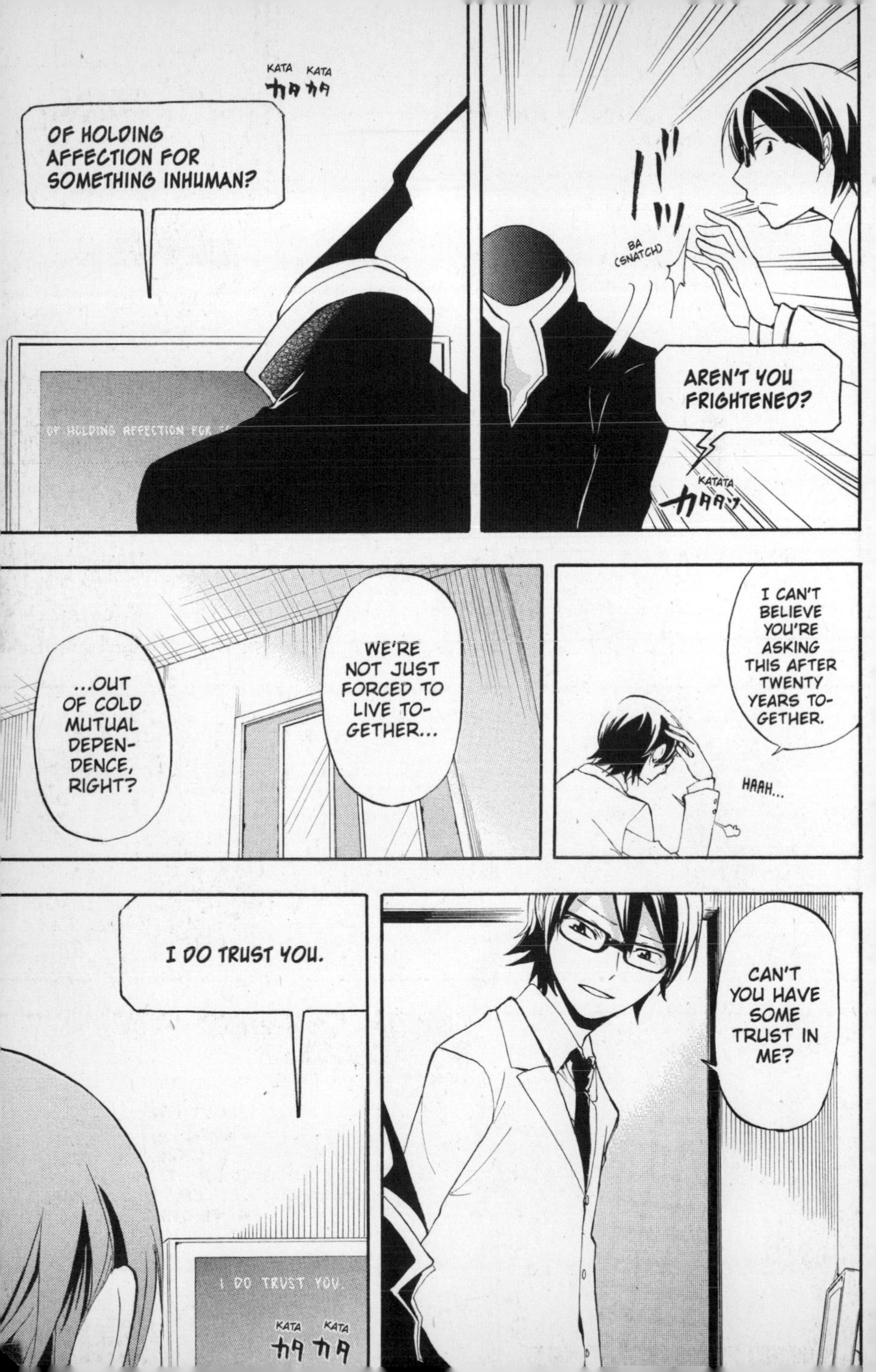
BA (SNATCH)
AREN'T YOU FRIGHTENED?
KATATA
カタタッ
KATA KATA
カタ カタ
OF HOLDING AFFECTION FOR SOMETHING INHUMAN?
OF HOLDING AFFECTION FOR
I CAN'T BELIEVE YOU'RE ASKING THIS AFTER TWENTY YEARS TO-GETHER.
HAAH...
WE'RE NOT JUST FORCED TO LIVE TO-GETHER...
...OUT OF COLD MUTUAL DEPEN-DENCE, RIGHT?
CAN'T YOU HAVE SOME TRUST IN ME?
I DO TRUST YOU.
I DO TRUST YOU.
KATA KATA
カタ カタ

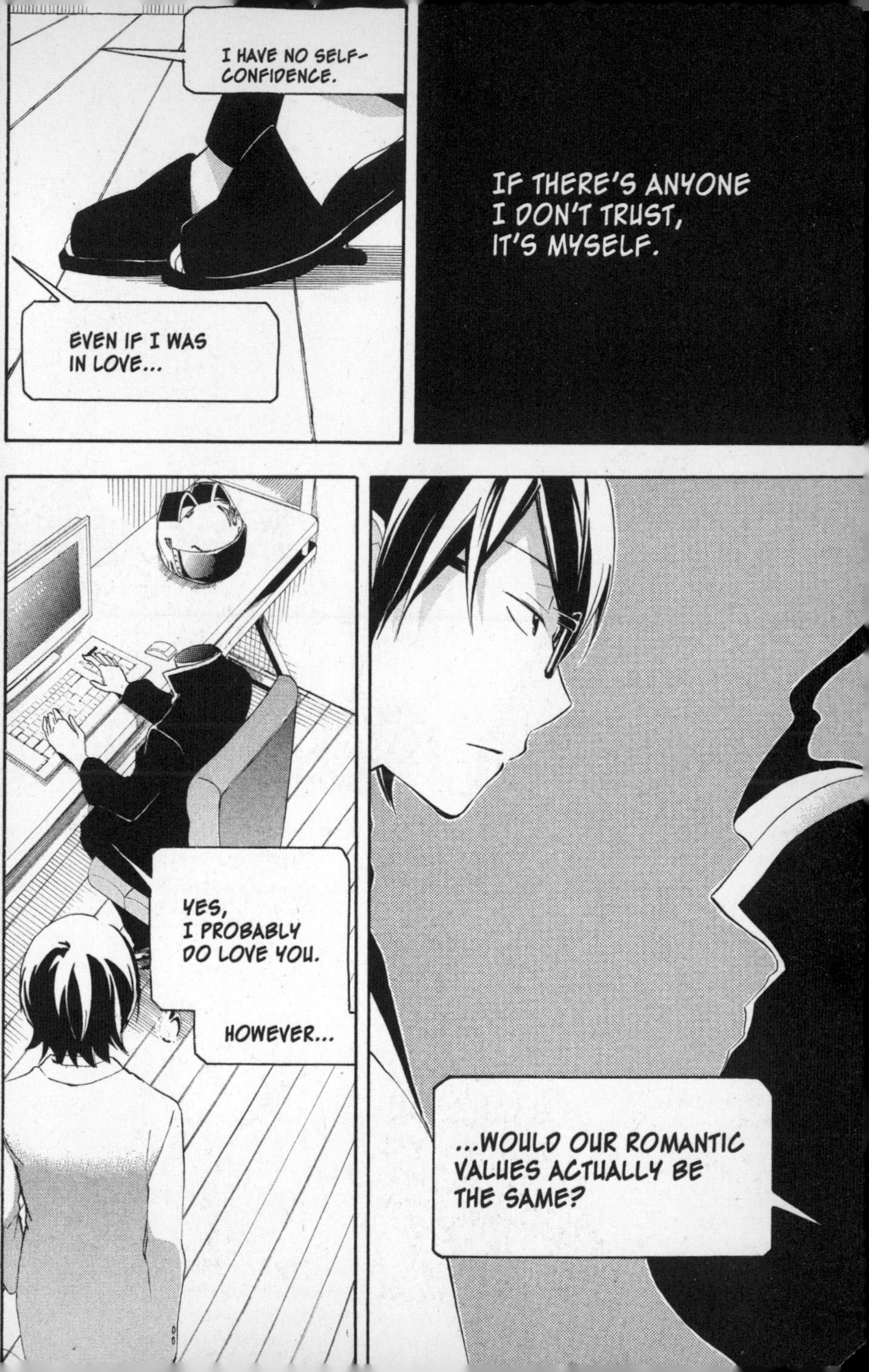
IF THERE'S ANYONE I DON'T TRUST, IT'S MYSELF.
I HAVE NO SELF-CONFIDENCE.
EVEN IF I WAS IN LOVE...
...WOULD OUR ROMANTIC VALUES ACTUALLY BE THE SAME?
YES, I PROBABLY DO LOVE YOU.
HOWEVER...

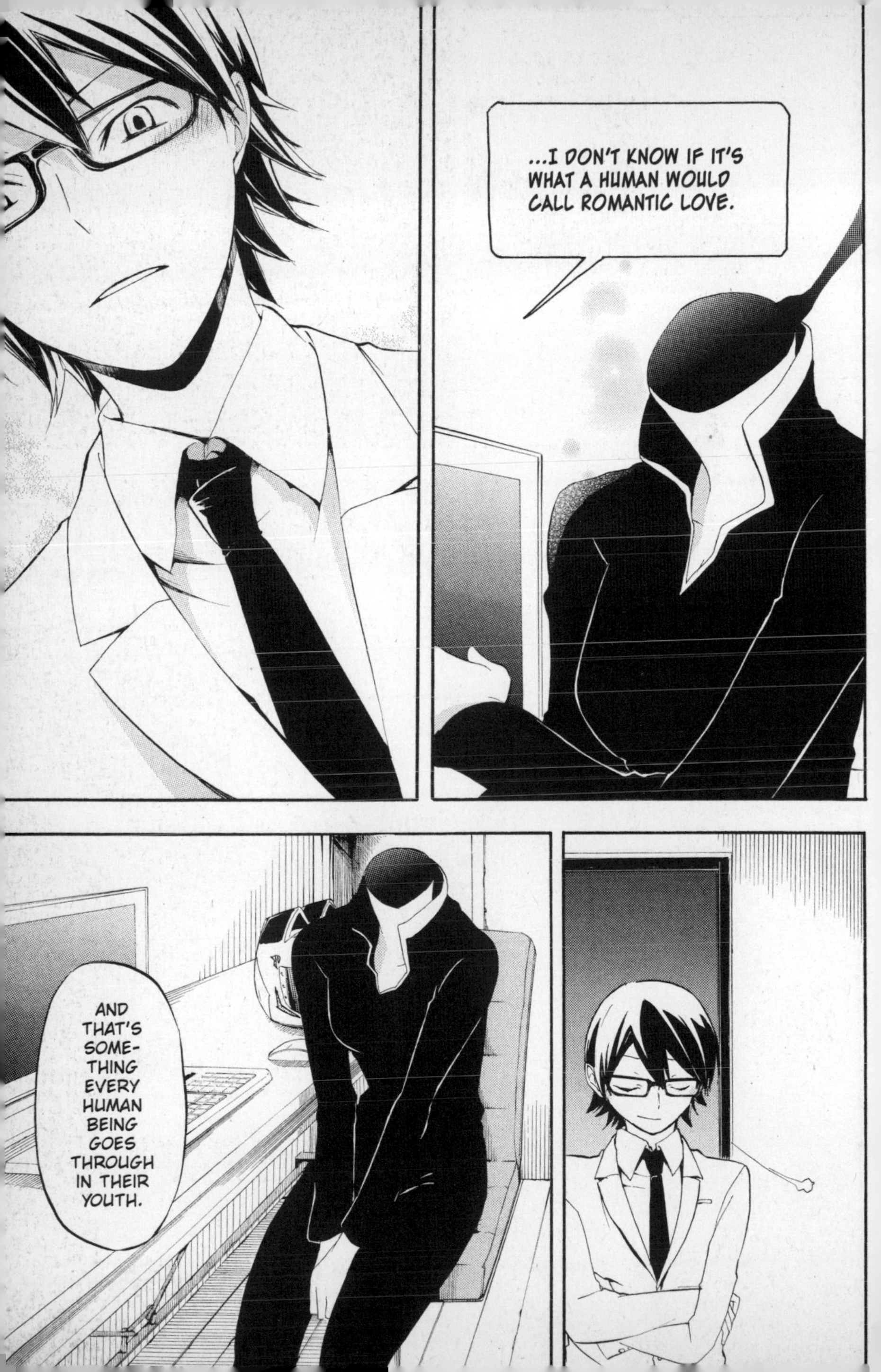
...I DON'T KNOW IF IT'S WHAT A HUMAN WOULD CALL ROMANTIC LOVE.
AND THAT'S SOME-THING EVERY HUMAN BEING GOES THROUGH IN THEIR YOUTH.

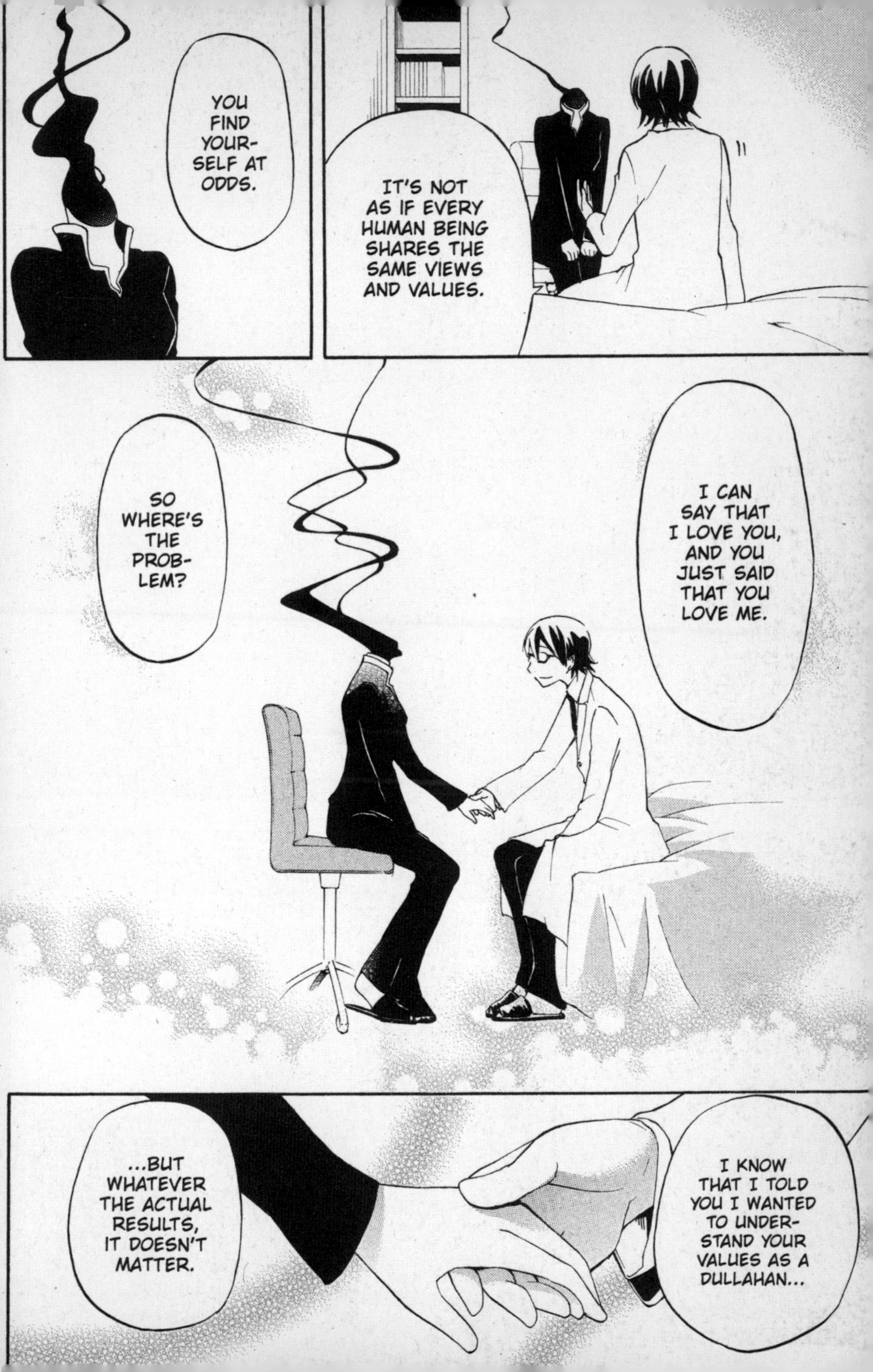
IT'S NOT AS IF EVERY HUMAN BEING SHARES THE SAME VIEWS AND VALUES.
YOU FIND YOUR-SELF AT ODDS.
I CAN SAY THAT I LOVE YOU, AND YOU JUST SAID THAT YOU LOVE ME.
SO WHERE'S THE PROB-LEM?
I KNOW THAT I TOLD YOU I WANTED TO UNDER-STAND YOUR VALUES AS A DULLAHAN...
...BUT WHATEVER THE ACTUAL RESULTS, IT DOESN'T MATTER.

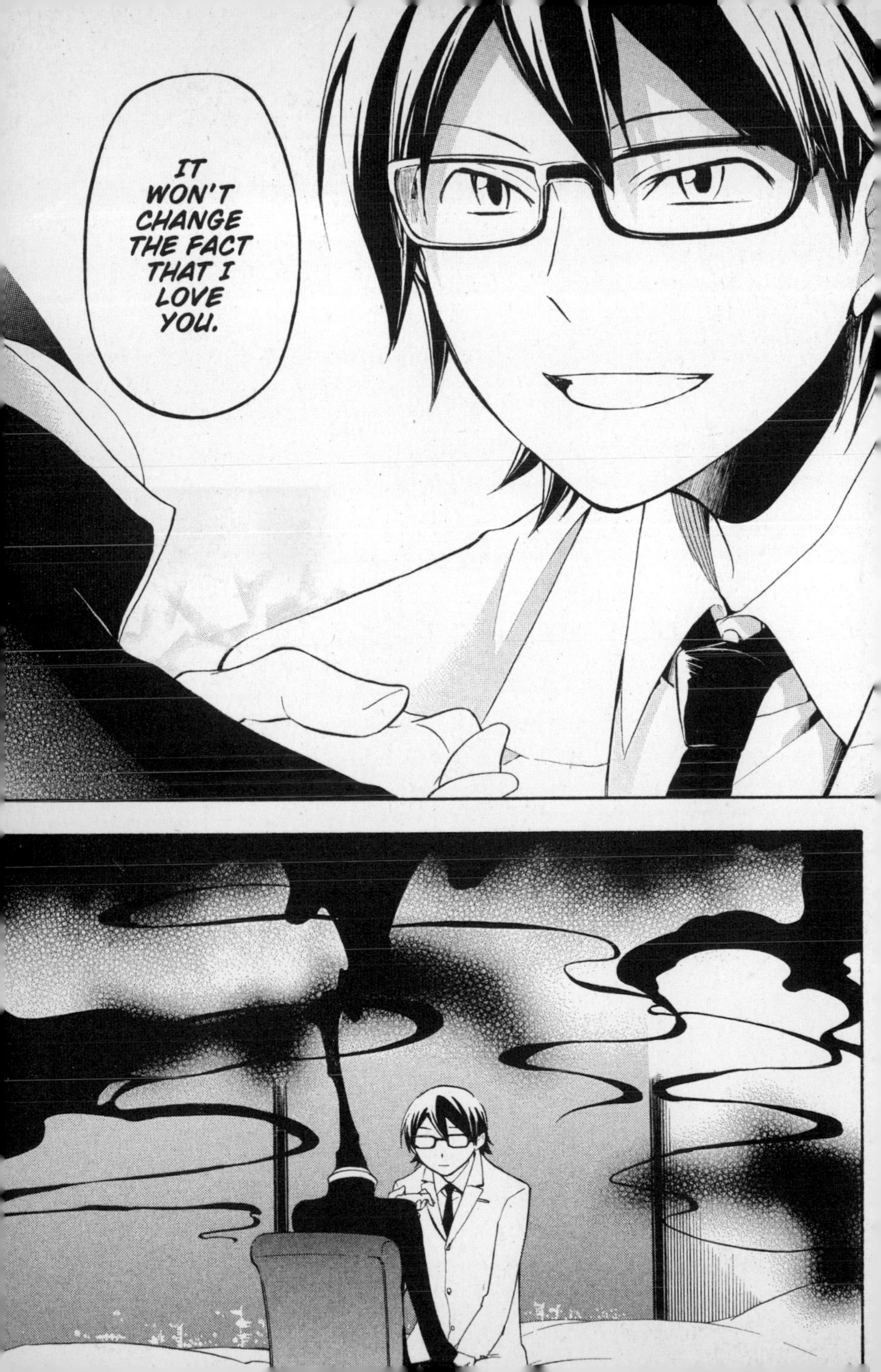
IT WON'T CHANGE THE FACT THAT I LOVE YOU.

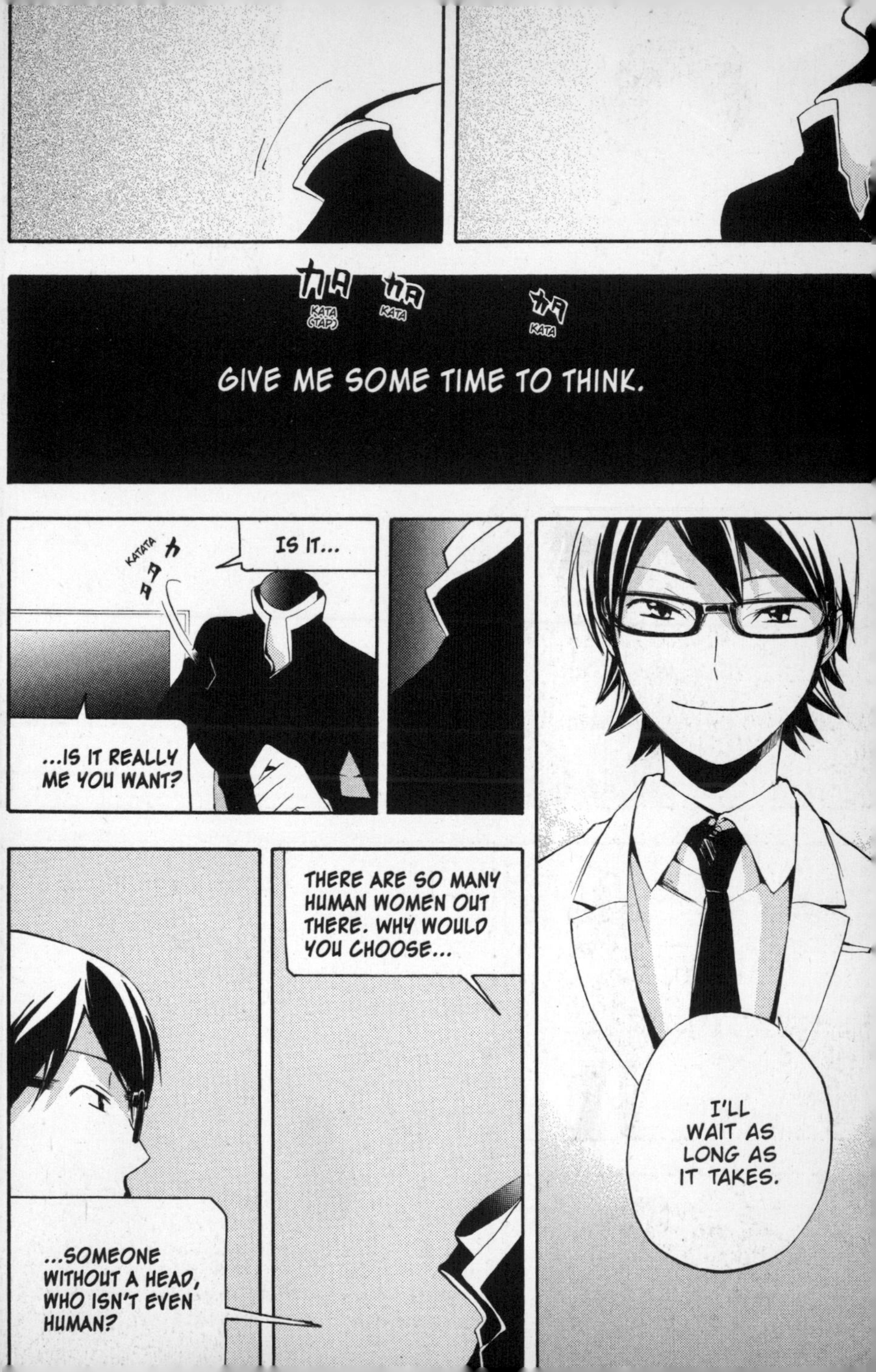
KATA
KATA
KATA (TAP)
GIVE ME SOME TIME TO THINK.
I'LL WAIT AS LONG AS IT TAKES.
KATATA
IS IT...
...IS IT REALLY ME YOU WANT?
THERE ARE SO MANY HUMAN WOMEN OUT THERE. WHY WOULD YOU CHOOSE...
...SOMEONE WITHOUT A HEAD, WHO ISN'T EVEN HUMAN?

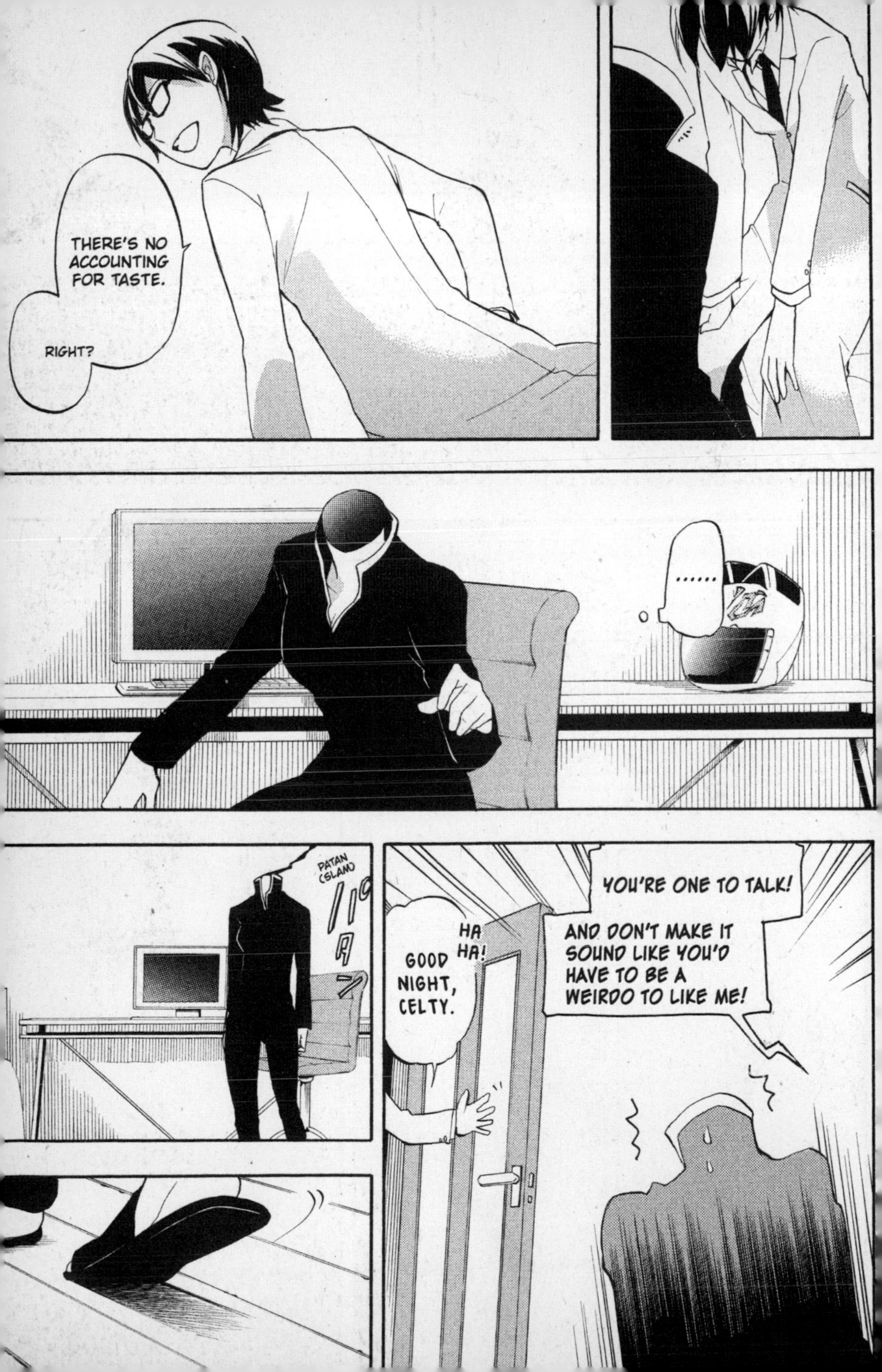
THERE'S NO ACCOUNTING FOR TASTE.
RIGHT?
......
YOU'RE ONE TO TALK!
AND DON'T MAKE IT SOUND LIKE YOU'D HAVE TO BE A WEIRDO TO LIKE ME!
HA HA!
GOOD NIGHT, CELTY.
PATAN (SLAM)

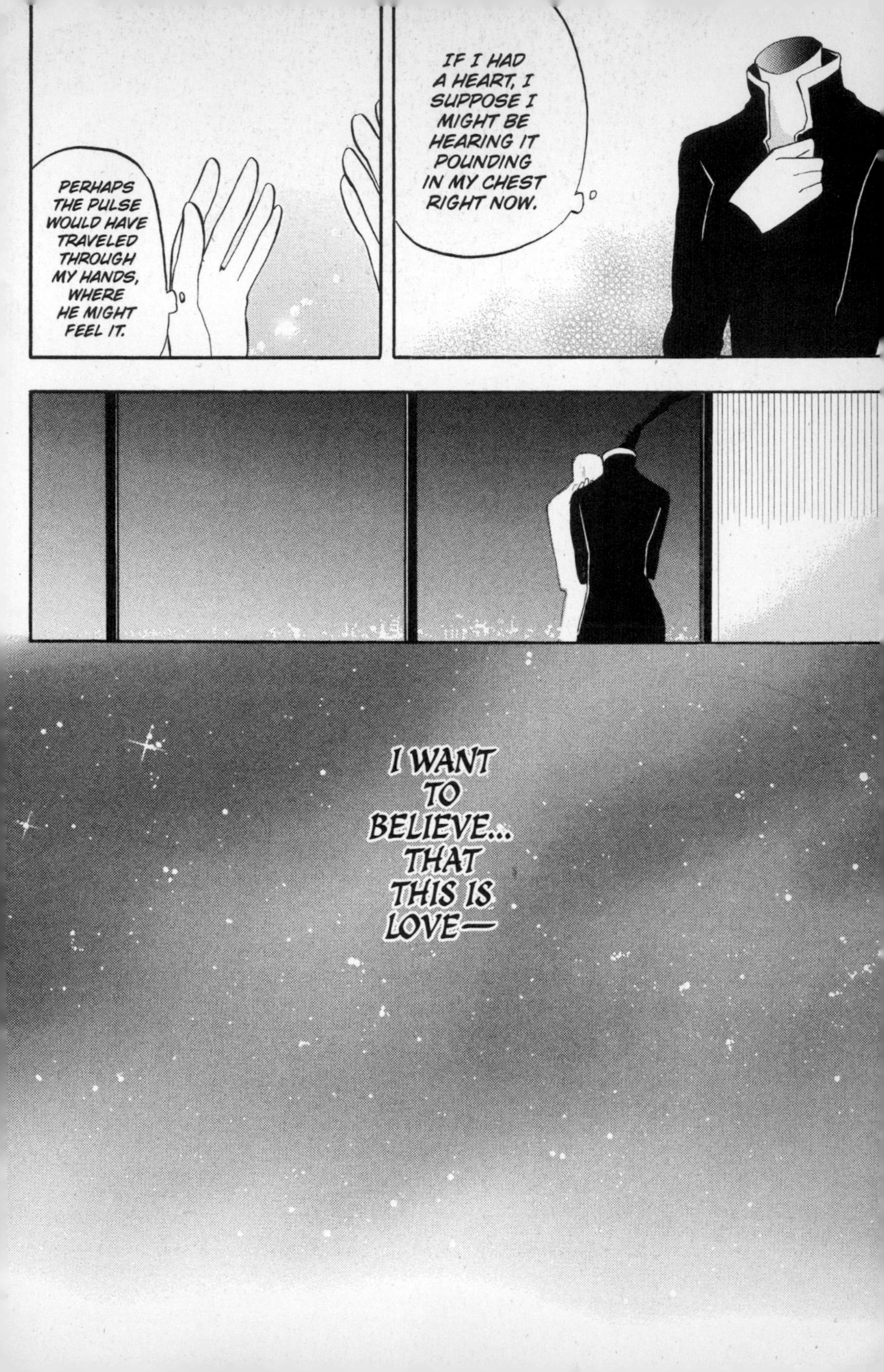
IF I HAD A HEART, I SUPPOSE I MIGHT BE HEARING IT POUNDING IN MY CHEST RIGHT NOW.
PERHAPS THE PULSE WOULD HAVE TRAVELED THROUGH MY HANDS, WHERE HE MIGHT FEEL IT.
I WANT TO BELIEVE... THAT THIS IS LOVE—

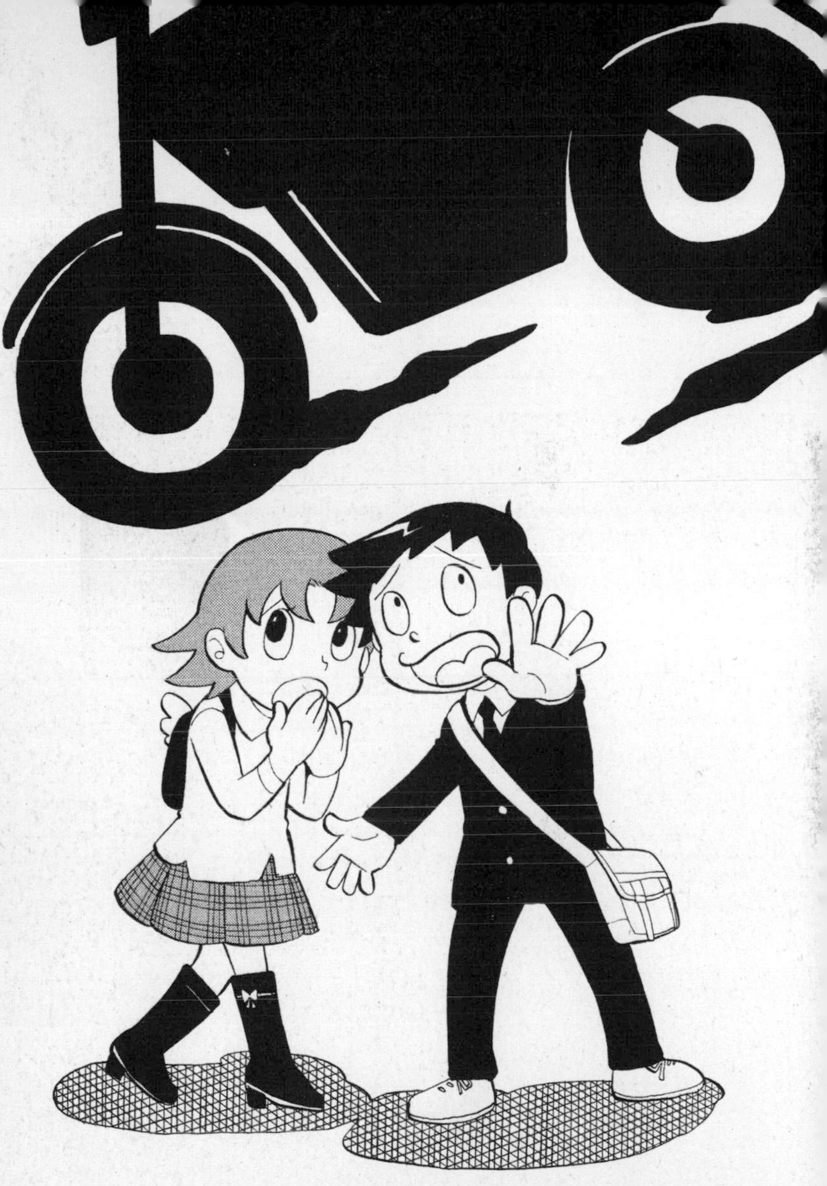

14: WAWAWAWAWAWAWAWAWAWAWAWAWAWAWAWA!!

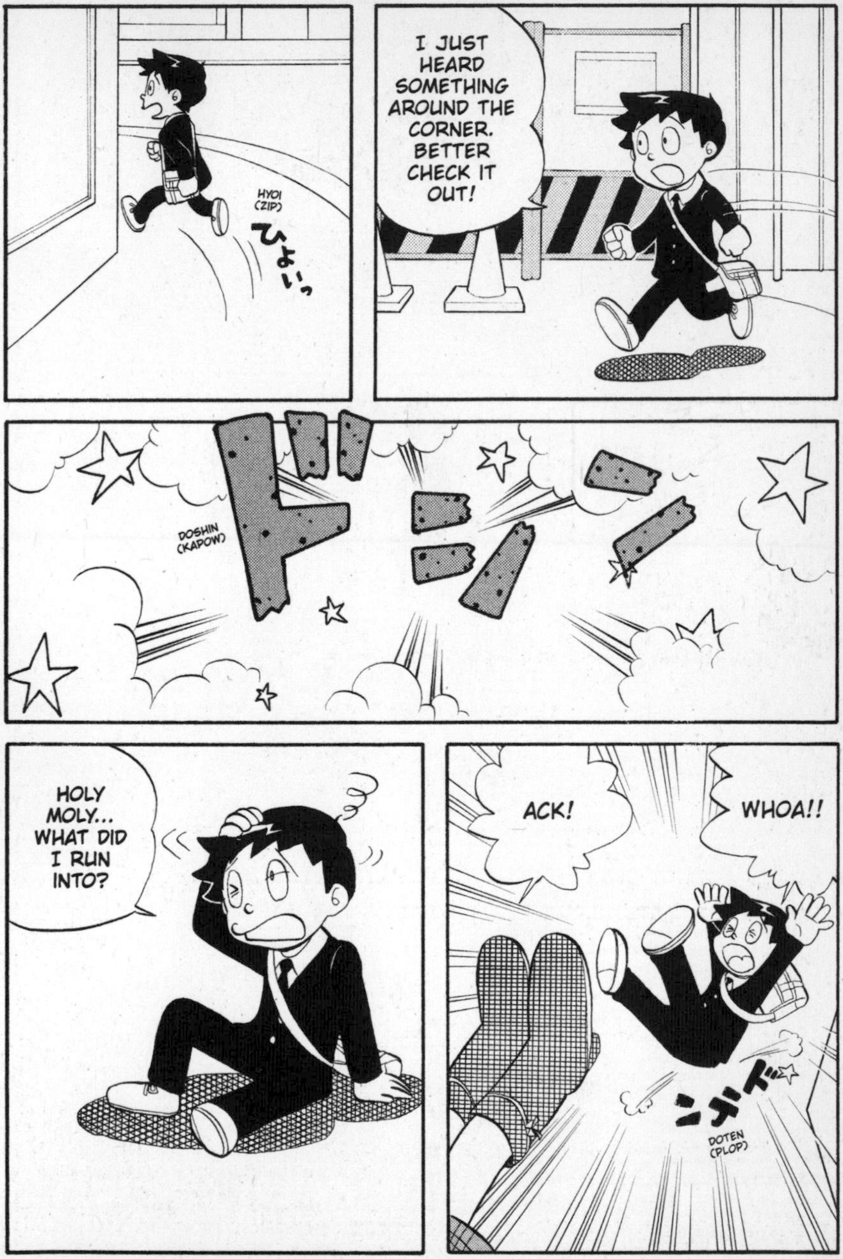
I JUST HEARD SOMETHING AROUND THE CORNER. BETTER CHECK IT OUT!
HYOI (ZIP)
ひょいっ
DOSHIN (KAPOW)
WHOA!!
ACK!
DOTEN (PLOP)
HOLY MOLY... WHAT DID I RUN INTO?

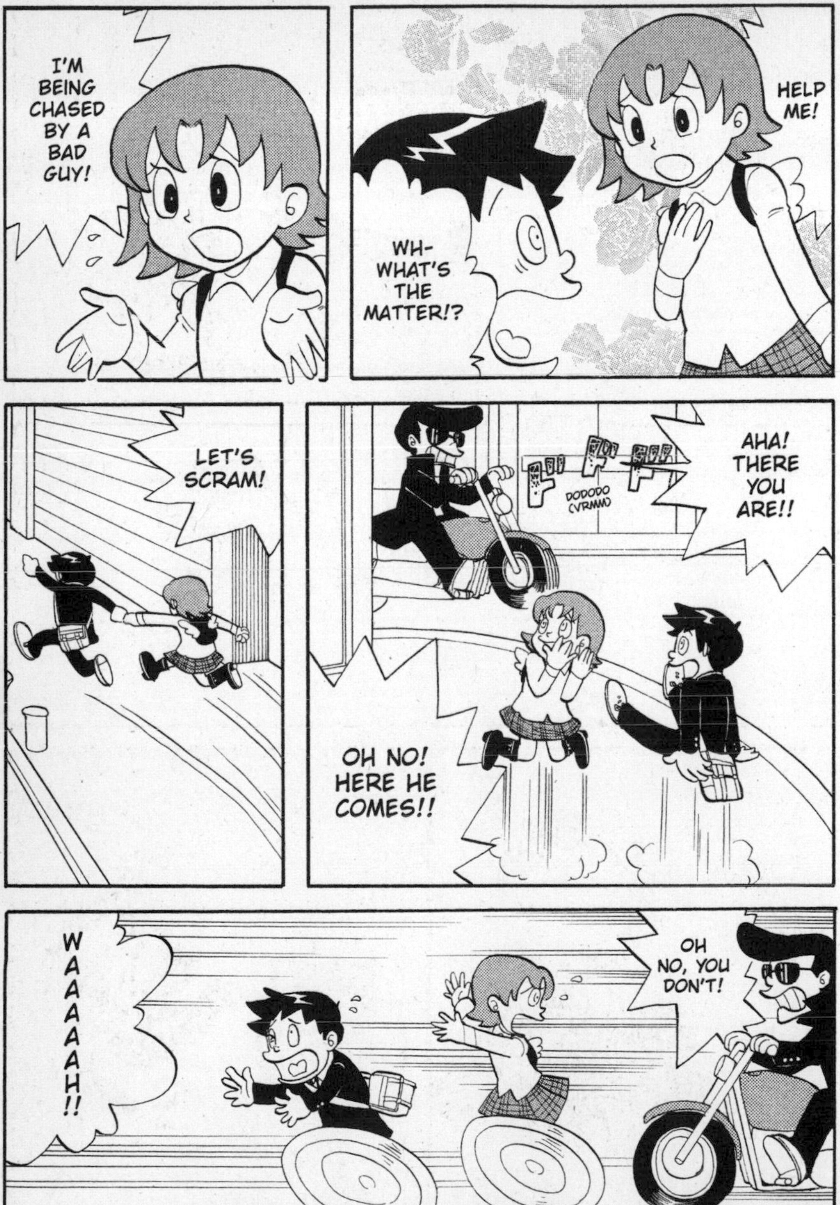
HELP ME!
WH- WHAT'S THE MATTER!?
I'M BEING CHASED BY A BAD GUY!
AHA! THERE YOU ARE!!
DODODO (VRMM)
OH NO! HERE HE COMES!!
LET'S SCRAM!
OH NO, YOU DON'T!
WAAAAAH!!

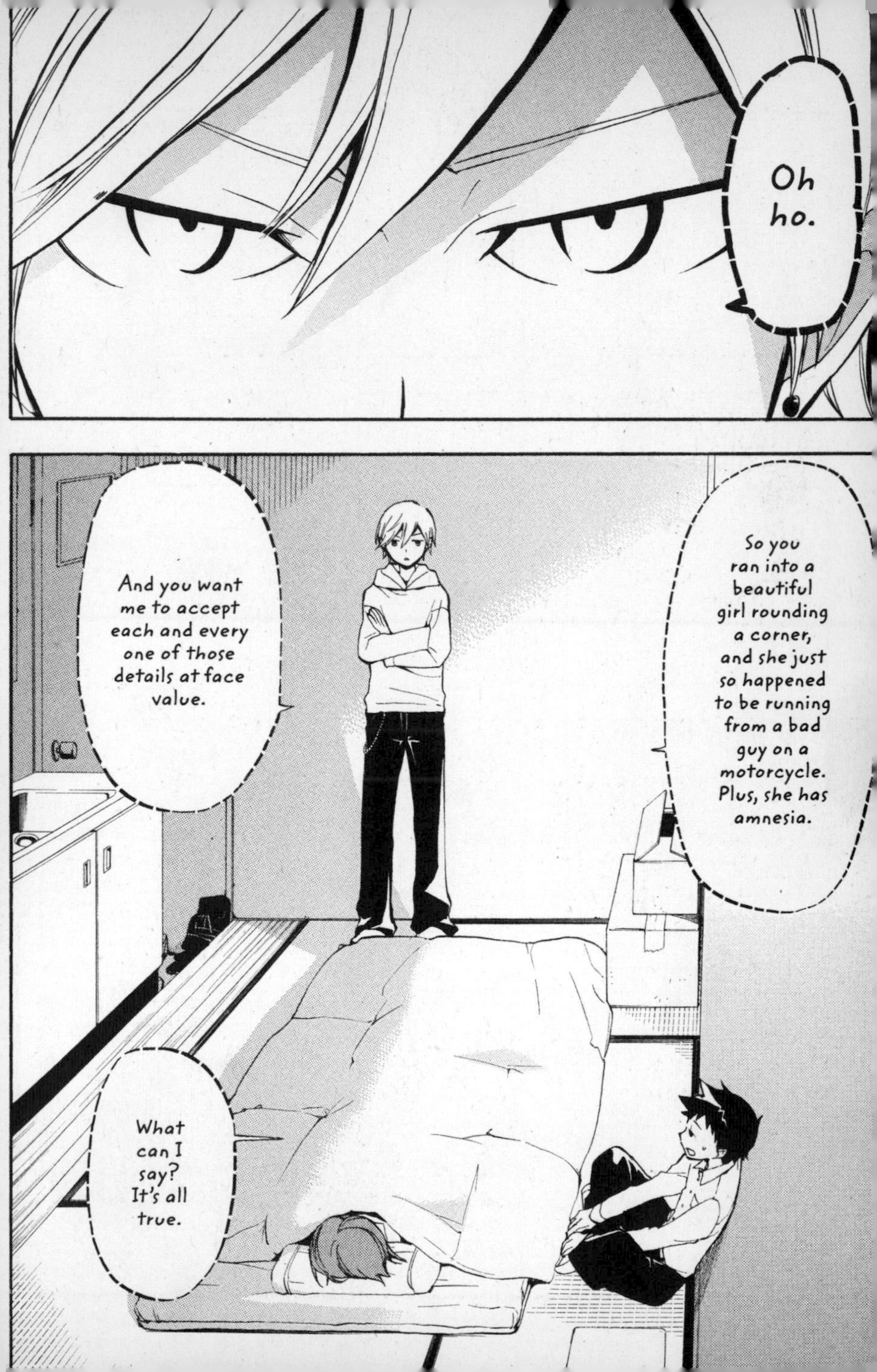
Oh ho.
So you ran into a beautiful girl rounding a corner, and she just so happened to be running from a bad guy on a motorcycle. Plus, she has amnesia.
And you want me to accept each and every one of those details at face value.
What can I say? It's all true.

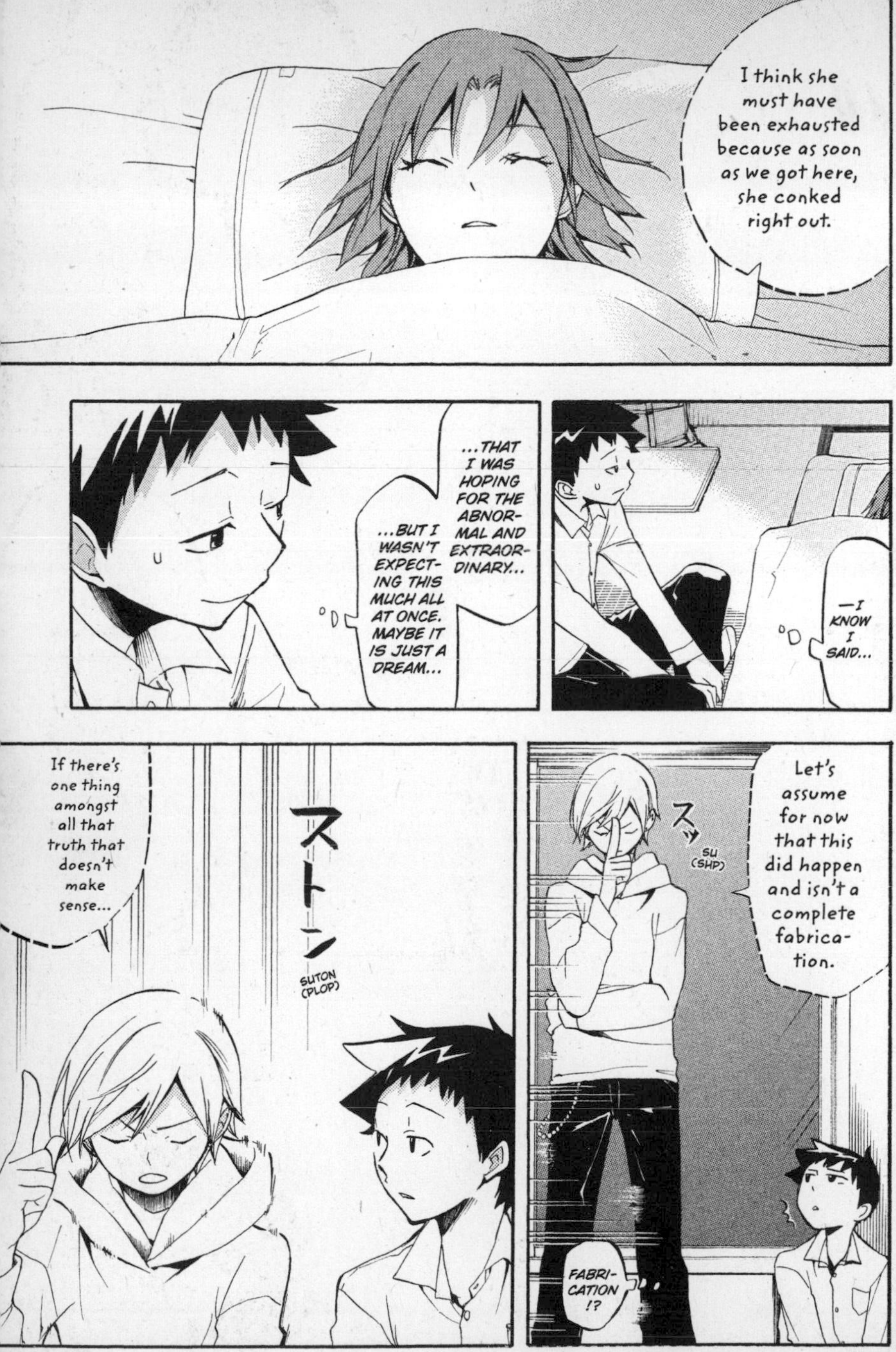
I think she must have been exhausted because as soon as we got here, she conked right out.
—I KNOW I SAID...
...THAT I WAS HOPING FOR THE ABNORMAL AND EXTRAORDINARY...
...BUT I WASN'T EXPECTING THIS MUCH ALL AT ONCE. MAYBE IT IS JUST A DREAM...
スッ
SU (SHP)
Let's assume for now that this did happen and isn't a complete fabrication.
FABRICATION!?
ストン
SUTON (PLOP)
If there's one thing amongst all that truth that doesn't make sense...

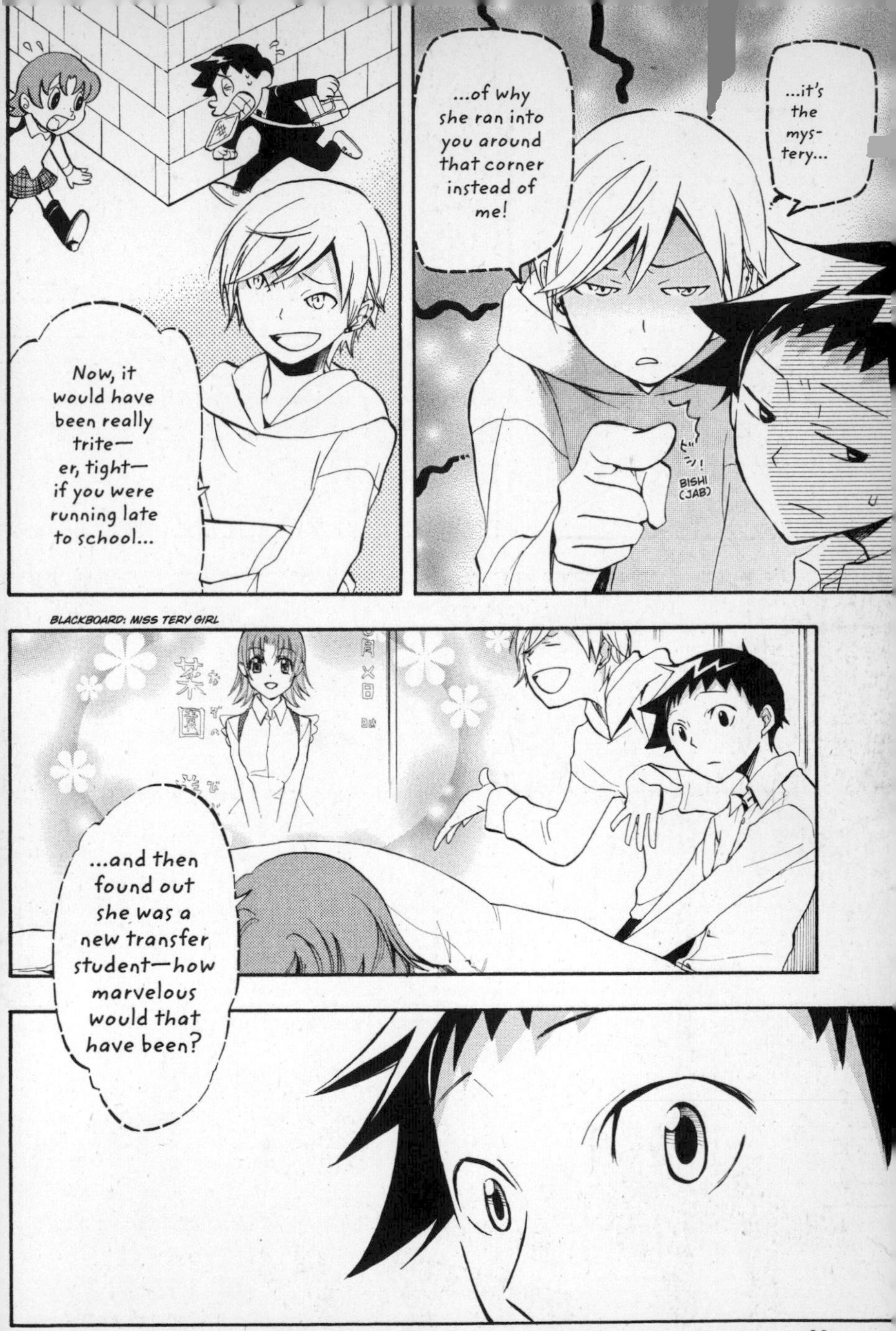
...it's the mys- tery...
...of why she ran into you around that corner instead of me!
BISHI (JAB)
Now, it would have been really trite— er, tight— if you were running late to school...
BLACKBOARD: MISS TERY GIRL
...and then found out she was a new transfer student—how marvelous would that have been?

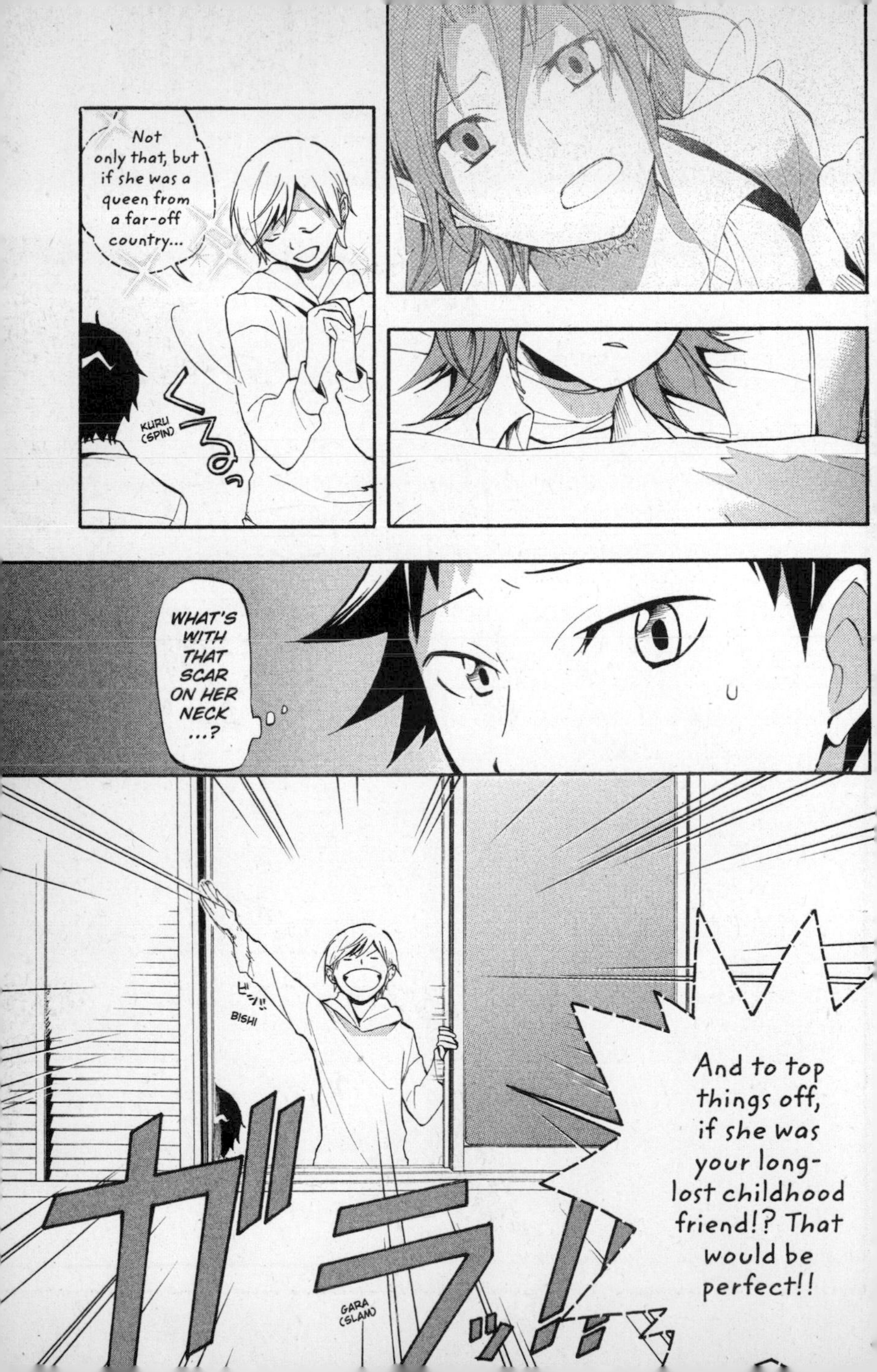
Not only that, but if she was a queen from a far-off country...
KURU (SPIN)
WHAT'S WITH THAT SCAR ON HER NECK ...?
ビッ!!
BISHI
And to top things off, if she was your long-lost childhood friend!? That would be perfect!!
GARA (SLAM)

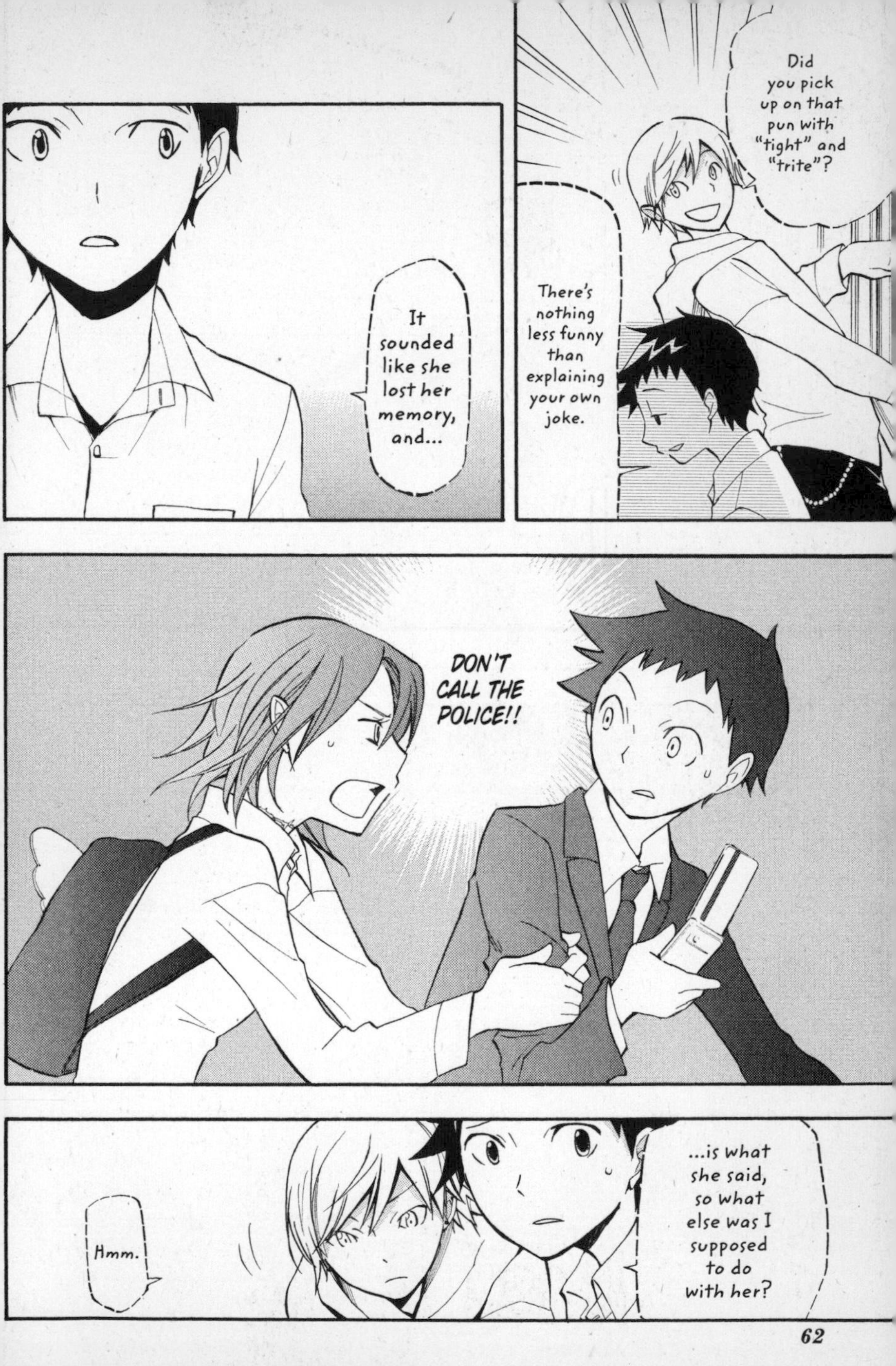
Did you pick up on that pun with "tight" and "trite"?
There's nothing less funny than explaining your own joke.
It sounded like she lost her memory, and...
DON'T CALL THE POLICE!!
...is what she said, so what else was I supposed to do with her?
Hmm.

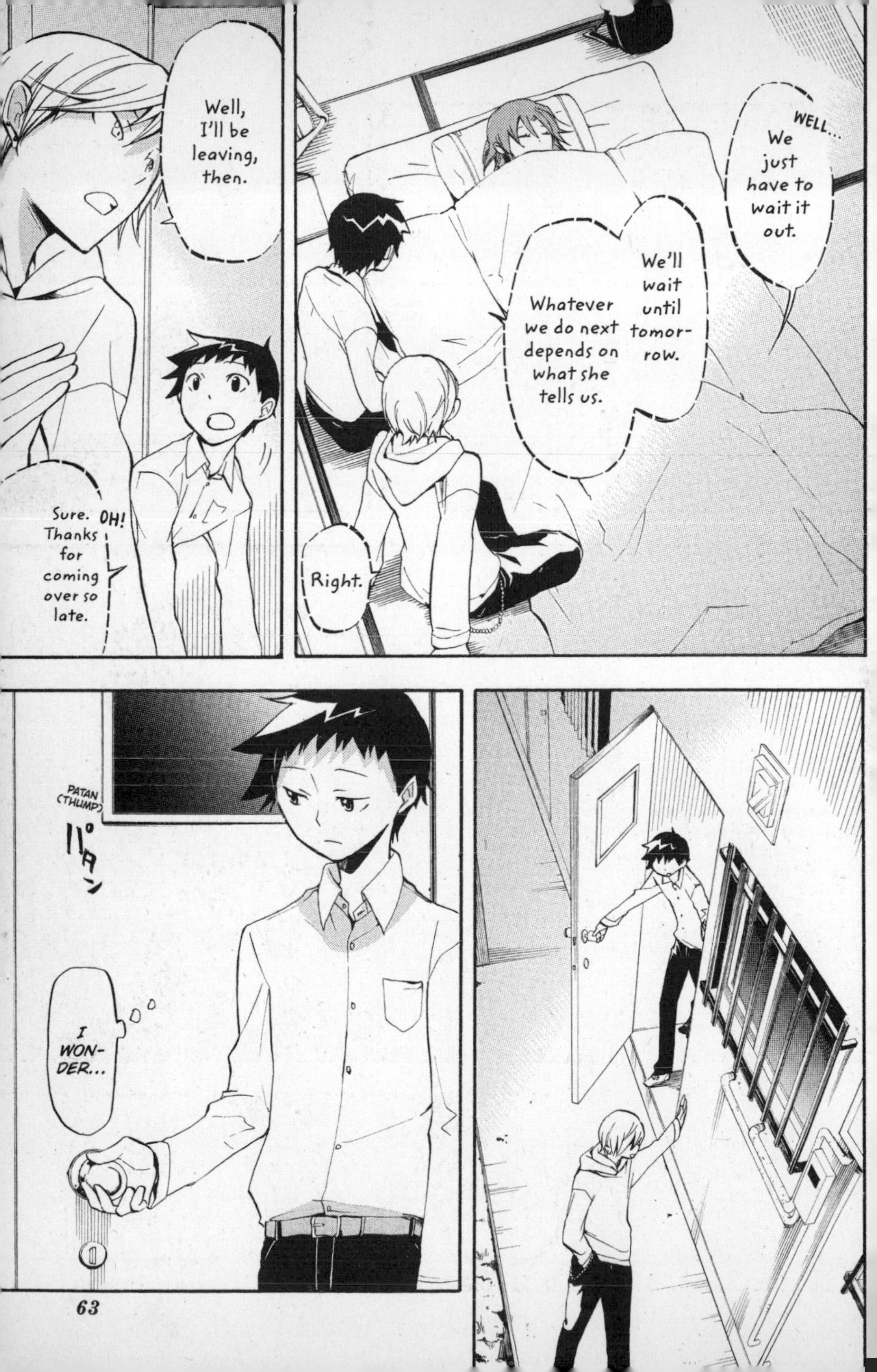
WELL...
We just have to wait it out.
We'll wait until tomor-row.
Whatever we do next depends on what she tells us.
Right.
Well, I'll be leaving, then.
Sure.
OH! Thanks for coming over so late.
PATAN (THUMP)
パタン
I WON-DER...

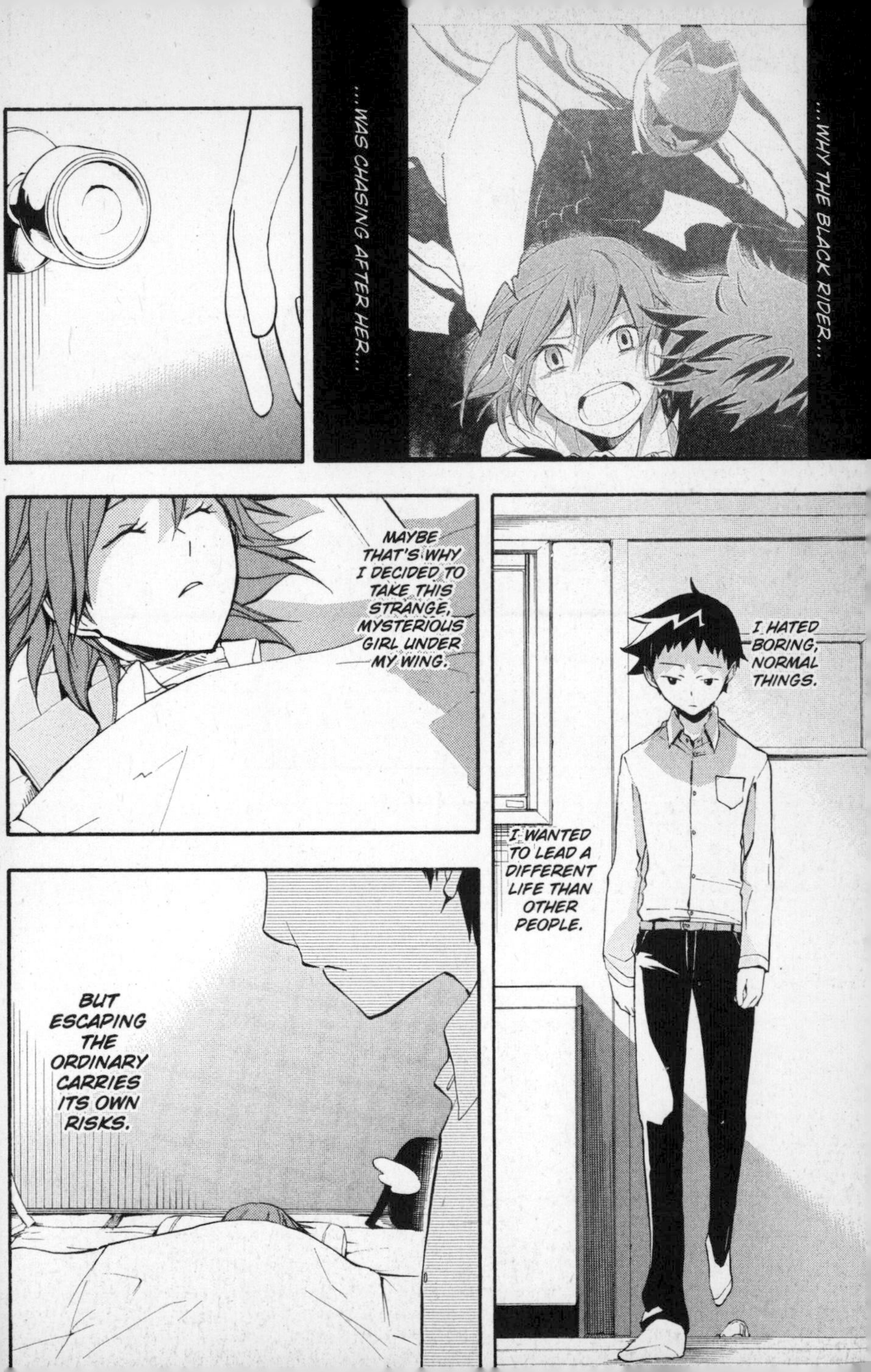
...WHY THE BLACK RIDER...
...WAS CHASING AFTER HER...
I HATED BORING, NORMAL THINGS.
I WANTED TO LEAD A DIFFERENT LIFE THAN OTHER PEOPLE.
MAYBE THAT'S WHY I DECIDED TO TAKE THIS STRANGE, MYSTERIOUS GIRL UNDER MY WING.
BUT ESCAPING THE ORDINARY CARRIES ITS OWN RISKS.

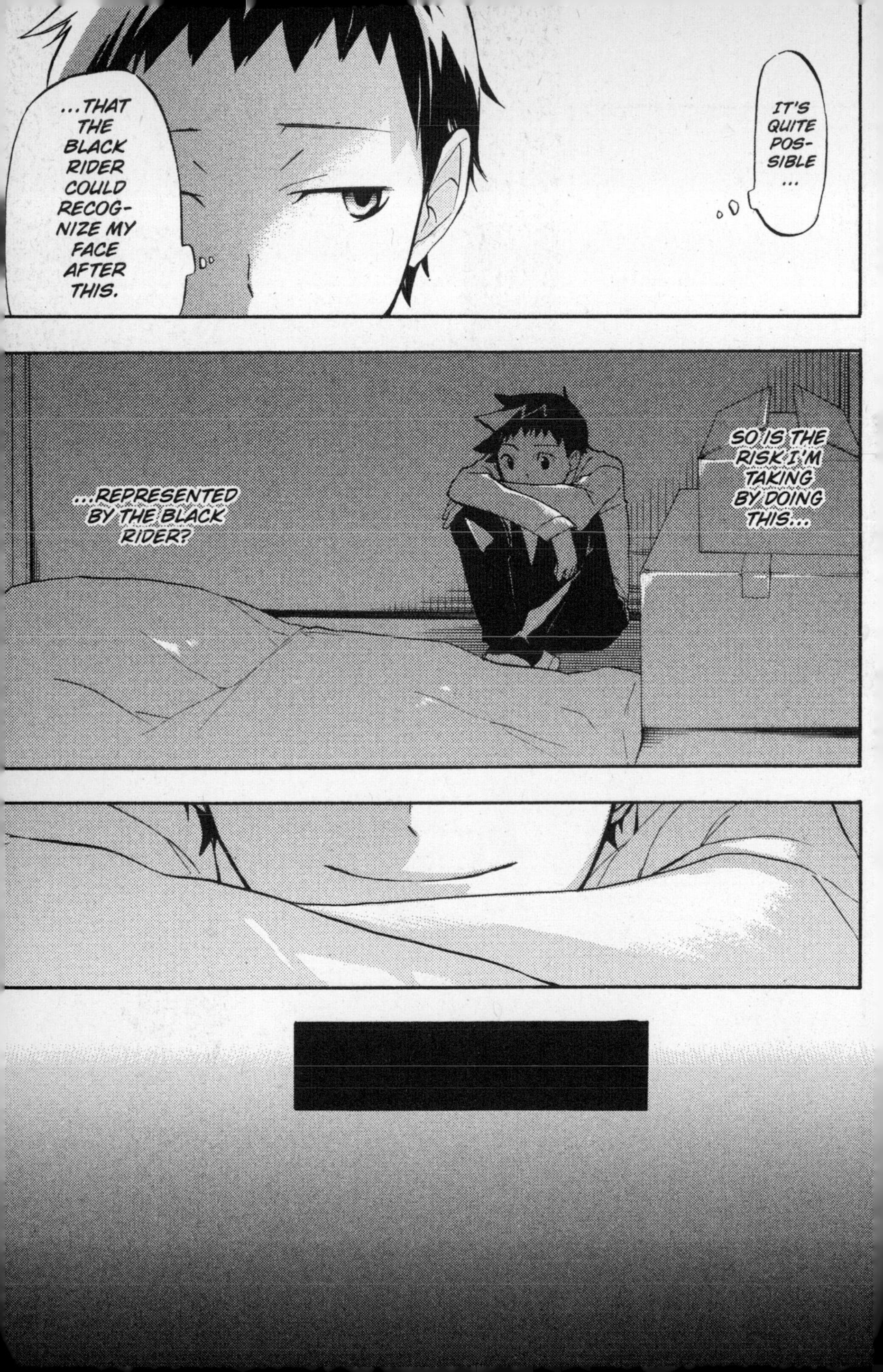
IT'S QUITE POS-SIBLE...
...THAT THE BLACK RIDER COULD RECOG-NIZE MY FACE AFTER THIS.
SO IS THE RISK I'M TAKING BY DOING THIS...
...REPRESENTED BY THE BLACK RIDER?
[redacted]

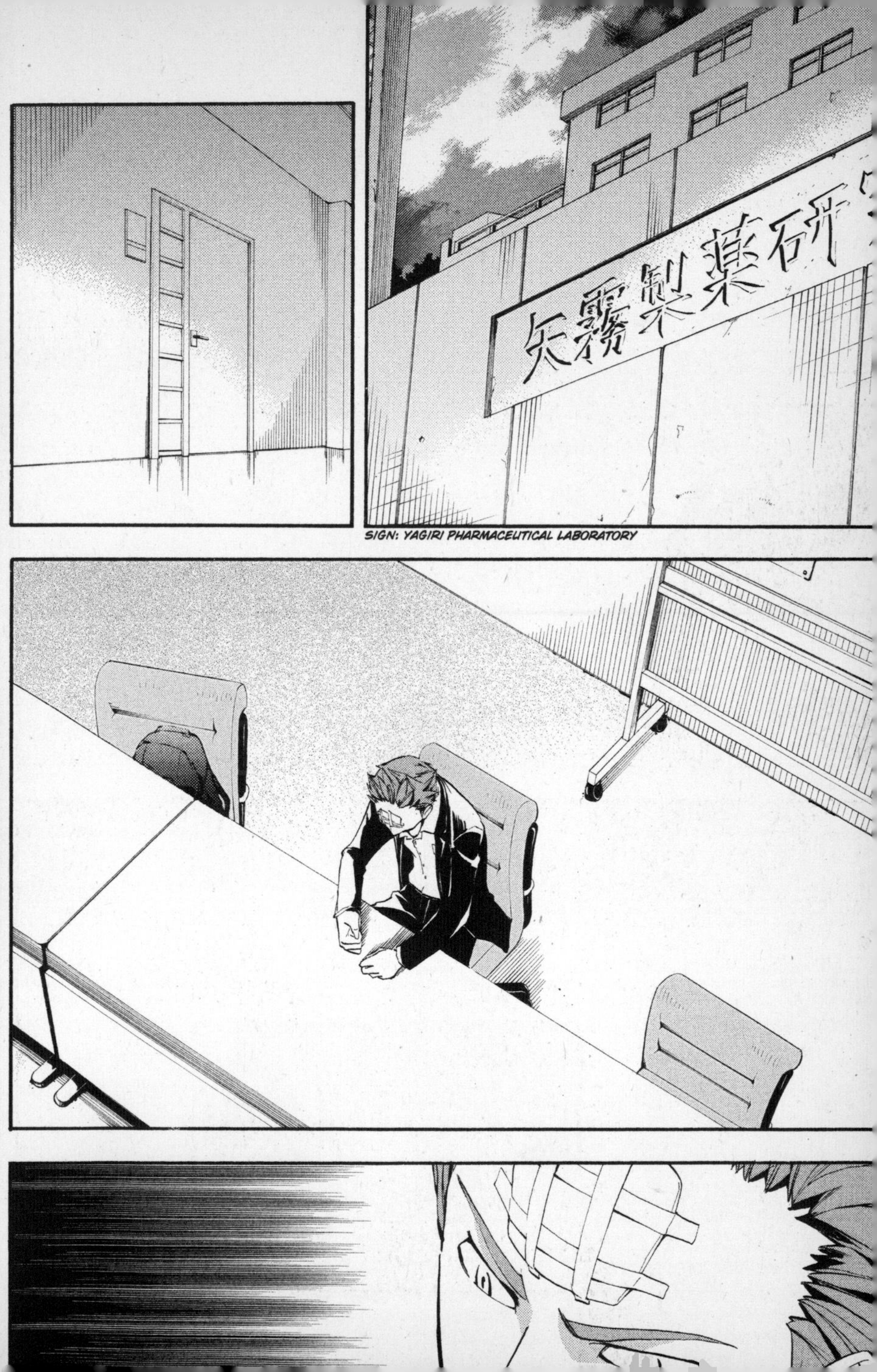
矢霧製薬研
SIGN: YAGIRI PHARMACEUTICAL LABORATORY

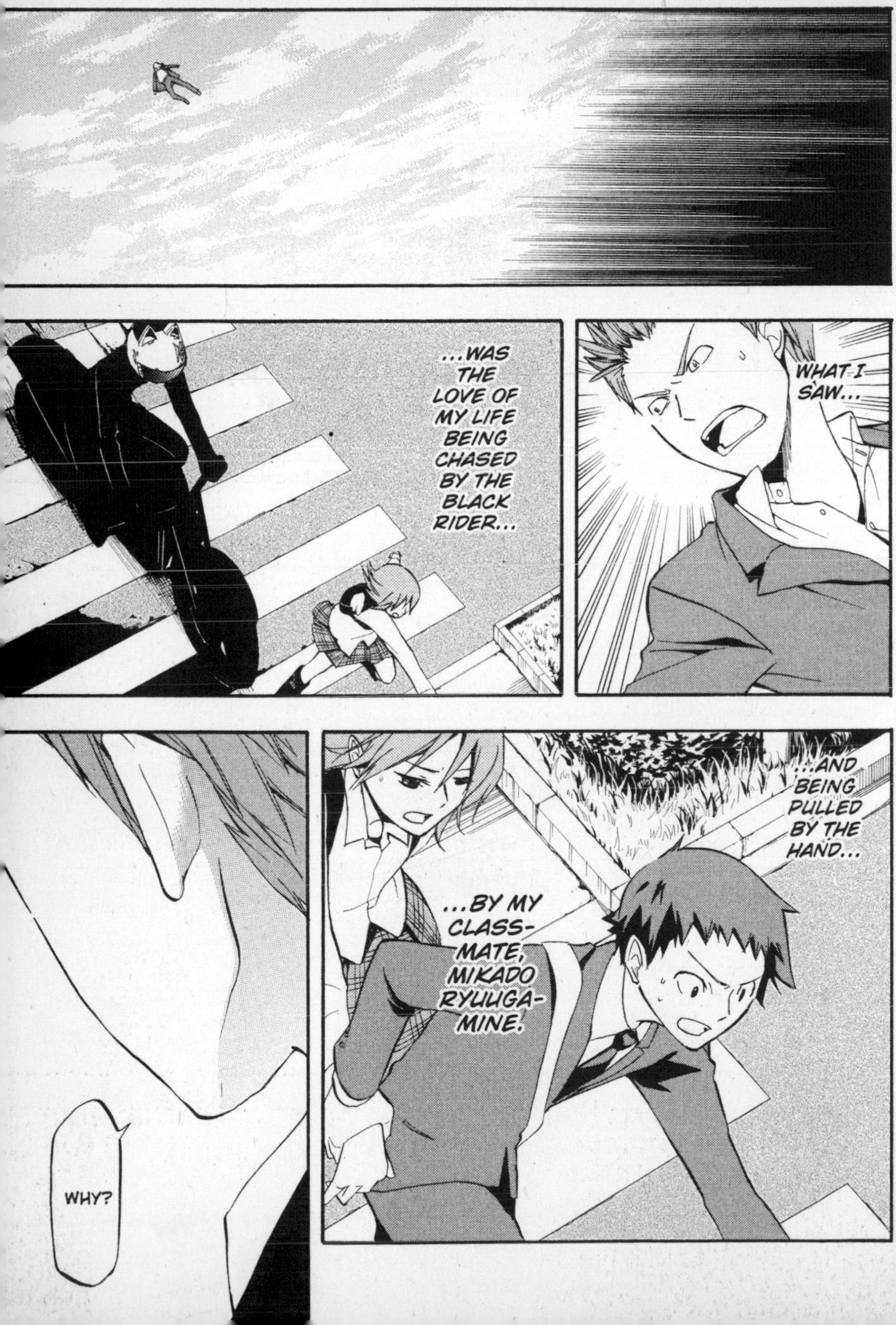
WHAT I SAW...
...WAS THE LOVE OF MY LIFE BEING CHASED BY THE BLACK RIDER...
...AND BEING PULLED BY THE HAND...
...BY MY CLASSMATE, MIKADO RYUUGAMINE.
WHY?

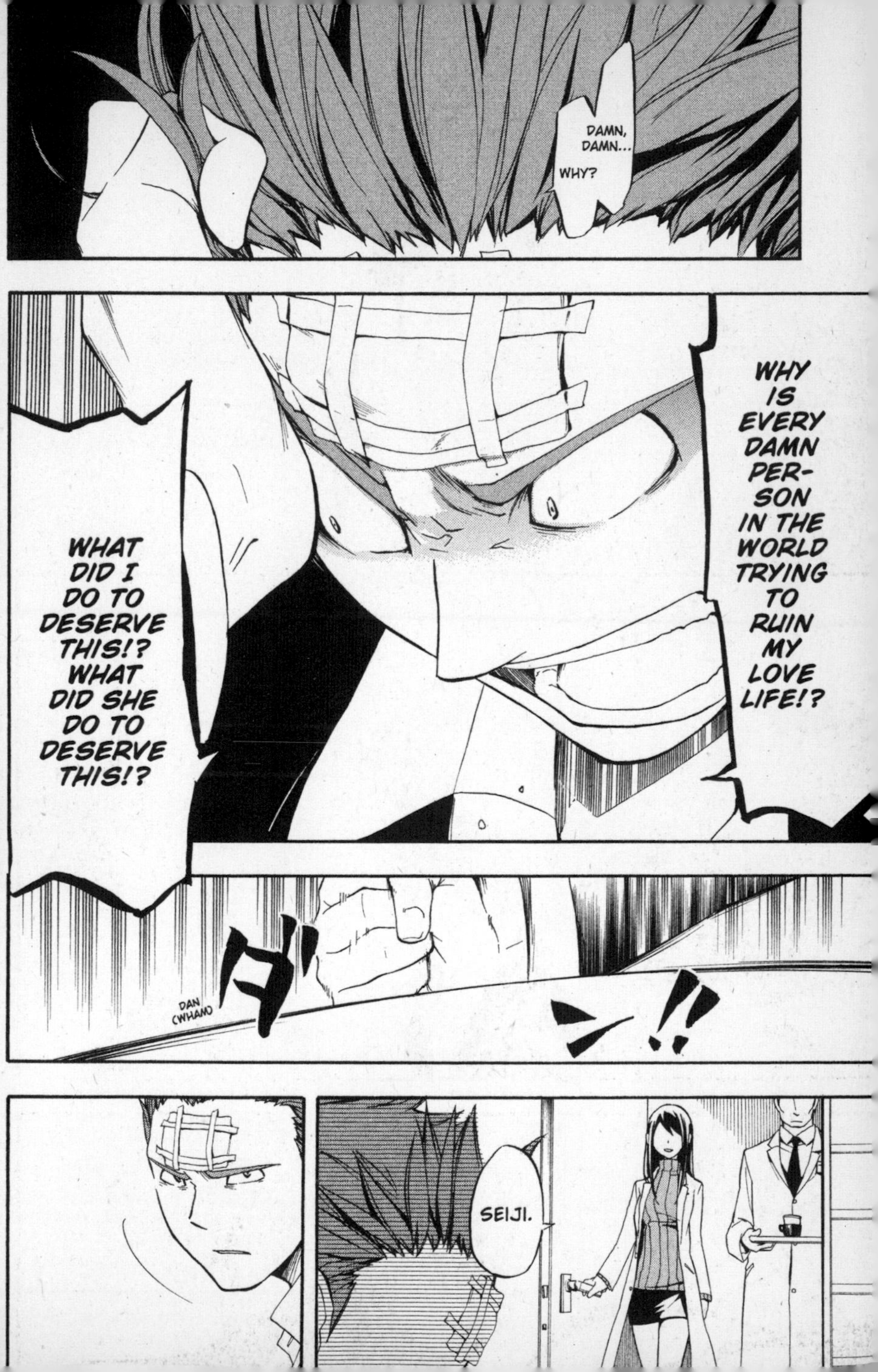
DAMN, DAMN...
WHY?
WHY IS EVERY DAMN PER-SON IN THE WORLD TRYING TO RUIN MY LOVE LIFE!?
WHAT DID I DO TO DESERVE THIS!? WHAT DID SHE DO TO DESERVE THIS!?
DAN (WHAM)
SEIJI.

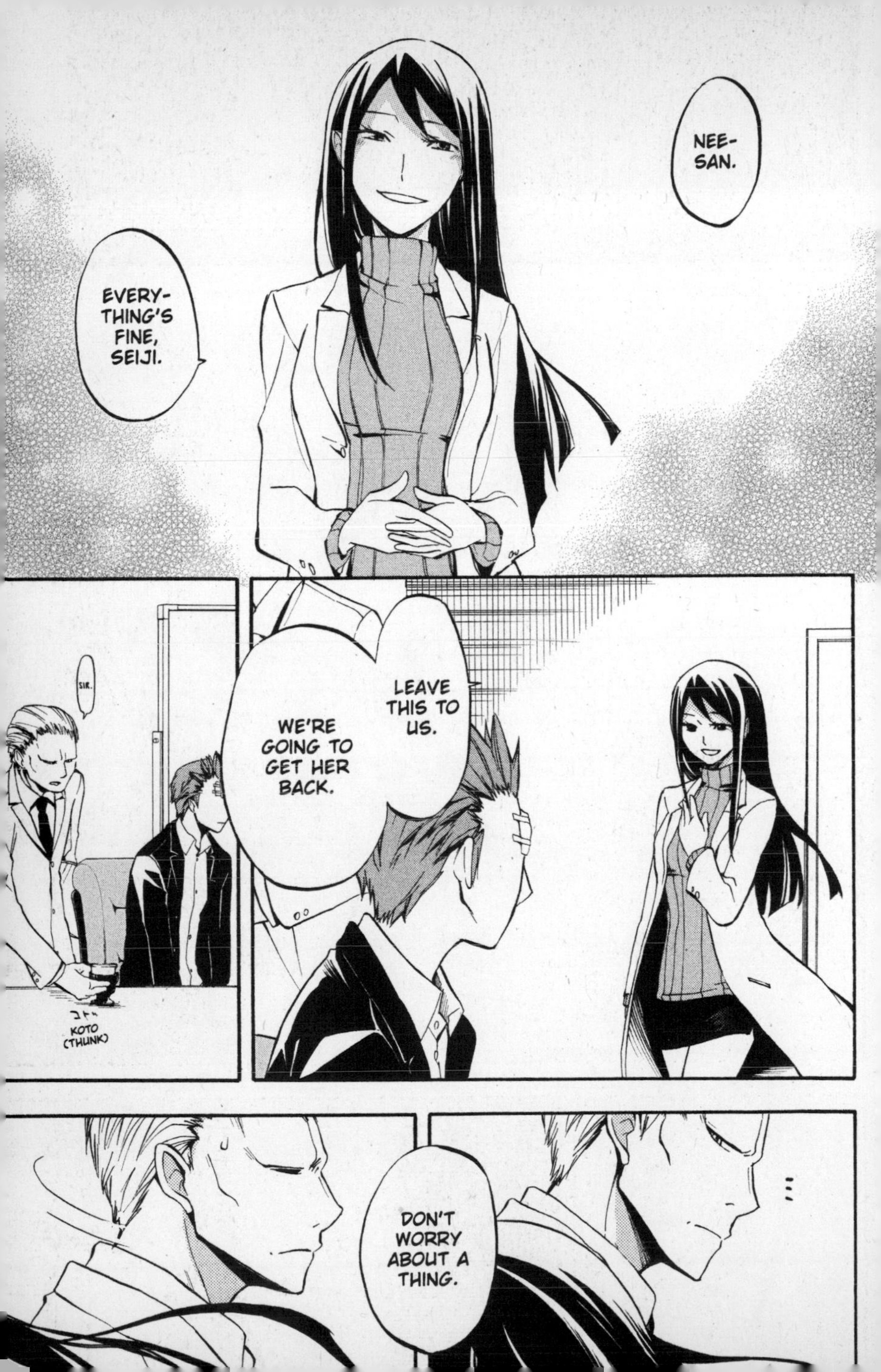
NEE-SAN.
EVERY-THING'S FINE, SEIJI.
LEAVE THIS TO US.
WE'RE GOING TO GET HER BACK.
SIR.
コトッ
KOTO (THUNK)
...
DON'T WORRY ABOUT A THING.

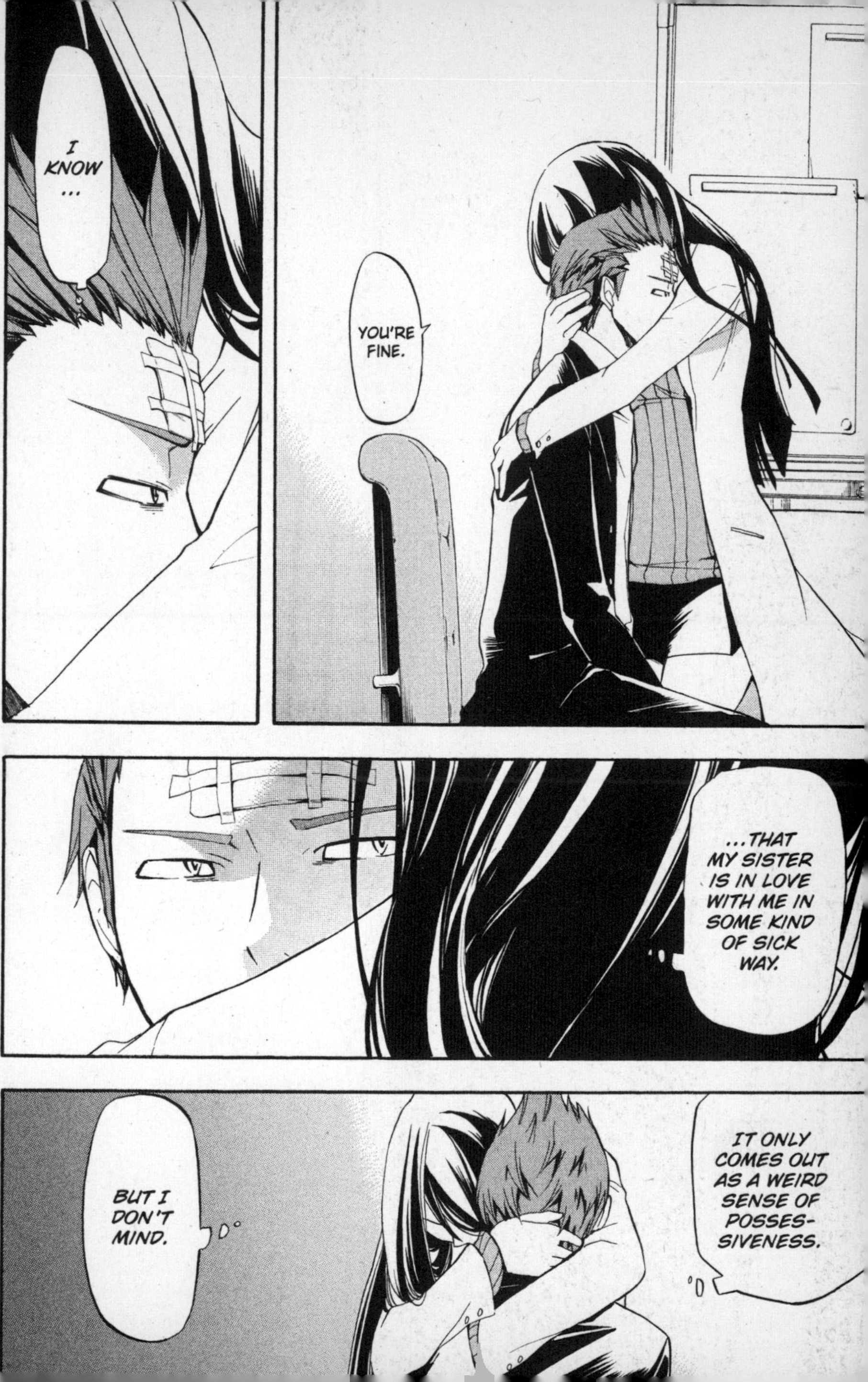
YOU'RE FINE.
I KNOW...
...THAT MY SISTER IS IN LOVE WITH ME IN SOME KIND OF SICK WAY.
IT ONLY COMES OUT AS A WEIRD SENSE OF POSSES-SIVENESS.
BUT I DON'T MIND.

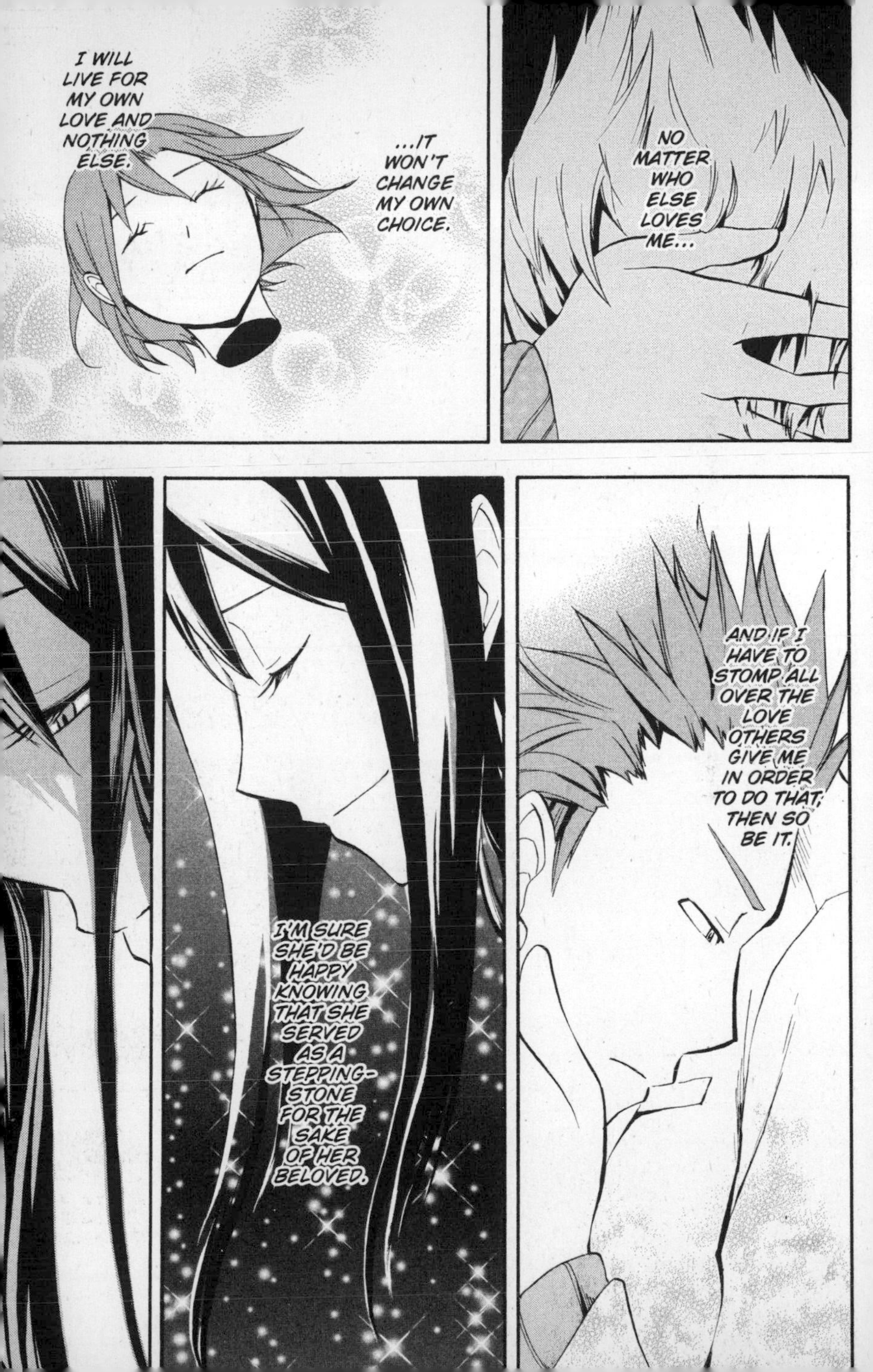
NO MATTER WHO ELSE LOVES ME...
...IT WON'T CHANGE MY OWN CHOICE.
I WILL LIVE FOR MY OWN LOVE AND NOTHING ELSE.
AND IF I HAVE TO STOMP ALL OVER THE LOVE OTHERS GIVE ME IN ORDER TO DO THAT, THEN SO BE IT.
I'M SURE SHE'D BE HAPPY KNOWING THAT SHE SERVED AS A STEPPING-STONE FOR THE SAKE OF HER BELOVED.

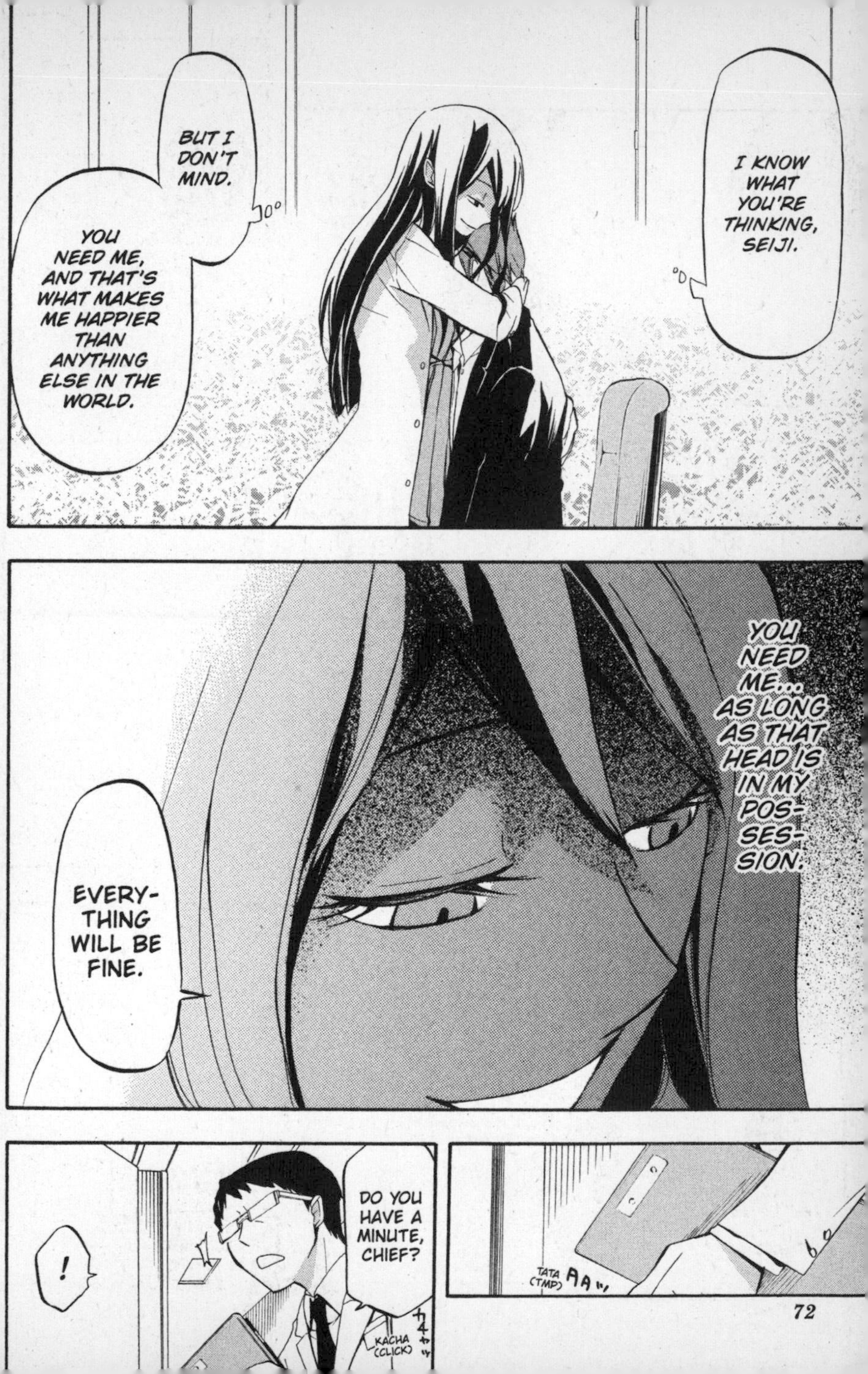
I KNOW WHAT YOU'RE THINKING, SEIJI.
BUT I DON'T MIND.
YOU NEED ME, AND THAT'S WHAT MAKES ME HAPPIER THAN ANYTHING ELSE IN THE WORLD.
YOU NEED ME... AS LONG AS THAT HEAD IS IN MY POS-SES-SION.
EVERY-THING WILL BE FINE.
TATA (TMP)
DO YOU HAVE A MINUTE, CHIEF?
KACHA (CLICK)
!

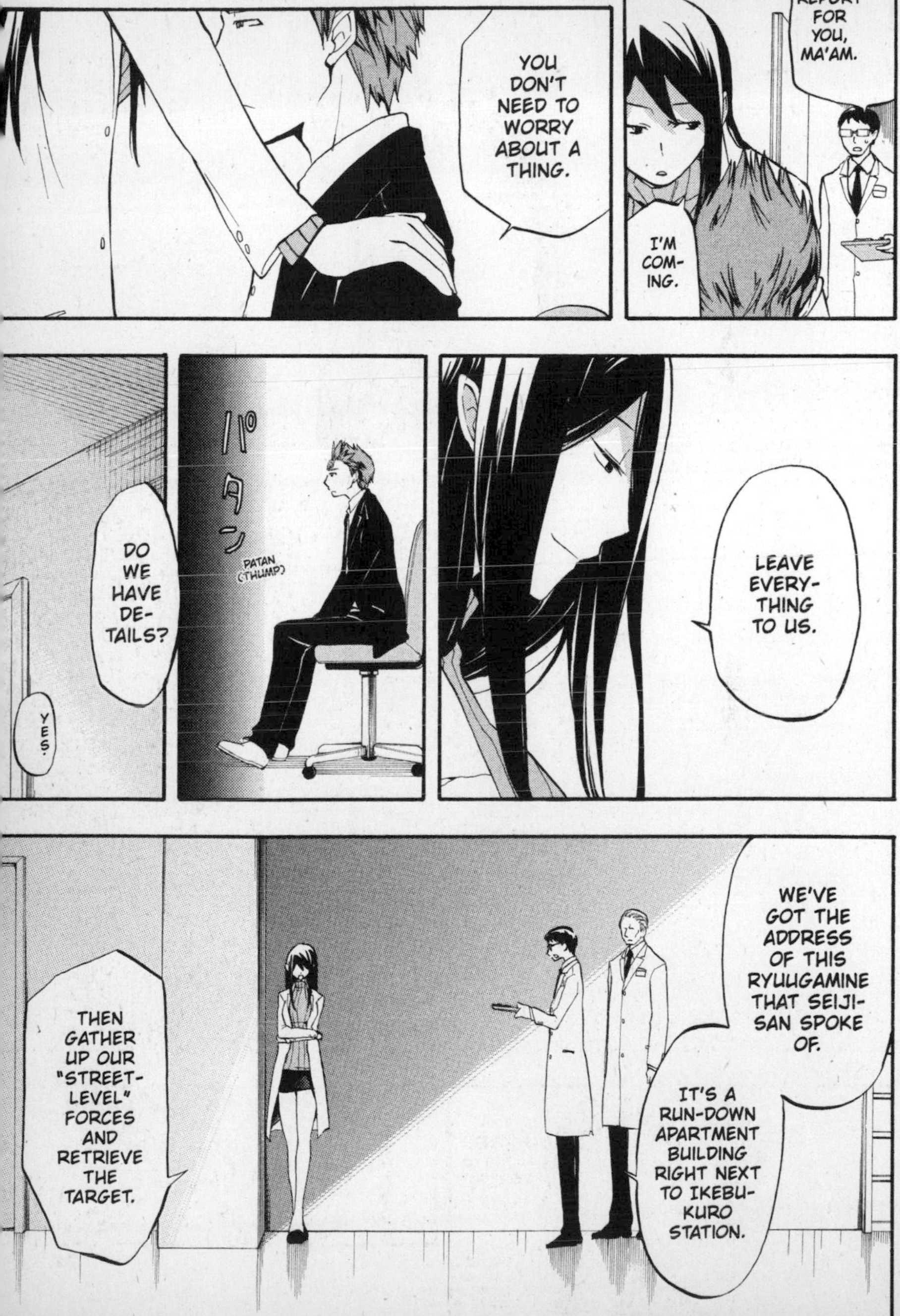
I HAVE A REPORT FOR YOU, MA'AM.
I'M COMING.
YOU DON'T NEED TO WORRY ABOUT A THING.
LEAVE EVERY-THING TO US.
パタン
PATAN (THUMP)
DO WE HAVE DE-TAILS?
YES.
WE'VE GOT THE ADDRESS OF THIS RYUUGAMINE THAT SEIJI-SAN SPOKE OF.
IT'S A RUN-DOWN APARTMENT BUILDING RIGHT NEXT TO IKEBU-KURO STATION.
THEN GATHER UP OUR "STREET-LEVEL" FORCES AND RETRIEVE THE TARGET.

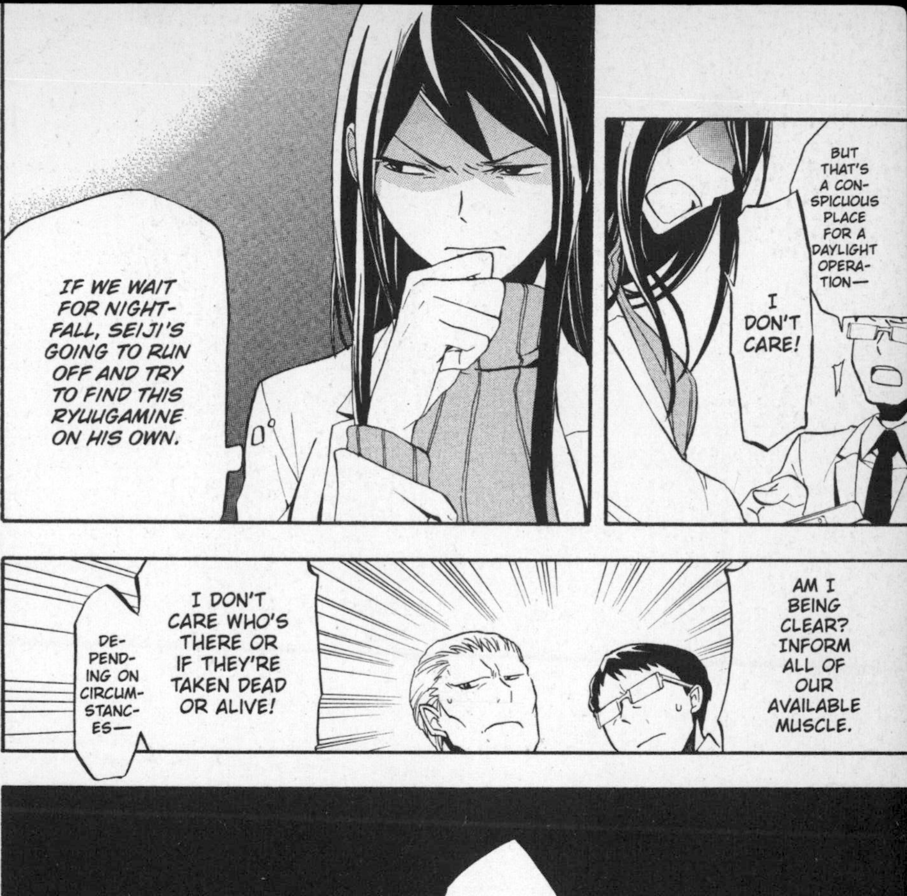
BUT THAT'S A CONSPICUOUS PLACE FOR A DAYLIGHT OPERATION—
I DON'T CARE!
IF WE WAIT FOR NIGHTFALL, SEIJI'S GOING TO RUN OFF AND TRY TO FIND THIS RYUUGAMINE ON HIS OWN.
AM I BEING CLEAR? INFORM ALL OF OUR AVAILABLE MUSCLE.
I DON'T CARE WHO'S THERE OR IF THEY'RE TAKEN DEAD OR ALIVE!
DEPENDING ON CIRCUMSTANCES—

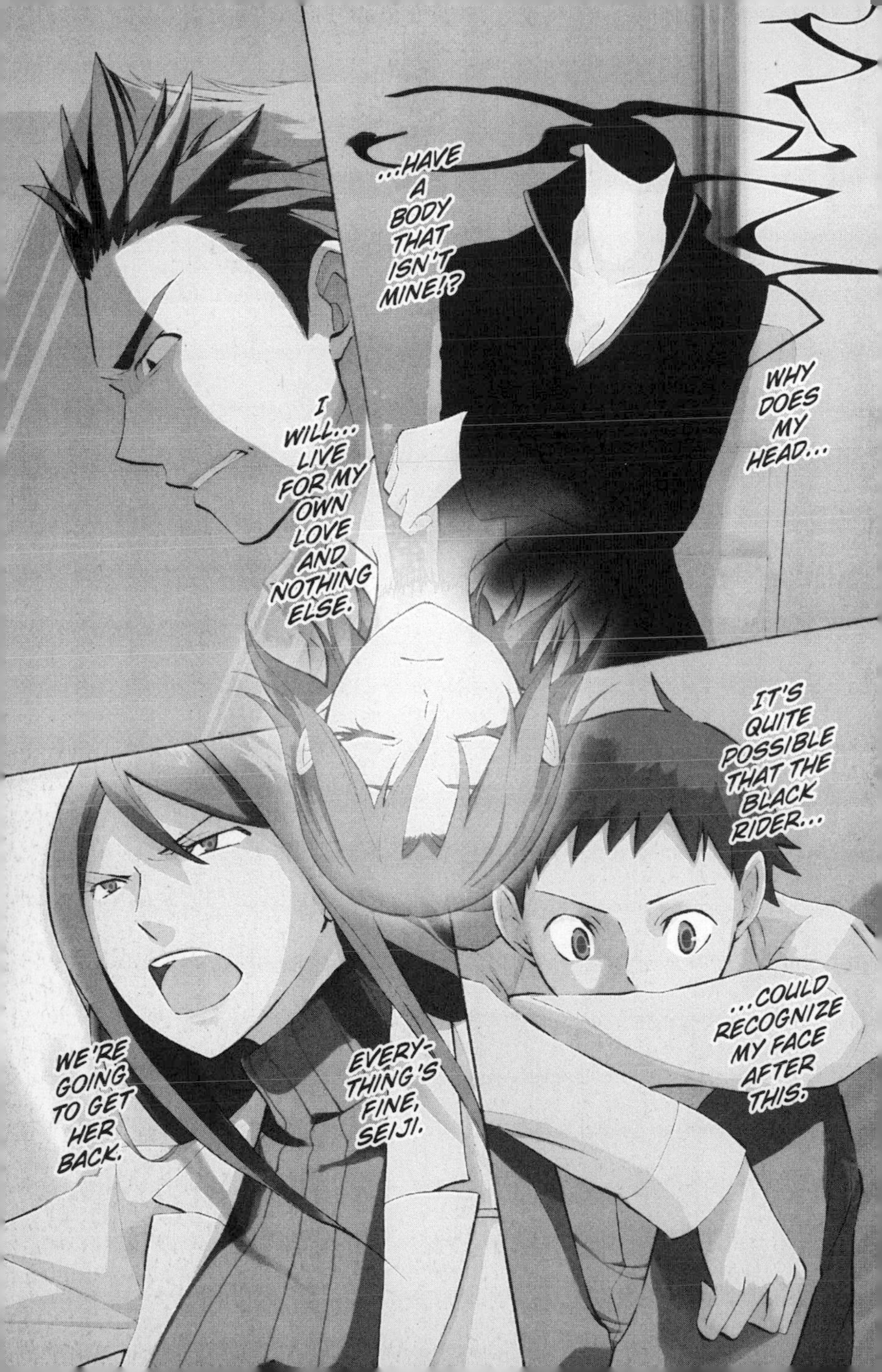
WHY DOES MY HEAD...
...HAVE A BODY THAT ISN'T MINE!?
I WILL... LIVE FOR MY OWN LOVE AND NOTHING ELSE.
IT'S QUITE POSSIBLE THAT THE BLACK RIDER...
...COULD RECOGNIZE MY FACE AFTER THIS.
EVERY-THING'S FINE, SEIJI.
WE'RE GOING TO GET HER BACK.

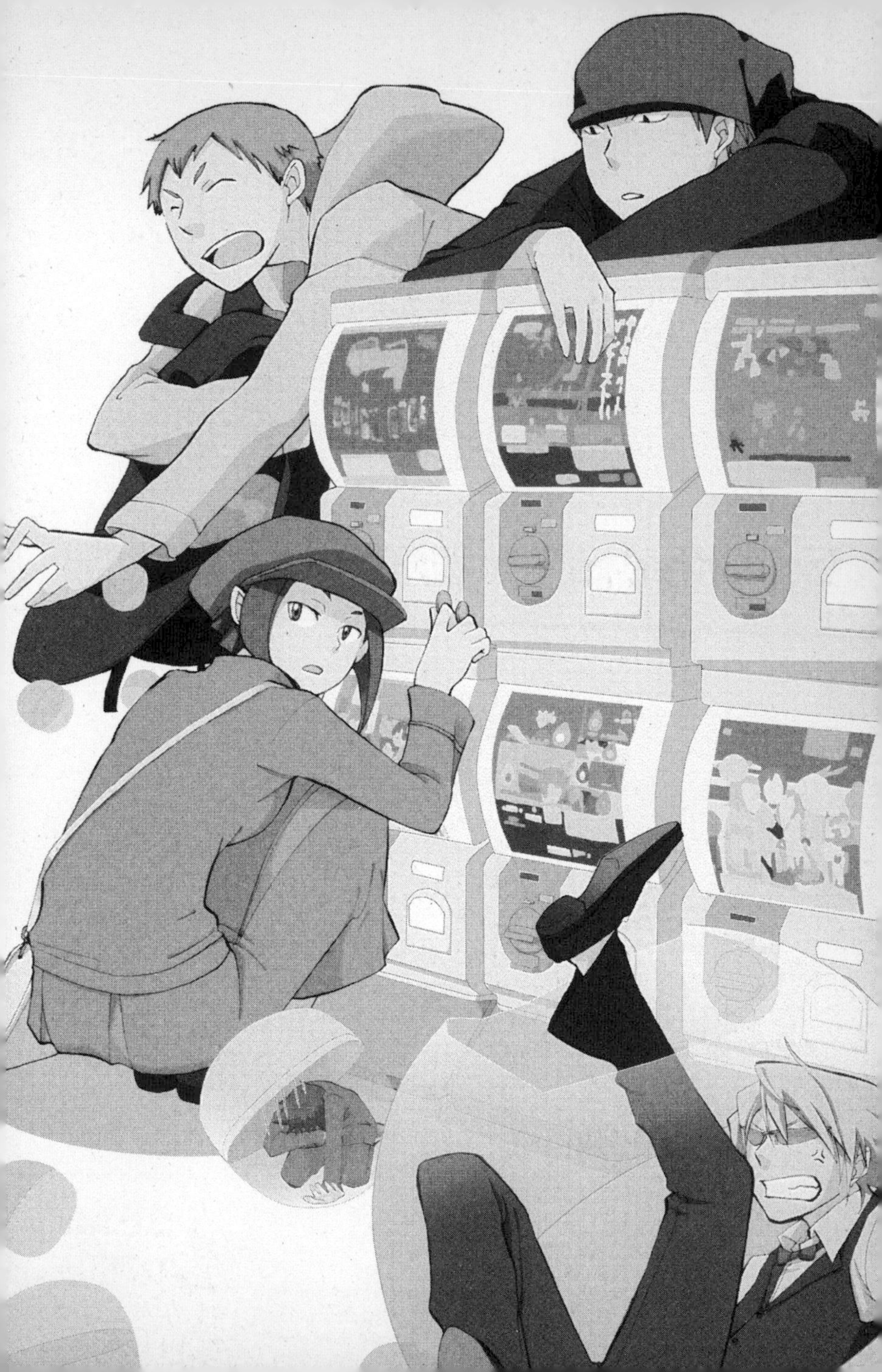

15: WAWAWAWAWAWAWAWAWAWAWAWAWAWAWA!!

DRRR!!

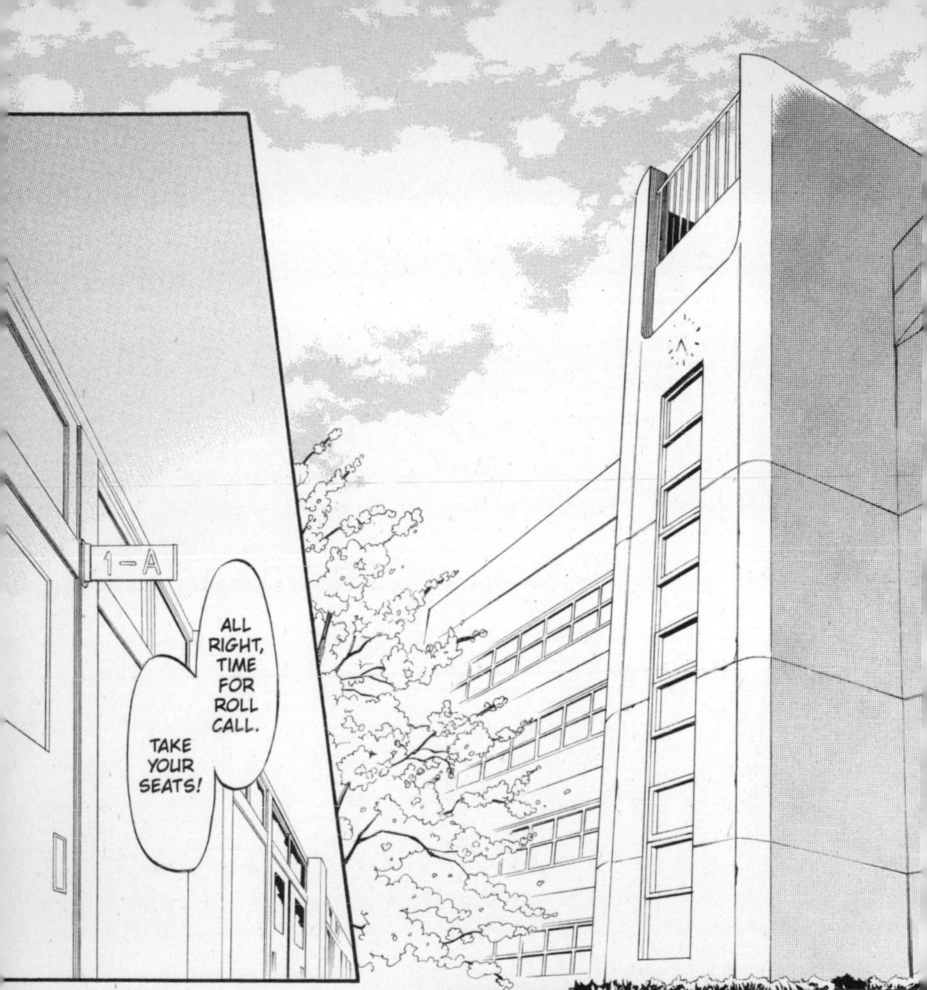
1-A
ALL RIGHT, TIME FOR ROLL CALL.
TAKE YOUR SEATS!
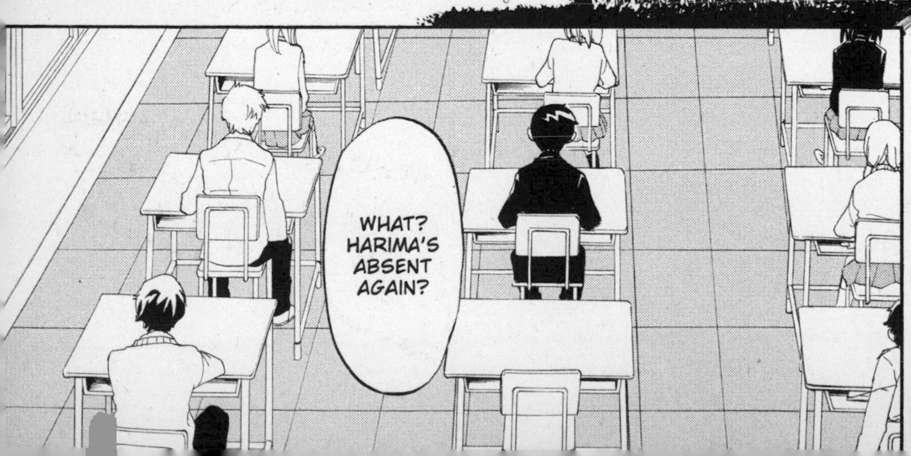
WHAT? HARIMA'S ABSENT AGAIN?

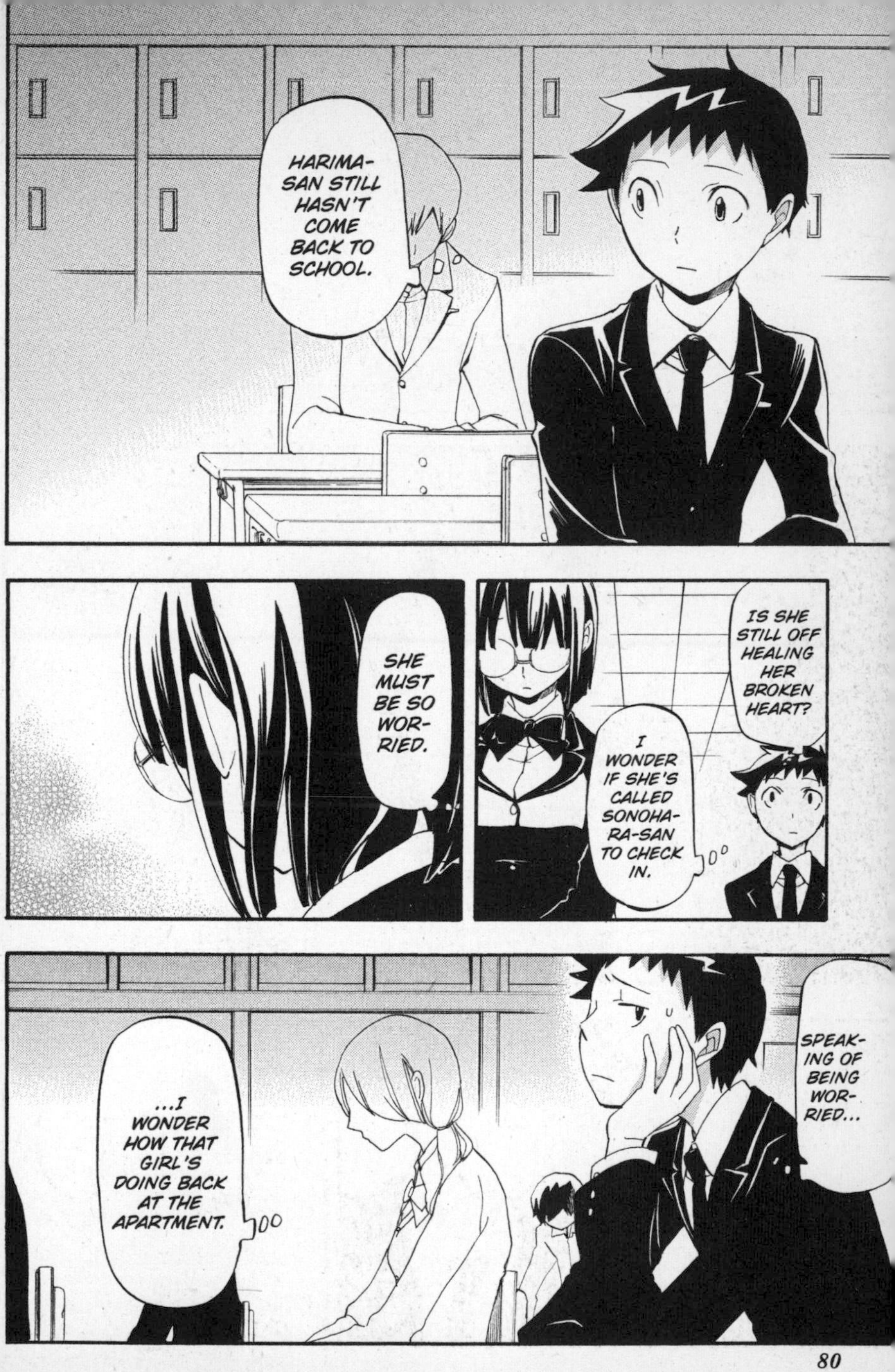
HARIMA-SAN STILL HASN'T COME BACK TO SCHOOL.
IS SHE STILL OFF HEALING HER BROKEN HEART?
I WONDER IF SHE'S CALLED SONOHARA-SAN TO CHECK IN.
SHE MUST BE SO WORRIED.
SPEAKING OF BEING WORRIED...
...I WONDER HOW THAT GIRL'S DOING BACK AT THE APARTMENT.

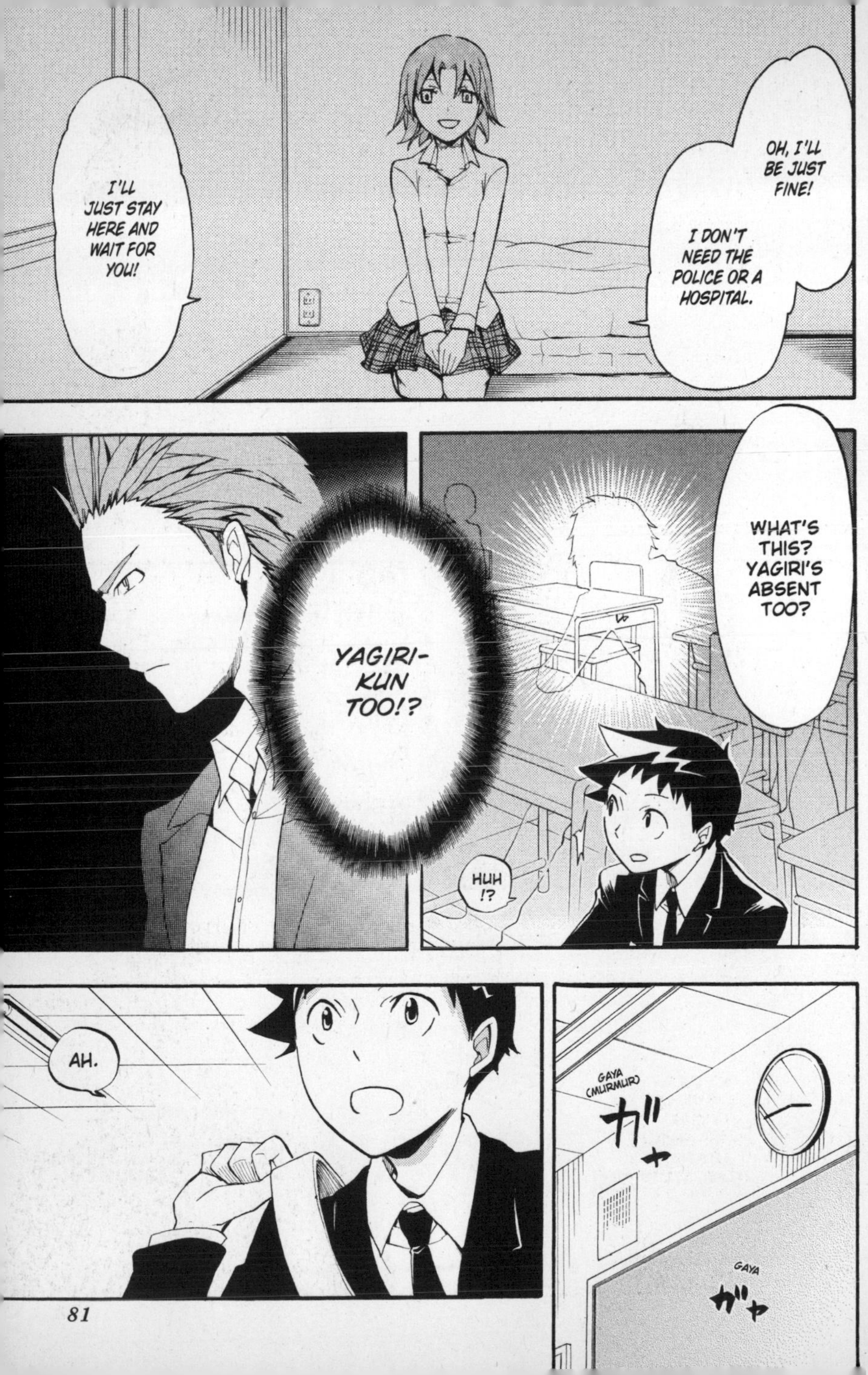

OH, I'LL BE JUST FINE!
I DON'T NEED THE POLICE OR A HOSPITAL.
I'LL JUST STAY HERE AND WAIT FOR YOU!
WHAT'S THIS? YAGIRI'S ABSENT TOO?
HUH !?
YAGIRI-KUN TOO!?
GAYA (MURMUR)
ガヤ
GAYA
ガヤ
AH.

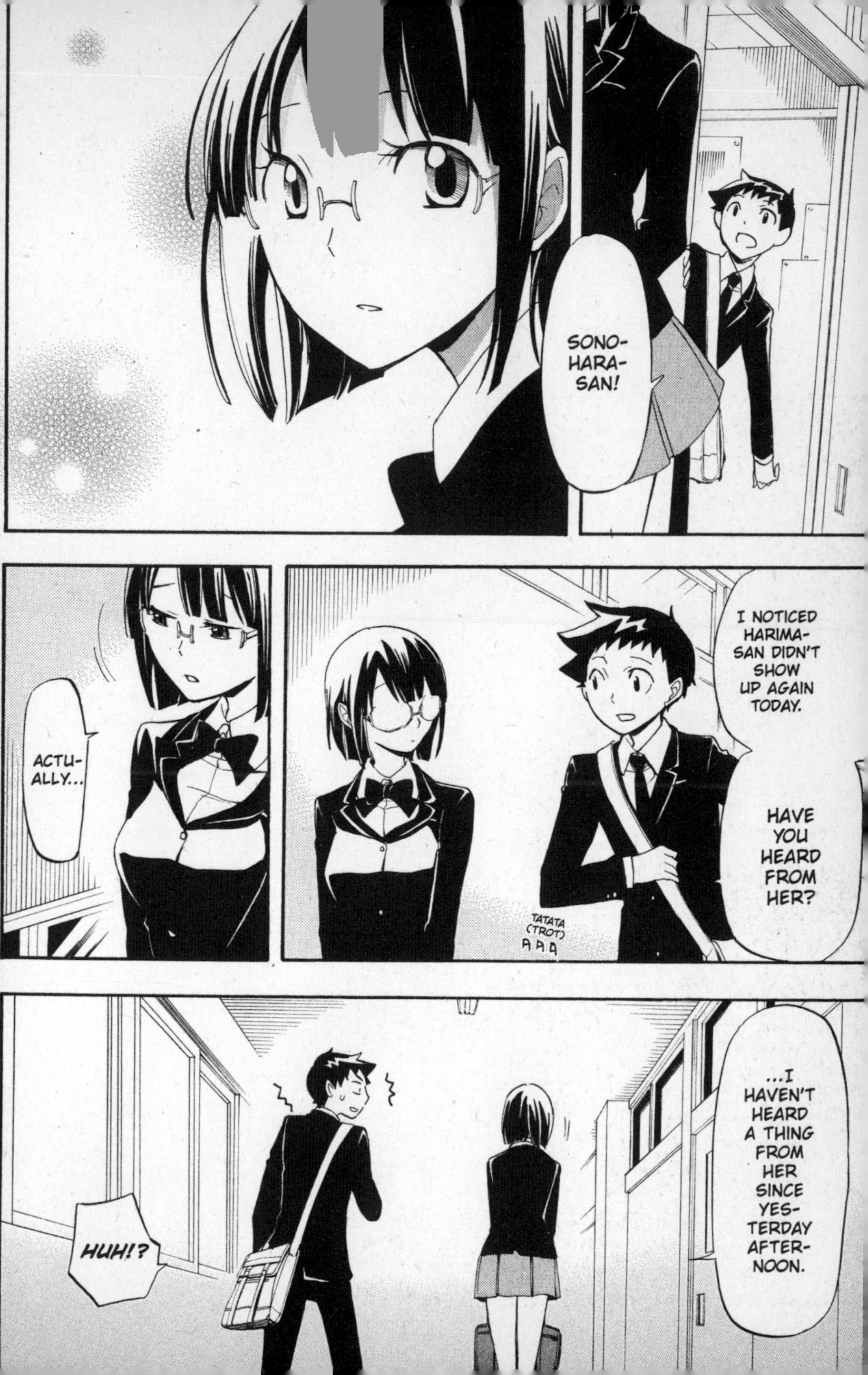
SONO-HARA-SAN!
I NOTICED HARIMA-SAN DIDN'T SHOW UP AGAIN TODAY.
HAVE YOU HEARD FROM HER?
TATATA (TROT)
ACTU-ALLY...
...I HAVEN'T HEARD A THING FROM HER SINCE YES-TERDAY AFTER-NOON.
HUH!?

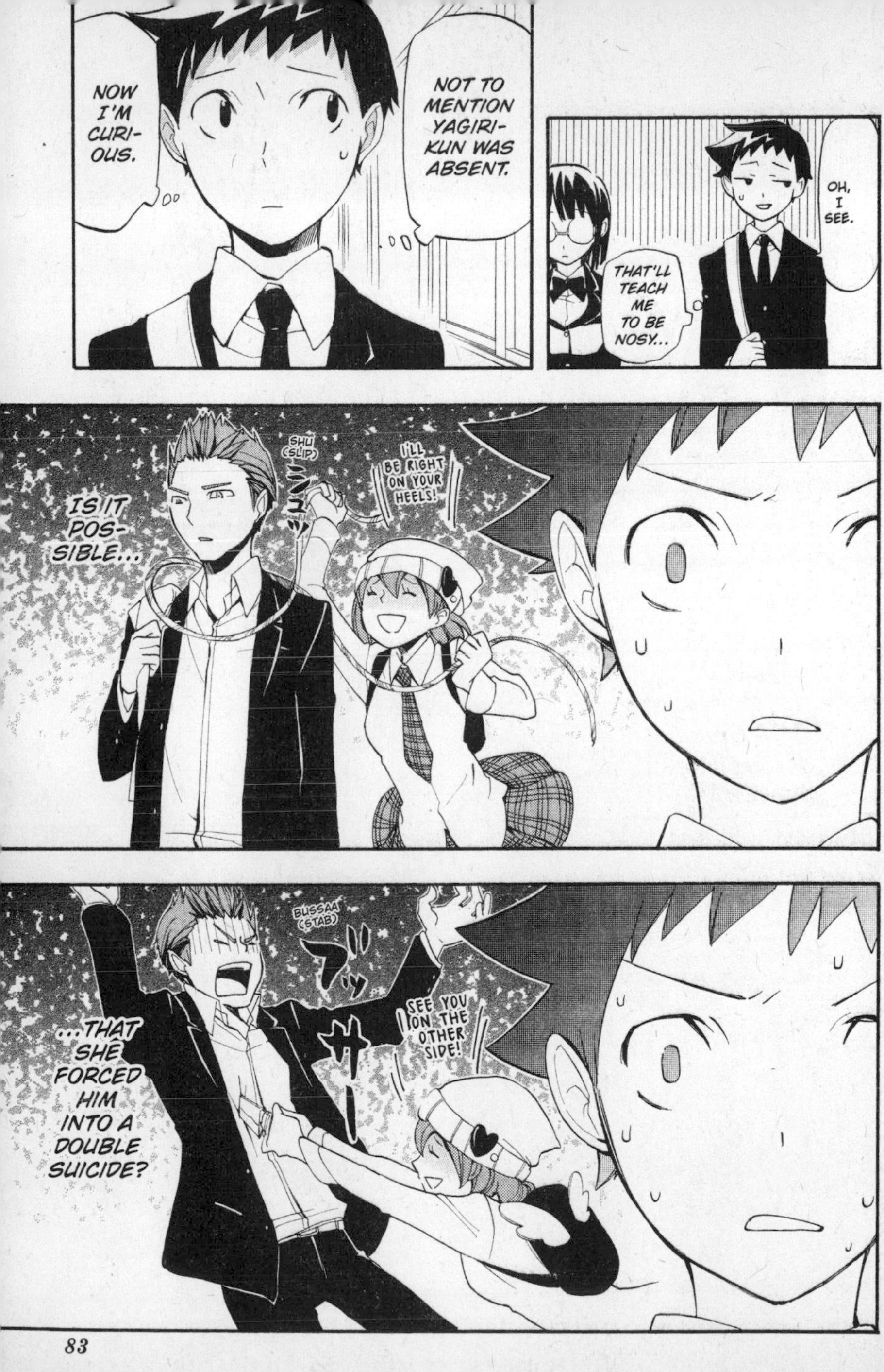
OH, I SEE.
THAT'LL TEACH ME TO BE NOSY...
NOT TO MENTION YAGIRI-KUN WAS ABSENT.
NOW I'M CURIOUS.
I'LL BE RIGHT ON YOUR HEELS!
SHU (SLIP)
IS IT POSSIBLE...
SEE YOU ON THE OTHER SIDE!
BUSSAA (STAB)
...THAT SHE FORCED HIM INTO A DOUBLE SUICIDE?

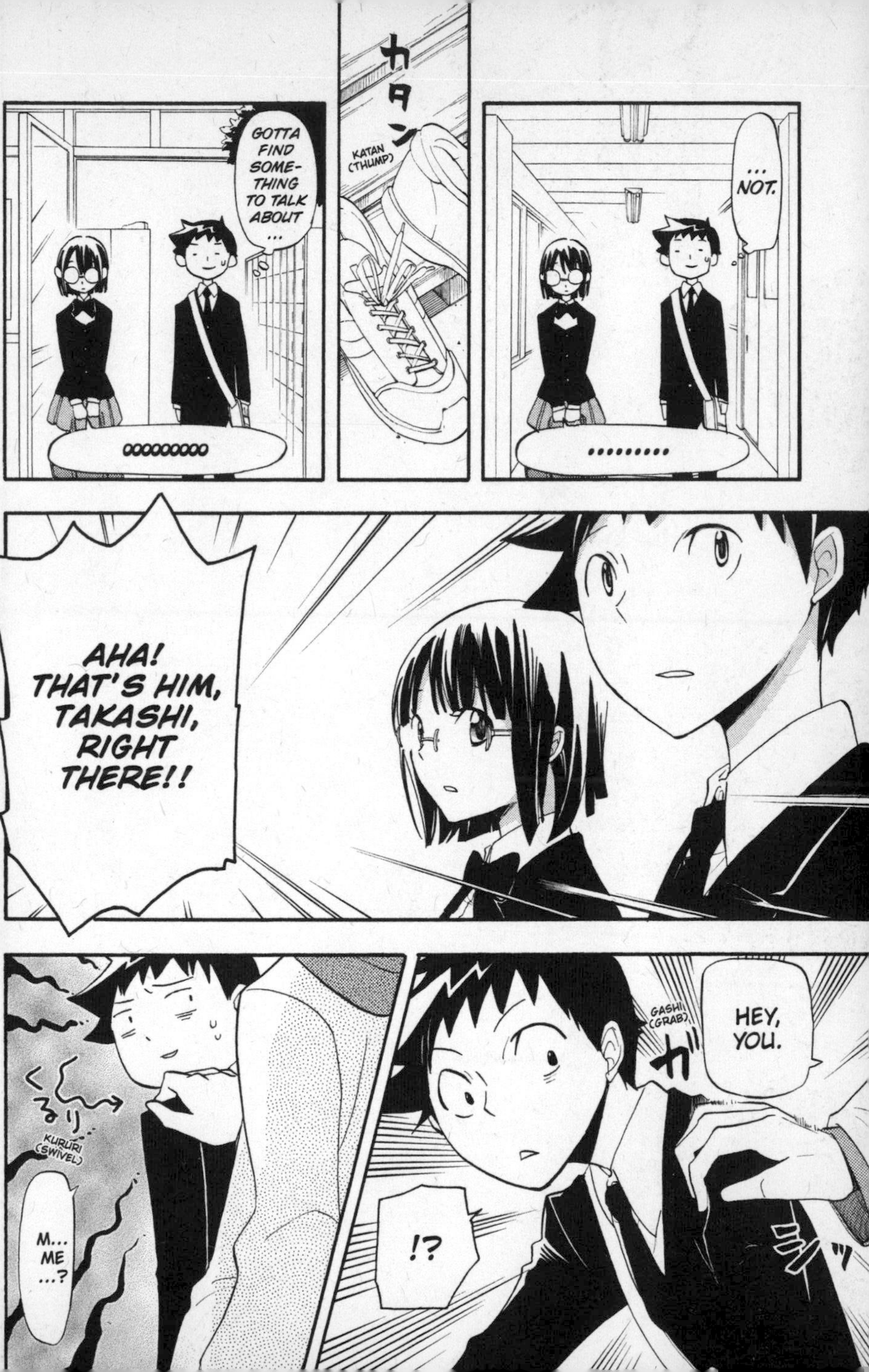
... NOT.
....
カタン
KATAN (THUMP)
GOTTA FIND SOME-THING TO TALK ABOUT ...
ooooooooo
AHA! THAT'S HIM, TAKASHI, RIGHT THERE!!
HEY, YOU.
GASHI (GRAB)
ガ
ミシッ
!?
くるり
KURURI (SWIVEL)
M... ME ...?

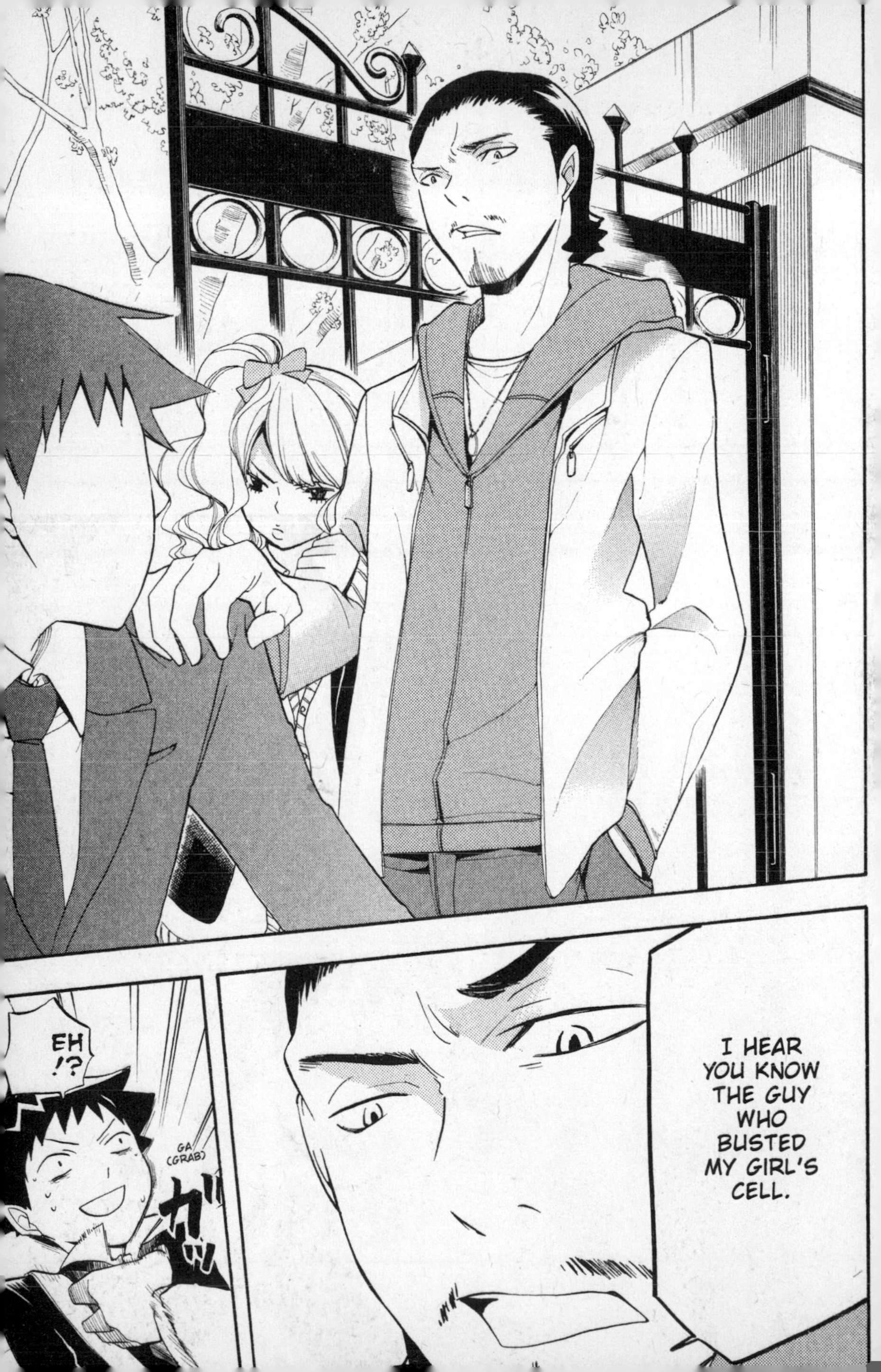
I HEAR YOU KNOW THE GUY WHO BUSTED MY GIRL'S CELL.
EH !?
GA (GRAB)
ガッ

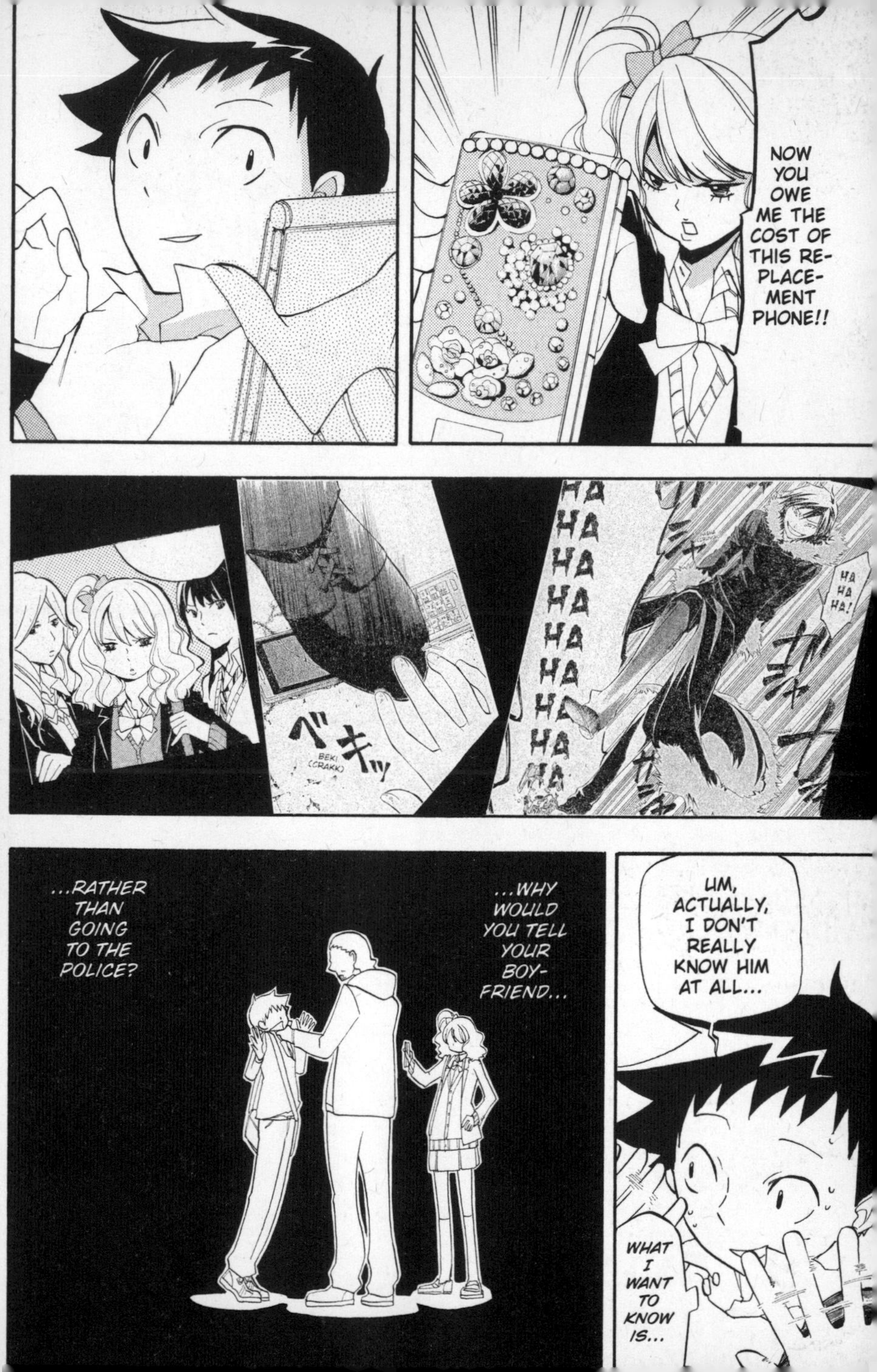
NOW YOU OWE ME THE COST OF THIS RE-PLACE-MENT PHONE!!
HA HA HA HA HA HA HA HA HA HA HA HA HA
HA HA HA!
ベキッ
BEKI (CRAKK)
UM, ACTUALLY, I DON'T REALLY KNOW HIM AT ALL...
WHAT I WANT TO KNOW IS...
...WHY WOULD YOU TELL YOUR BOY-FRIEND...
...RATHER THAN GOING TO THE POLICE?

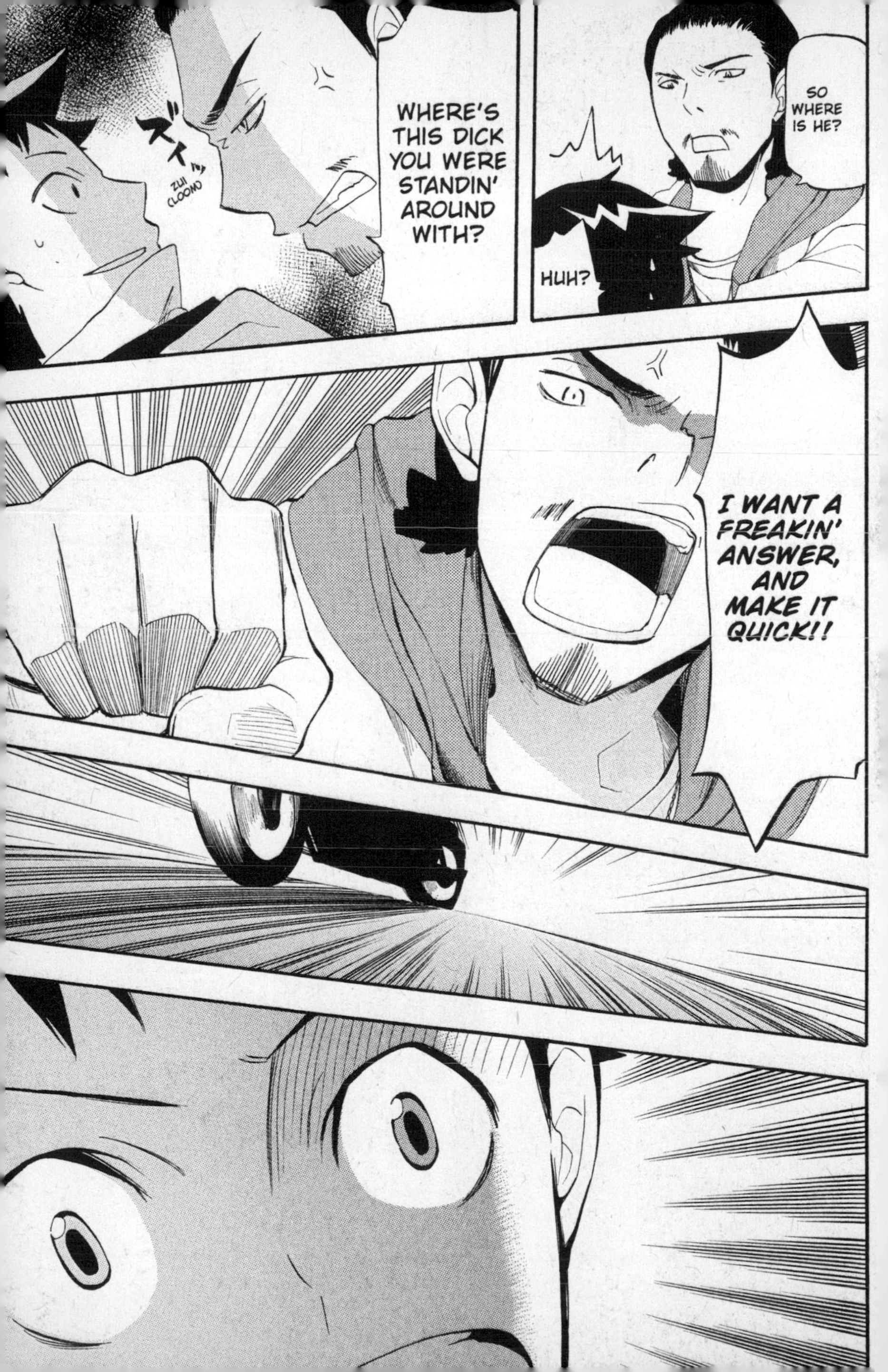
SO WHERE IS HE?
HUH?
WHERE'S THIS DICK YOU WERE STANDIN' AROUND WITH?
ZUI (LOOM)
I WANT A FREAKIN' ANSWER, AND MAKE IT QUICK!!

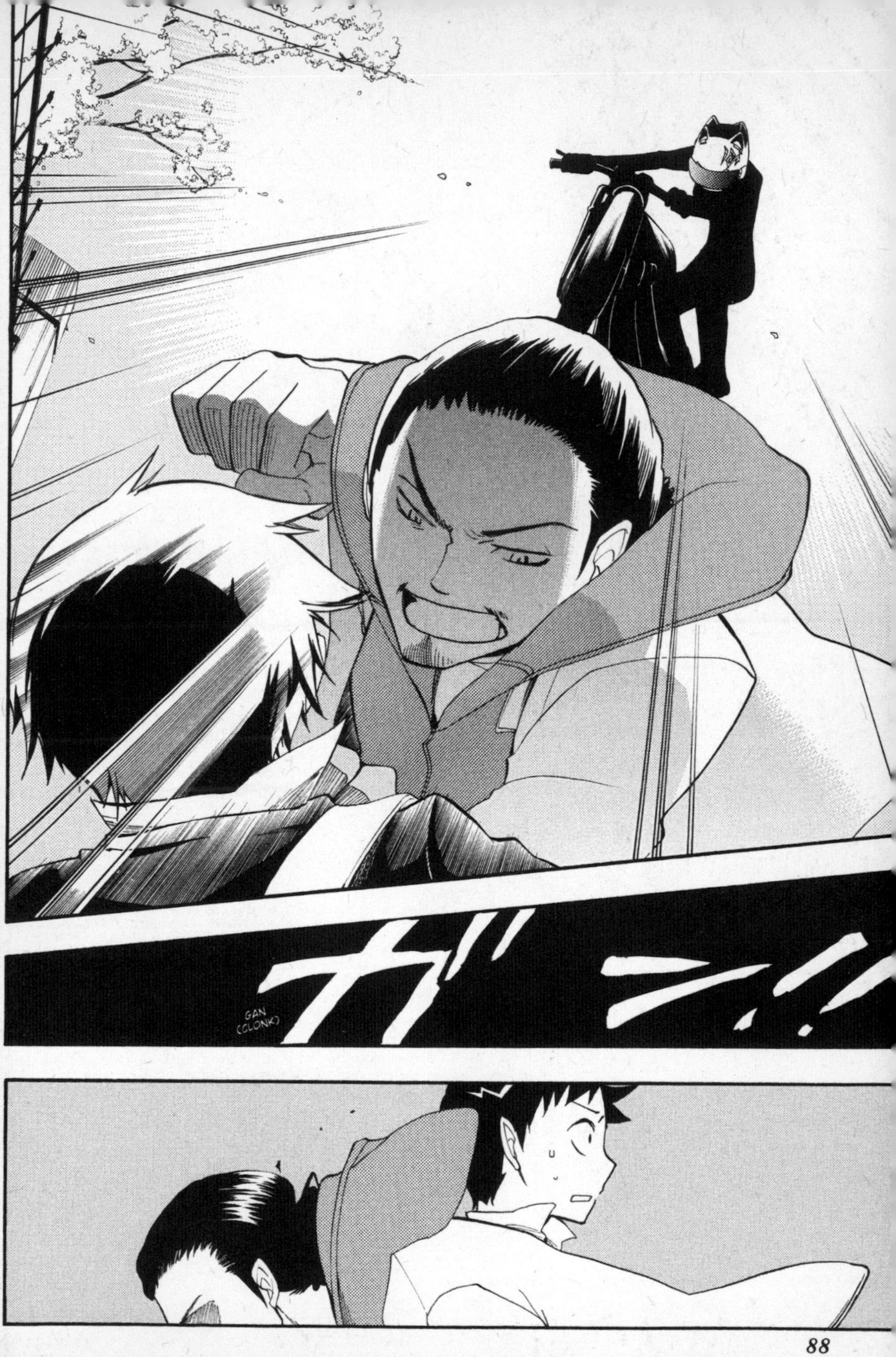
ガン!!
GAN
(CLONK)

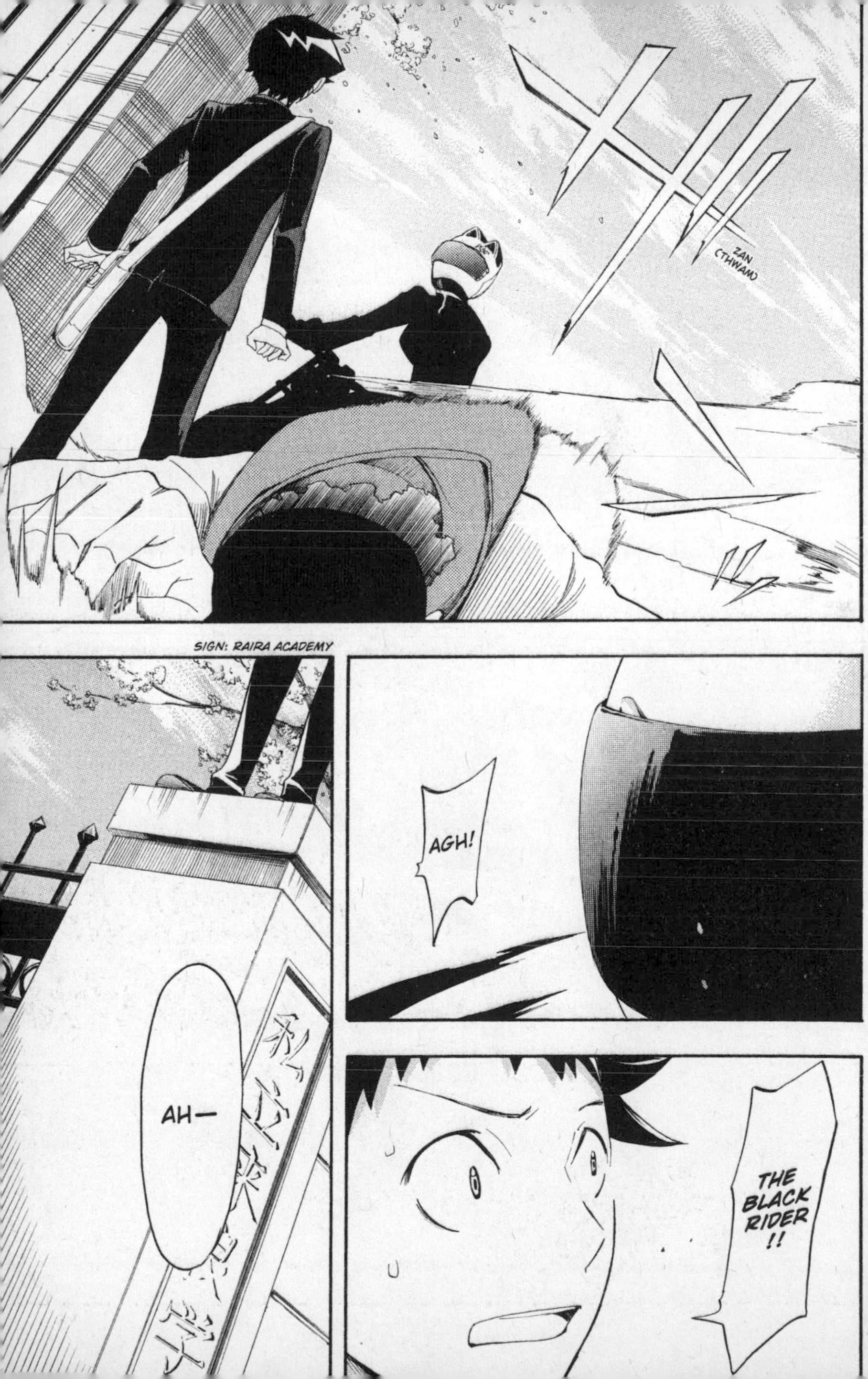
ZAN (THWAM)
AGH!
THE BLACK RIDER!!
SIGN: RAIRA ACADEMY
AH—

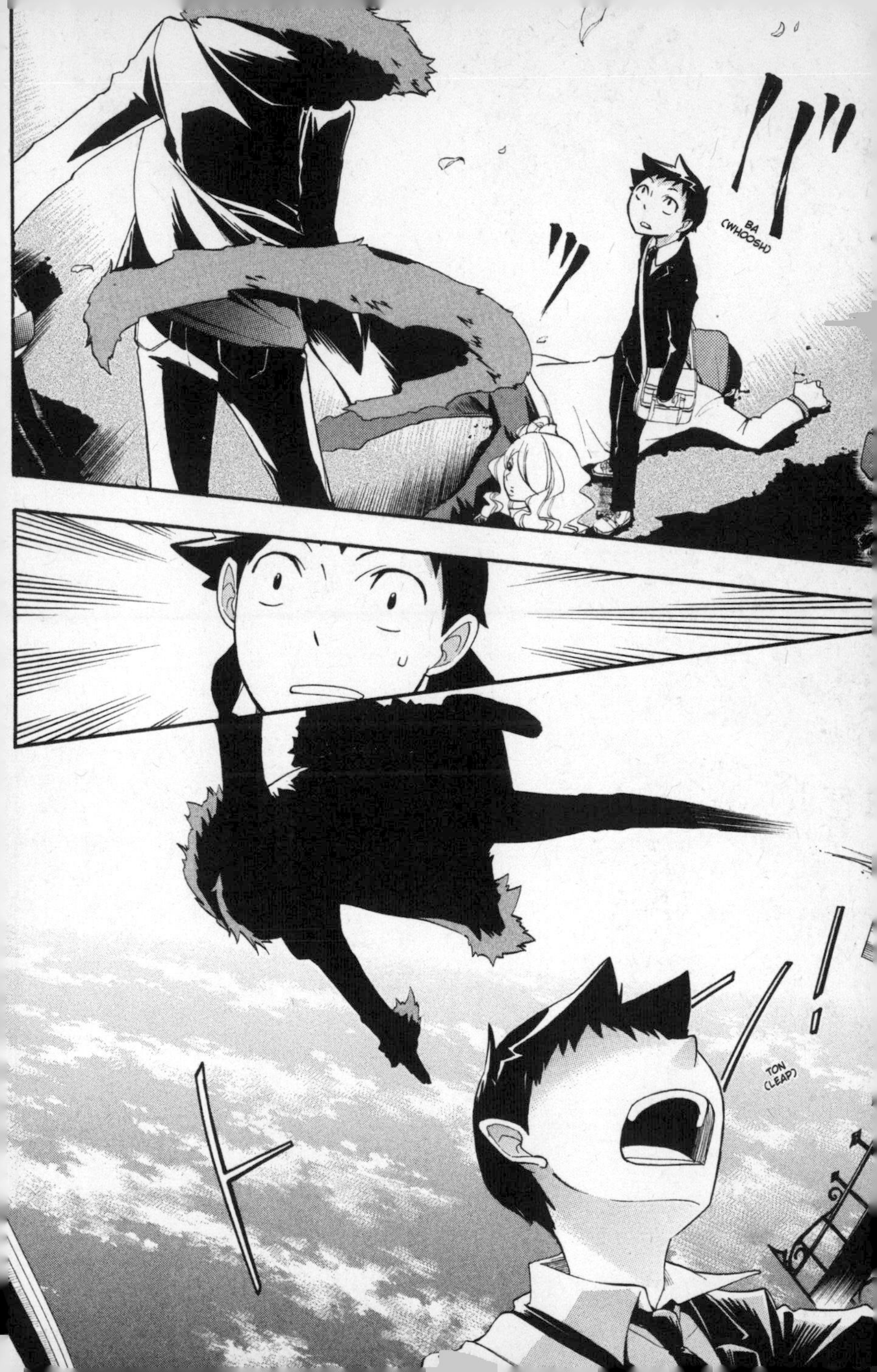
BA
(WHOOSH)
TON
(LEAP)

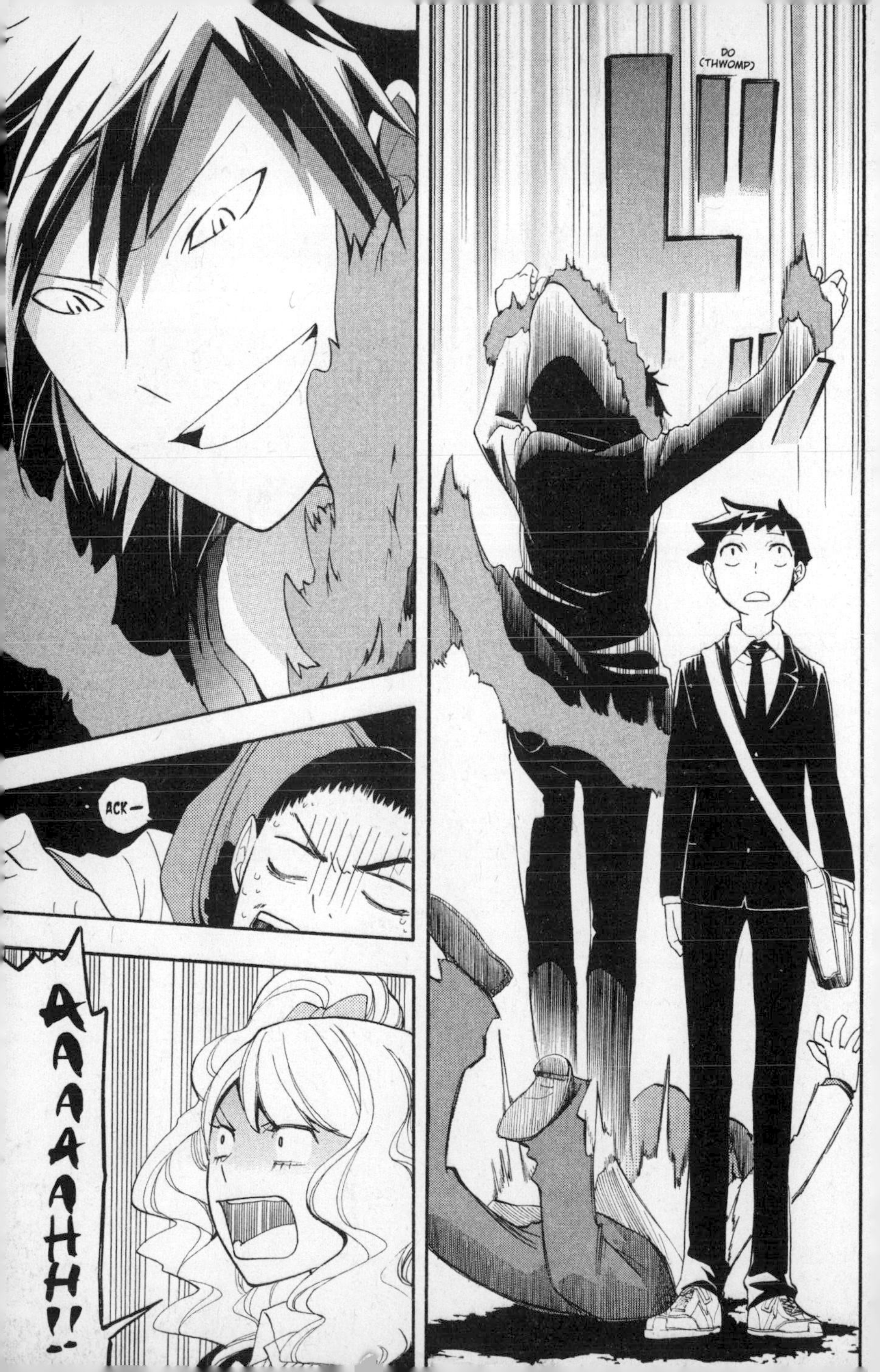
DO
(THWOMP)
ACK—
AAAAAAHH!!

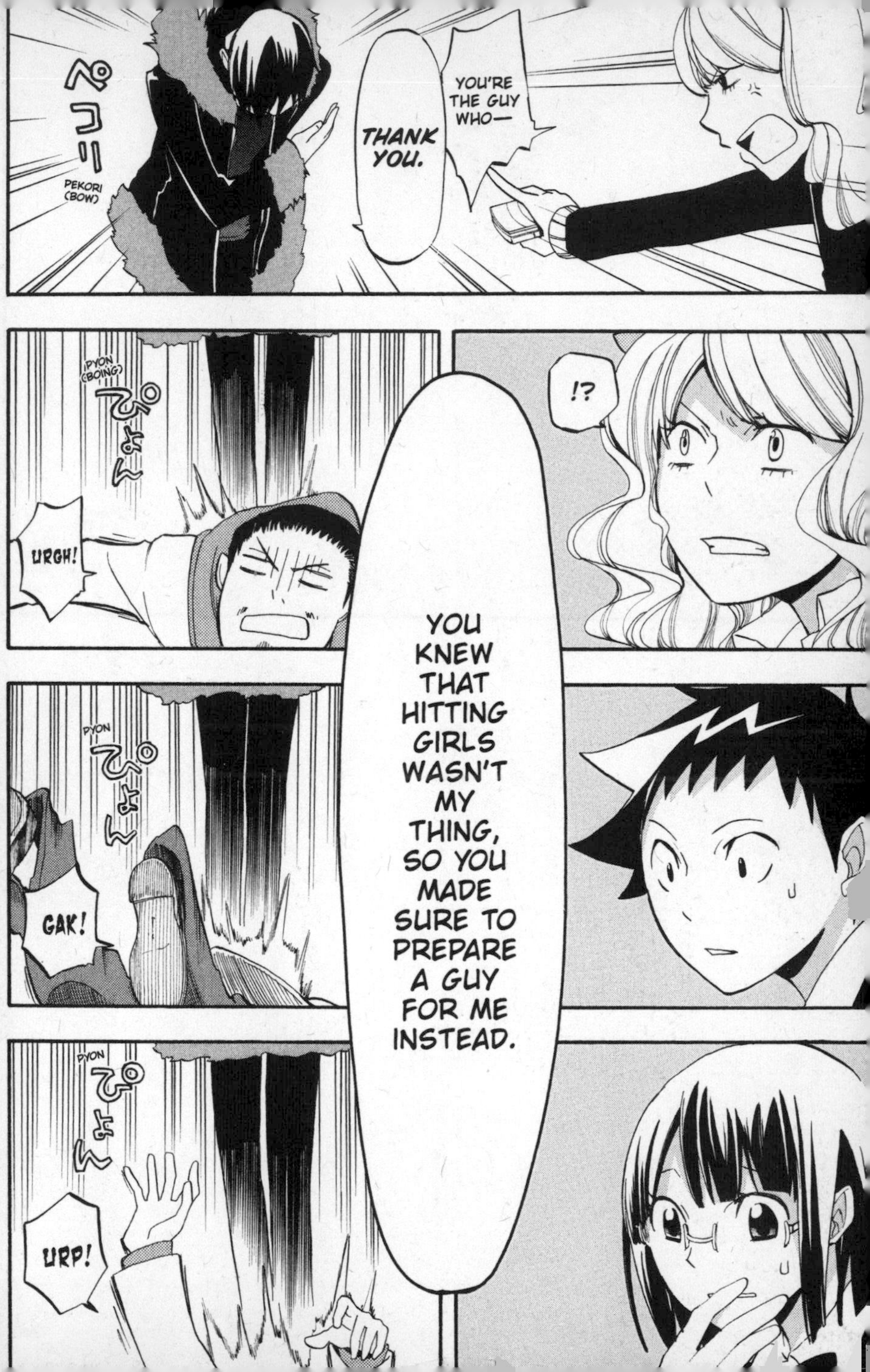
YOU'RE THE GUY WHO—
THANK YOU.
ペコーリ
PEKORI (BOW)
!?
YOU KNEW THAT HITTING GIRLS WASN'T MY THING, SO YOU MADE SURE TO PREPARE A GUY FOR ME INSTEAD.
ぴょん
PYON (BOING)
URGH!
ぴょん～
PYON
GAK!
ぴょん
PYON
URP!

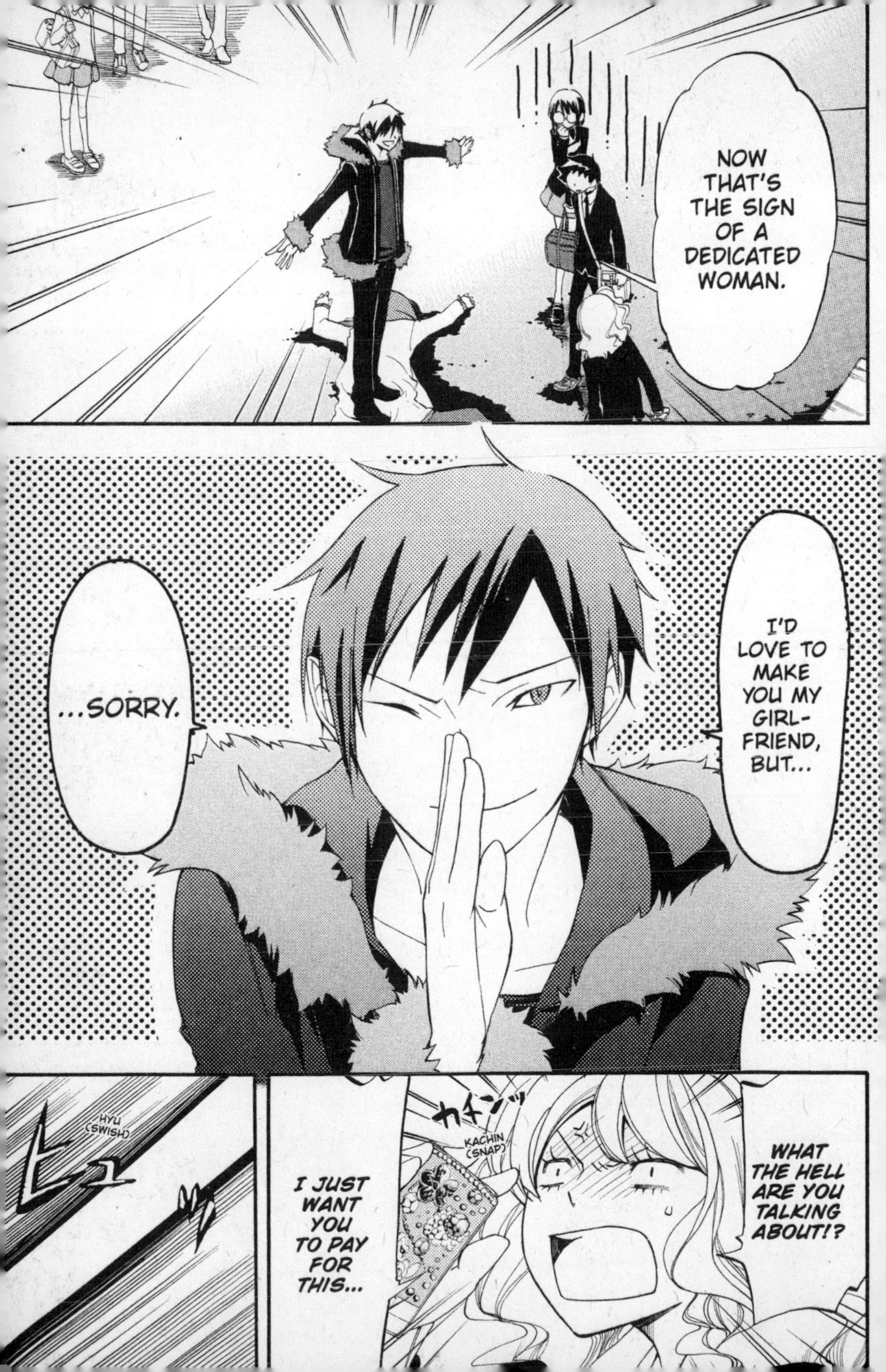
NOW THAT'S THE SIGN OF A DEDICATED WOMAN.
I'D LOVE TO MAKE YOU MY GIRL-FRIEND, BUT...
...SORRY.
WHAT THE HELL ARE YOU TALKING ABOUT!?
KACHIN (SNAP)
I JUST WANT YOU TO PAY FOR THIS...
HYU (SWISH)

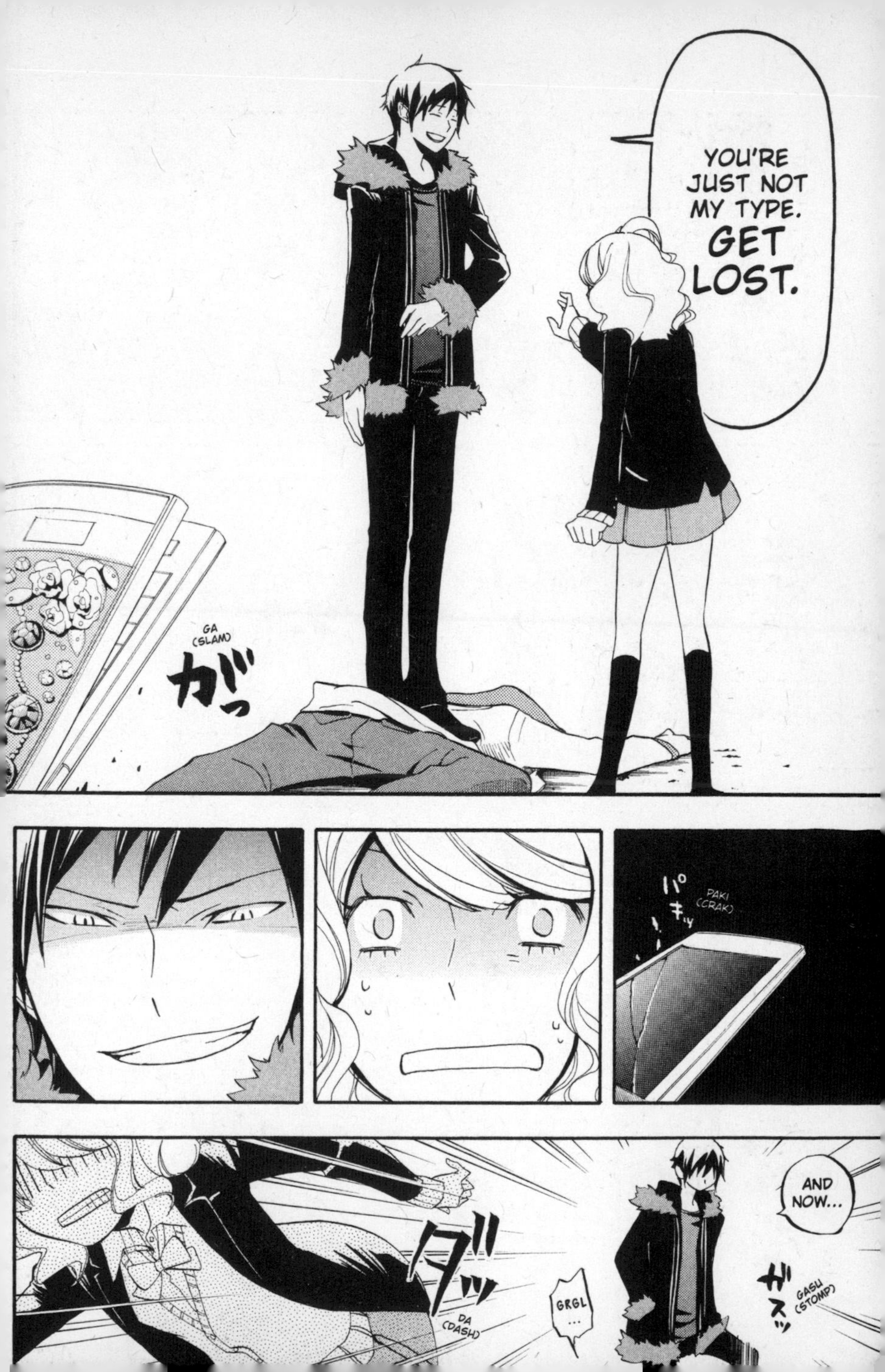
YOU'RE JUST NOT MY TYPE. GET LOST.
ガッ
GA (SLAM)
パキッ
PAKI (CRAK)
AND NOW...
ガスッ
GASU (STOMP)
GRGL ...
ダッ
DA (DASH)

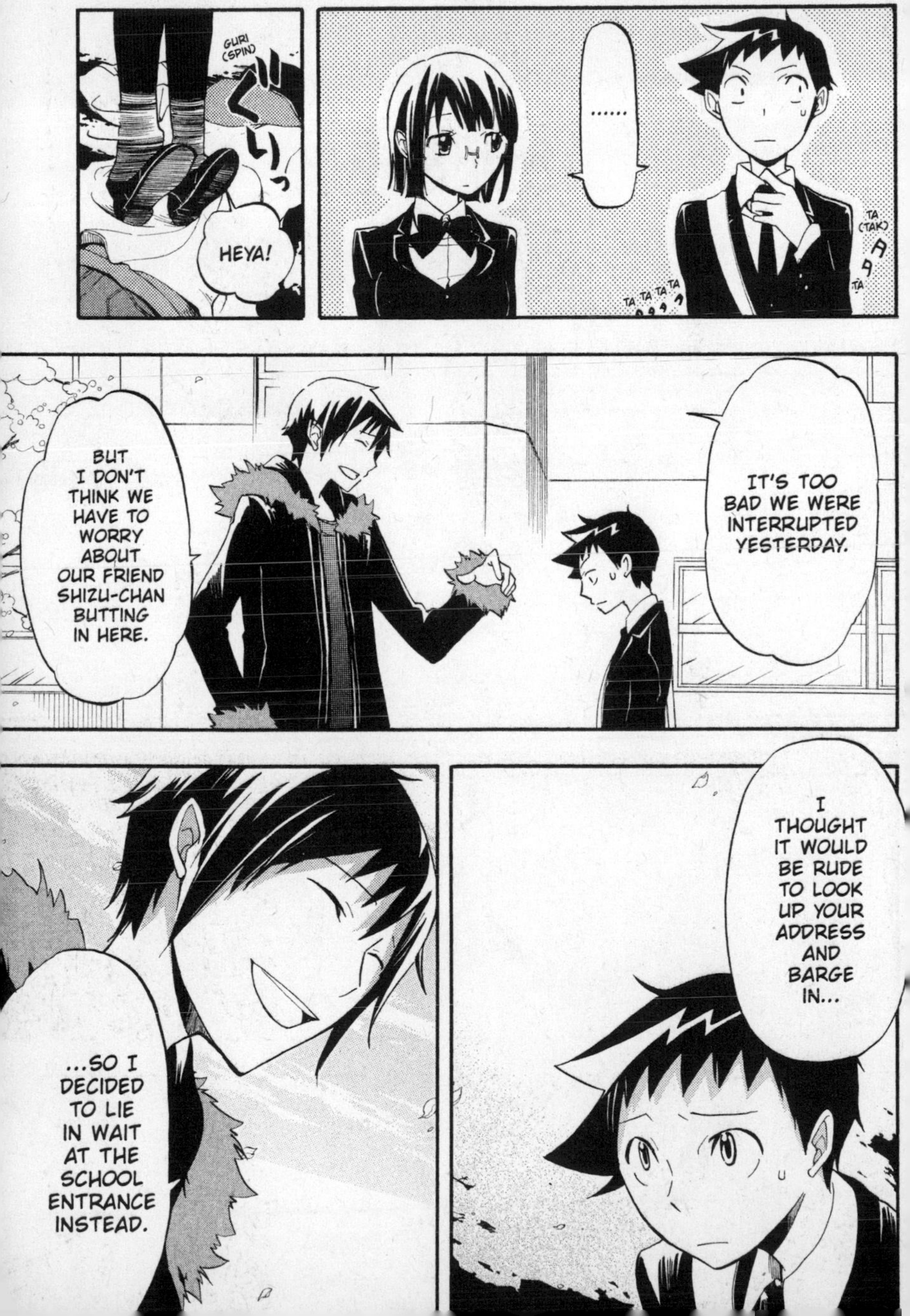
......
TA (TAK) TA TA
TA TA TA TA
GURI (SPIND)
HEYA!
IT'S TOO BAD WE WERE INTERRUPTED YESTERDAY.
BUT I DON'T THINK WE HAVE TO WORRY ABOUT OUR FRIEND SHIZU-CHAN BUTTING IN HERE.
I THOUGHT IT WOULD BE RUDE TO LOOK UP YOUR ADDRESS AND BARGE IN...
...SO I DECIDED TO LIE IN WAIT AT THE SCHOOL ENTRANCE INSTEAD.

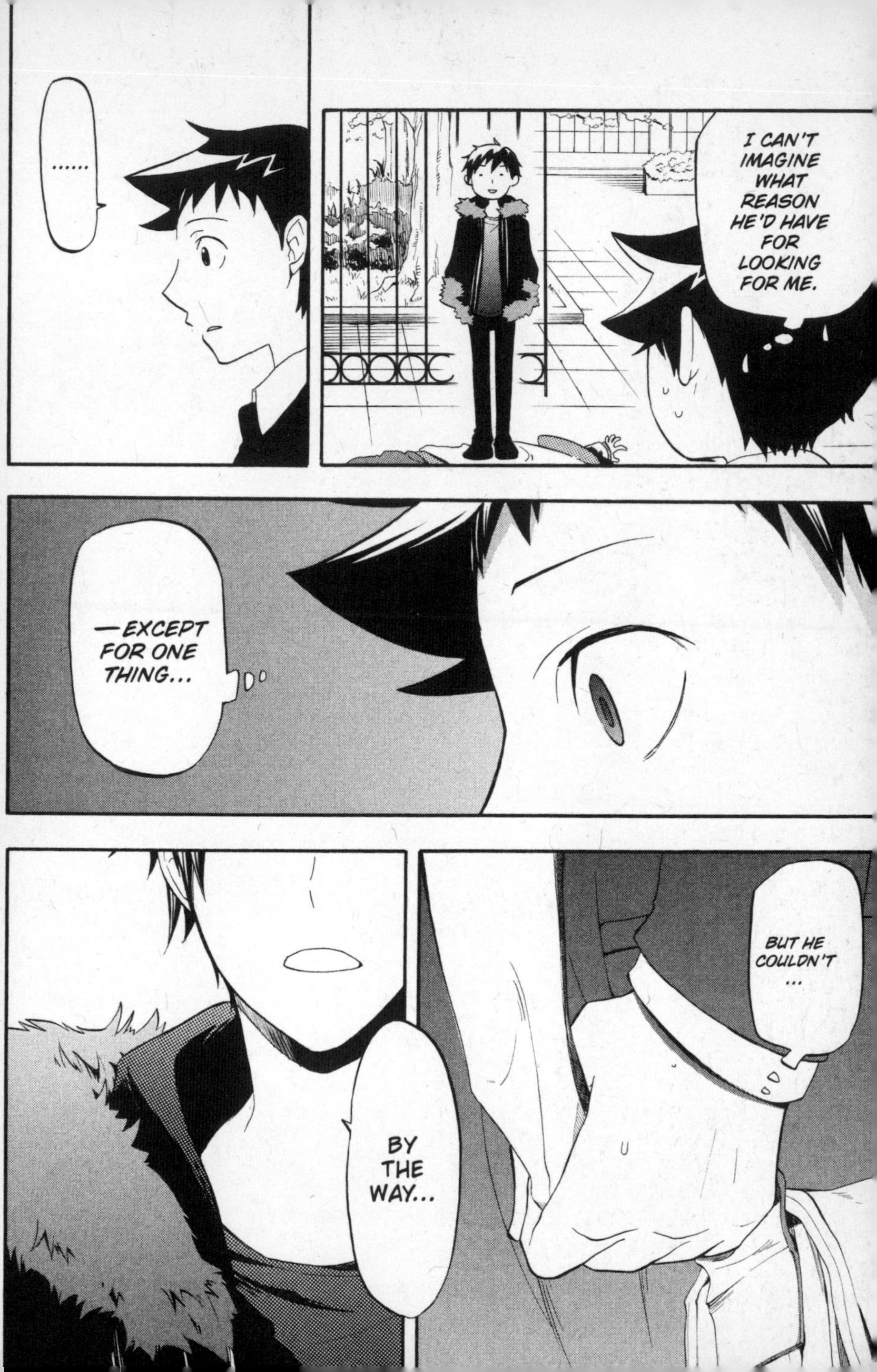
I CAN'T IMAGINE WHAT REASON HE'D HAVE FOR LOOKING FOR ME.
......
—EXCEPT FOR ONE THING...
BUT HE COULDN'T ...
BY THE WAY...

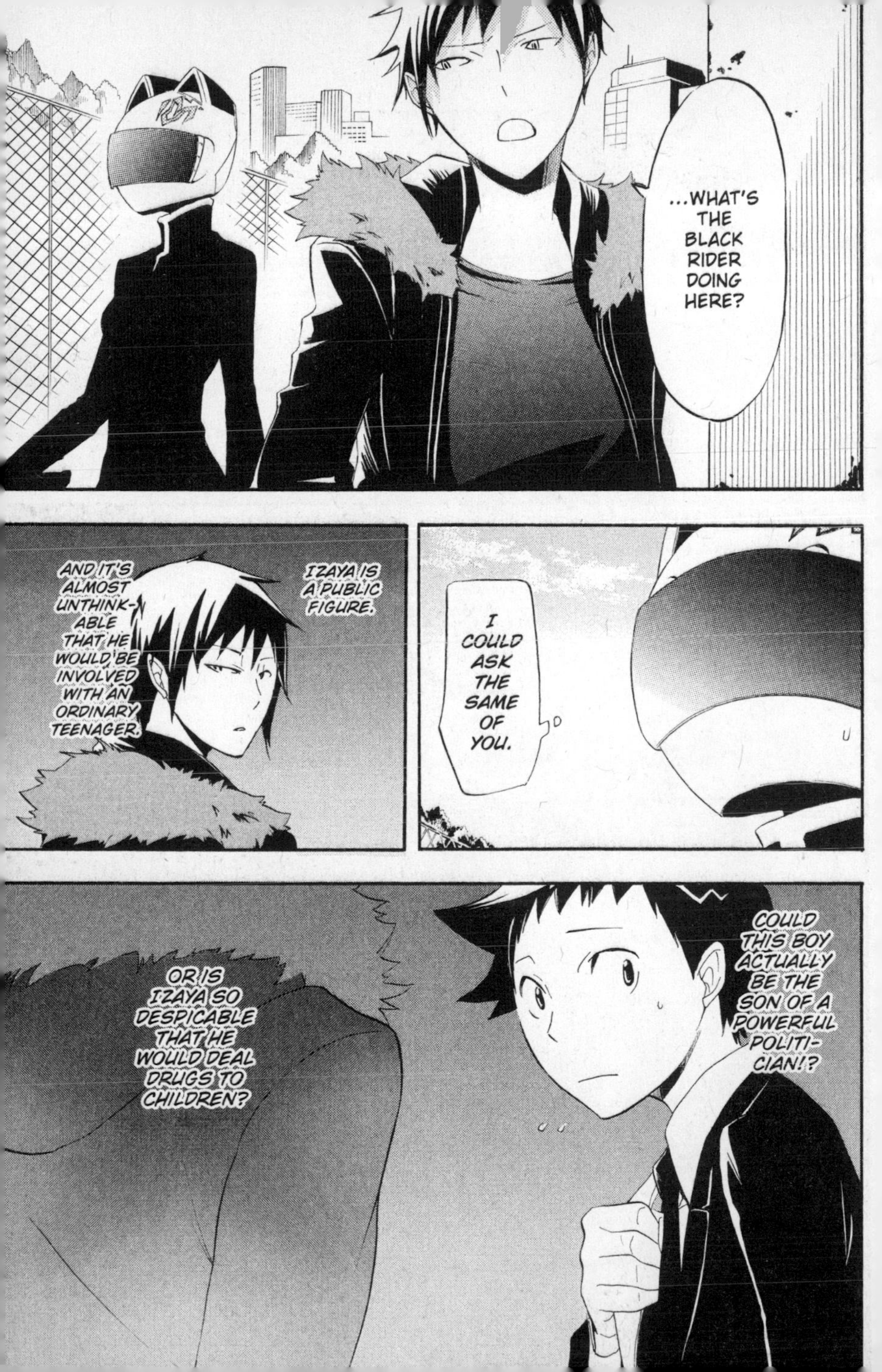
...WHAT'S THE BLACK RIDER DOING HERE?
I COULD ASK THE SAME OF YOU.
IZAYA IS A PUBLIC FIGURE.
AND IT'S ALMOST UNTHINK-ABLE THAT HE WOULD BE INVOLVED WITH AN ORDINARY TEENAGER.
COULD THIS BOY ACTUALLY BE THE SON OF A POWERFUL POLITI-CIAN!?
OR IS IZAYA SO DESPICABLE THAT HE WOULD DEAL DRUGS TO CHILDREN?

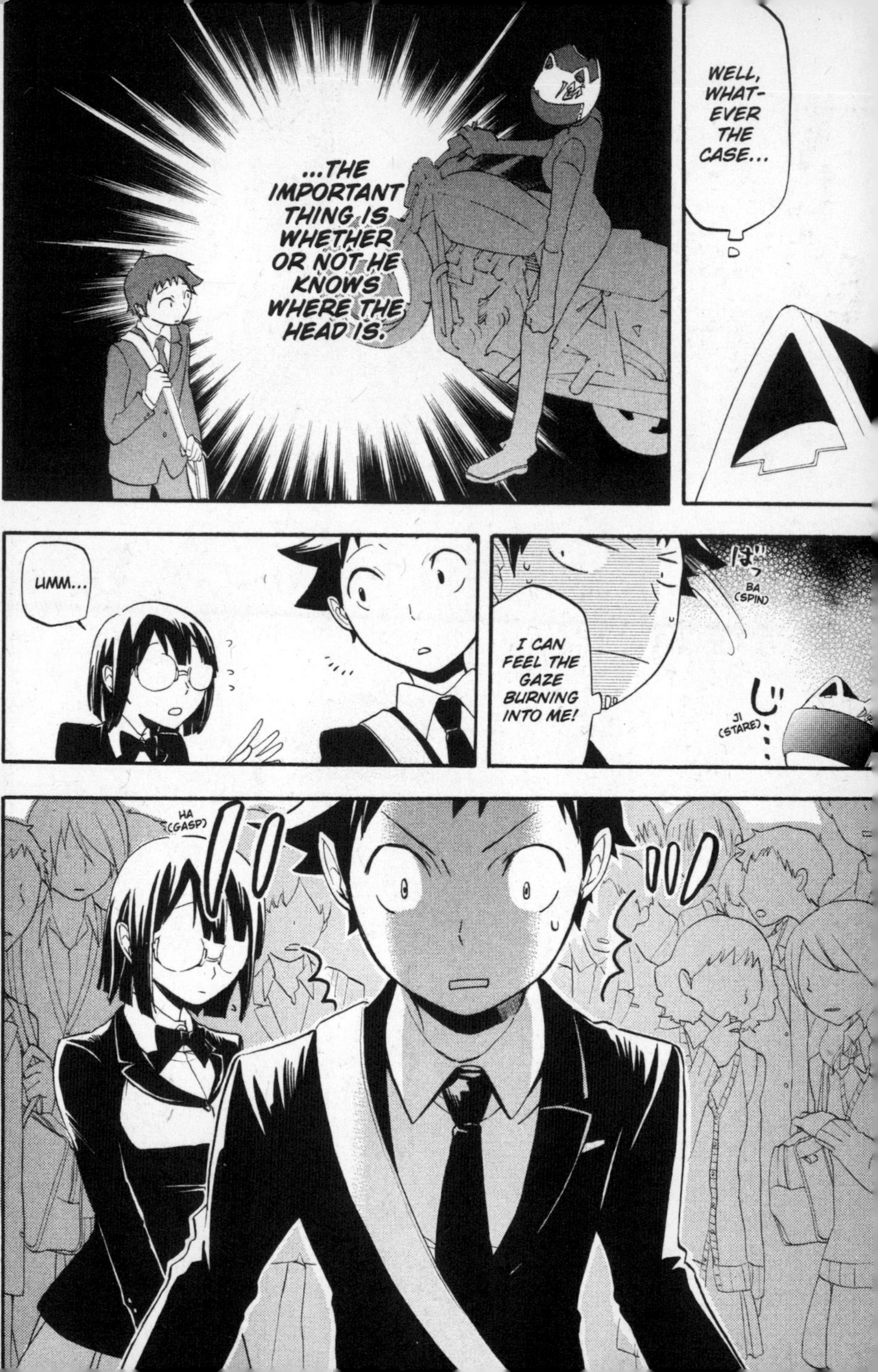
WELL, WHATEVER THE CASE...
...THE IMPORTANT THING IS WHETHER OR NOT HE KNOWS WHERE THE HEAD IS.
ばっ
BA (SPIN)
I CAN FEEL THE GAZE BURNING INTO ME!
じ
JI (STARE)
UMM...
HA (GASP)

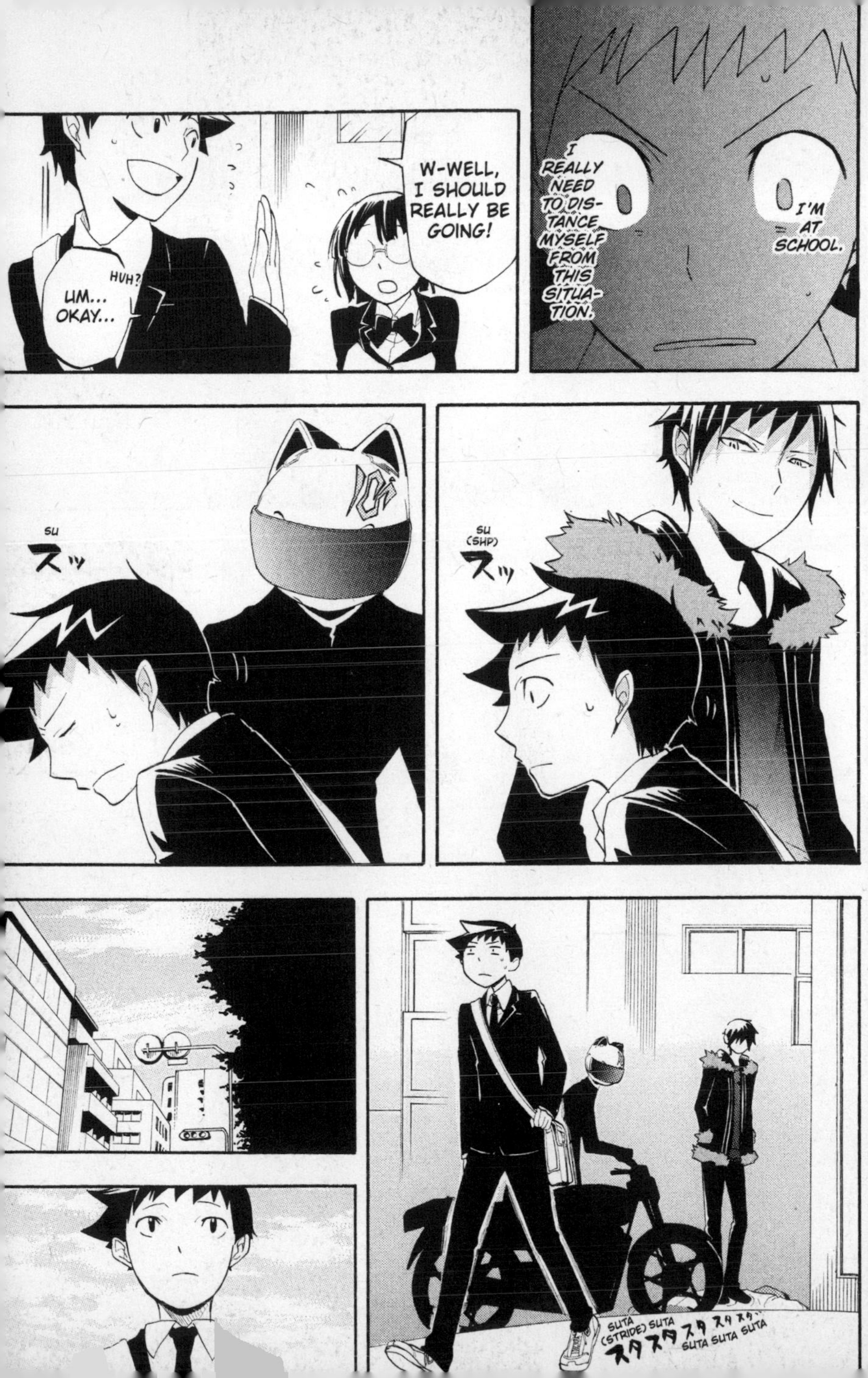
I'M AT SCHOOL.
I REALLY NEED TO DIS-TANCE MYSELF FROM THIS SITUA-TION.
W-WELL, I SHOULD REALLY BE GOING!
HUH?
UM... OKAY...
SU (SHP)
スッ
SU
スッ
SUTA (STRIDE) SUTA
スタスタ スタ スタ スタ
SUTA SUTA SUTA

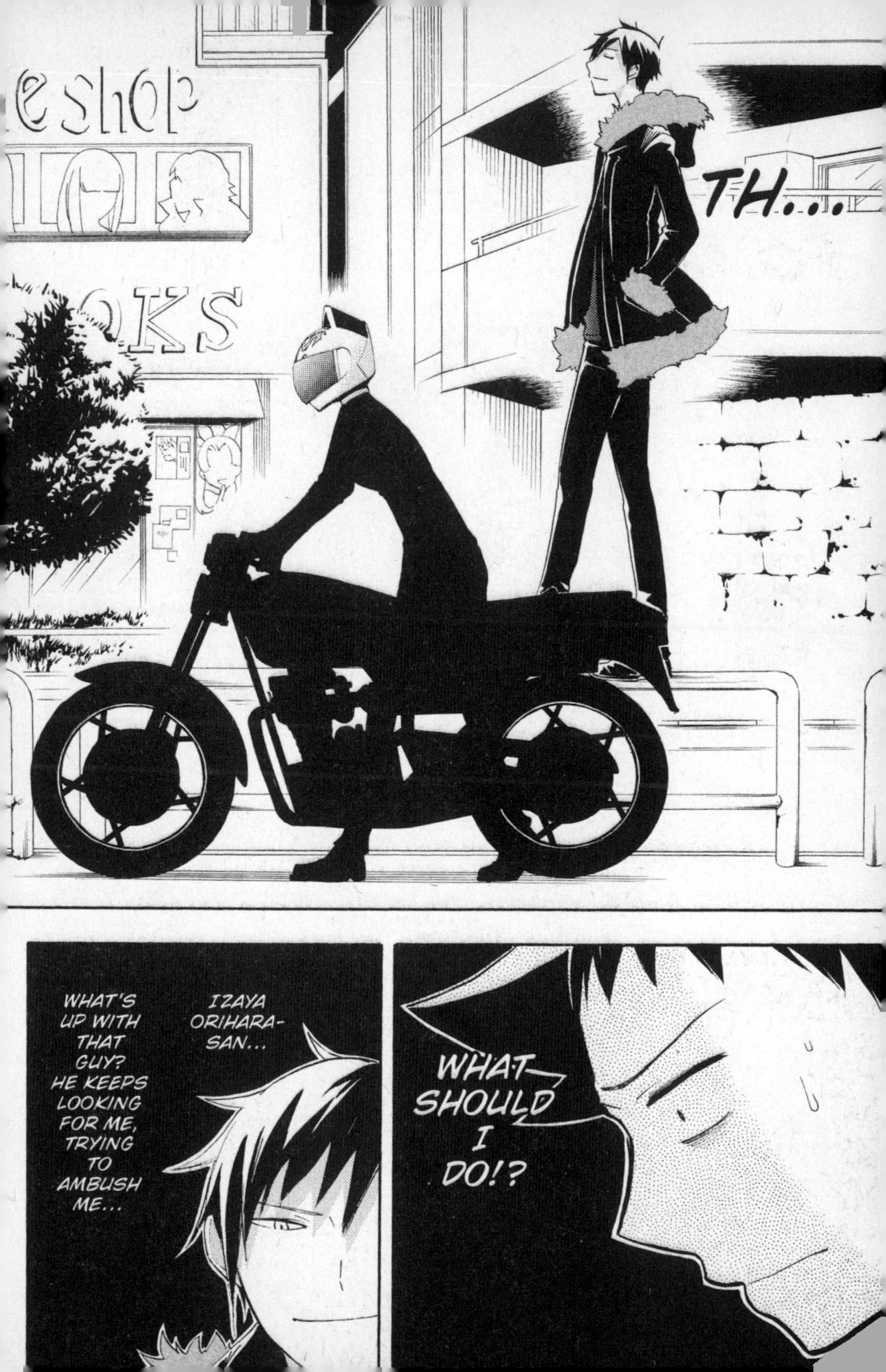
e shop
OKS
TH...
WHAT SHOULD I DO!?
IZAYA ORIHARA-SAN...
WHAT'S UP WITH THAT GUY? HE KEEPS LOOKING FOR ME, TRYING TO AMBUSH ME...

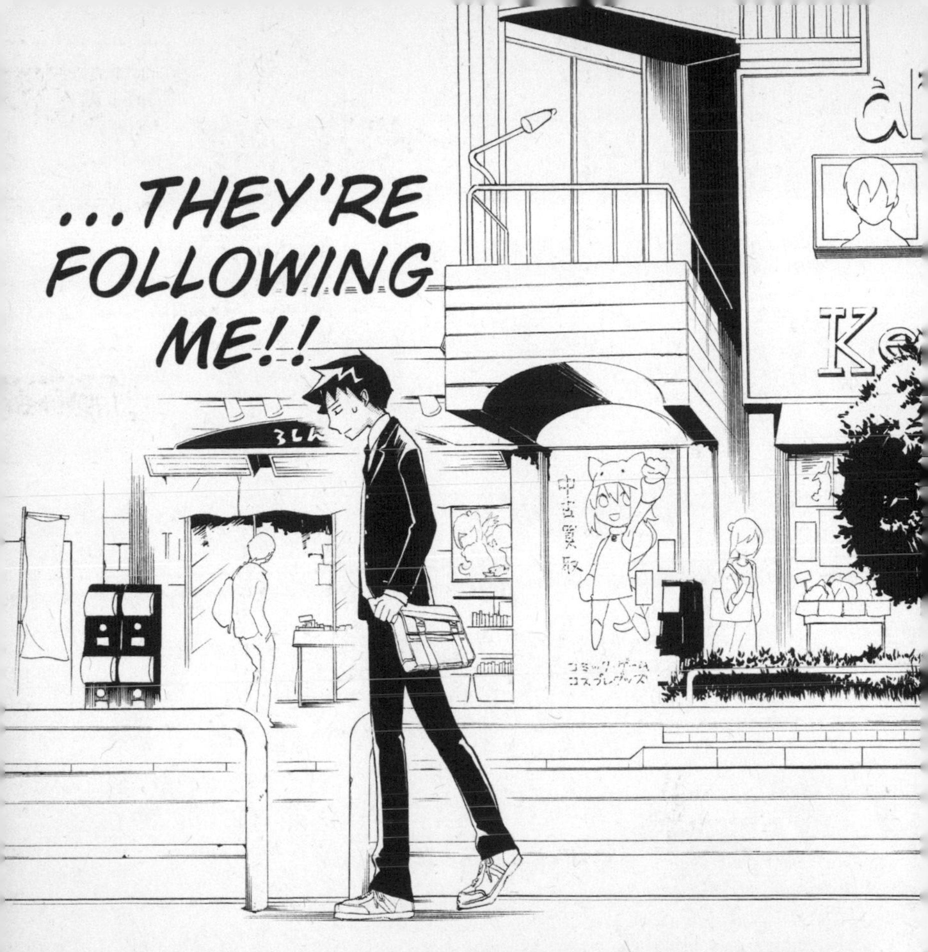
...THEY'RE FOLLOWING ME!!

SIGN: WE BUY USED COMICS — GAMES — COSPLAY GOODS

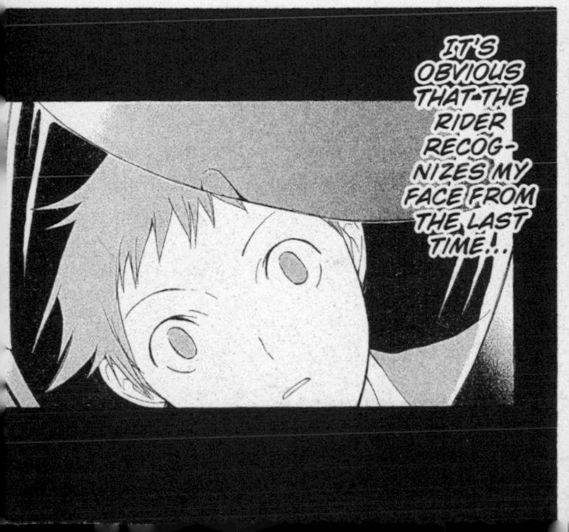
IT'S OBVIOUS THAT THE RIDER RECOG-NIZES MY FACE FROM THE LAST TIME...

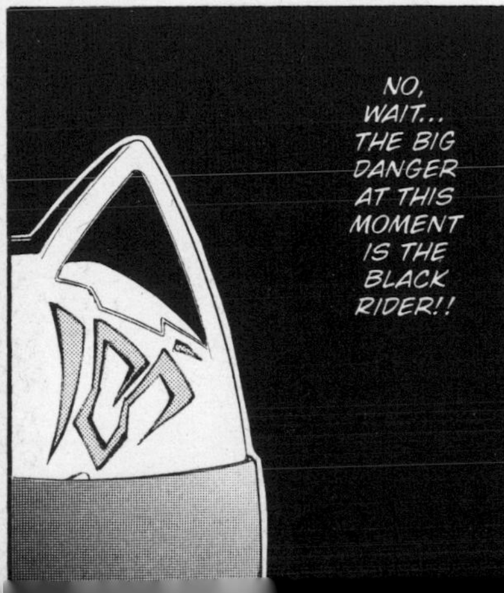
NO, WAIT... THE BIG DANGER AT THIS MOMENT IS THE BLACK RIDER!!

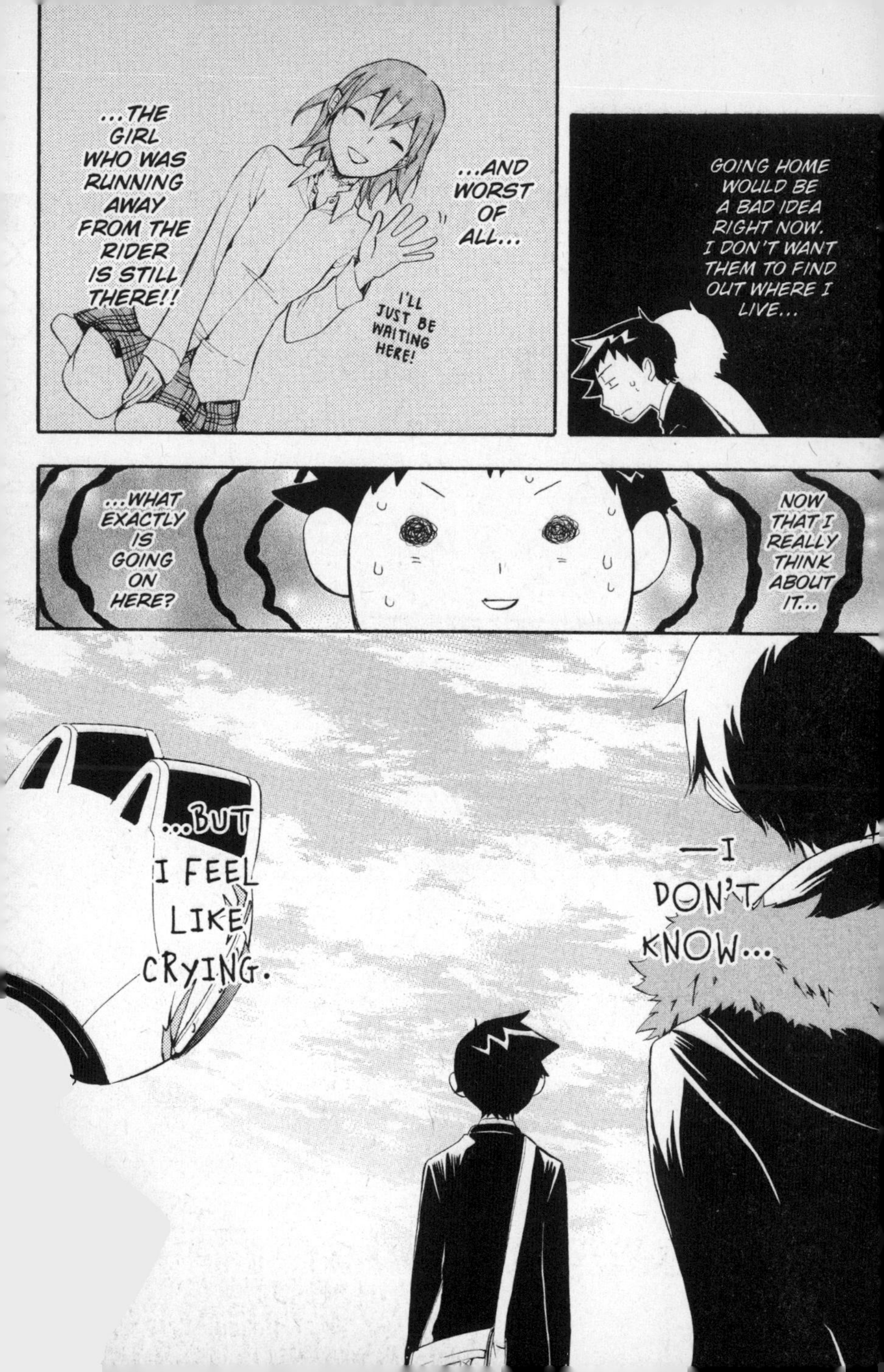
GOING HOME WOULD BE A BAD IDEA RIGHT NOW. I DON'T WANT THEM TO FIND OUT WHERE I LIVE...
...AND WORST OF ALL...
...THE GIRL WHO WAS RUNNING AWAY FROM THE RIDER IS STILL THERE!!
I'LL JUST BE WAITING HERE!
NOW THAT I REALLY THINK ABOUT IT...
...WHAT EXACTLY IS GOING ON HERE?
—I DON'T KNOW...
...BUT I FEEL LIKE CRYING.

16: WAWAWAWAWAWAWAWAWAWAWAWAWAWAWA!!

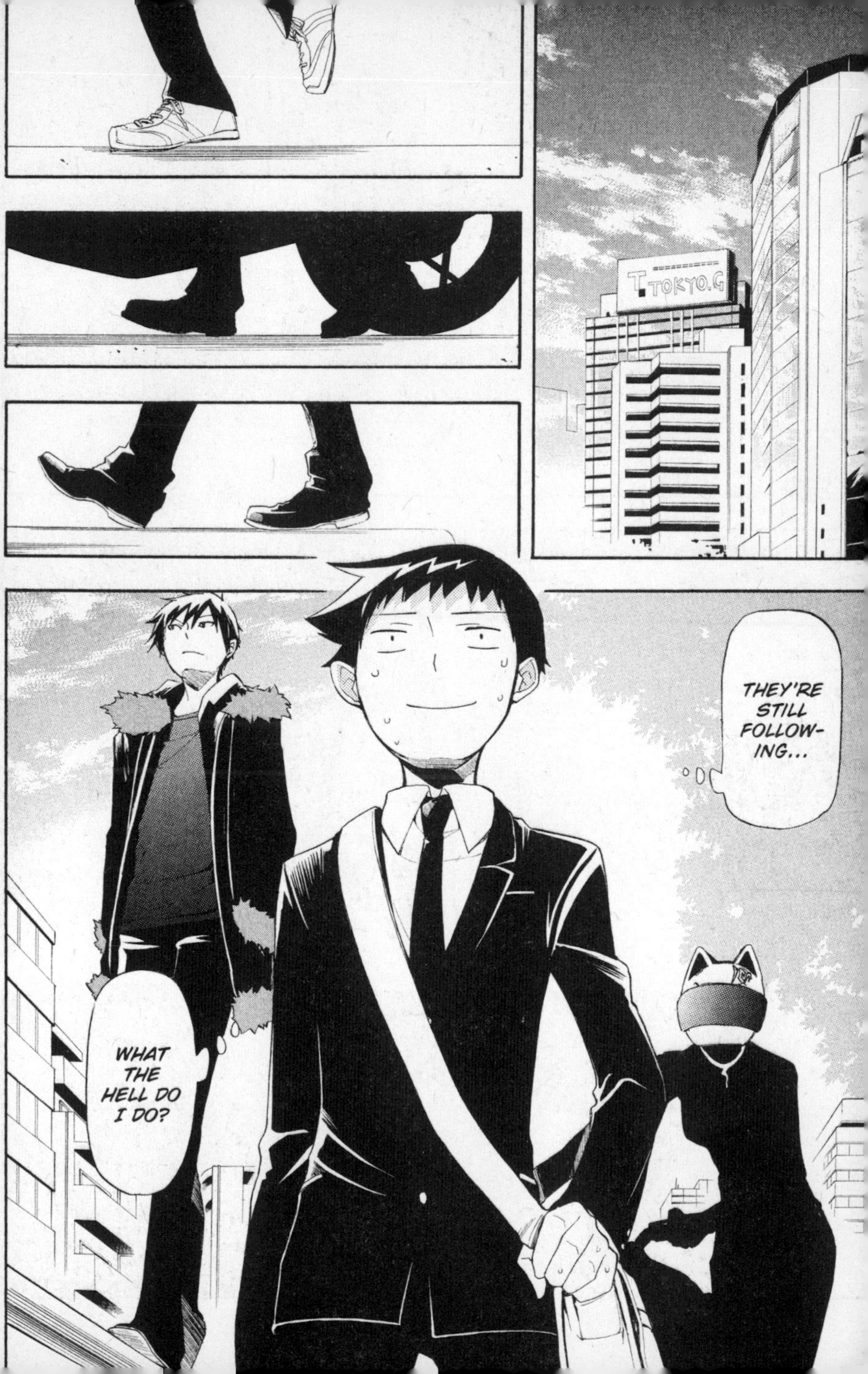
TOKYO.G
THEY'RE STILL FOLLOW-ING...
WHAT THE HELL DO I DO?

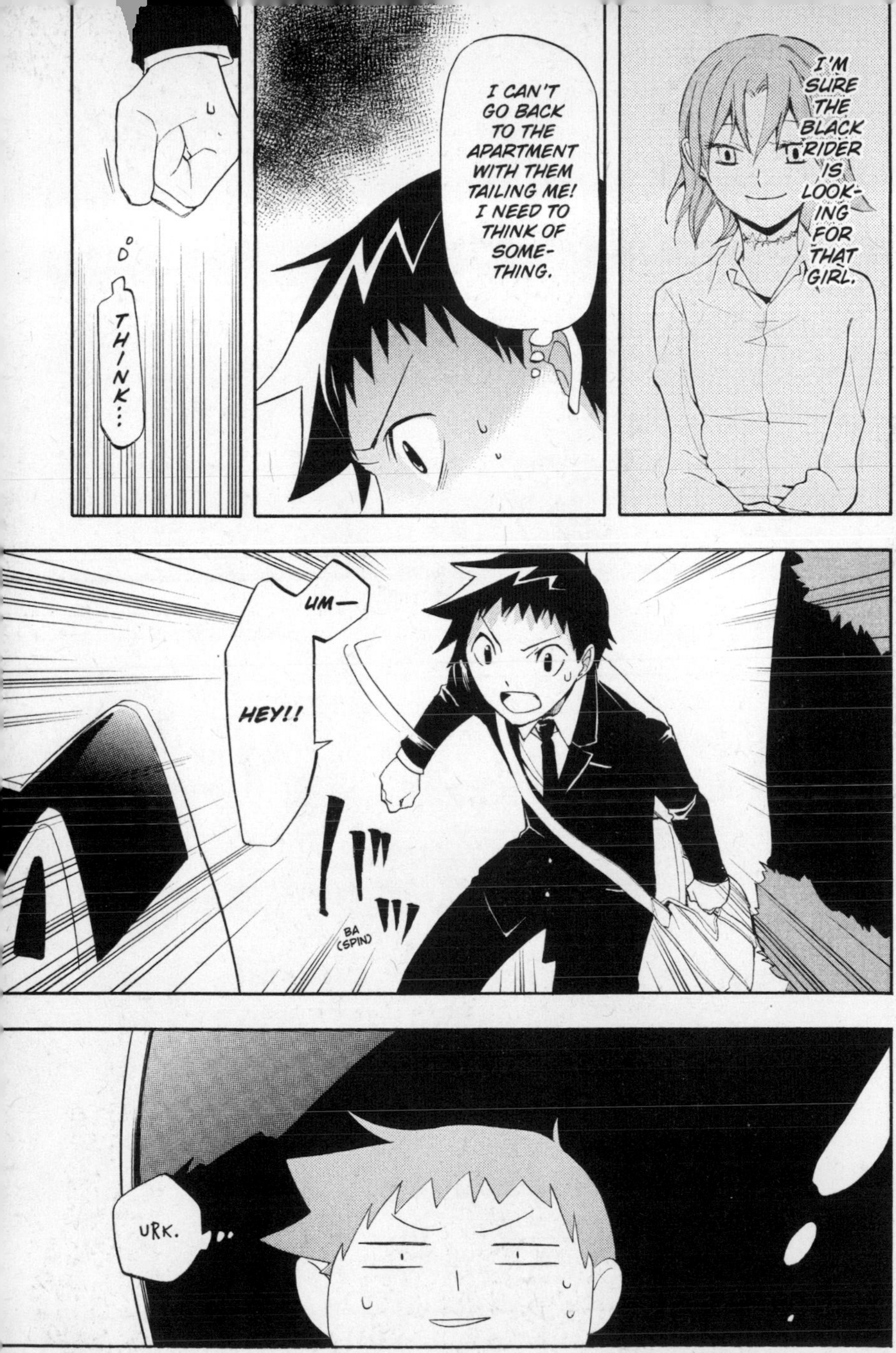
I'M SURE THE BLACK RIDER IS LOOKING FOR THAT GIRL.
I CAN'T GO BACK TO THE APARTMENT WITH THEM TAILING ME! I NEED TO THINK OF SOMETHING.
THINK...
UM—
HEY!!
BA (SPIN)
URK.

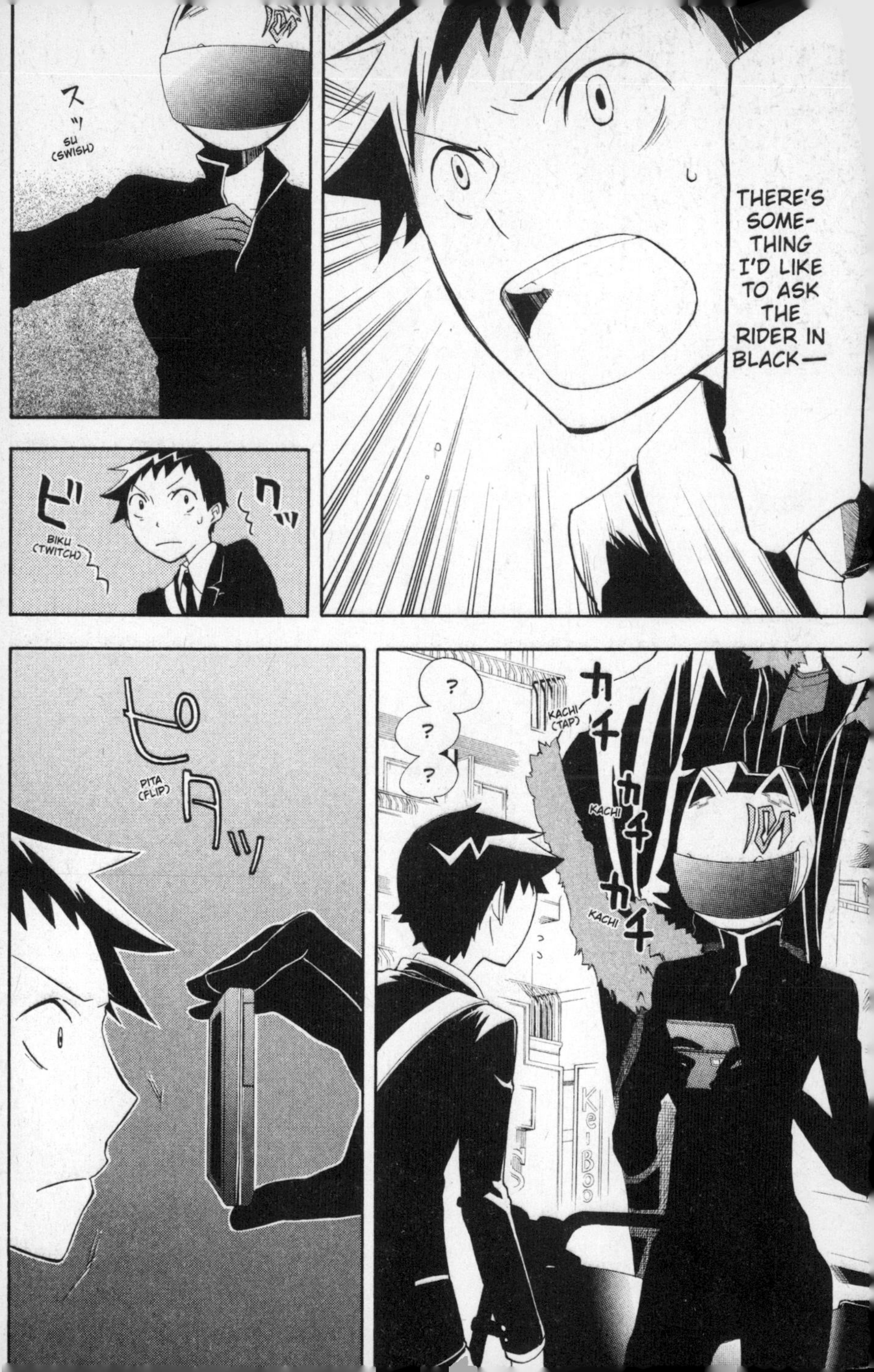
THERE'S SOMETHING I'D LIKE TO ASK THE RIDER IN BLACK—
スッ
SU (SWISH)
ビクッ
BIKU (TWITCH)
? ? ?
カチ
KACHI (TAP)
カチ
KACHI
カチ
KACHI
Kei BOO
ピタッ
PITA (FLIP)

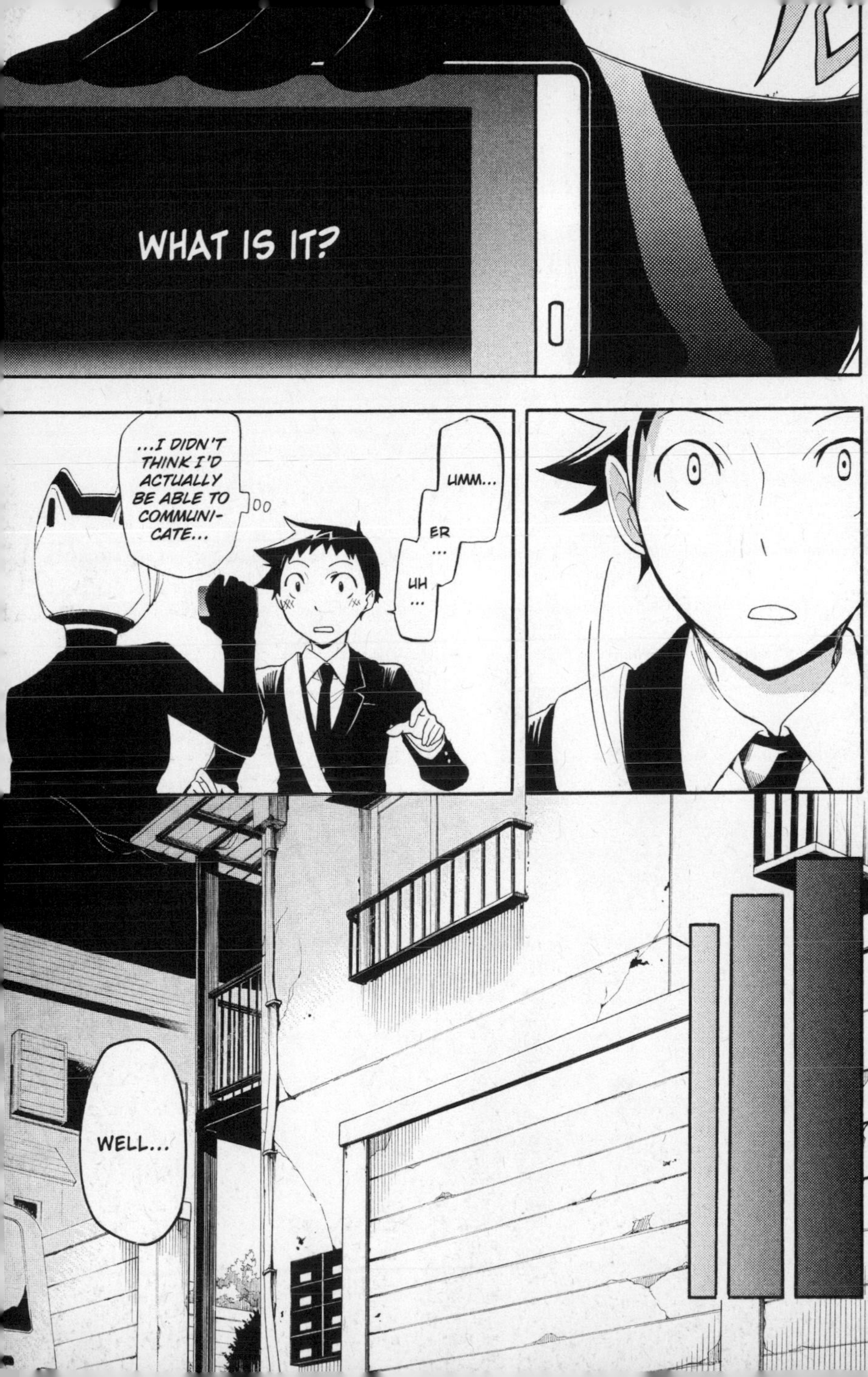
WHAT IS IT?
UMMM... ER ... UH ...
...I DIDN'T THINK I'D ACTUALLY BE ABLE TO COMMUNI-CATE...
WELL...

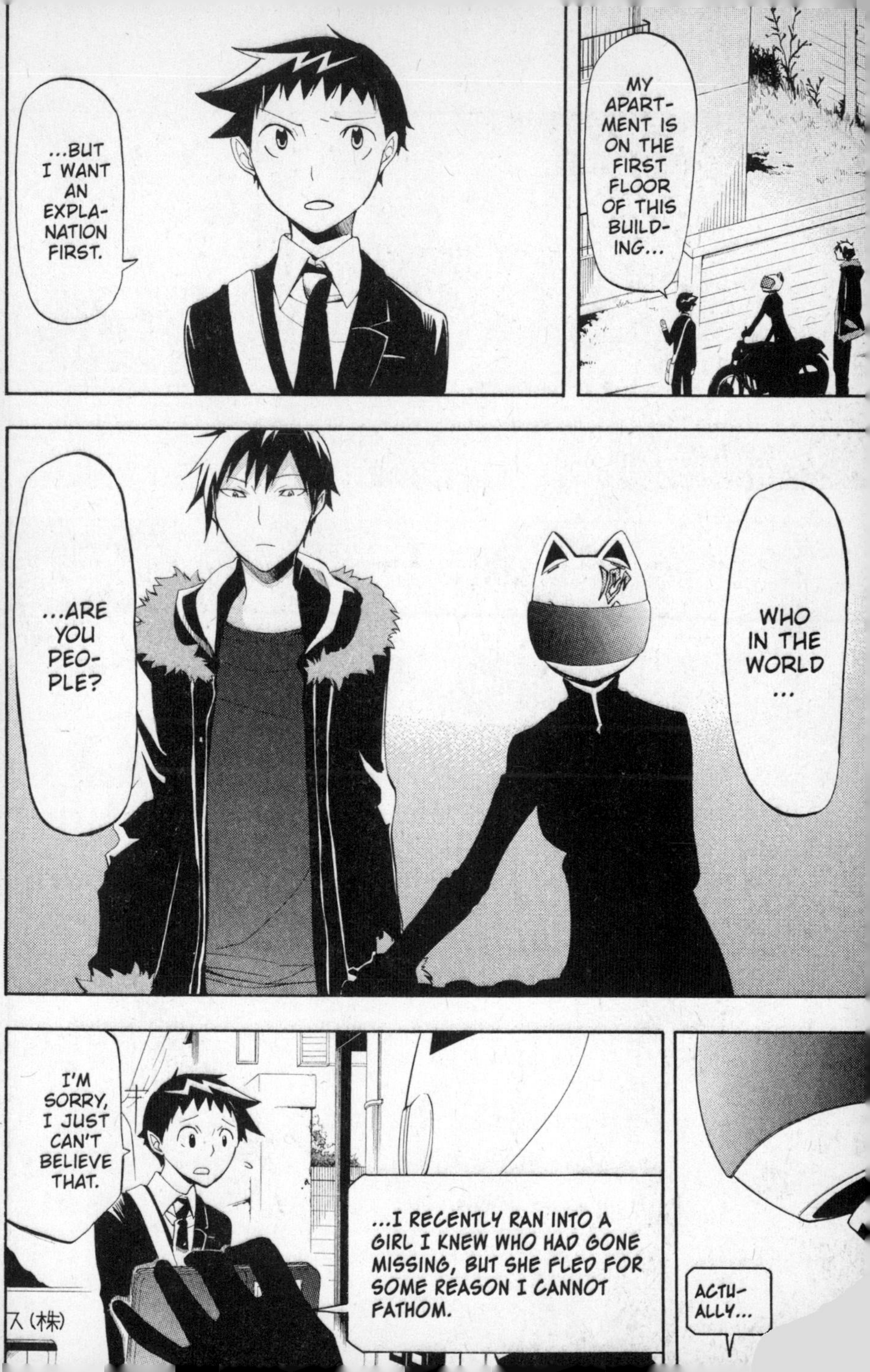
MY APARTMENT IS ON THE FIRST FLOOR OF THIS BUILDING...
...BUT I WANT AN EXPLANATION FIRST.
WHO IN THE WORLD...
...ARE YOU PEOPLE?
ACTUALLY...
...I RECENTLY RAN INTO A GIRL I KNEW WHO HAD GONE MISSING, BUT SHE FLED FOR SOME REASON I CANNOT FATHOM.
I'M SORRY, I JUST CAN'T BELIEVE THAT.
ス(株)

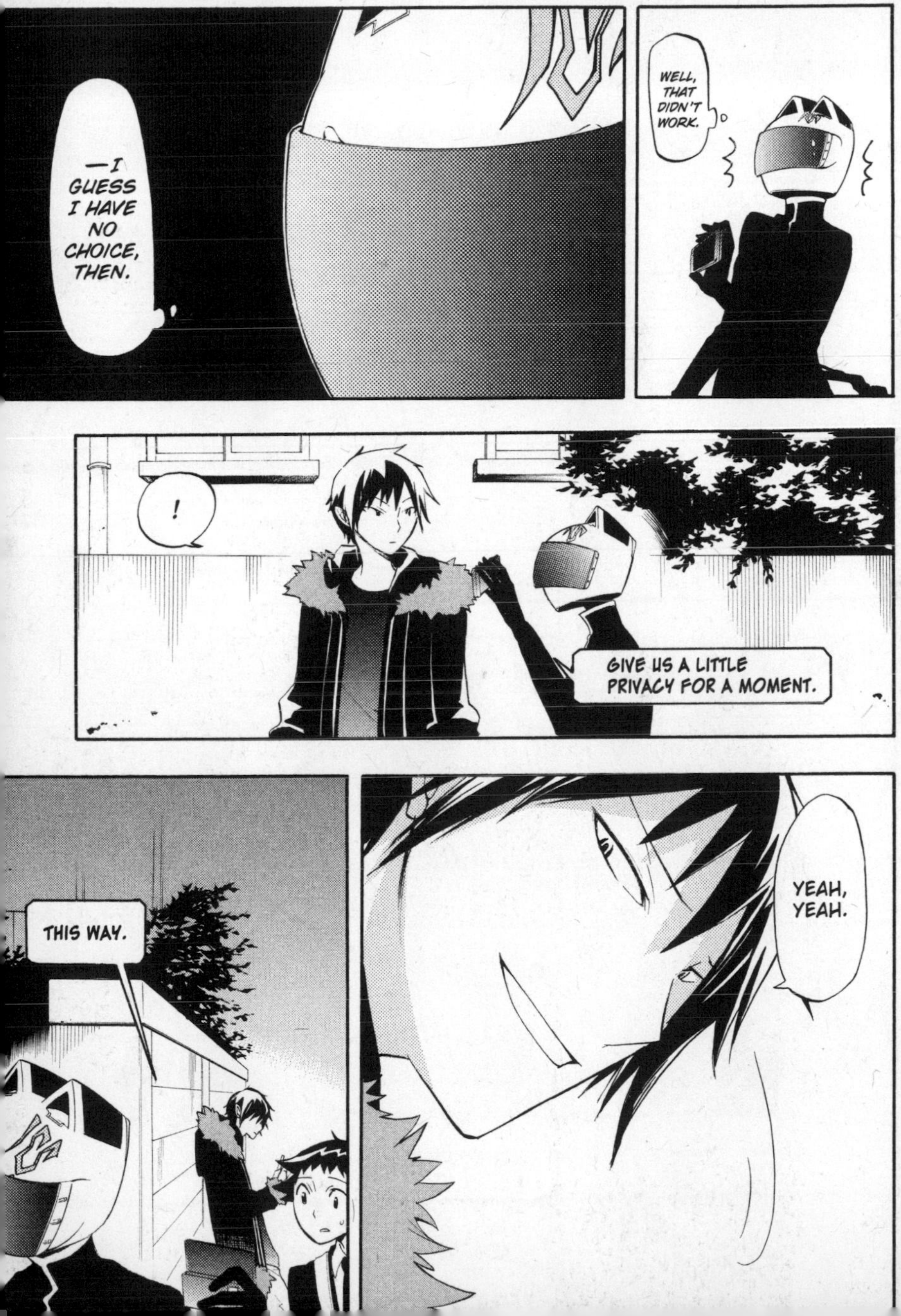
WELL, THAT DIDN'T WORK.
—I GUESS I HAVE NO CHOICE, THEN.
!
GIVE US A LITTLE PRIVACY FOR A MOMENT.
YEAH, YEAH.
THIS WAY.

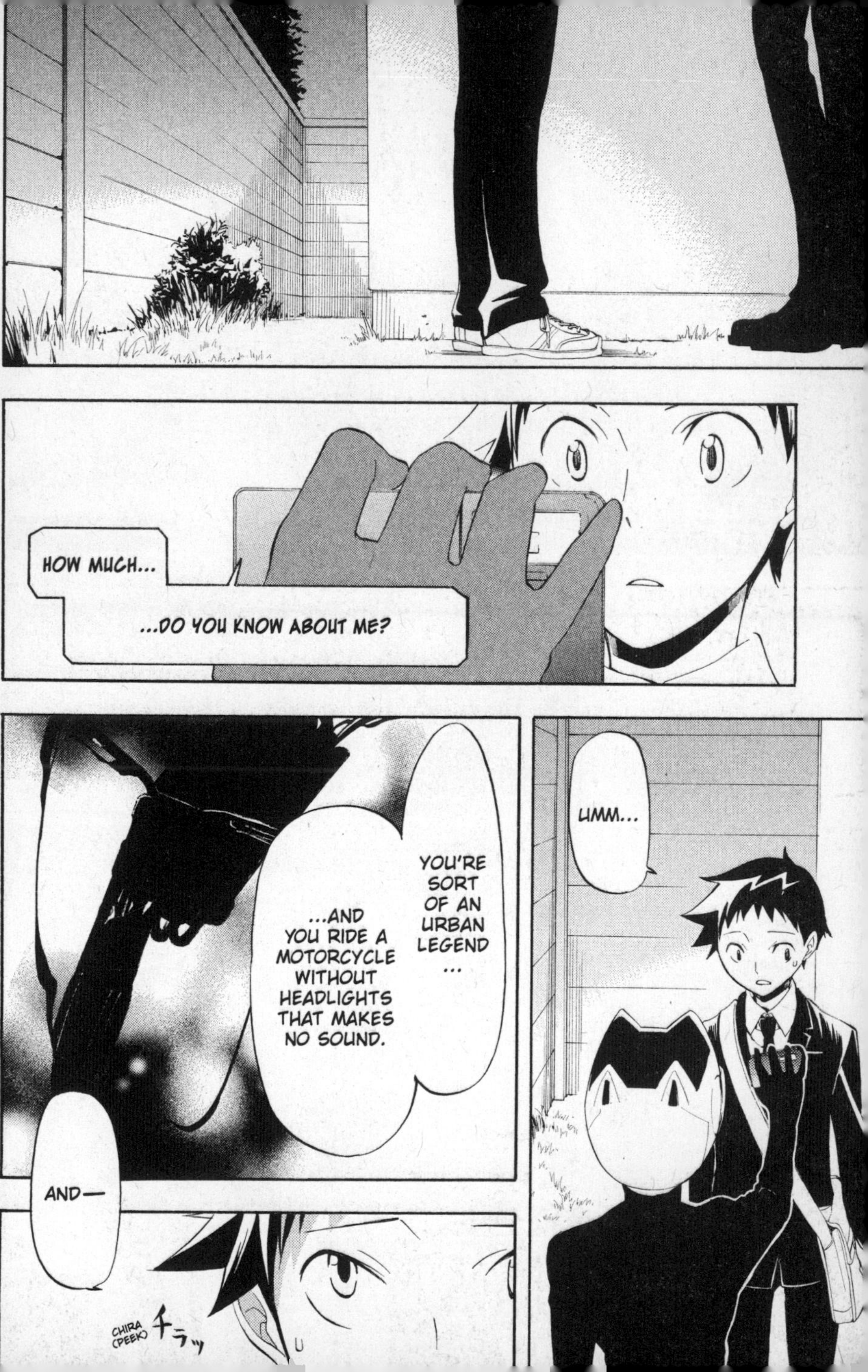
HOW MUCH...
...DO YOU KNOW ABOUT ME?
UMM...
YOU'RE SORT OF AN URBAN LEGEND...
...AND YOU RIDE A MOTORCYCLE WITHOUT HEADLIGHTS THAT MAKES NO SOUND.
AND—
チラッ
CHIRA (PEEK)

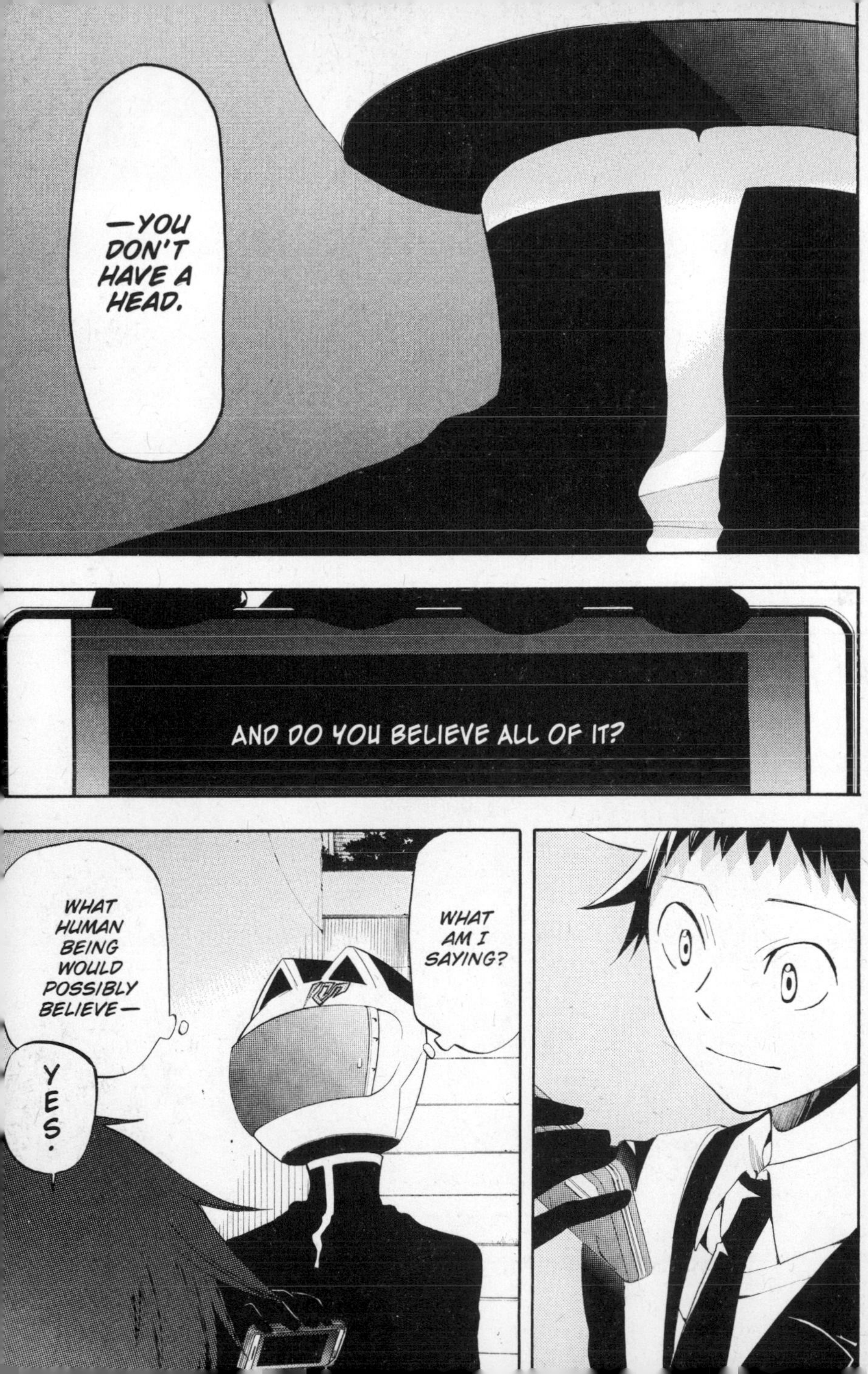
—YOU DON'T HAVE A HEAD.
AND DO YOU BELIEVE ALL OF IT?
WHAT AM I SAYING?
WHAT HUMAN BEING WOULD POSSIBLY BELIEVE—
YES.

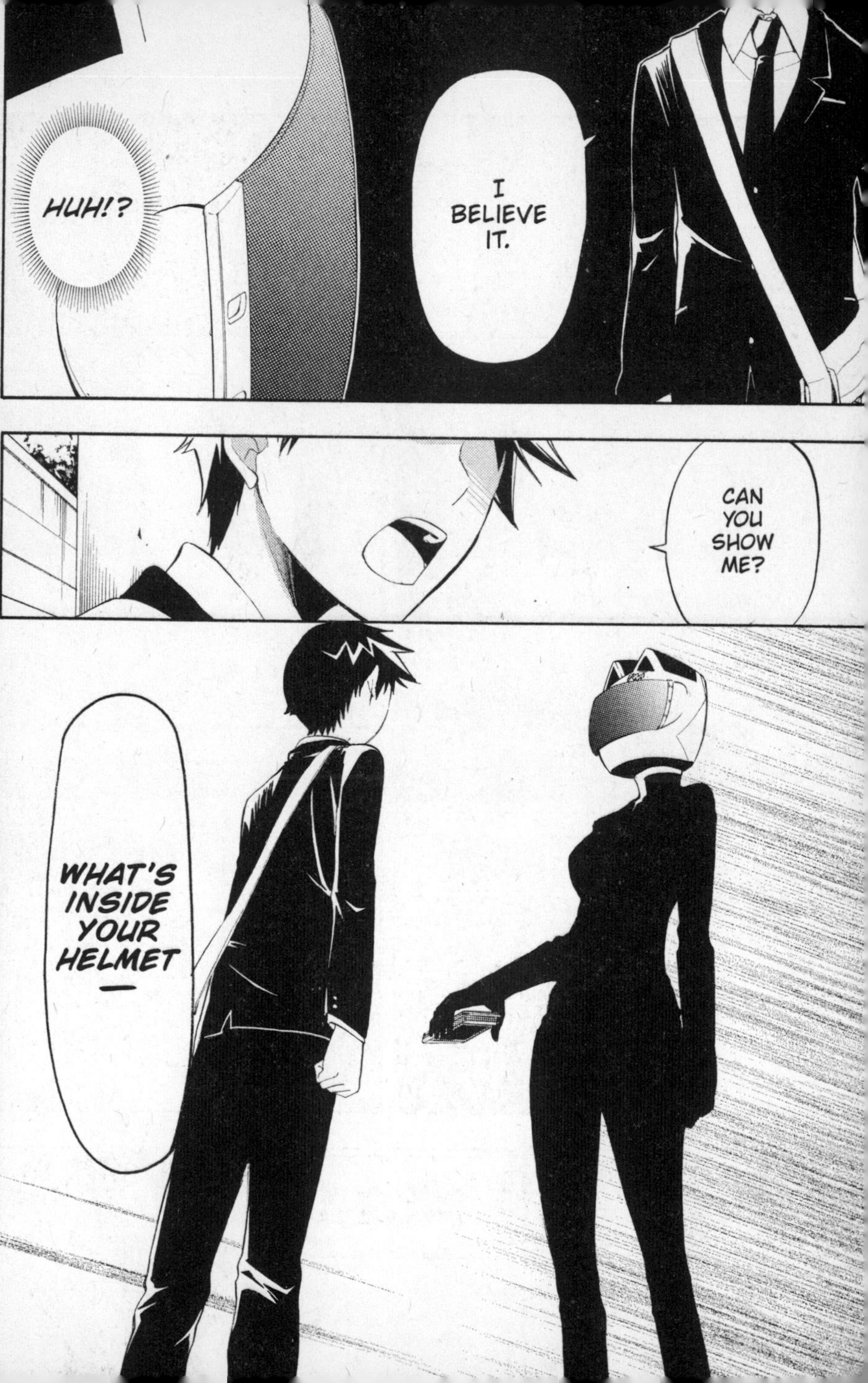
I BELIEVE IT.
HUH!?
CAN YOU SHOW ME?
WHAT'S INSIDE YOUR HELMET —

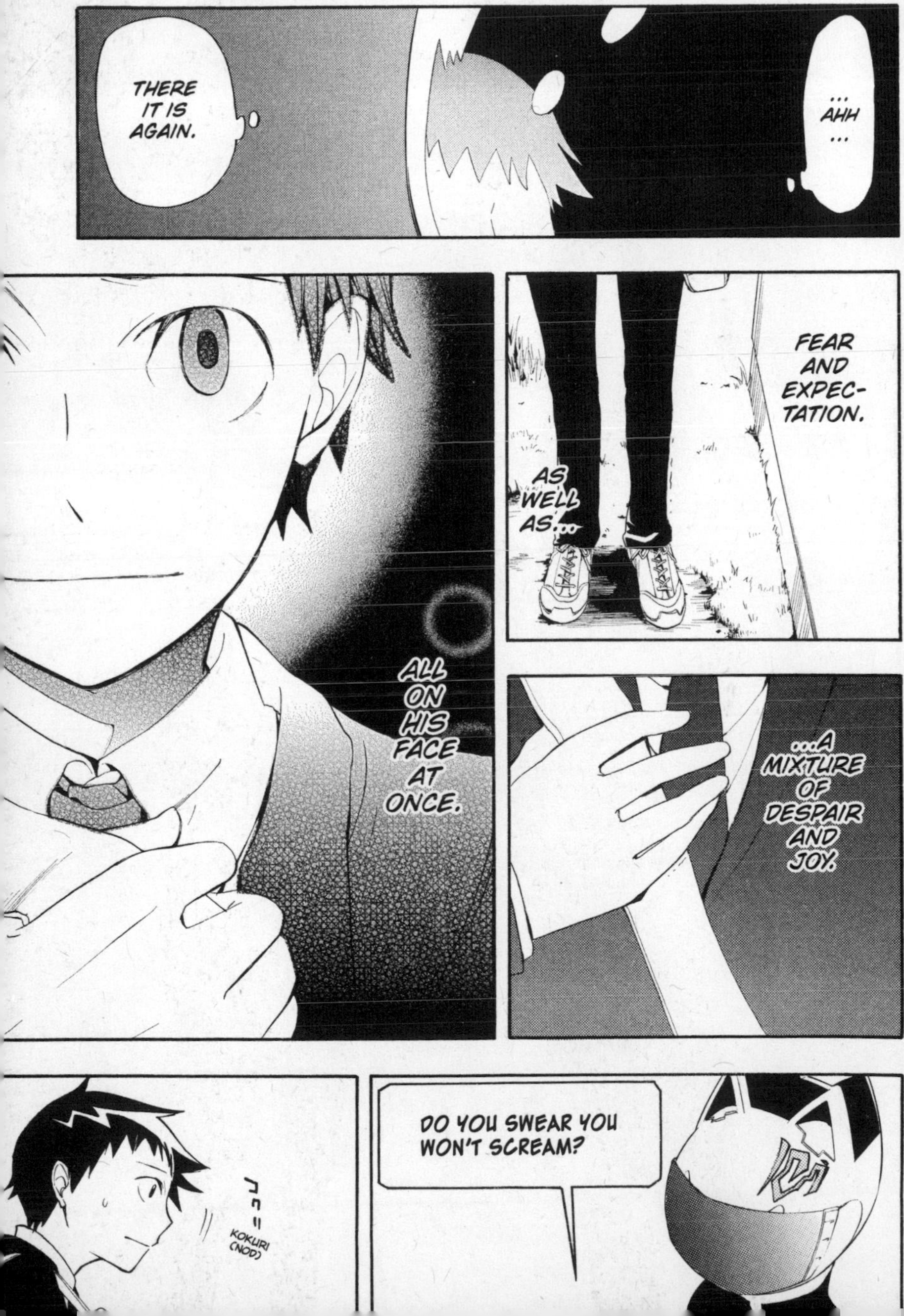
...AHH...
THERE IT IS AGAIN.
FEAR AND EXPECTATION.
AS WELL AS...
...A MIXTURE OF DESPAIR AND JOY.
ALL ON HIS FACE AT ONCE.
DO YOU SWEAR YOU WON'T SCREAM?
KOKURI (NOD)

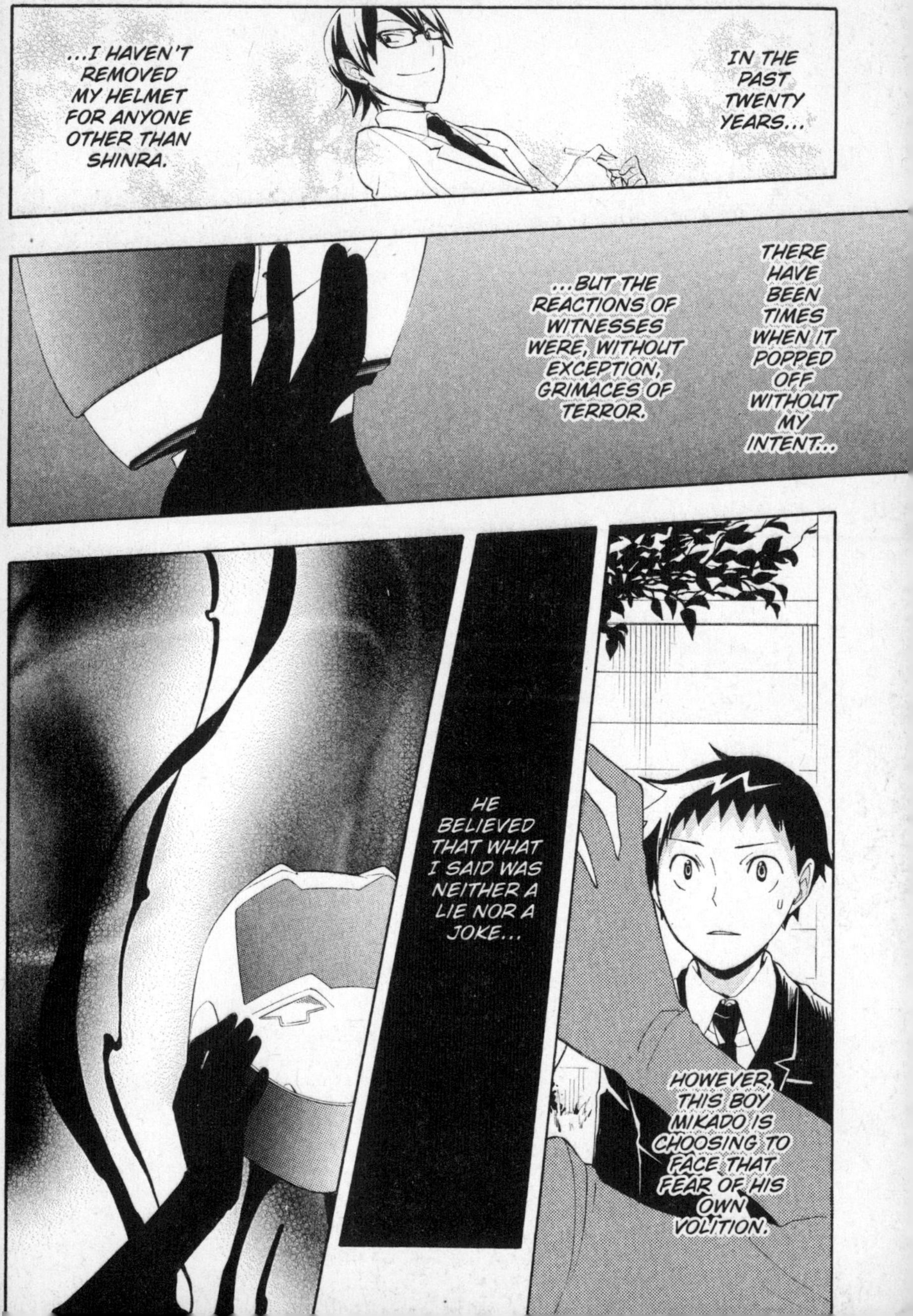
IN THE PAST TWENTY YEARS...
...I HAVEN'T REMOVED MY HELMET FOR ANYONE OTHER THAN SHINRA.
THERE HAVE BEEN TIMES WHEN IT POPPED OFF WITHOUT MY INTENT...
...BUT THE REACTIONS OF WITNESSES WERE, WITHOUT EXCEPTION, GRIMACES OF TERROR.
HOWEVER, THIS BOY MIKADO IS CHOOSING TO FACE THAT FEAR OF HIS OWN VOLITION.
HE BELIEVED THAT WHAT I SAID WAS NEITHER A LIE NOR A JOKE...

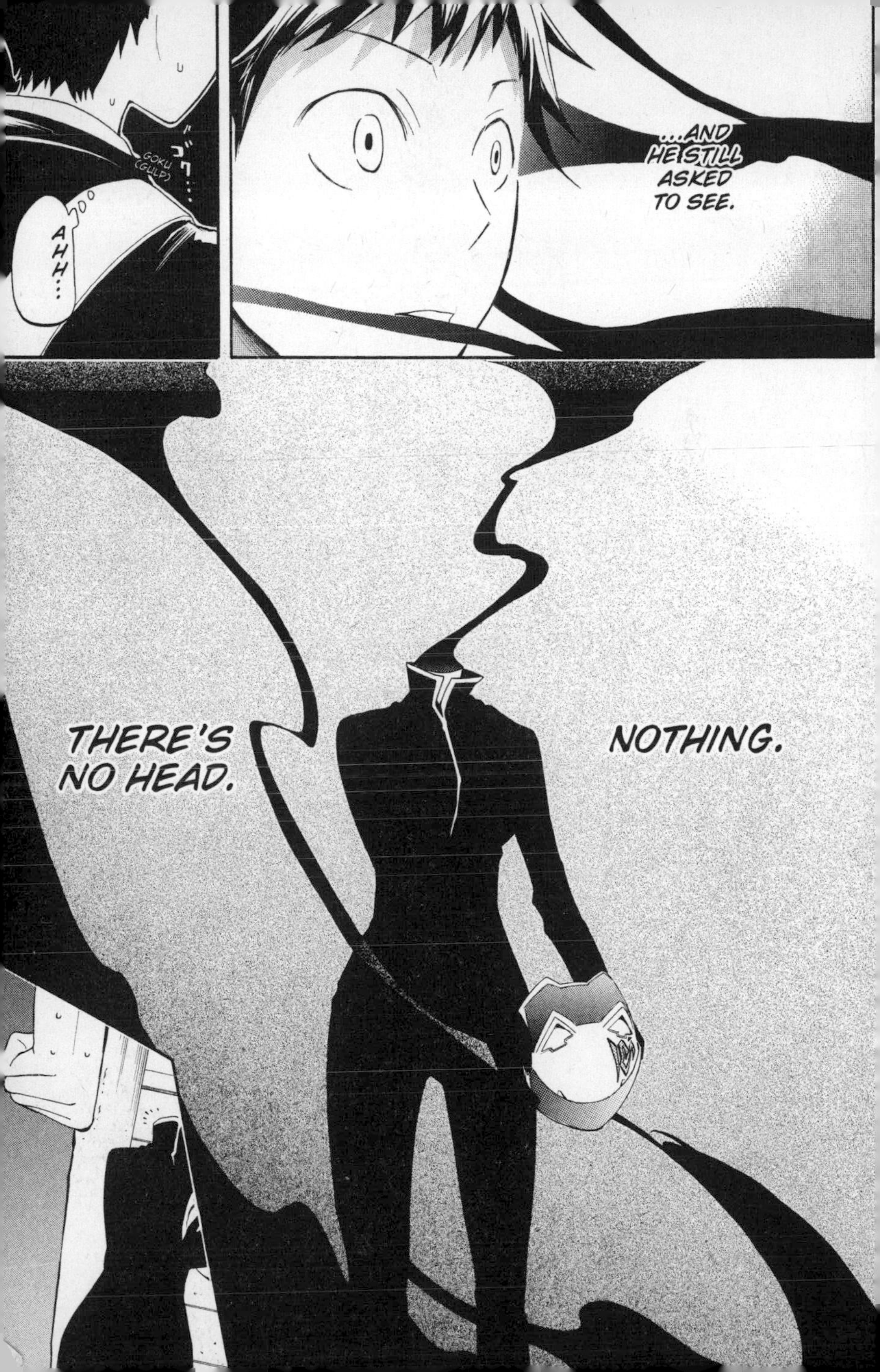
...AND HE STILL ASKED TO SEE.
GOKU (GULP)
AHH...
NOTHING.
THERE'S NO HEAD.

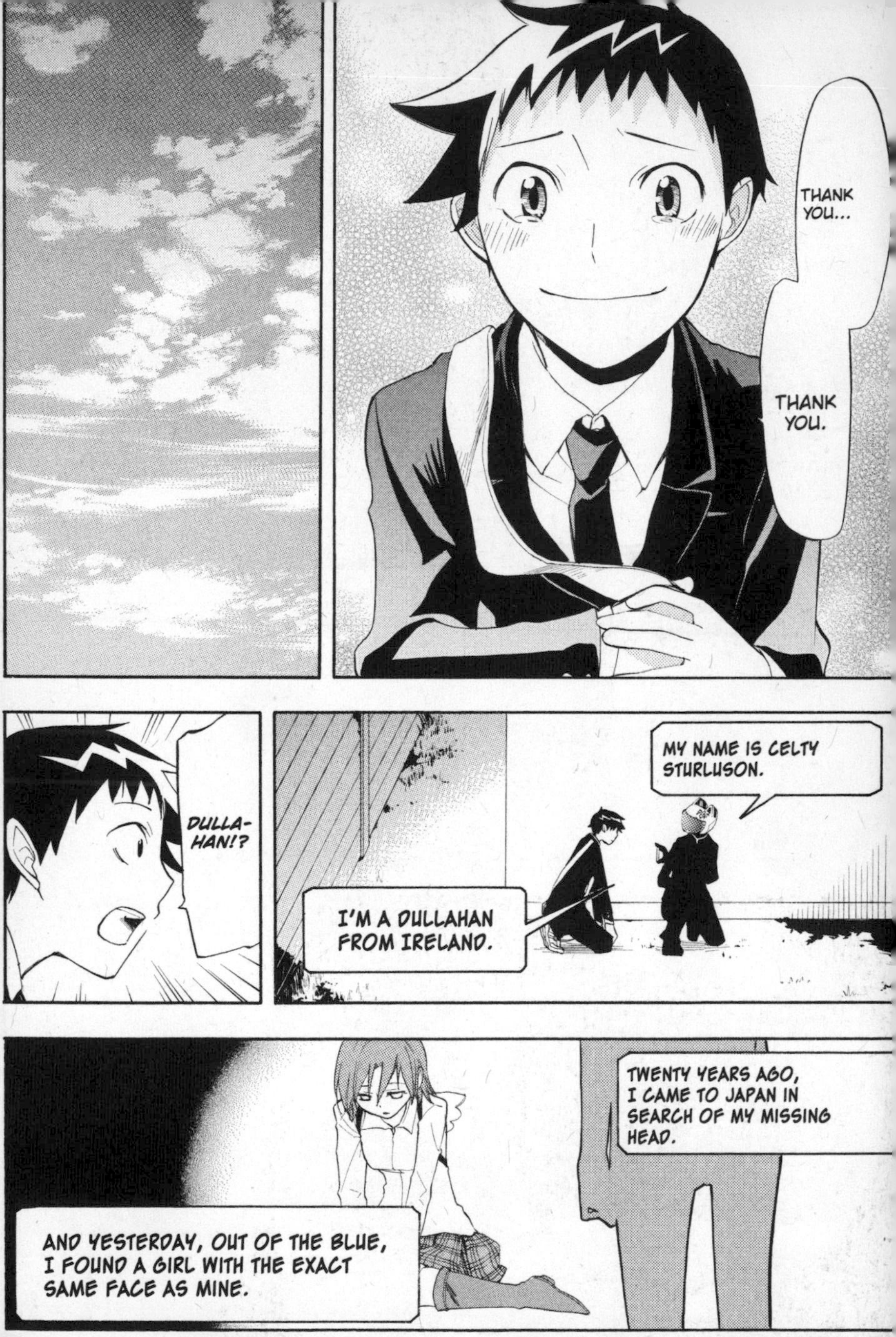
THANK YOU...
THANK YOU.
MY NAME IS CELTY STURLUSON.
I'M A DULLAHAN FROM IRELAND.
DULLA-HAN!?
TWENTY YEARS AGO, I CAME TO JAPAN IN SEARCH OF MY MISSING HEAD.
AND YESTERDAY, OUT OF THE BLUE, I FOUND A GIRL WITH THE EXACT SAME FACE AS MINE.

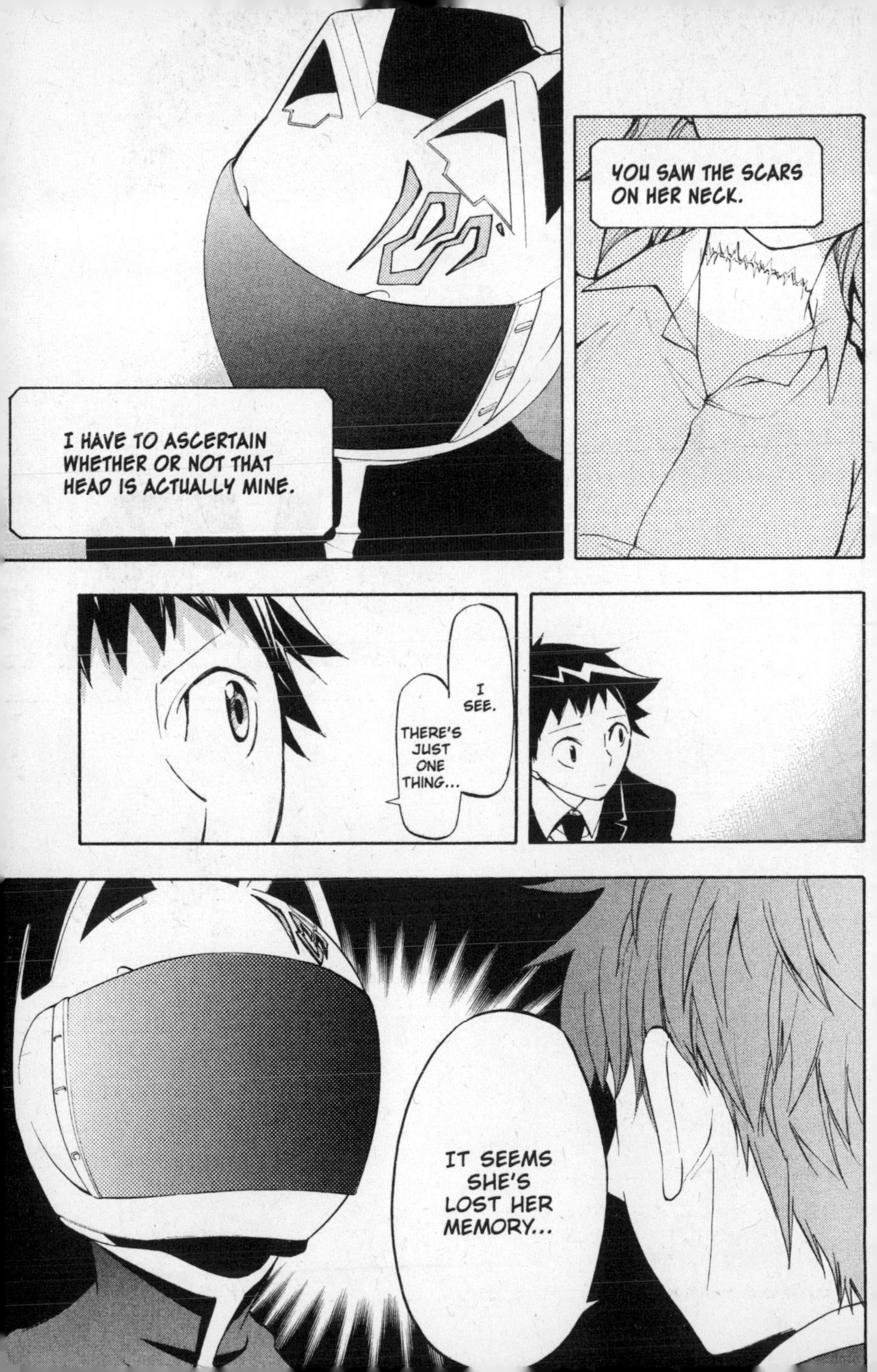
YOU SAW THE SCARS ON HER NECK.
I HAVE TO ASCERTAIN WHETHER OR NOT THAT HEAD IS ACTUALLY MINE.
I SEE. THERE'S JUST ONE THING...
IT SEEMS SHE'S LOST HER MEMORY...

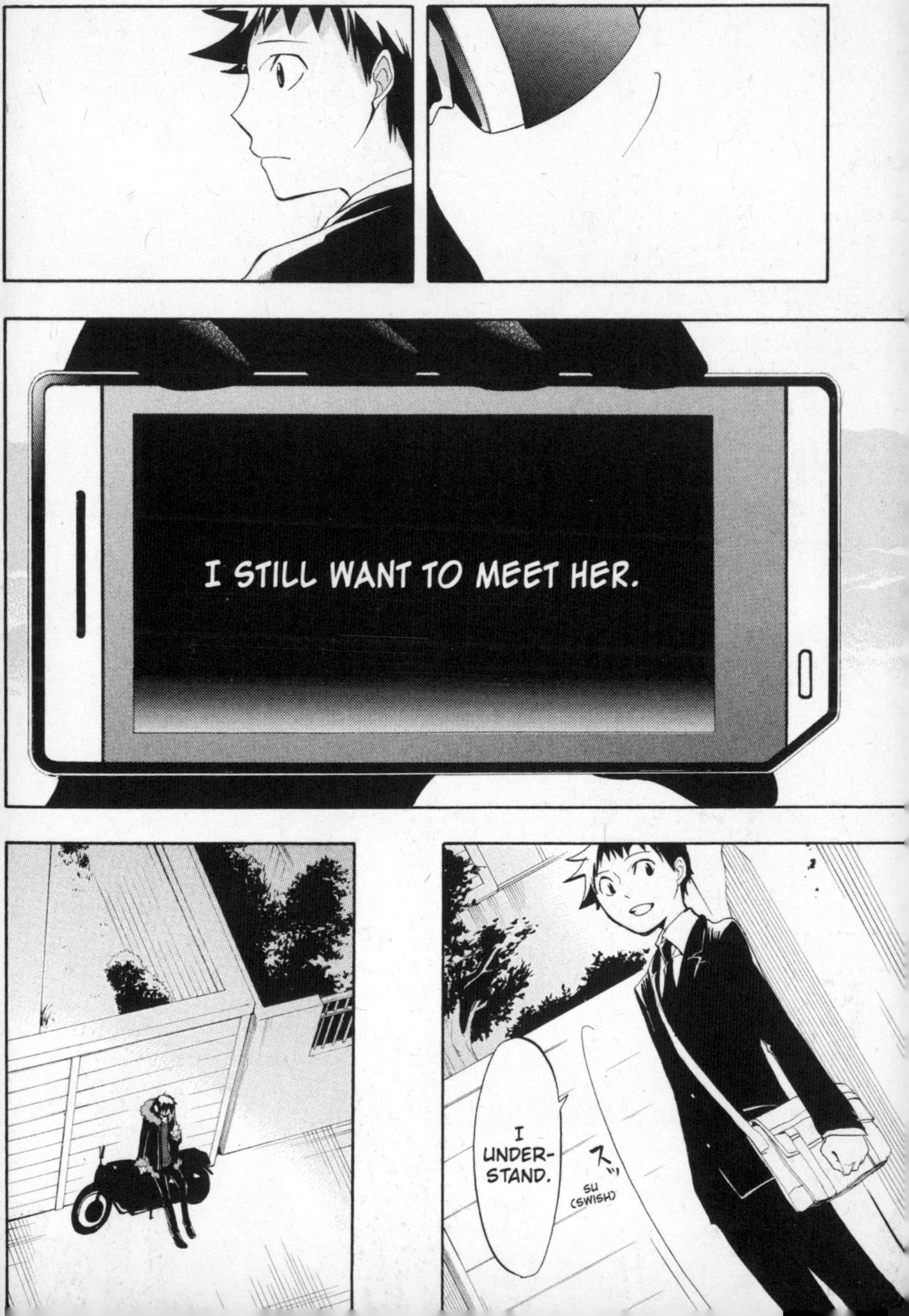
I STILL WANT TO MEET HER.
I UNDER-STAND.
スッ
SU (SWISH)

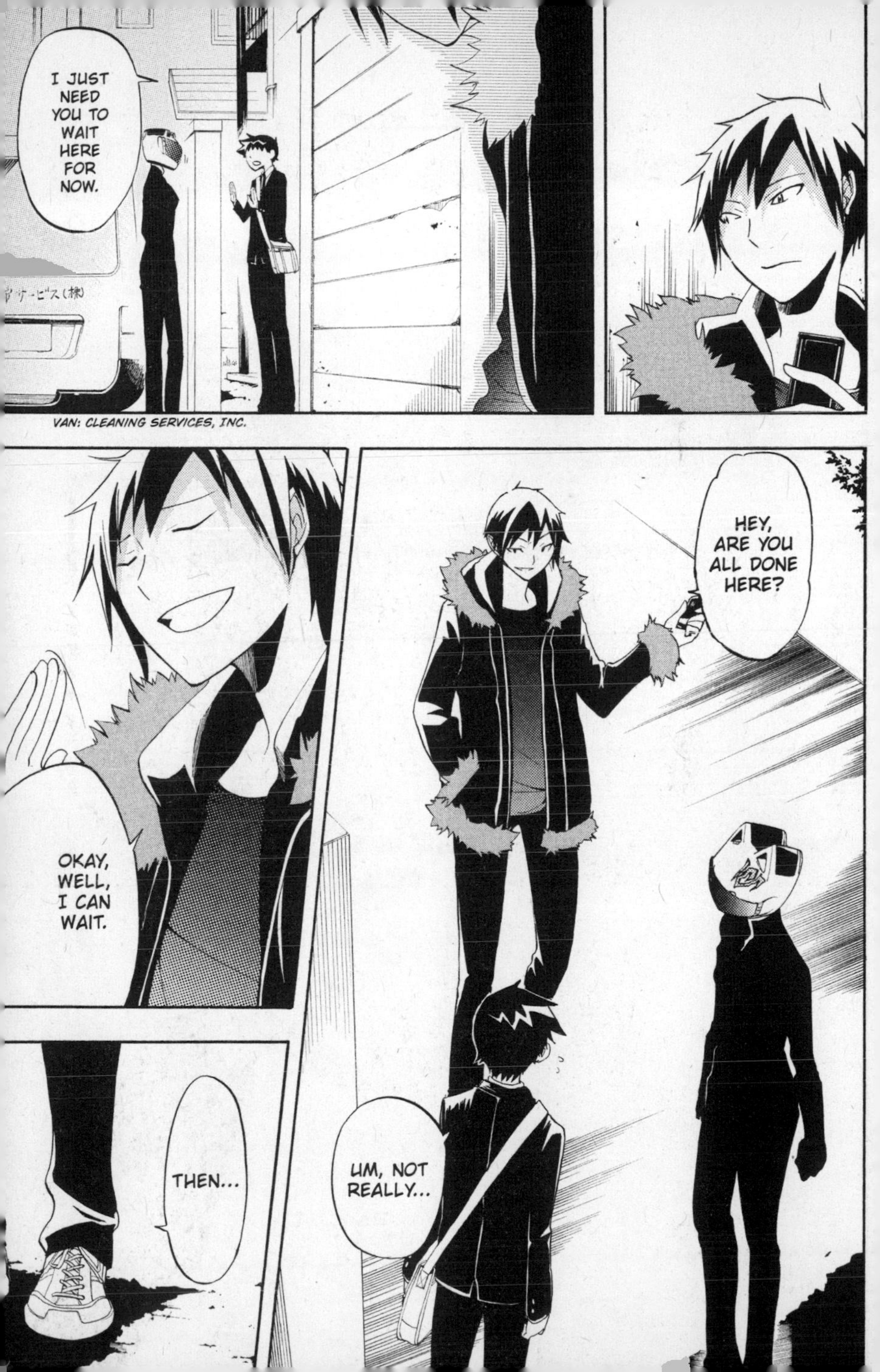
I JUST NEED YOU TO WAIT HERE FOR NOW.
サービス(株)
VAN: CLEANING SERVICES, INC.
HEY, ARE YOU ALL DONE HERE?
UM, NOT REALLY...
OKAY, WELL, I CAN WAIT.
THEN...

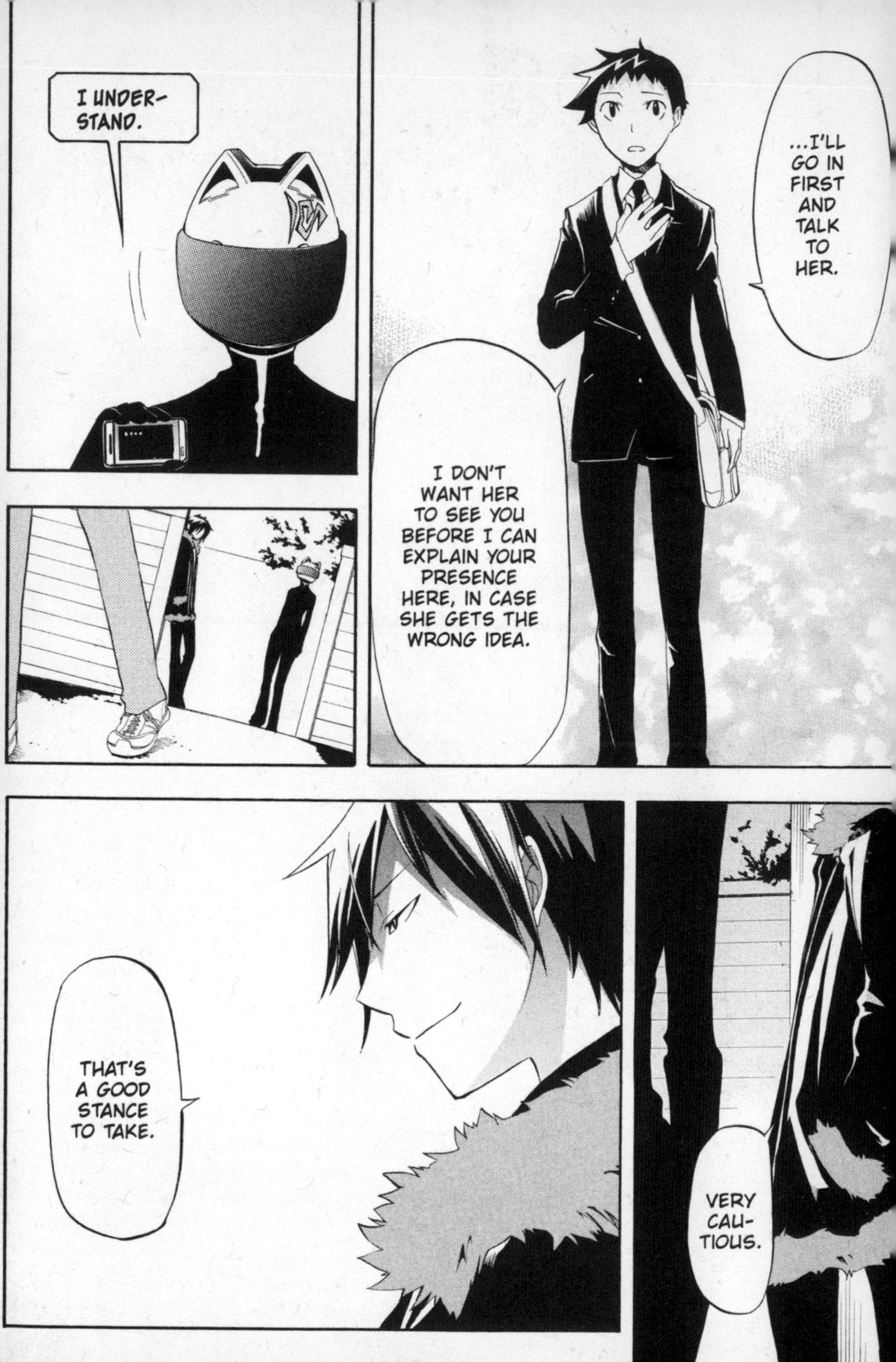
...I'LL GO IN FIRST AND TALK TO HER.
I DON'T WANT HER TO SEE YOU BEFORE I CAN EXPLAIN YOUR PRESENCE HERE, IN CASE SHE GETS THE WRONG IDEA.
I UNDER-STAND.
VERY CAU-TIOUS.
THAT'S A GOOD STANCE TO TAKE.

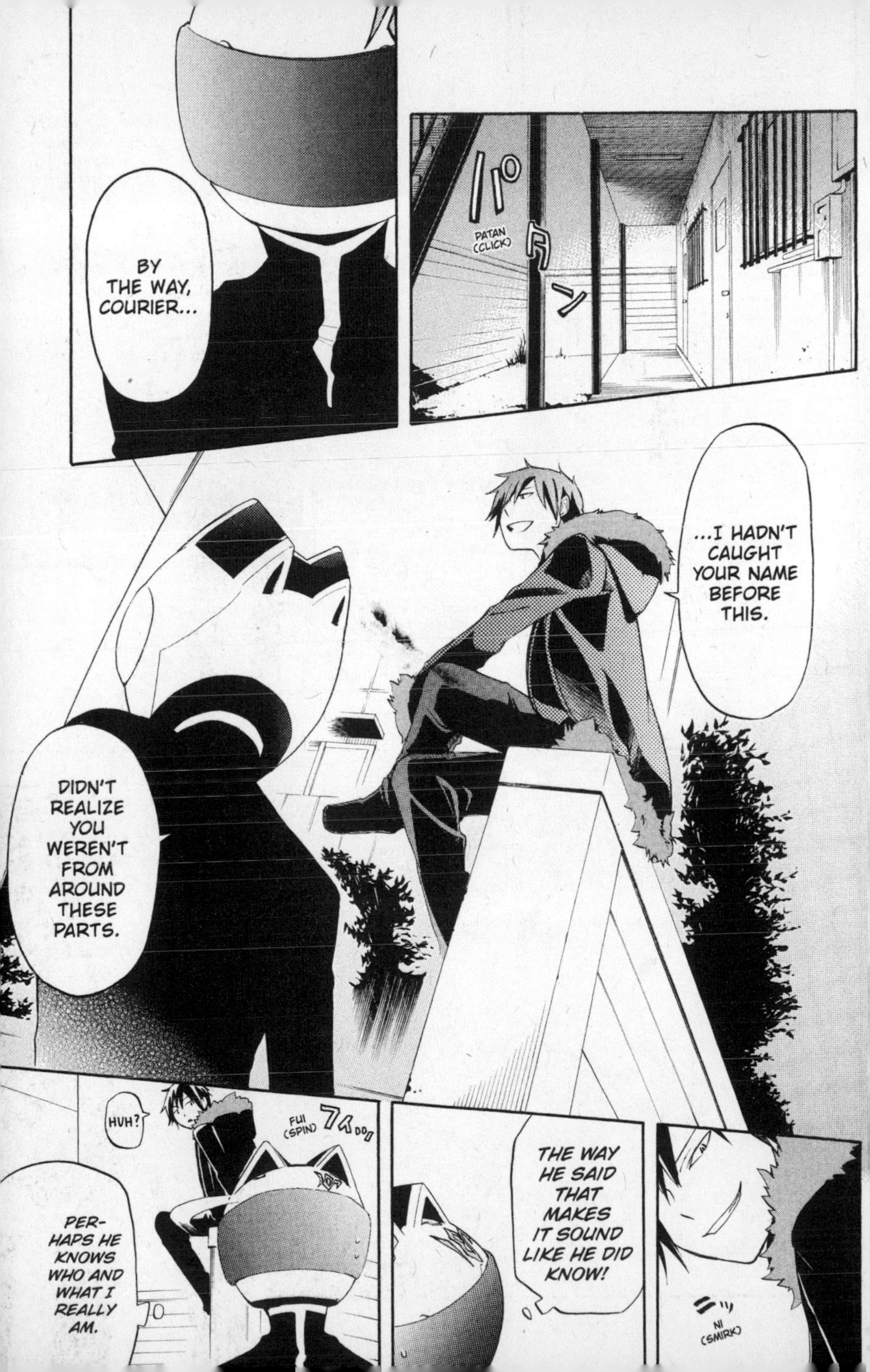
PATAN (CLICK)
BY THE WAY, COURIER...
...I HADN'T CAUGHT YOUR NAME BEFORE THIS.
DIDN'T REALIZE YOU WEREN'T FROM AROUND THESE PARTS.
NI (SMIRK)
THE WAY HE SAID THAT MAKES IT SOUND LIKE HE DID KNOW!
FUI (SPIN)
HUH?
PER-HAPS HE KNOWS WHO AND WHAT I REALLY AM.

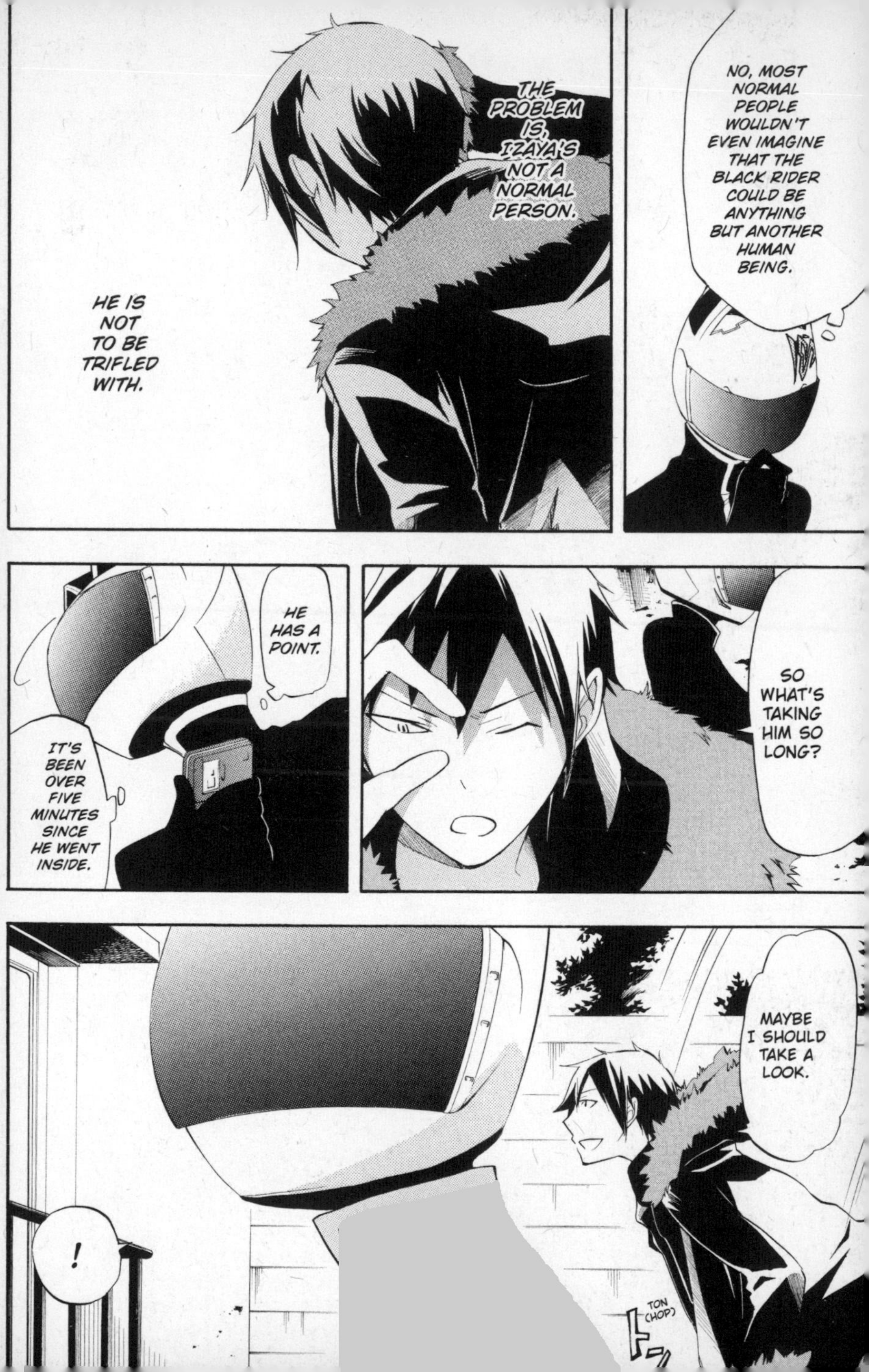
NO, MOST NORMAL PEOPLE WOULDN'T EVEN IMAGINE THAT THE BLACK RIDER COULD BE ANYTHING BUT ANOTHER HUMAN BEING.
THE PROBLEM IS, IZAYA'S NOT A NORMAL PERSON.
HE IS NOT TO BE TRIFLED WITH.
SO WHAT'S TAKING HIM SO LONG?
HE HAS A POINT.
IT'S BEEN OVER FIVE MINUTES SINCE HE WENT INSIDE.
MAYBE I SHOULD TAKE A LOOK.
TON (HOP)
!

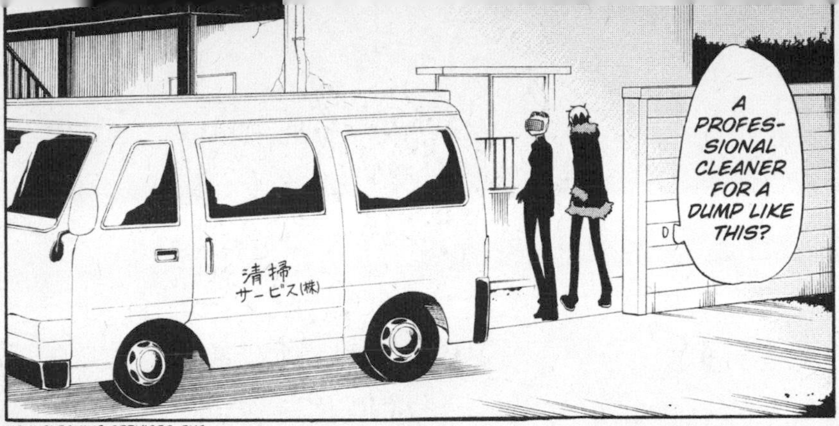
清掃
サービス(株)
A PROFES-SIONAL CLEANER FOR A DUMP LIKE THIS?

VAN: CLEANING SERVICES, INC.

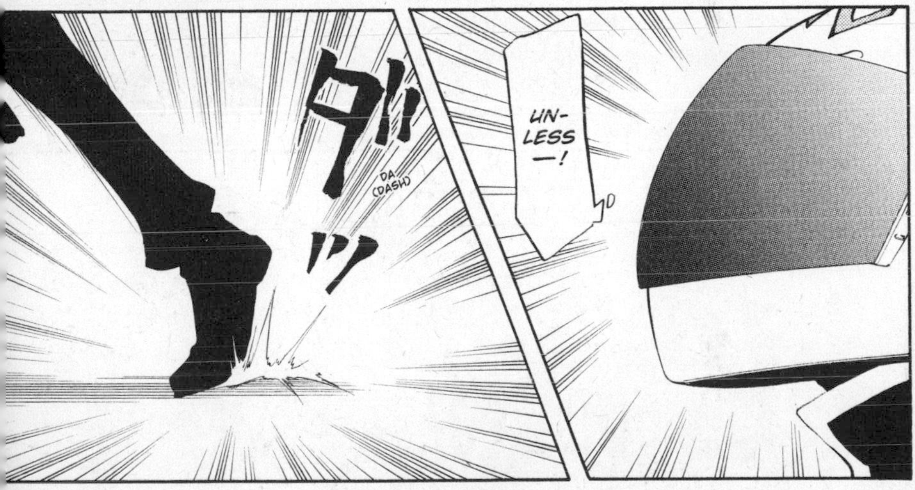
UN-LESS—!
DA (DASH)

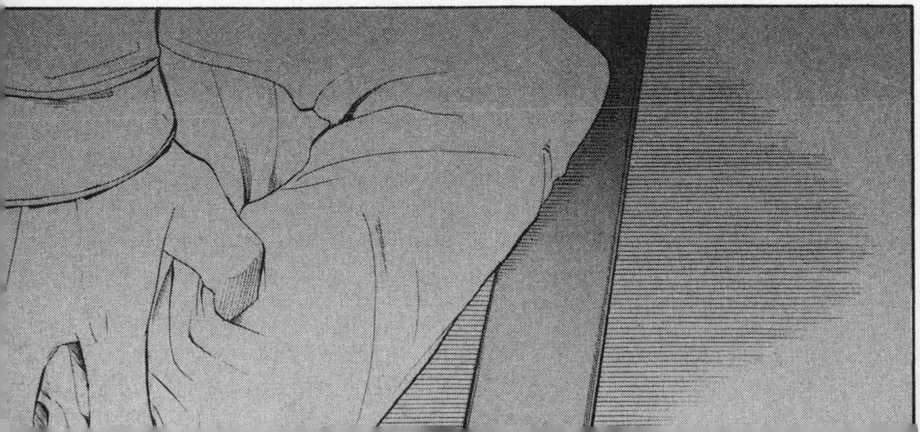

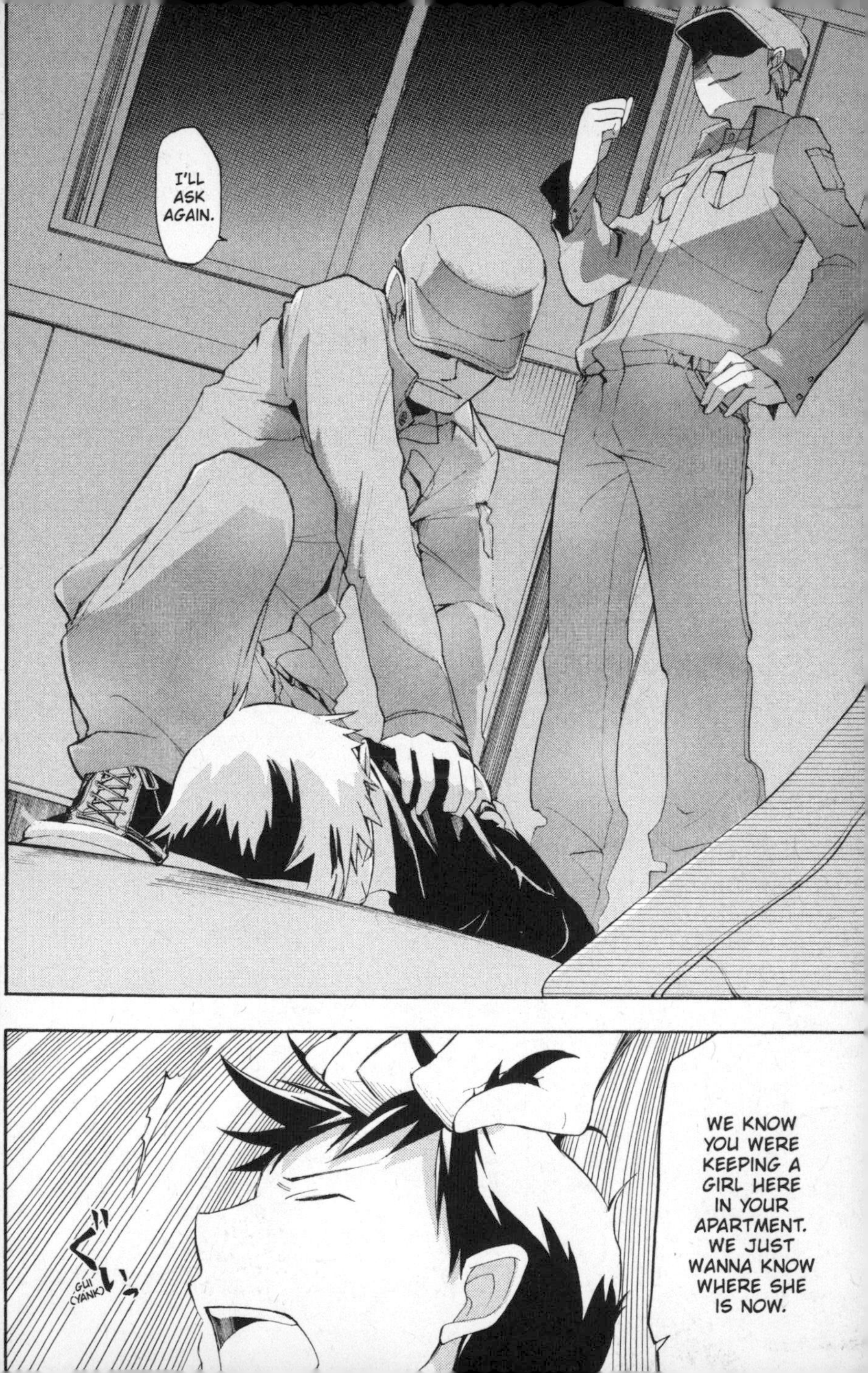
I'LL ASK AGAIN.
WE KNOW YOU WERE KEEPING A GIRL HERE IN YOUR APARTMENT. WE JUST WANNA KNOW WHERE SHE IS NOW.
ぐいっ
GUI (YANK)

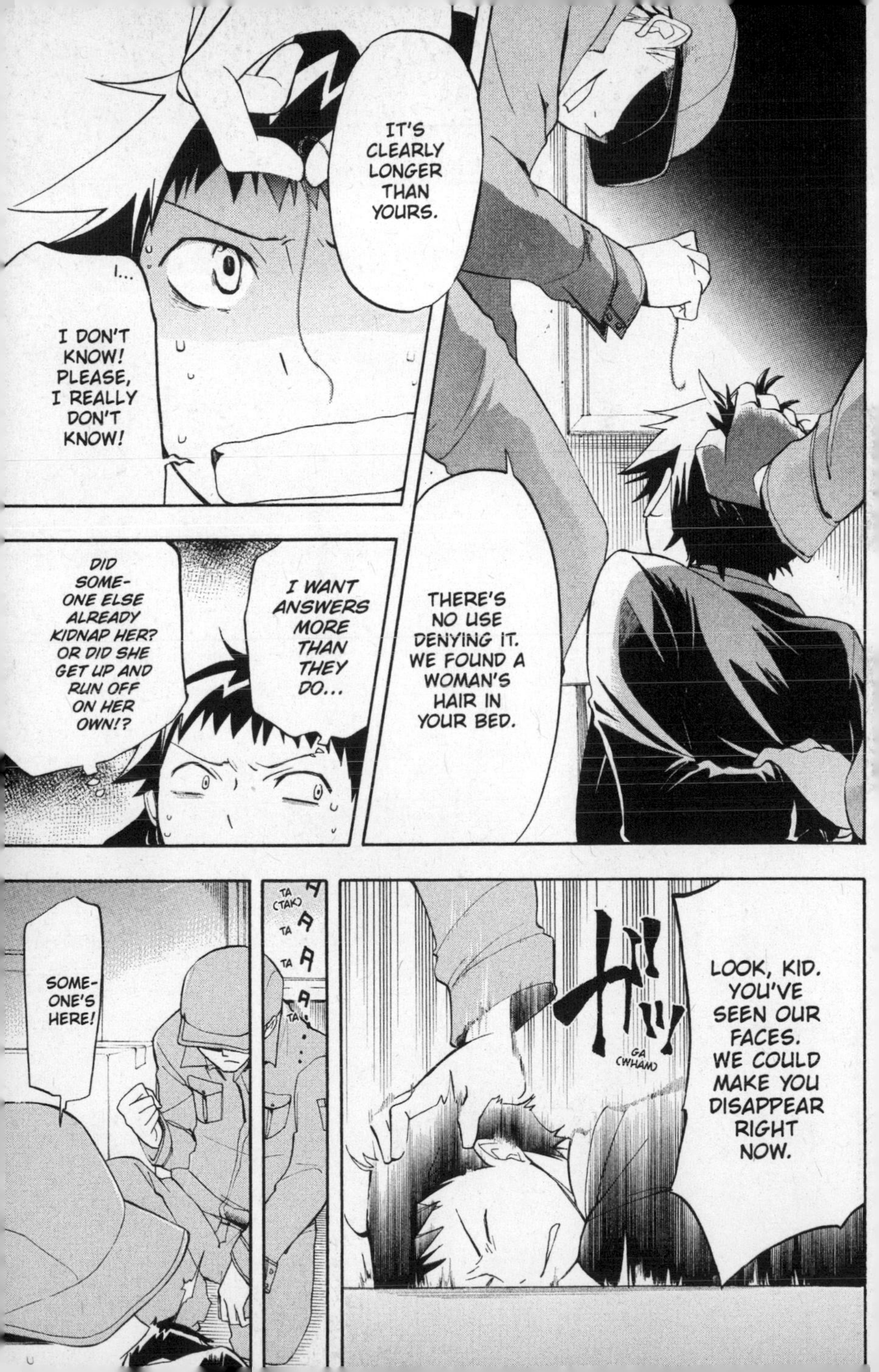
IT'S CLEARLY LONGER THAN YOURS.
THERE'S NO USE DENYING IT. WE FOUND A WOMAN'S HAIR IN YOUR BED.
I...
I DON'T KNOW! PLEASE, I REALLY DON'T KNOW!
I WANT ANSWERS MORE THAN THEY DO...
DID SOME-ONE ELSE ALREADY KIDNAP HER? OR DID SHE GET UP AND RUN OFF ON HER OWN!?
LOOK, KID. YOU'VE SEEN OUR FACES. WE COULD MAKE YOU DISAPPEAR RIGHT NOW.
GA (WHAM)
TA (TAK) TA TA TA
SOME-ONE'S HERE!

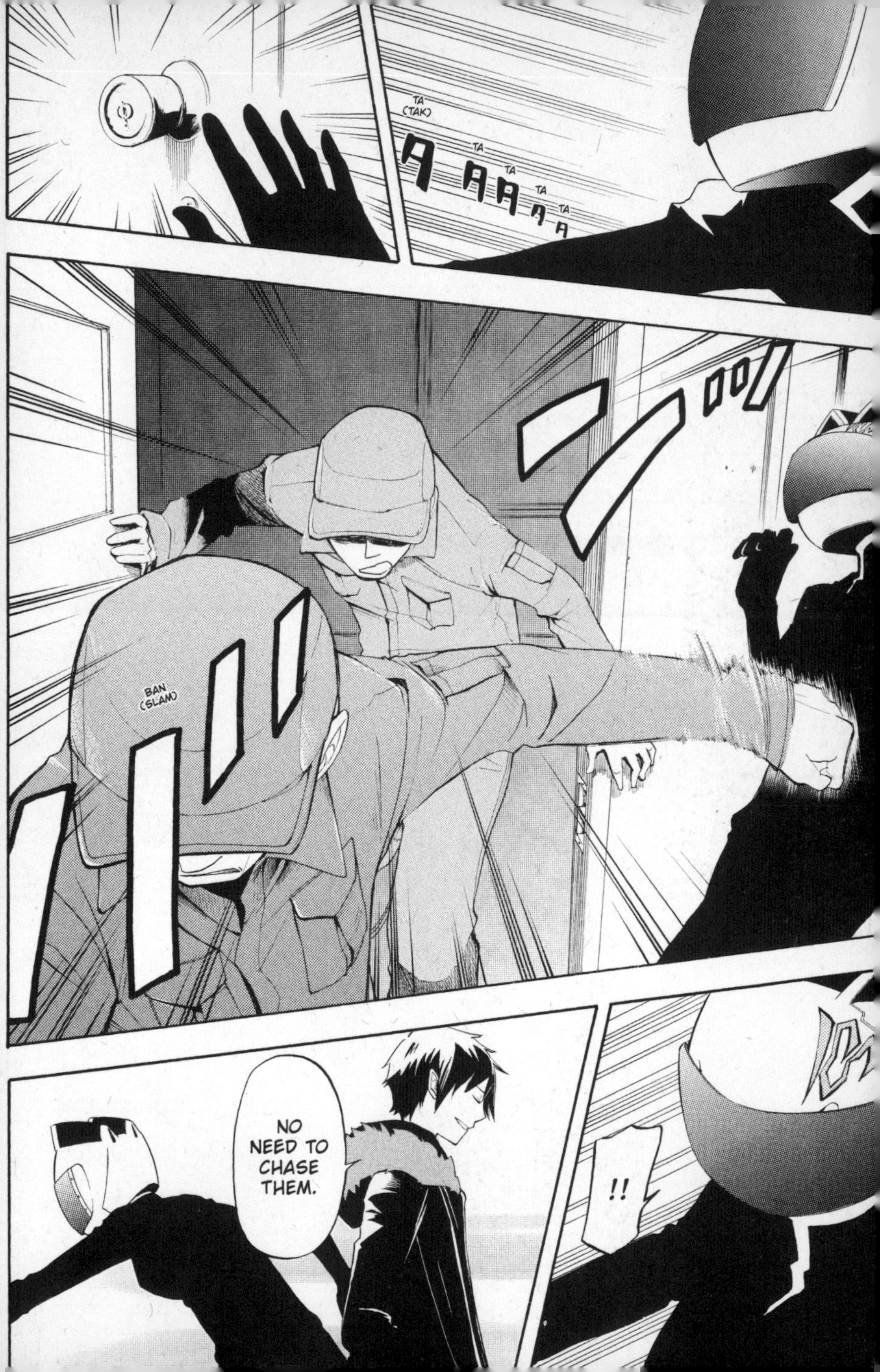
TA
(TAK)
TA
TA
TA
TA
BAN
(SLAM)
!!
NO NEED TO CHASE THEM.

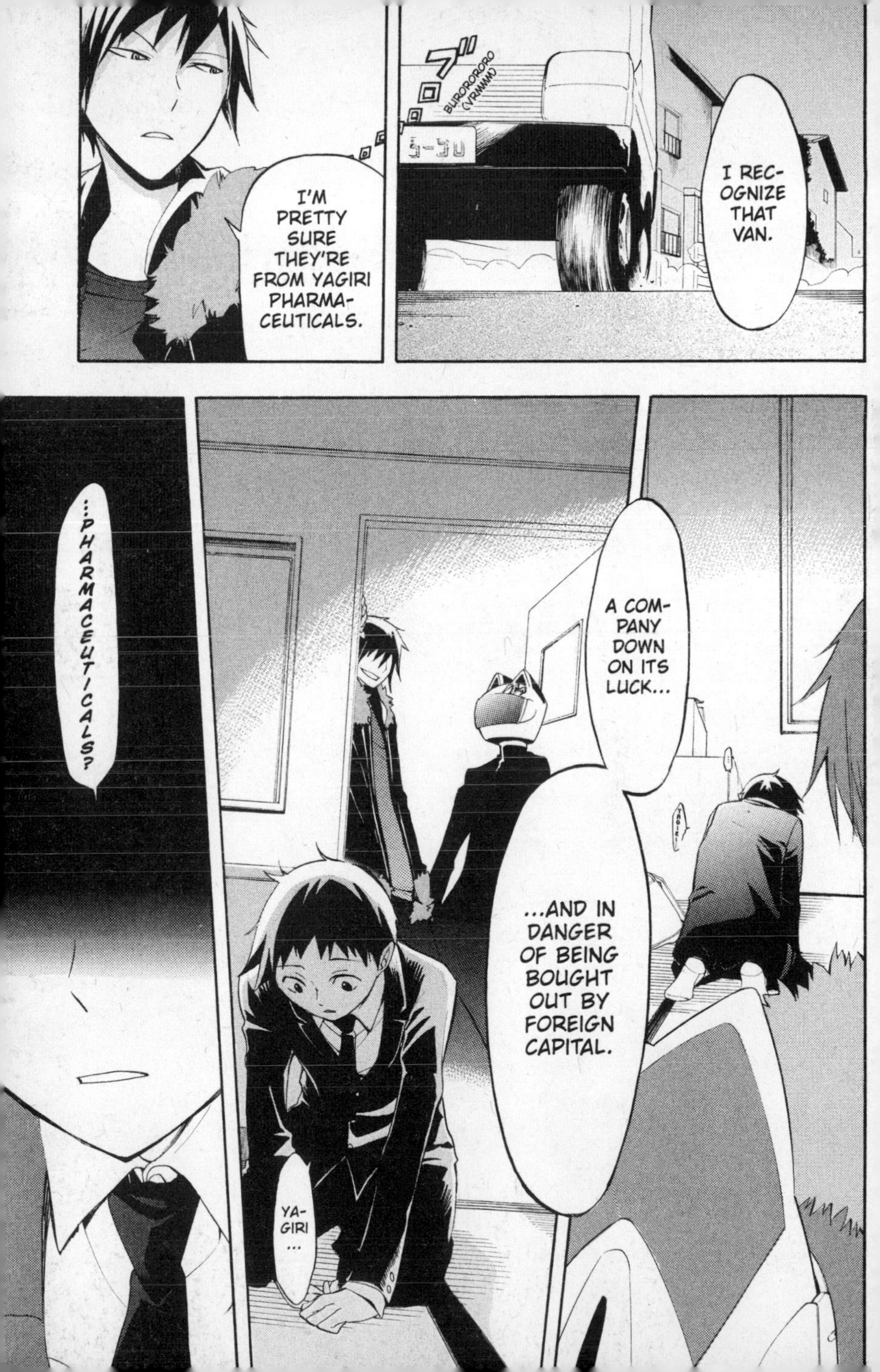

I RECOGNIZE THAT VAN.
BUROROROROR (VRMMM)
I'M PRETTY SURE THEY'RE FROM YAGIRI PHARMACEUTICALS.
A COMPANY DOWN ON ITS LUCK...
...AND IN DANGER OF BEING BOUGHT OUT BY FOREIGN CAPITAL.
YAGIRI!
YAGIRI...
...PHARMACEUTICALS?

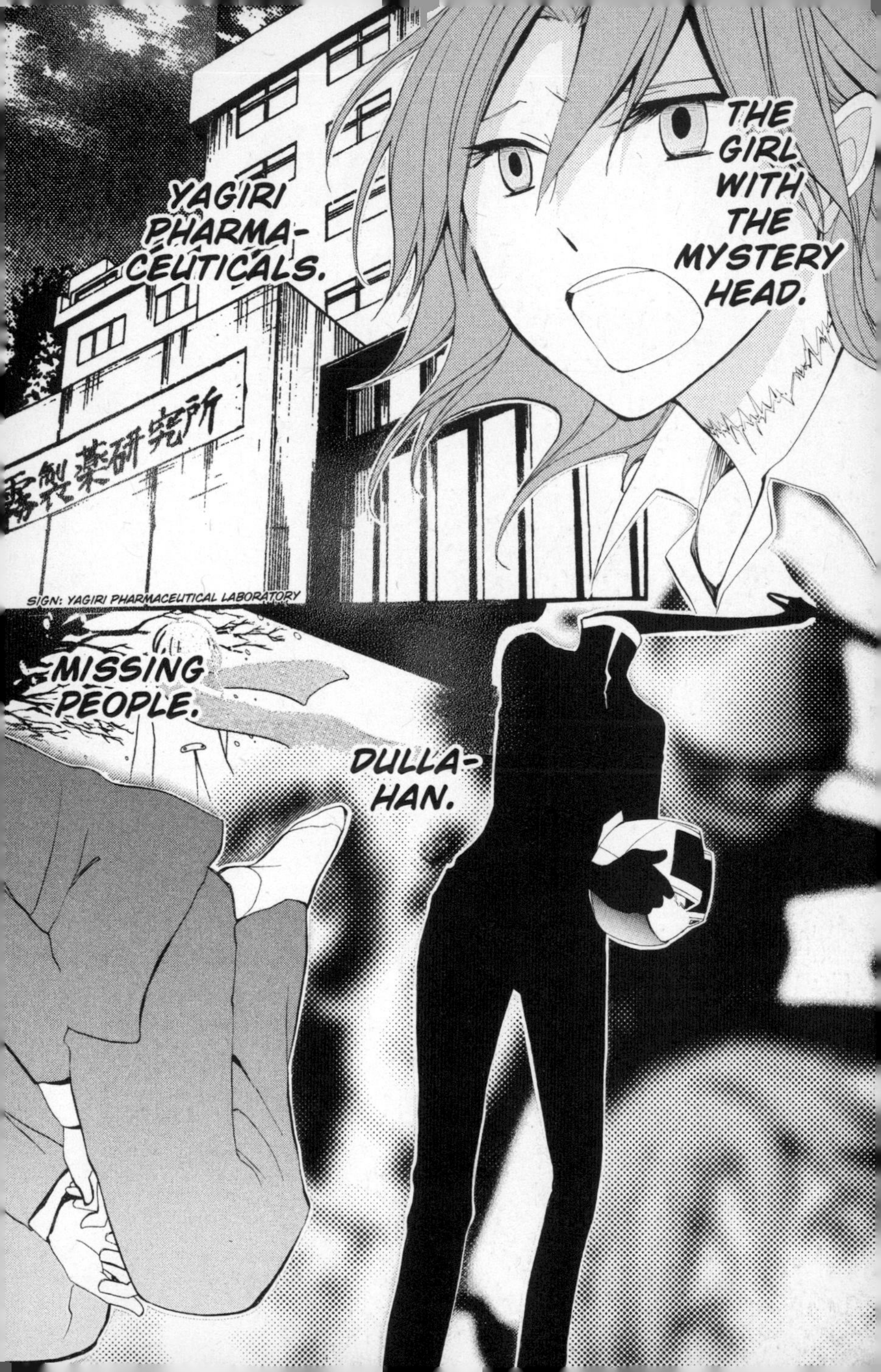
THE GIRL WITH THE MYSTERY HEAD.
YAGIRI PHARMA-CEUTICALS.
SIGN: YAGIRI PHARMACEUTICAL LABORATORY
DULLA-HAN.
MISSING PEOPLE.

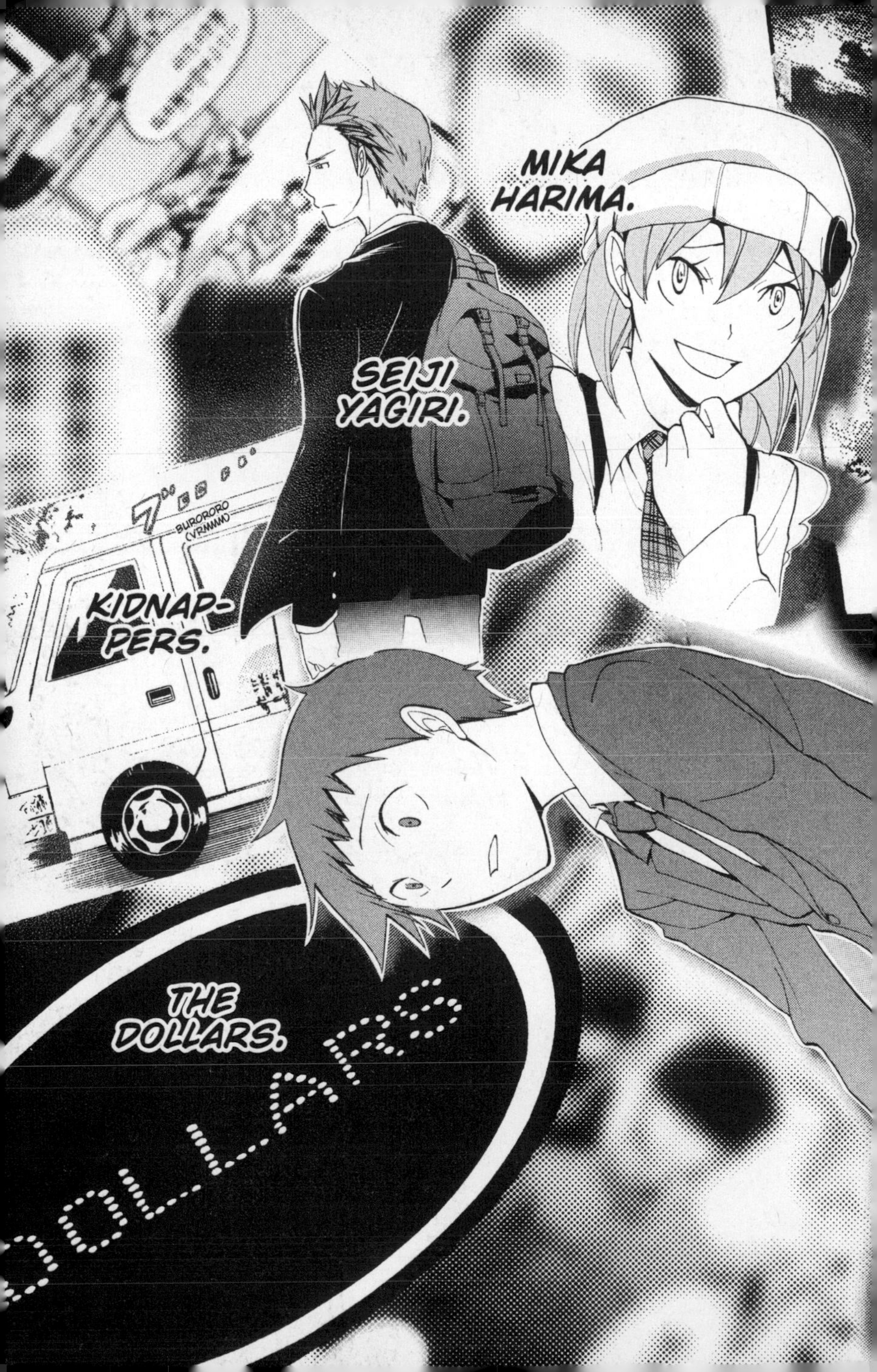
MIKA HARIMA.
SEIJI YAGIRI.
BURORORO (VRMMM)
KIDNAP-PERS.
THE DOLLARS.
DOLLARS

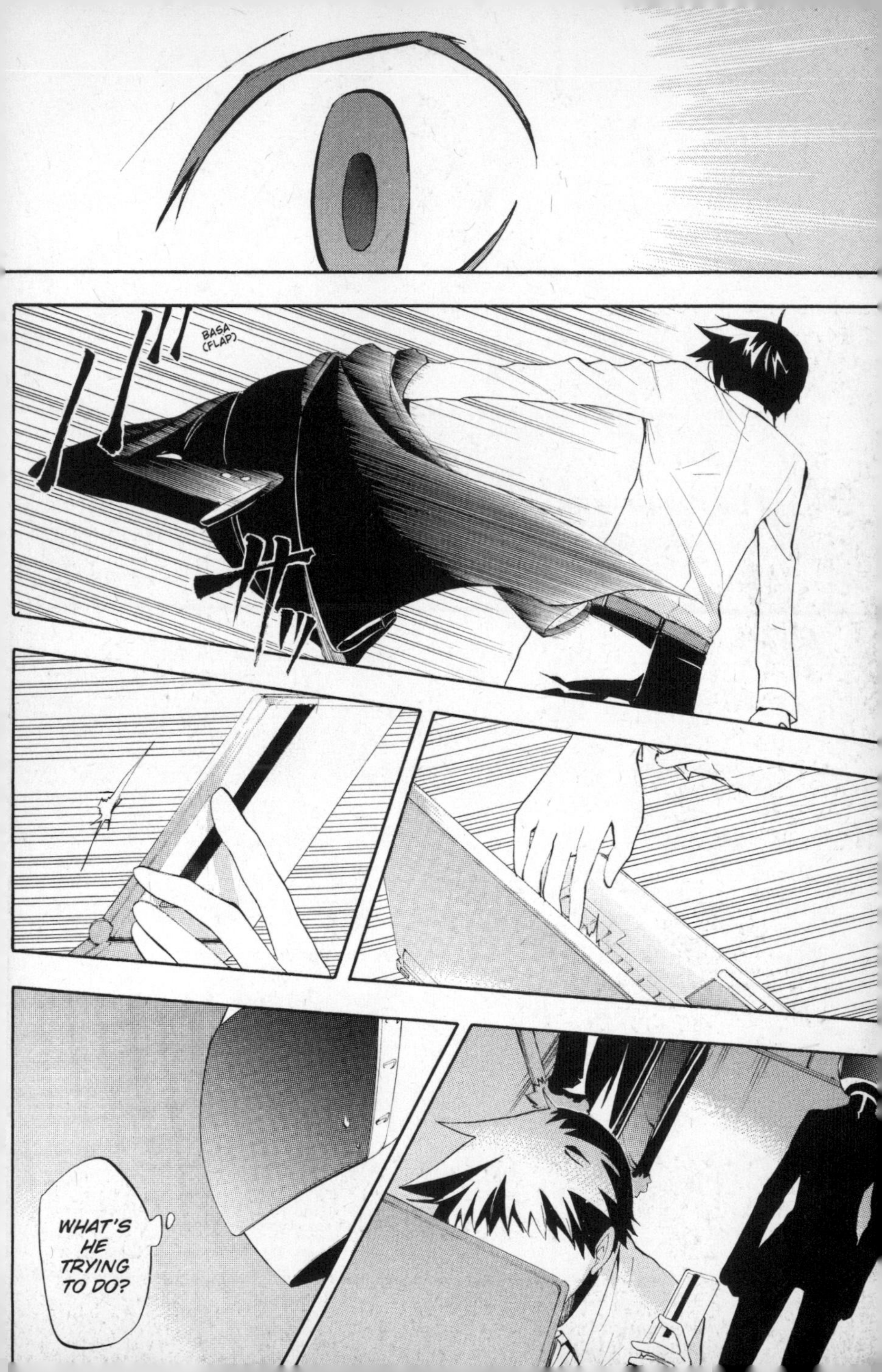
BASA (FLAP)
WHAT'S HE TRYING TO DO?

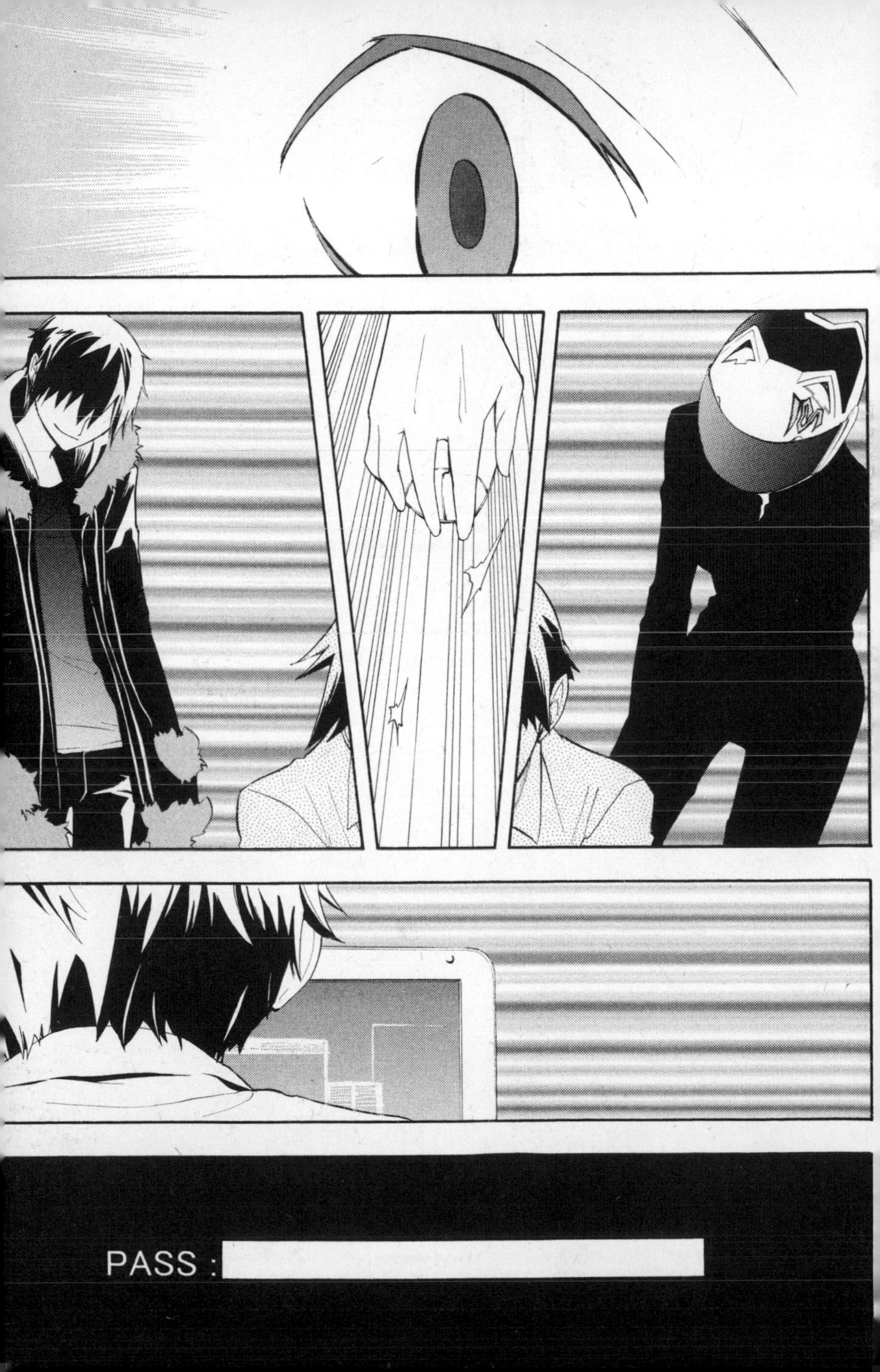
PASS :

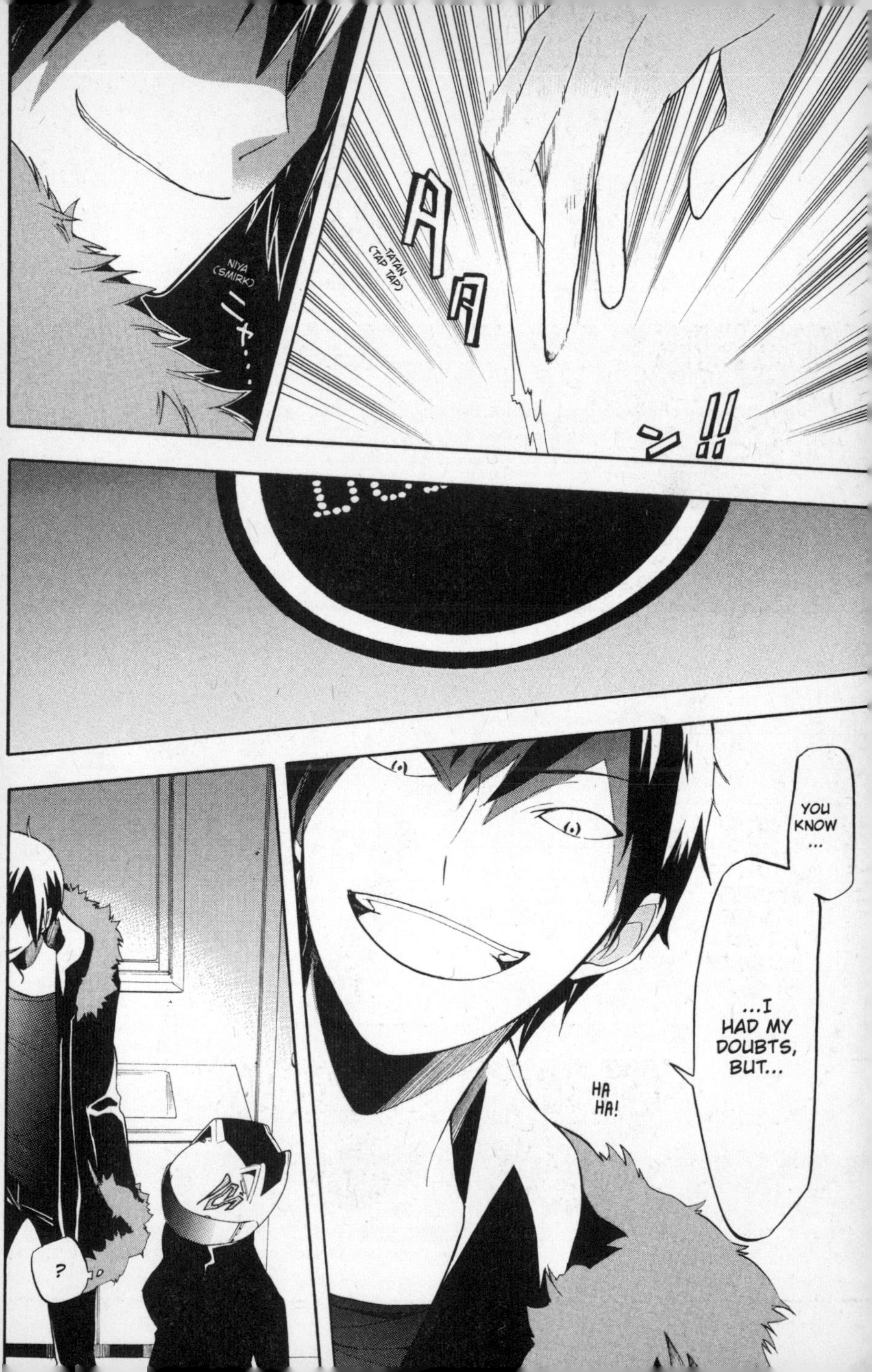
TATAN (TAP TAP)
NIYA (SMIRK)
ニヤ…
YOU KNOW ...
...I HAD MY DOUBTS, BUT...
HA HA!
?

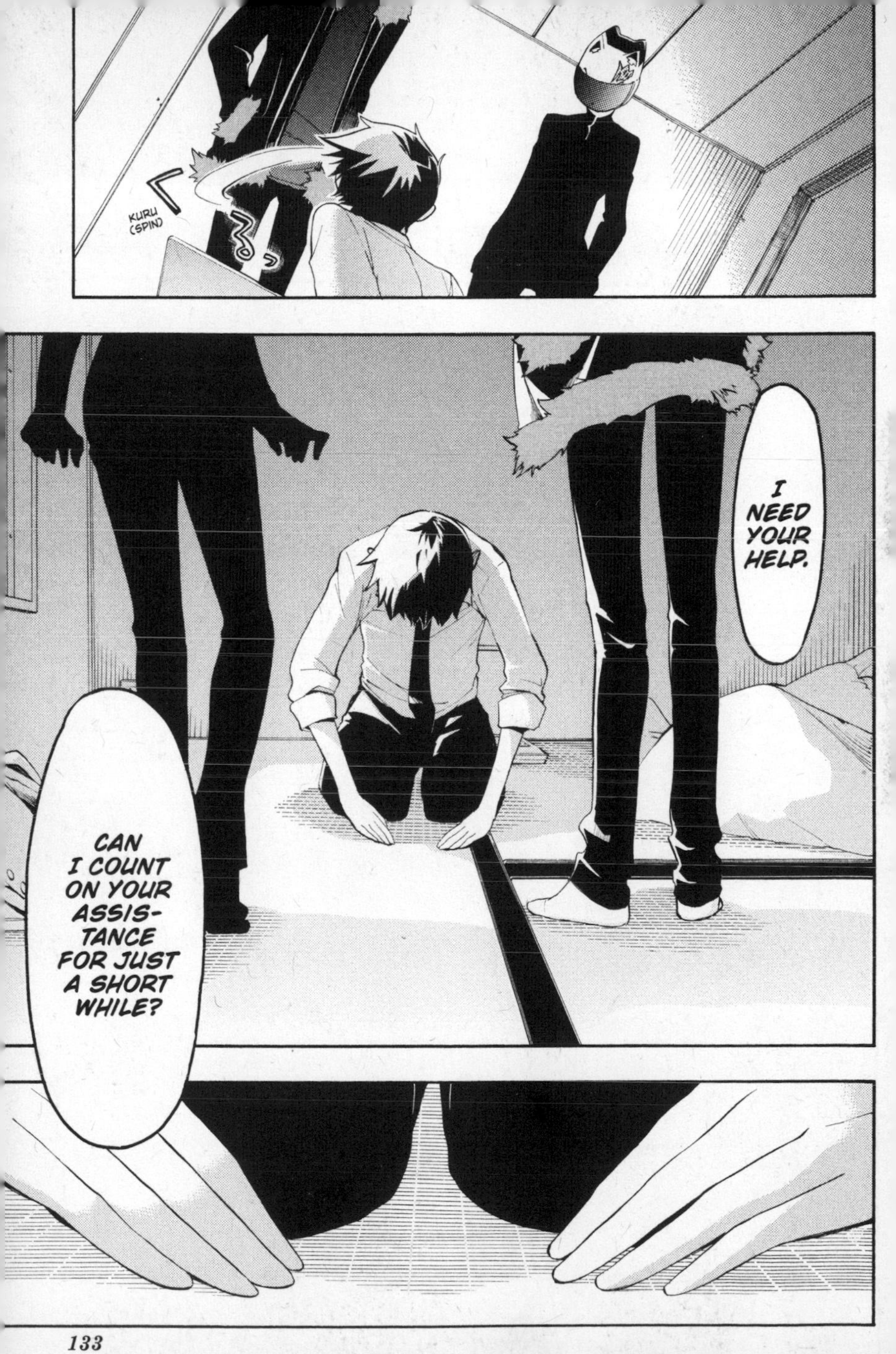
KURU (SPIN)
I NEED YOUR HELP.
CAN I COUNT ON YOUR ASSIS-TANCE FOR JUST A SHORT WHILE?

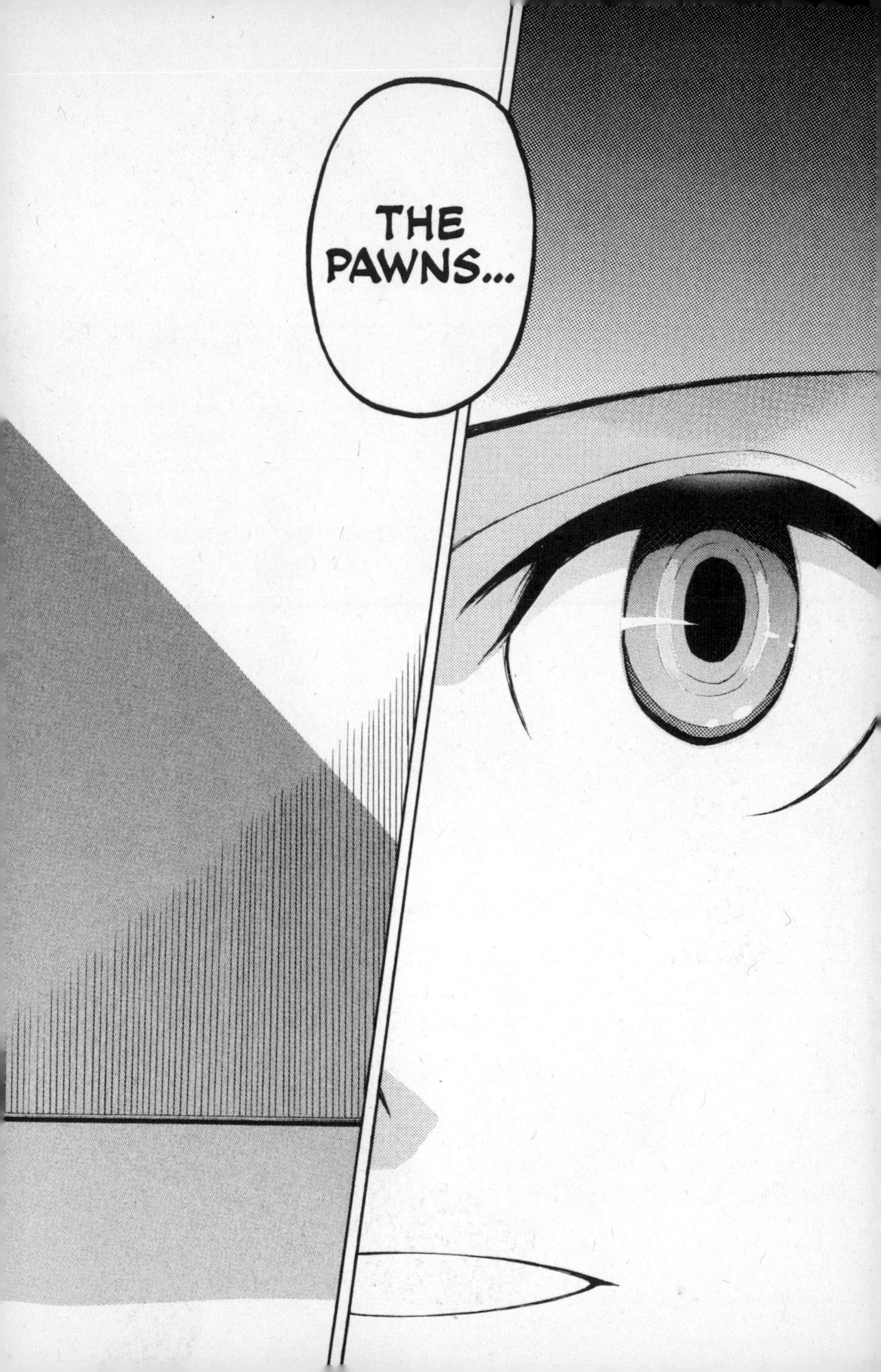
THE PAWNS...

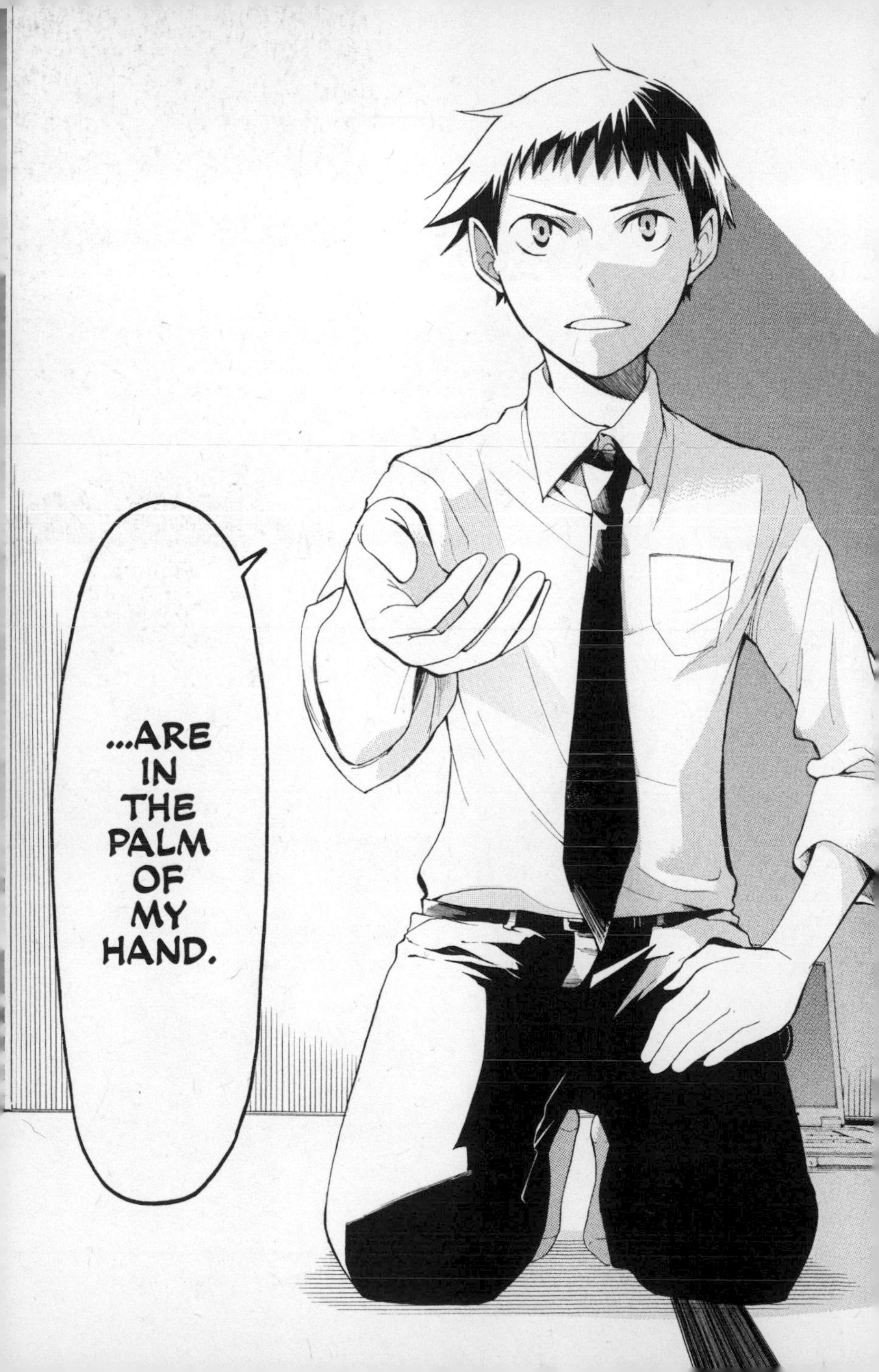
...ARE IN THE PALM OF MY HAND.

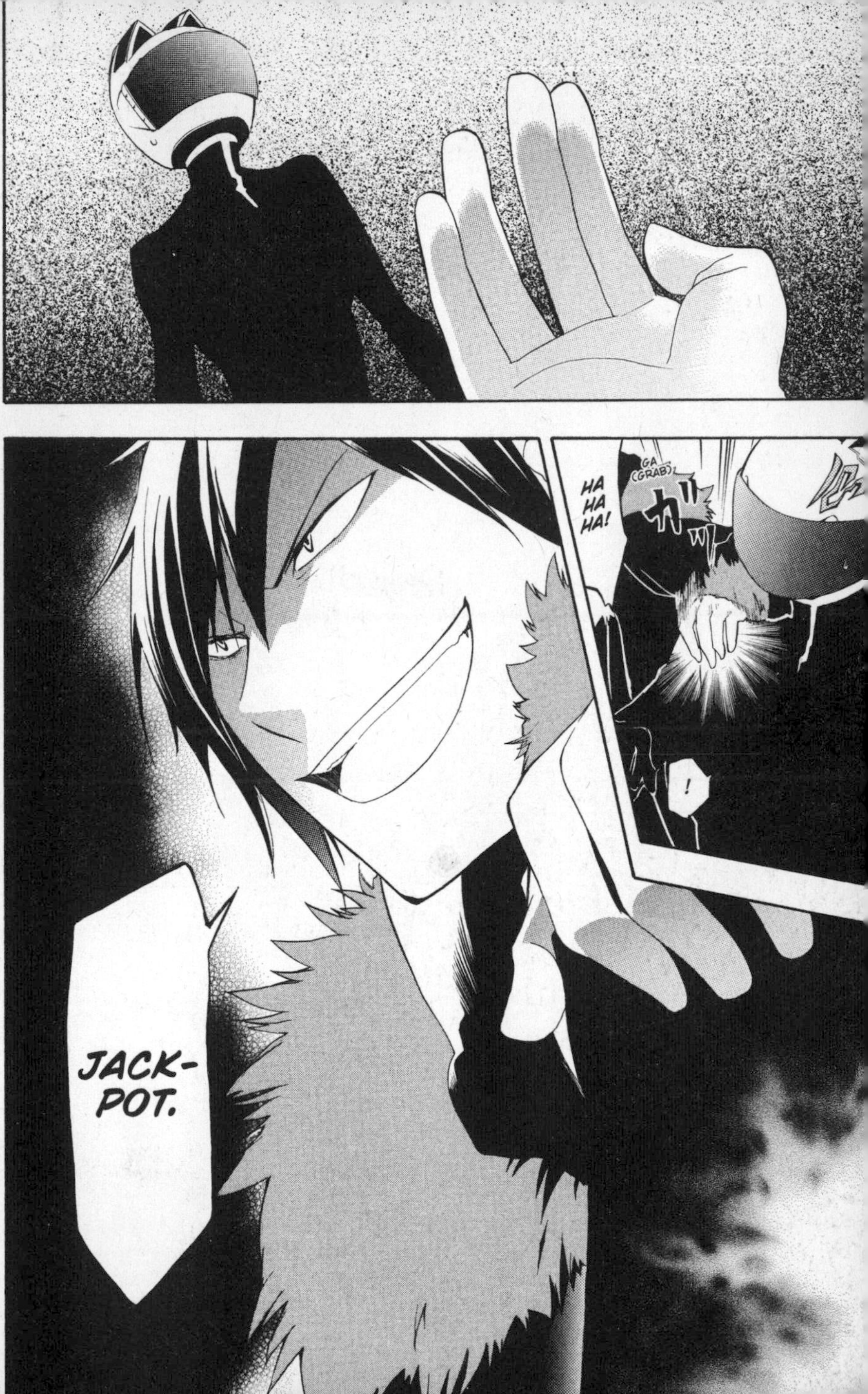
HA HA HA!
GA (GRAB)
!
JACK-POT.

17: WAWAWAWAWAWAWAWAWAWAWAWAWAWAWAWAWAWAWAWA!!

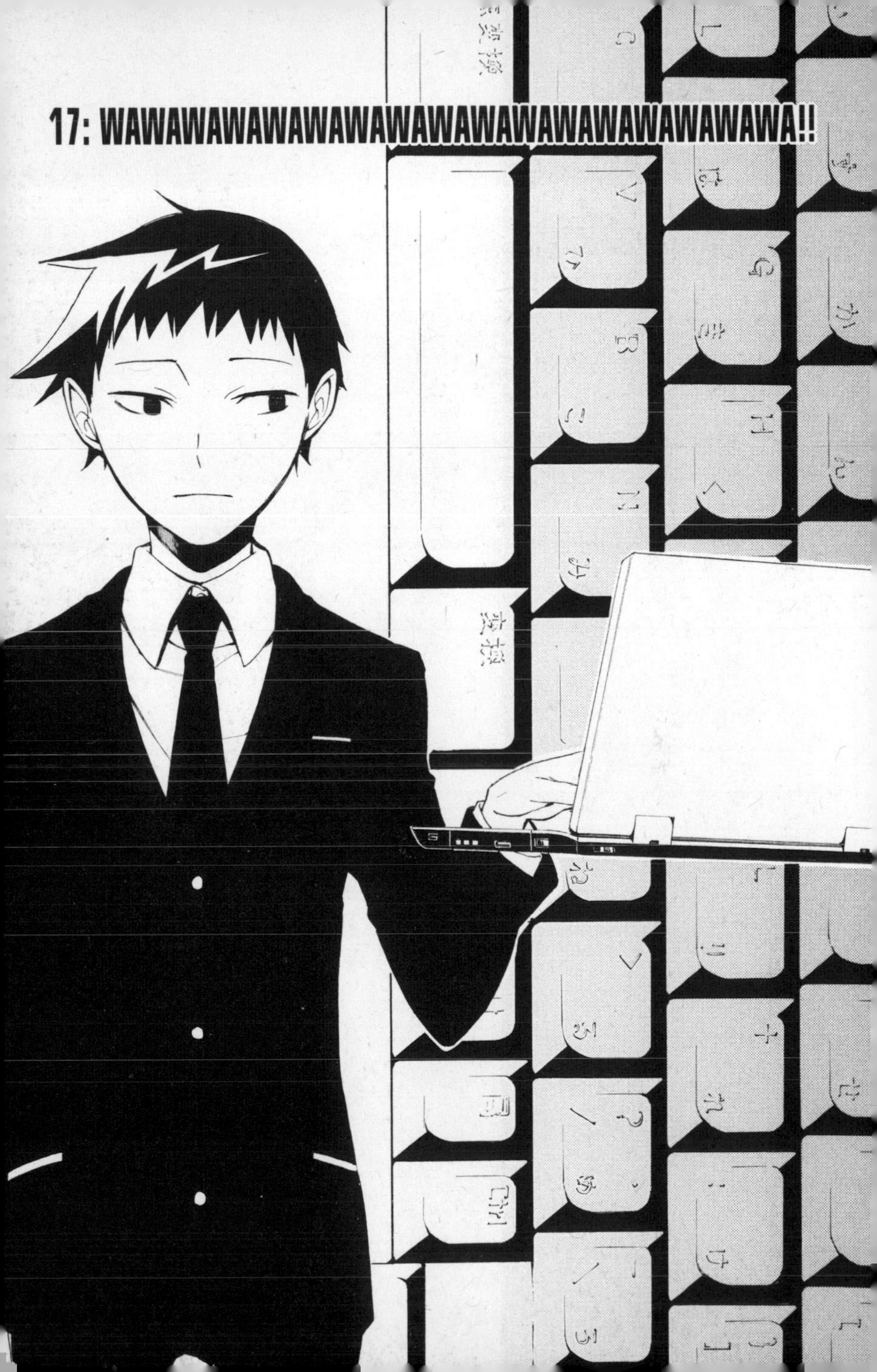

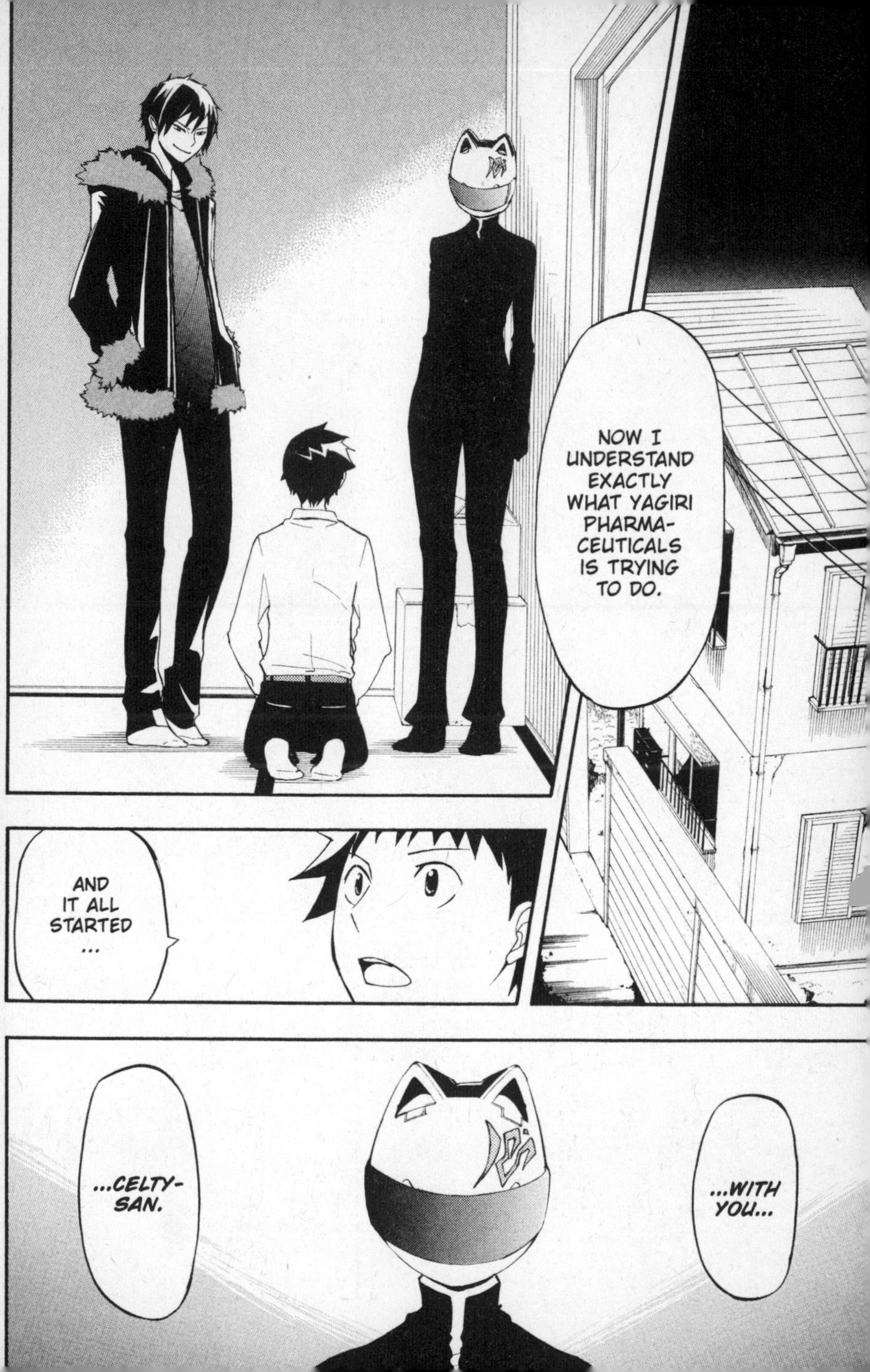
NOW I UNDERSTAND EXACTLY WHAT YAGIRI PHARMA-CEUTICALS IS TRYING TO DO.
AND IT ALL STARTED ...
...WITH YOU...
...CELTY-SAN.

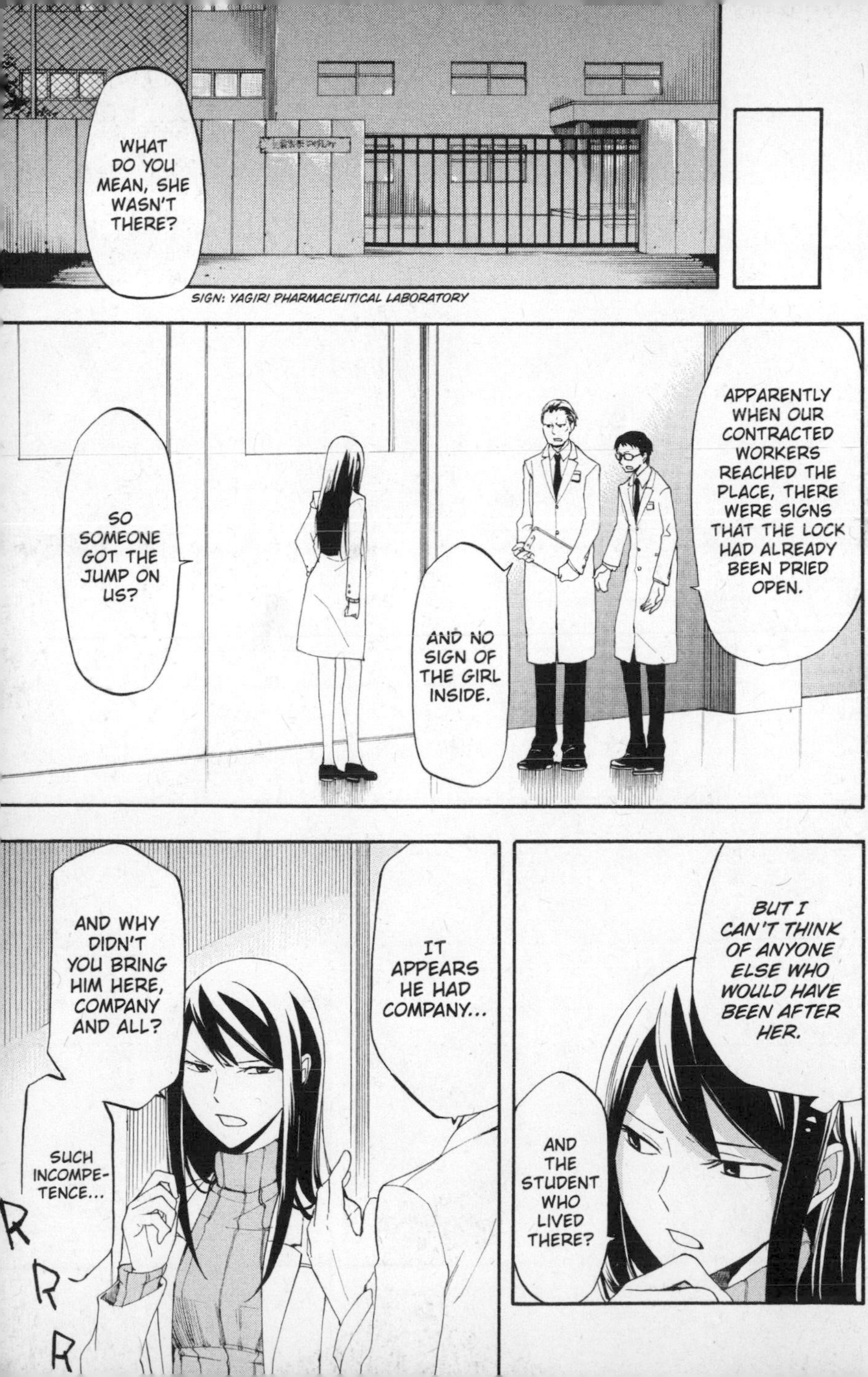
WHAT DO YOU MEAN, SHE WASN'T THERE?
SIGN: YAGIRI PHARMACEUTICAL LABORATORY
APPARENTLY WHEN OUR CONTRACTED WORKERS REACHED THE PLACE, THERE WERE SIGNS THAT THE LOCK HAD ALREADY BEEN PRIED OPEN.
AND NO SIGN OF THE GIRL INSIDE.
SO SOMEONE GOT THE JUMP ON US?
BUT I CAN'T THINK OF ANYONE ELSE WHO WOULD HAVE BEEN AFTER HER.
AND THE STUDENT WHO LIVED THERE?
IT APPEARS HE HAD COMPANY...
AND WHY DIDN'T YOU BRING HIM HERE, COMPANY AND ALL?
SUCH INCOMPETENCE...
RRR

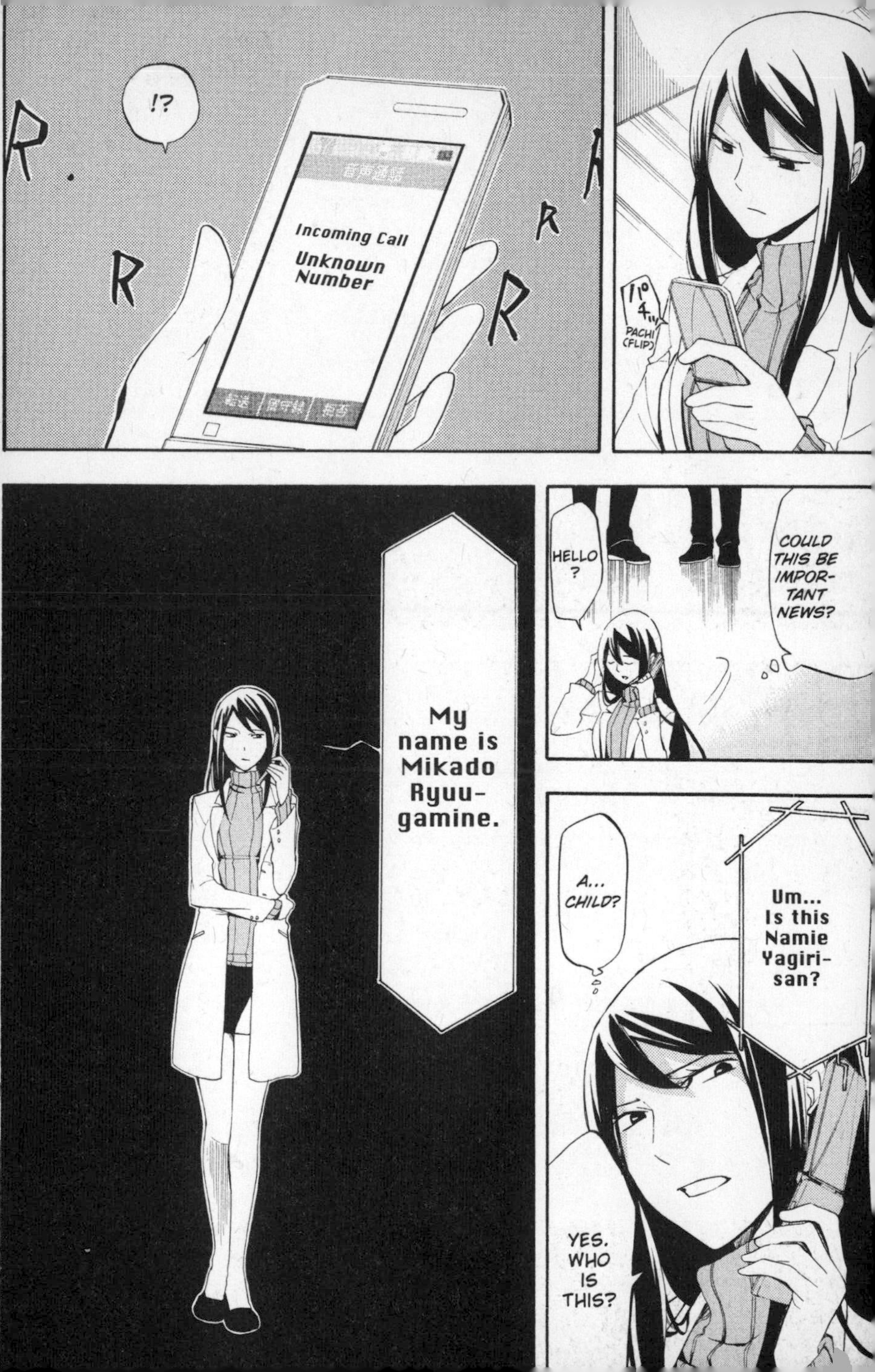

PACHI (FLIP)
R
R
R
R
!?
Incoming Call
Unknown Number
COULD THIS BE IMPORTANT NEWS?
HELLO?
Um... Is this Namie Yagiri-san?
A... CHILD?
YES. WHO IS THIS?
My name is Mikado Ryuugamine.

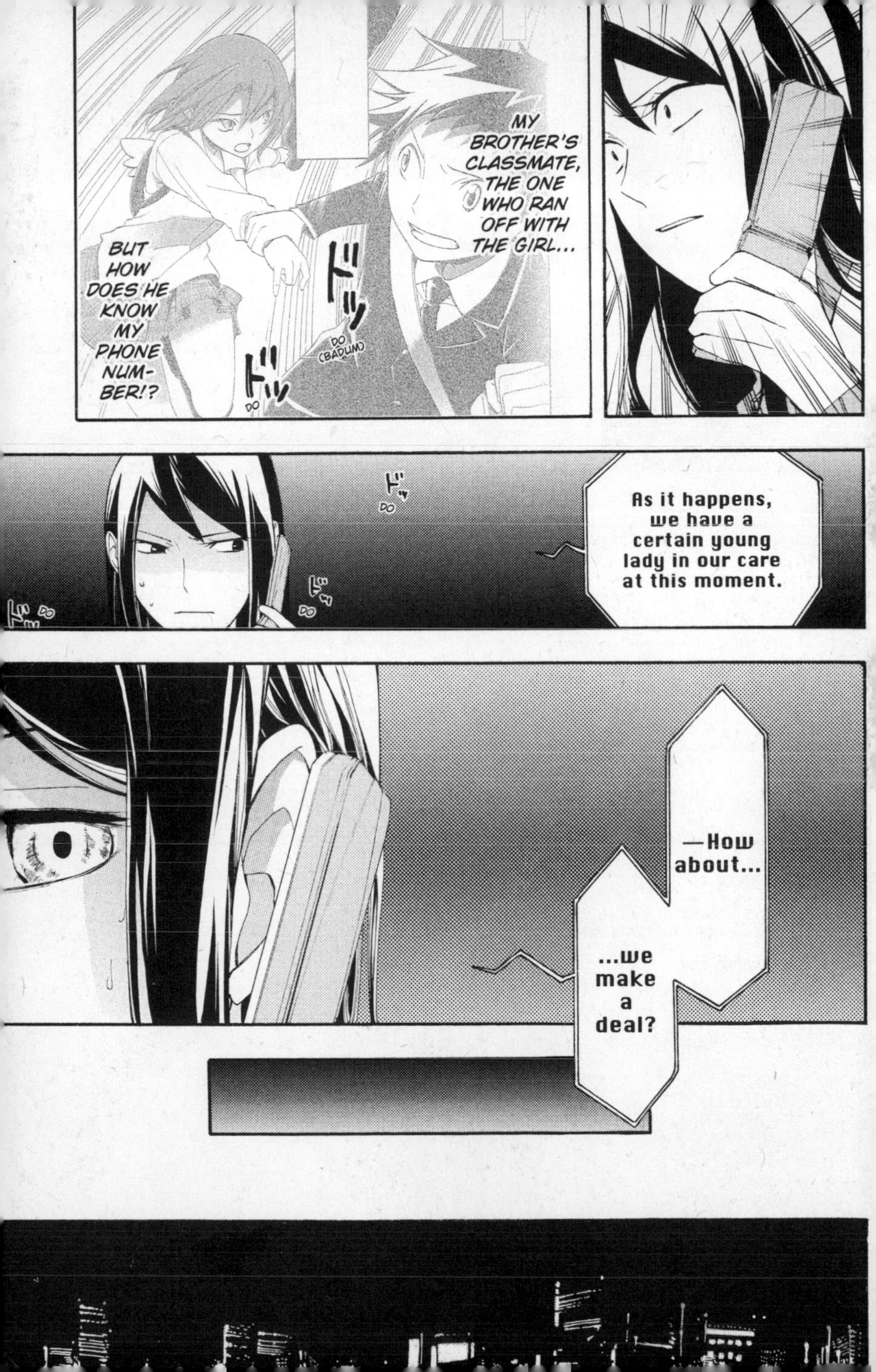
MY BROTHER'S CLASSMATE, THE ONE WHO RAN OFF WITH THE GIRL...
BUT HOW DOES HE KNOW MY PHONE NUMBER!?
ドッ
DO (BADUM)
ドッ
DO
As it happens, we have a certain young lady in our care at this moment.
ドッ
DO
ドッ
DO
ドッ
DO
—How about...
...we make a deal?

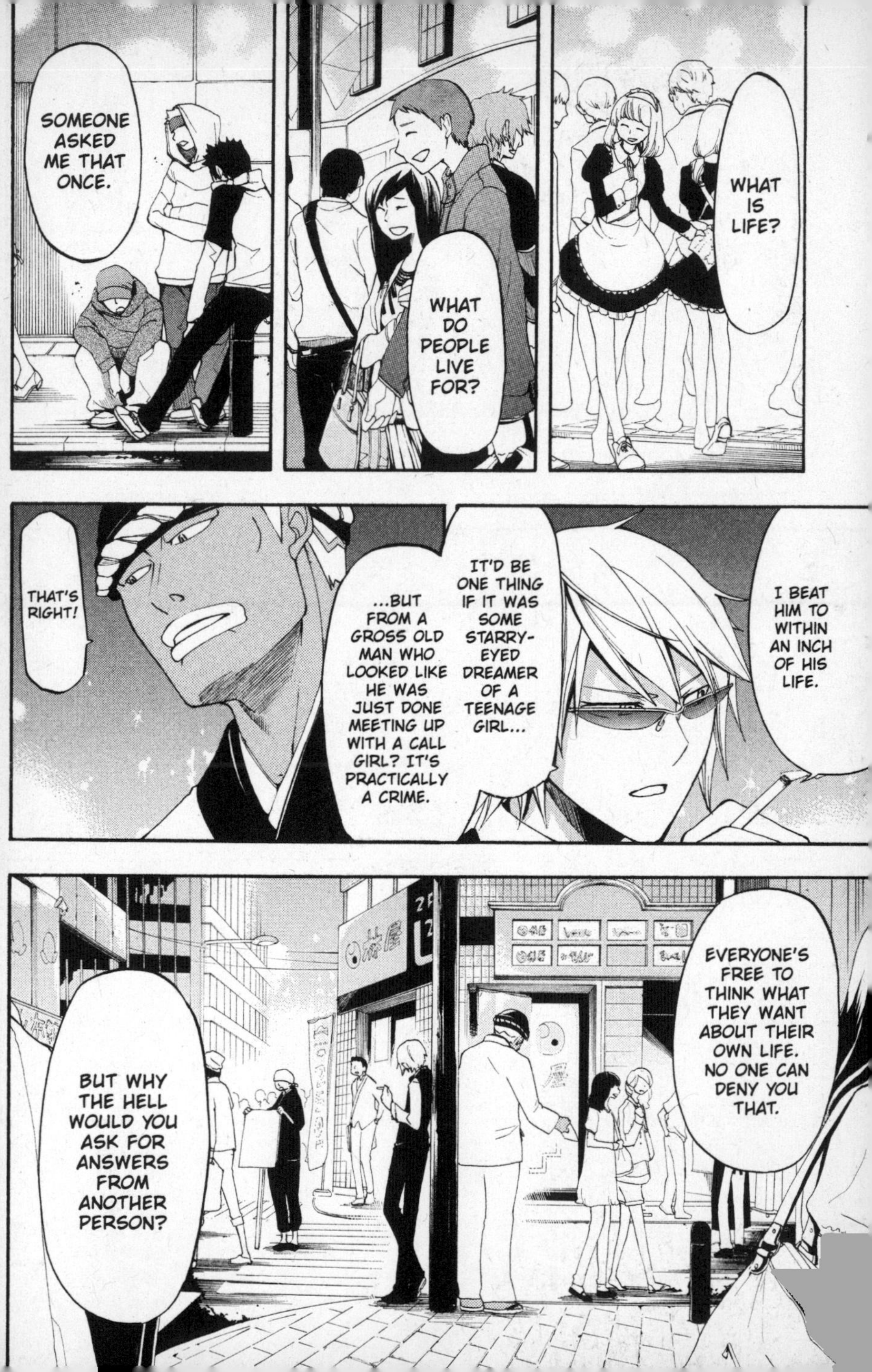
WHAT IS LIFE?
WHAT DO PEOPLE LIVE FOR?
SOMEONE ASKED ME THAT ONCE.
I BEAT HIM TO WITHIN AN INCH OF HIS LIFE.
IT'D BE ONE THING IF IT WAS SOME STARRY-EYED DREAMER OF A TEENAGE GIRL...
...BUT FROM A GROSS OLD MAN WHO LOOKED LIKE HE WAS JUST DONE MEETING UP WITH A CALL GIRL? IT'S PRACTICALLY A CRIME.
THAT'S RIGHT!
EVERYONE'S FREE TO THINK WHAT THEY WANT ABOUT THEIR OWN LIFE. NO ONE CAN DENY YOU THAT.
BUT WHY THE HELL WOULD YOU ASK FOR ANSWERS FROM ANOTHER PERSON?

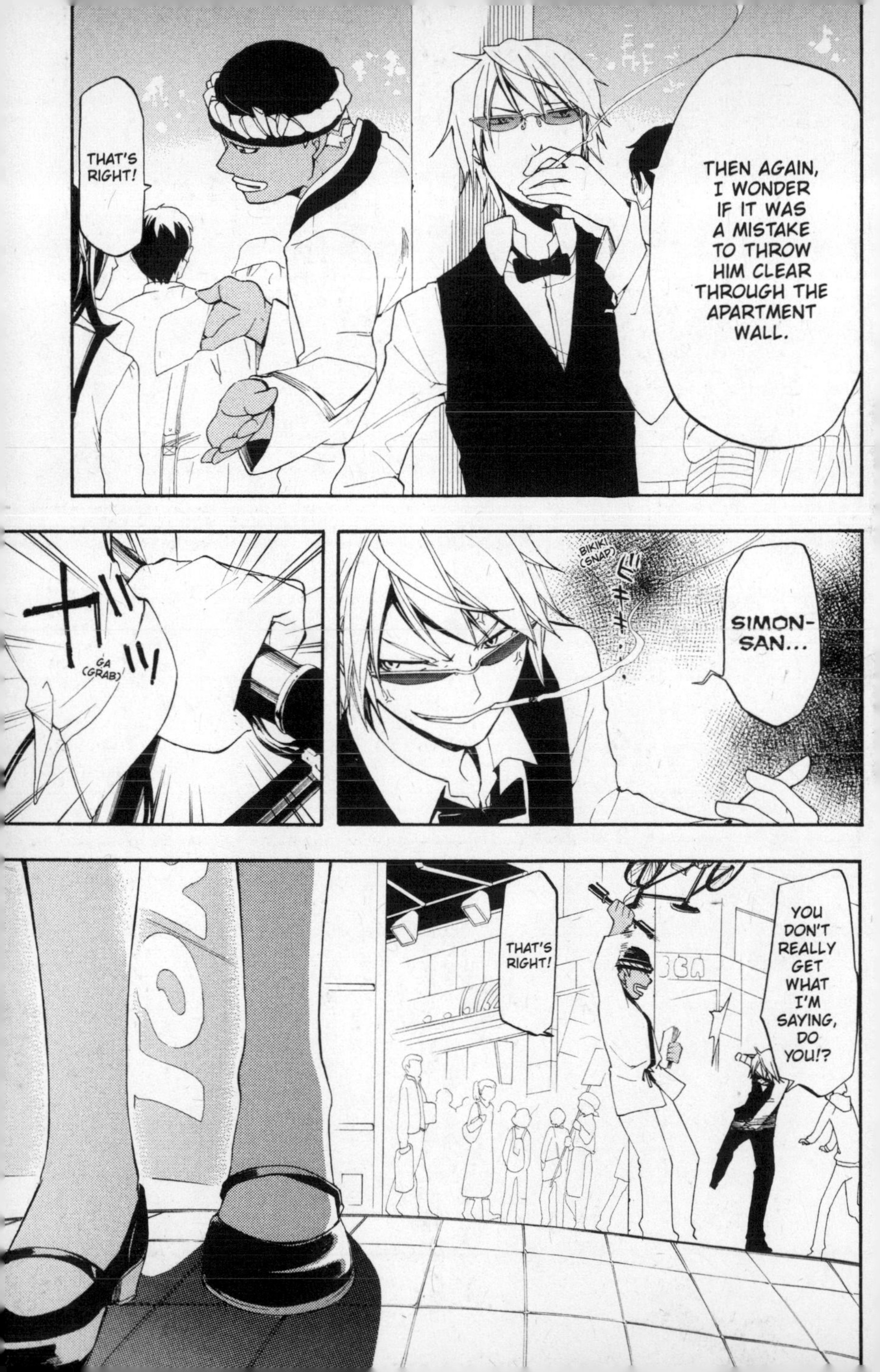
THEN AGAIN, I WONDER IF IT WAS A MISTAKE TO THROW HIM CLEAR THROUGH THE APARTMENT WALL.
THAT'S RIGHT!
BIKIKI (SNAP)
SIMON-SAN...
GA (GRAB)
YOU DON'T REALLY GET WHAT I'M SAYING, DO YOU!?
THAT'S RIGHT!

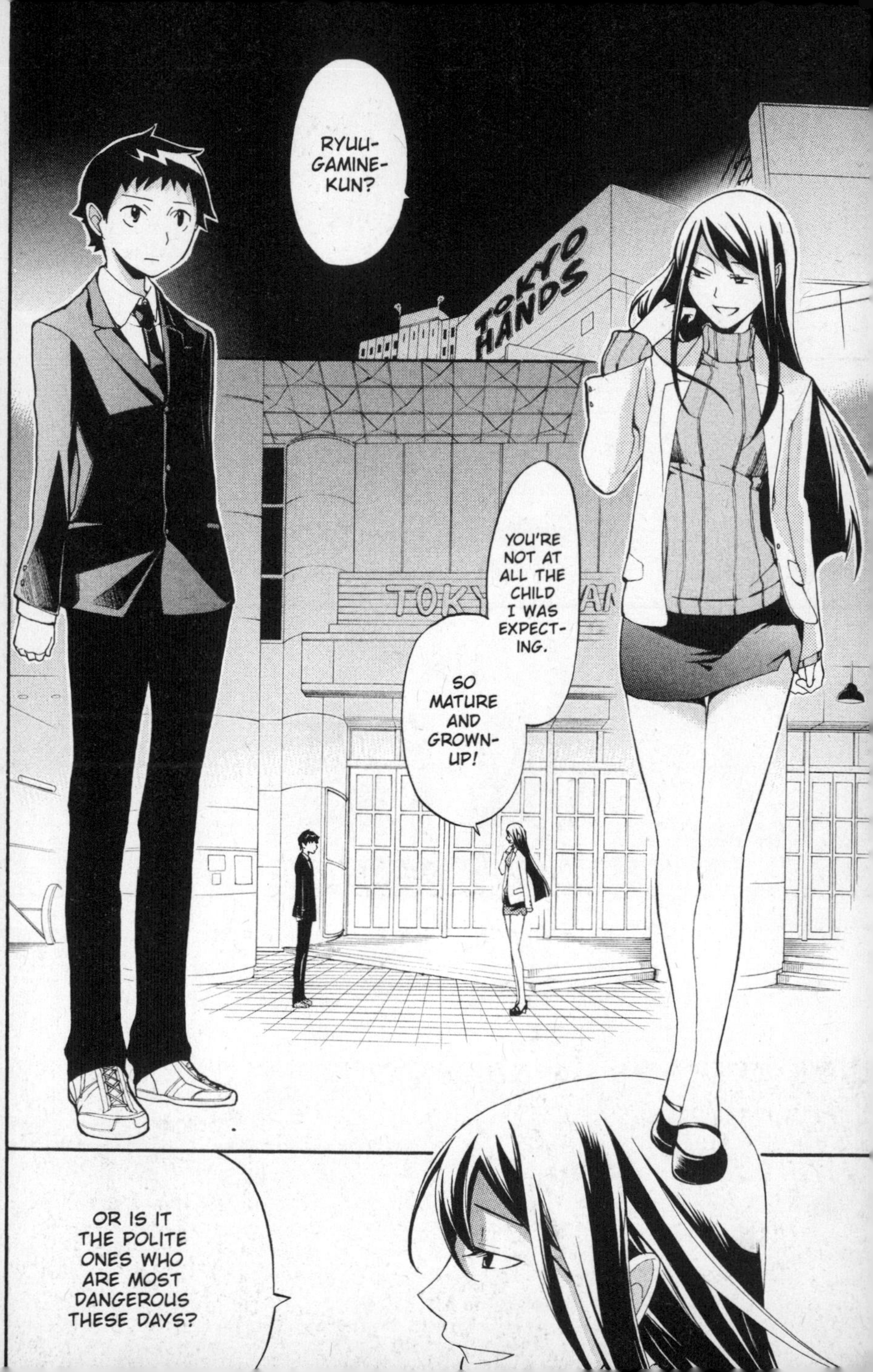
TOKYO HANDS
RYUU-GAMINE-KUN?
YOU'RE NOT AT ALL THE CHILD I WAS EXPECTING.
SO MATURE AND GROWN-UP!
OR IS IT THE POLITE ONES WHO ARE MOST DANGEROUS THESE DAYS?

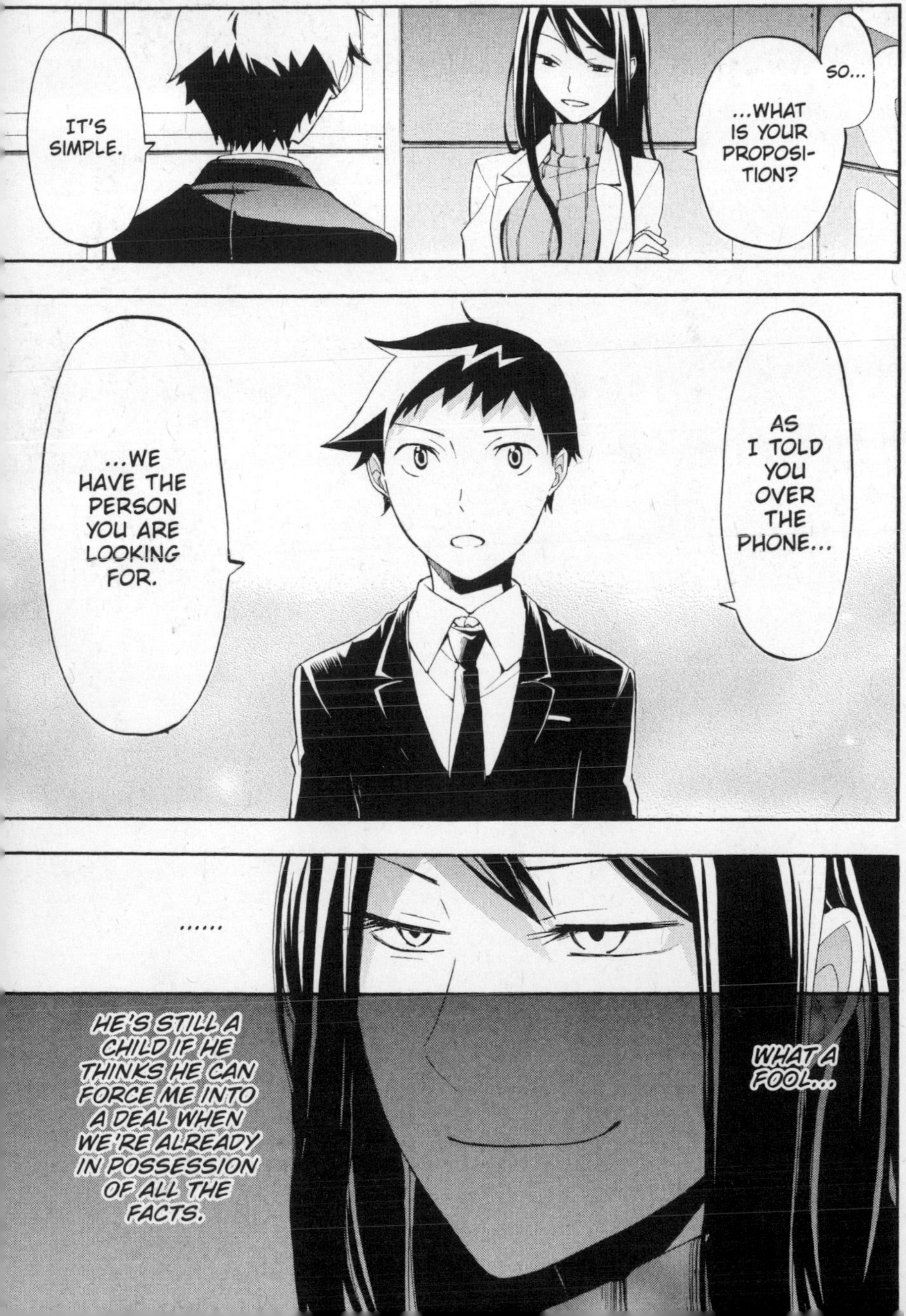
SO...
...WHAT IS YOUR PROPOSITION?
IT'S SIMPLE.
AS I TOLD YOU OVER THE PHONE...
...WE HAVE THE PERSON YOU ARE LOOKING FOR.
......
WHAT A FOOL...
HE'S STILL A CHILD IF HE THINKS HE CAN FORCE ME INTO A DEAL WHEN WE'RE ALREADY IN POSSESSION OF ALL THE FACTS.

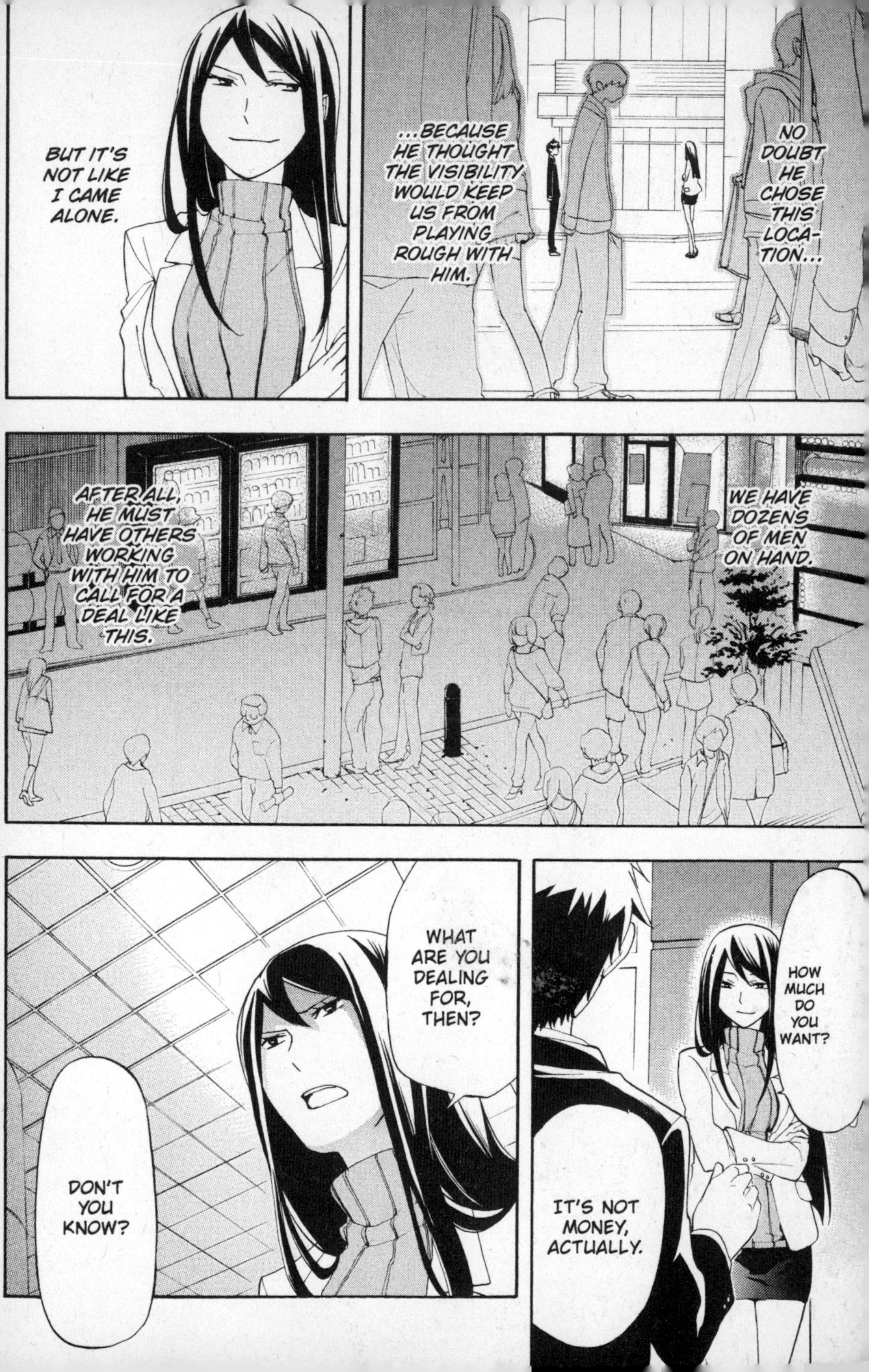
NO DOUBT HE CHOSE THIS LOCATION...
...BECAUSE HE THOUGHT THE VISIBILITY WOULD KEEP US FROM PLAYING ROUGH WITH HIM.
BUT IT'S NOT LIKE I CAME ALONE.
WE HAVE DOZENS OF MEN ON HAND.
AFTER ALL, HE MUST HAVE OTHERS WORKING WITH HIM TO CALL FOR A DEAL LIKE THIS.
HOW MUCH DO YOU WANT?
IT'S NOT MONEY, ACTUALLY.
WHAT ARE YOU DEALING FOR, THEN?
DON'T YOU KNOW?

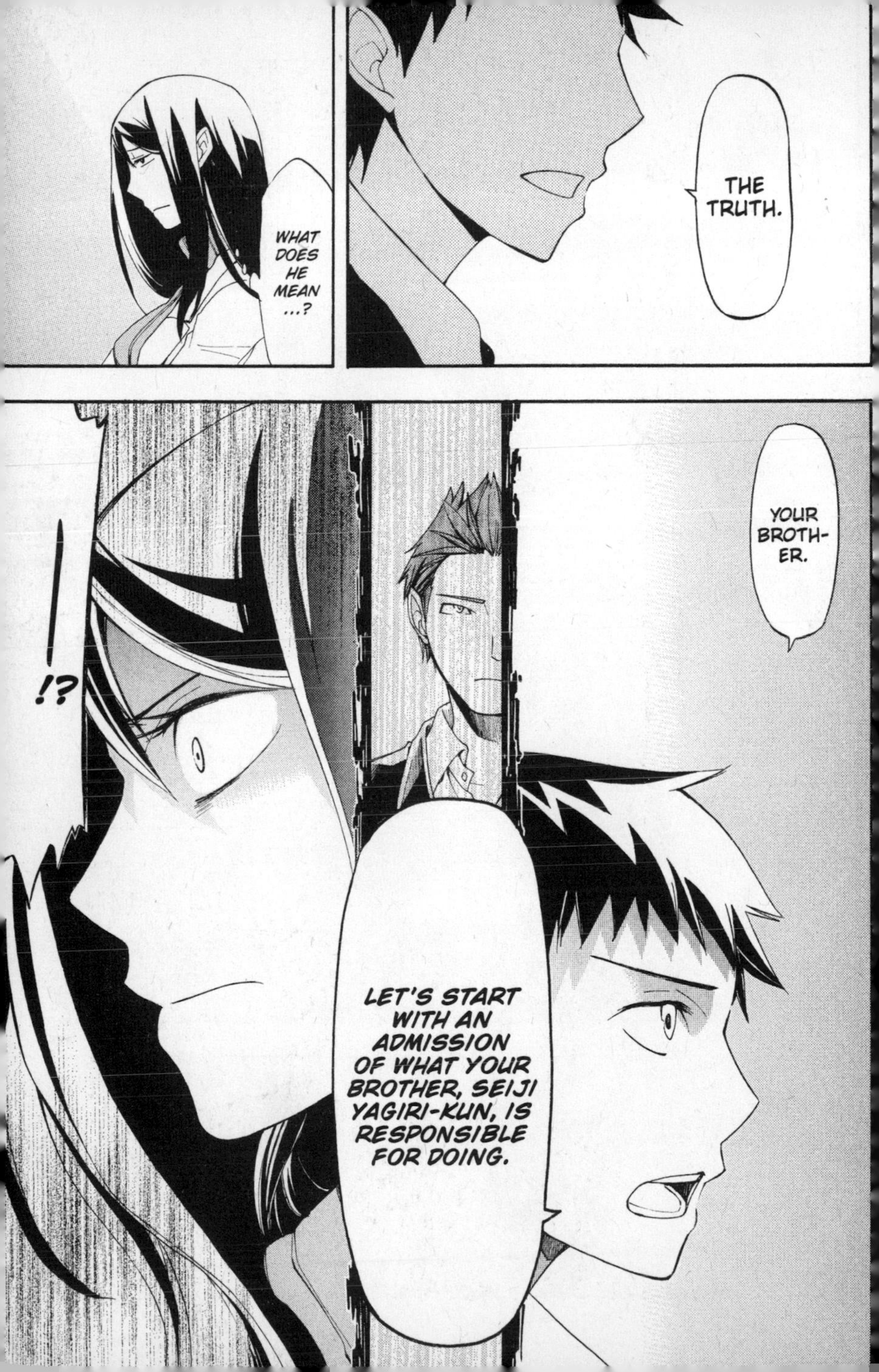
THE TRUTH.
WHAT DOES HE MEAN ...?
YOUR BROTH-ER.
!?
LET'S START WITH AN ADMISSION OF WHAT YOUR BROTHER, SEIJI YAGIRI-KUN, IS RESPONSIBLE FOR DOING.

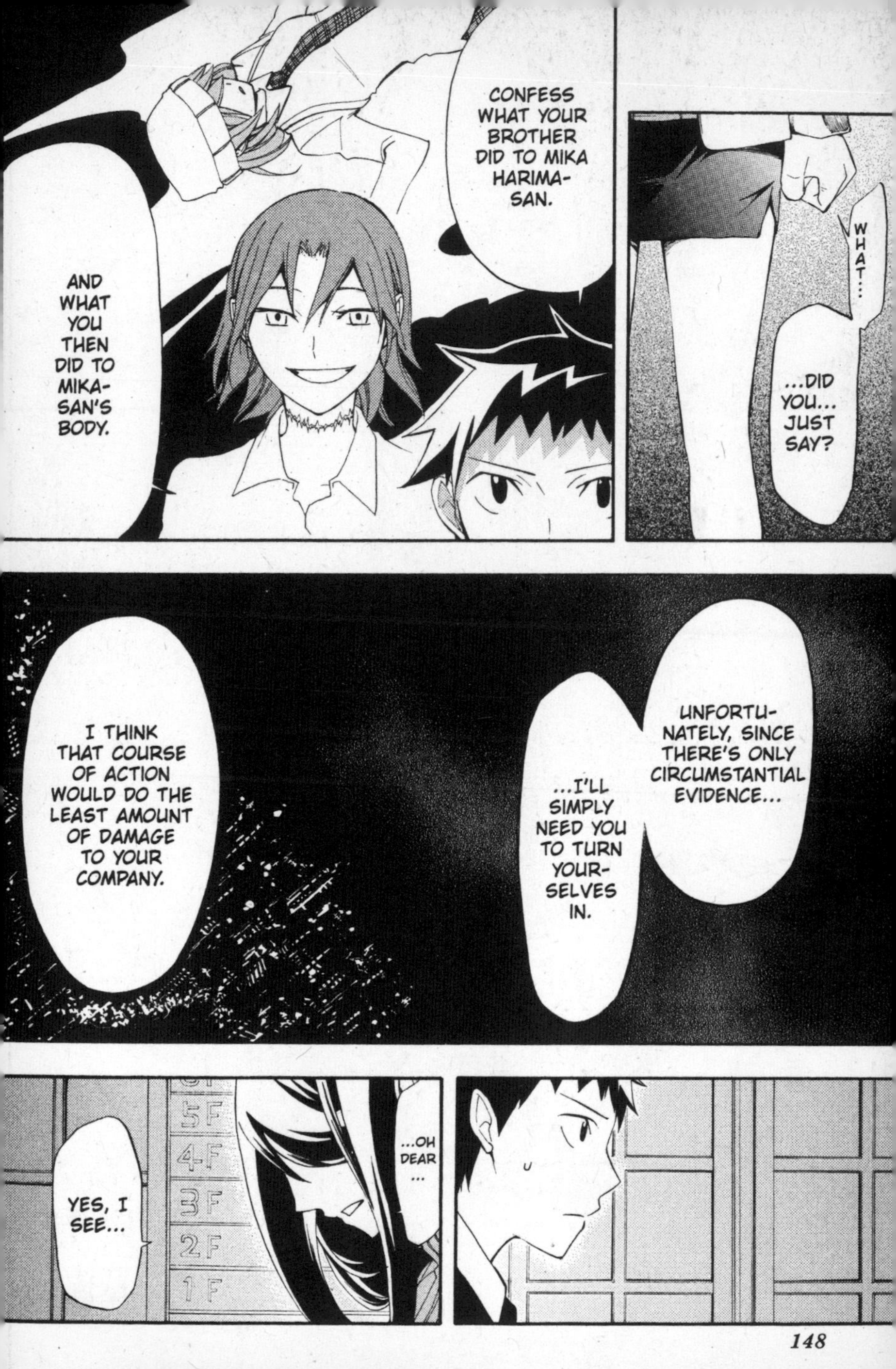
WHAT...
...DID YOU... JUST SAY?
CONFESS WHAT YOUR BROTHER DID TO MIKA HARIMA-SAN.
AND WHAT YOU THEN DID TO MIKA-SAN'S BODY.
UNFORTU-NATELY, SINCE THERE'S ONLY CIRCUMSTANTIAL EVIDENCE...
...I'LL SIMPLY NEED YOU TO TURN YOUR-SELVES IN.
I THINK THAT COURSE OF ACTION WOULD DO THE LEAST AMOUNT OF DAMAGE TO YOUR COMPANY.
...OH DEAR...
YES, I SEE...
5F
4F
3F
2F
1F

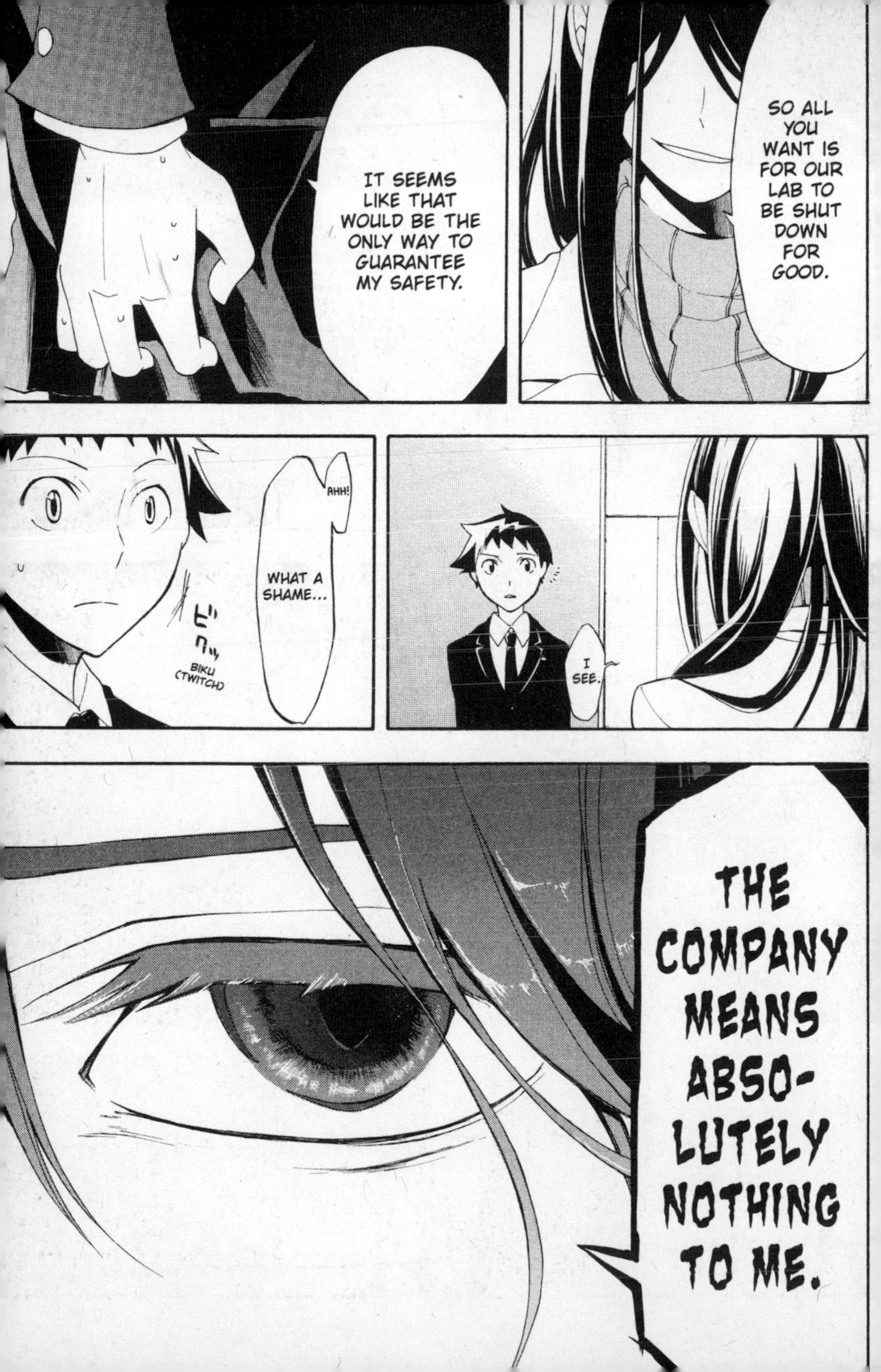
SO ALL YOU WANT IS FOR OUR LAB TO BE SHUT DOWN FOR GOOD.
IT SEEMS LIKE THAT WOULD BE THE ONLY WAY TO GUARANTEE MY SAFETY.
I SEE.
AHH!
WHAT A SHAME...
ビクッ
BIKU (TWITCH)
THE COMPANY MEANS ABSO-LUTELY NOTHING TO ME.

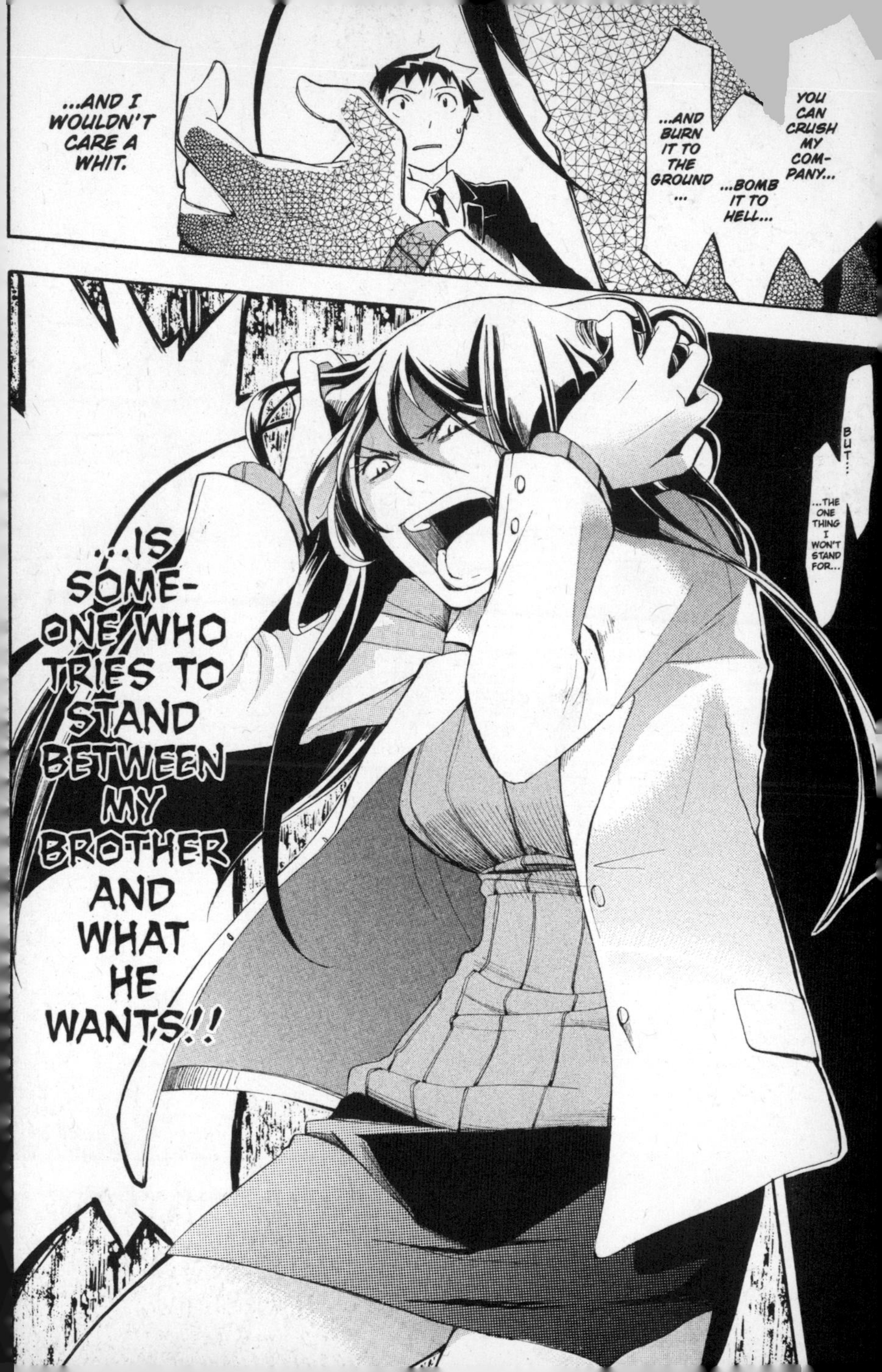
YOU CAN CRUSH MY COM-PANY...
...BOMB IT TO HELL...
...AND BURN IT TO THE GROUND ...
...AND I WOULDN'T CARE A WHIT.
BUT...
...THE ONE THING I WON'T STAND FOR...
...IS SOME-ONE WHO TRIES TO STAND BETWEEN MY BROTHER AND WHAT HE WANTS!!

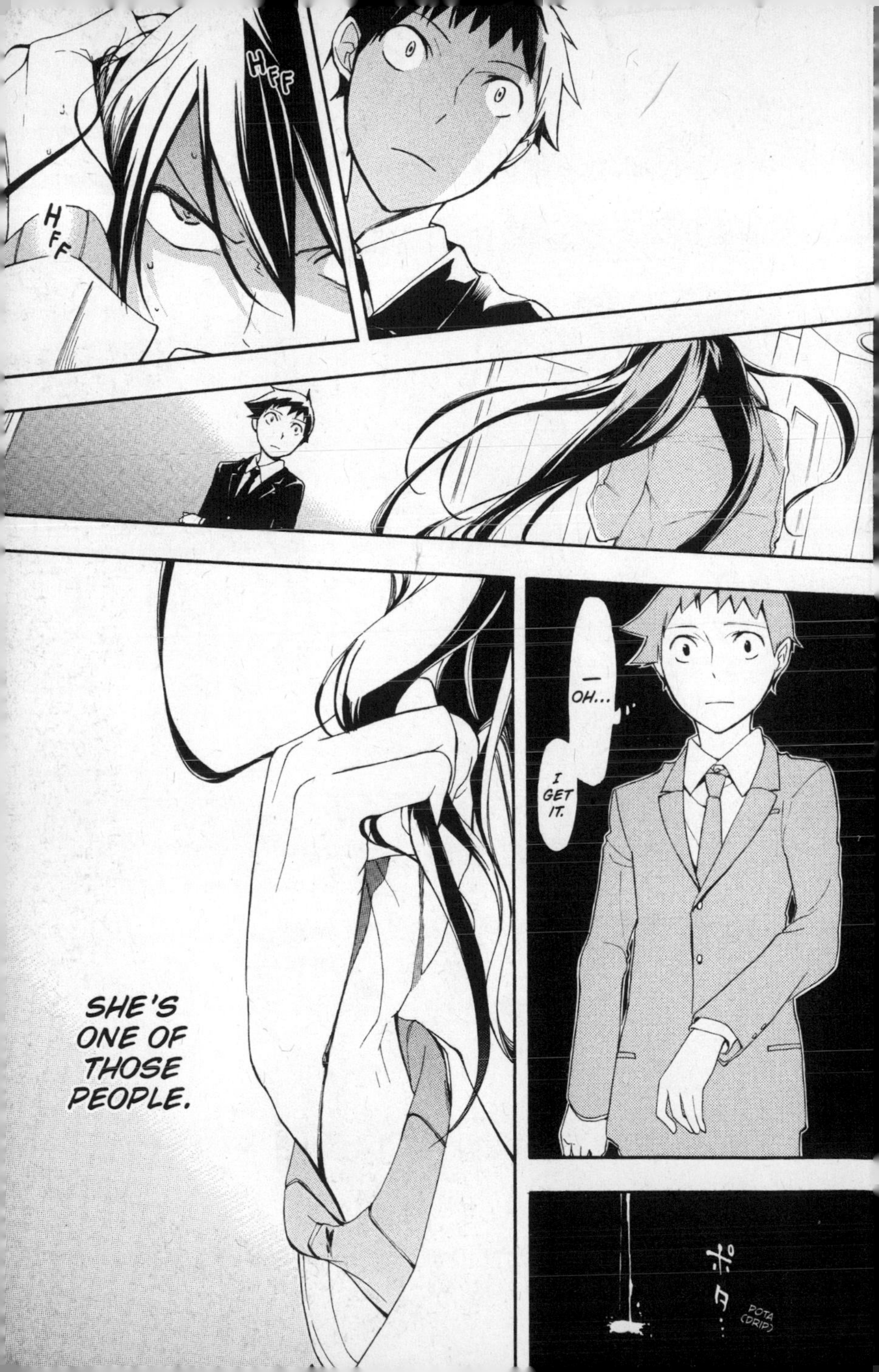
HFF
HFF
—OH...
I GET IT.
SHE'S ONE OF THOSE PEOPLE.
POTA (DRIP)

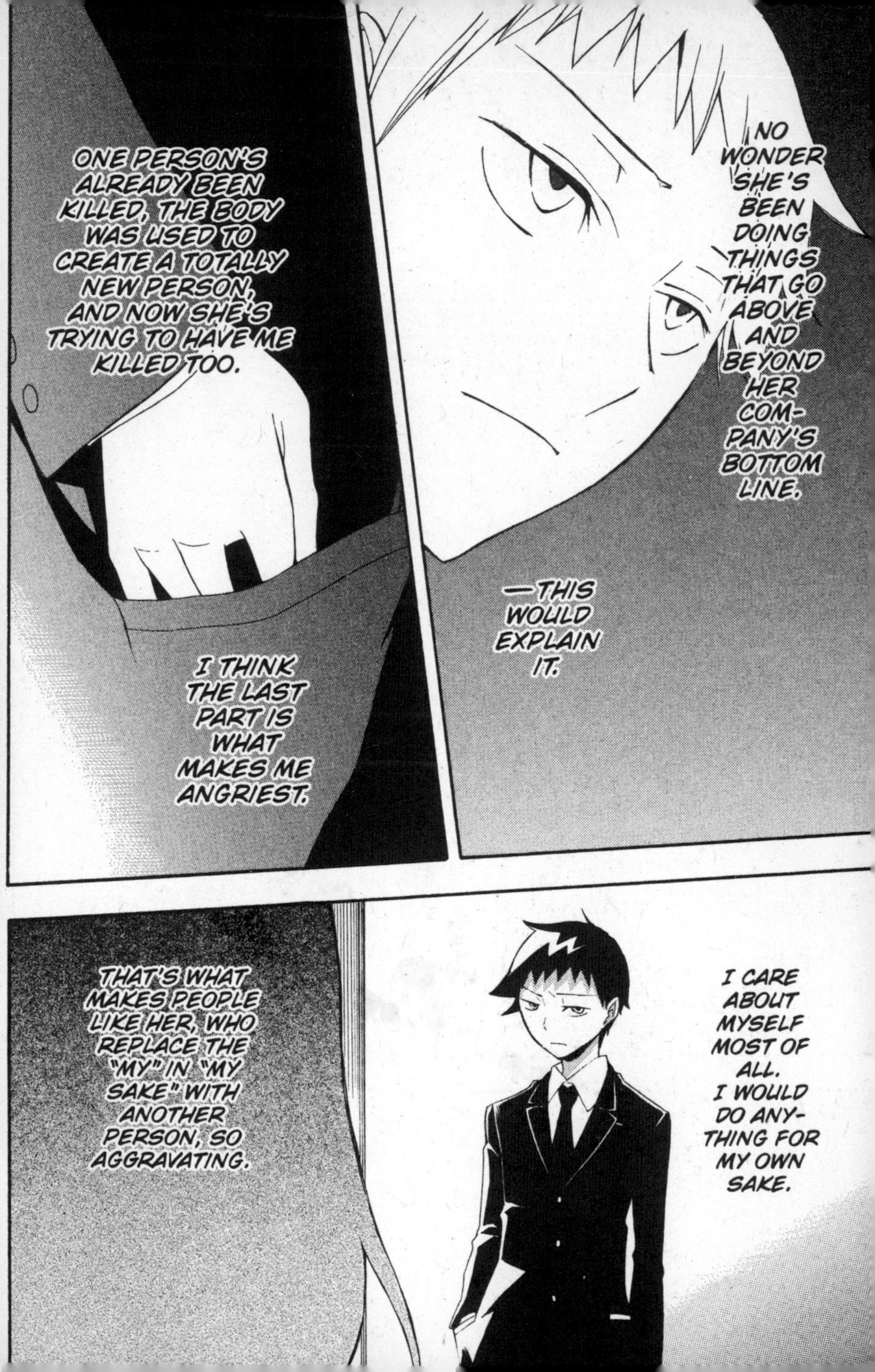
NO WONDER SHE'S BEEN DOING THINGS THAT GO ABOVE AND BEYOND HER COM-PANY'S BOTTOM LINE.
—THIS WOULD EXPLAIN IT.
ONE PERSON'S ALREADY BEEN KILLED, THE BODY WAS USED TO CREATE A TOTALLY NEW PERSON, AND NOW SHE'S TRYING TO HAVE ME KILLED TOO.
I THINK THE LAST PART IS WHAT MAKES ME ANGRIEST.
I CARE ABOUT MYSELF MOST OF ALL. I WOULD DO ANY-THING FOR MY OWN SAKE.
THAT'S WHAT MAKES PEOPLE LIKE HER, WHO REPLACE THE "MY" IN "MY SAKE" WITH ANOTHER PERSON, SO AGGRAVATING.

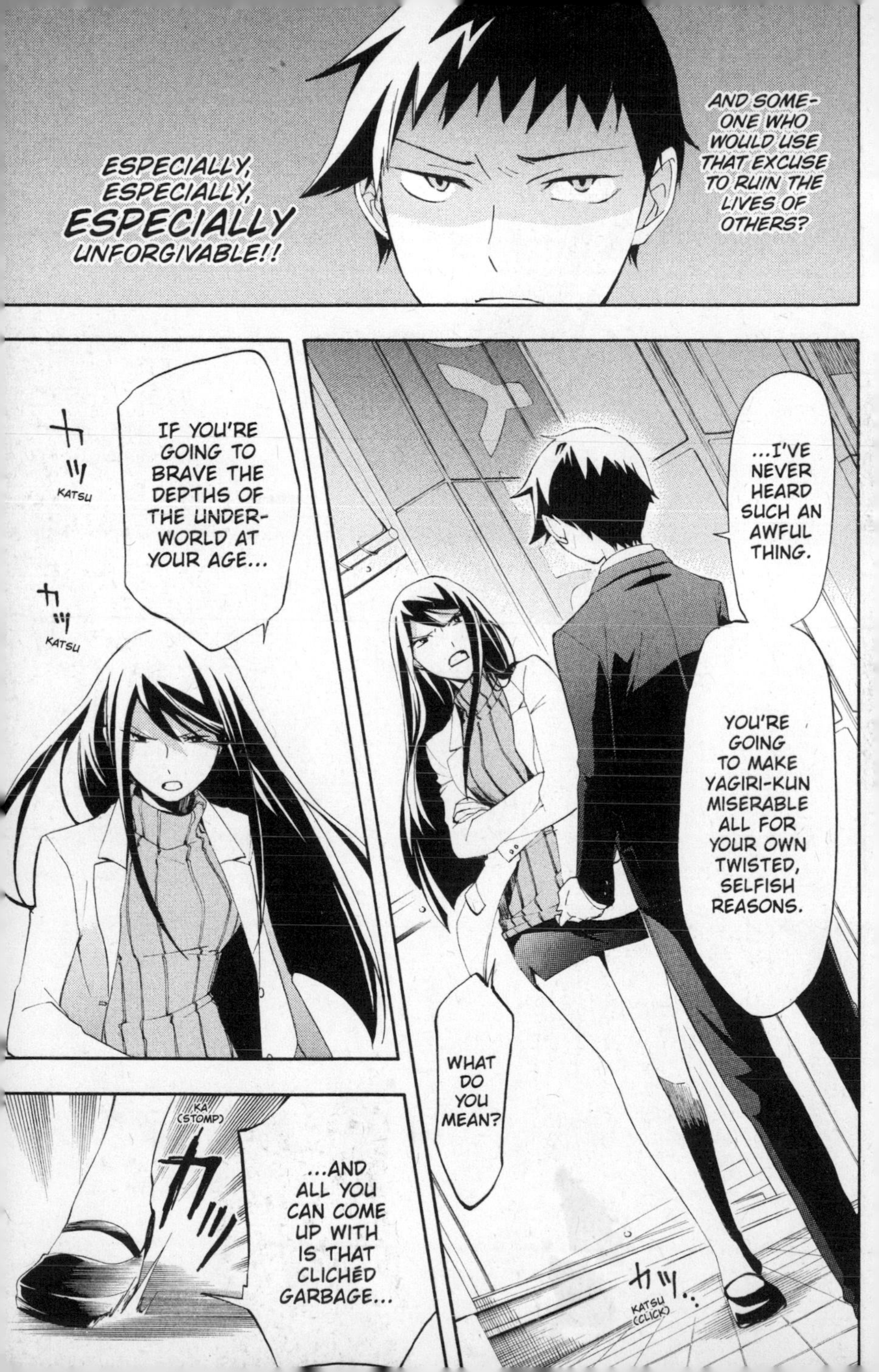
AND SOME-ONE WHO WOULD USE THAT EXCUSE TO RUIN THE LIVES OF OTHERS?
ESPECIALLY, ESPECIALLY, ESPECIALLY UNFORGIVABLE!!
...I'VE NEVER HEARD SUCH AN AWFUL THING.
YOU'RE GOING TO MAKE YAGIRI-KUN MISERABLE ALL FOR YOUR OWN TWISTED, SELFISH REASONS.
WHAT DO YOU MEAN?
カッ
KATSU (CLICK)
カッ
KATSU
カッ
KATSU
IF YOU'RE GOING TO BRAVE THE DEPTHS OF THE UNDER-WORLD AT YOUR AGE...
KA (STOMP)
カッ
...AND ALL YOU CAN COME UP WITH IS THAT CLICHÉD GARBAGE...

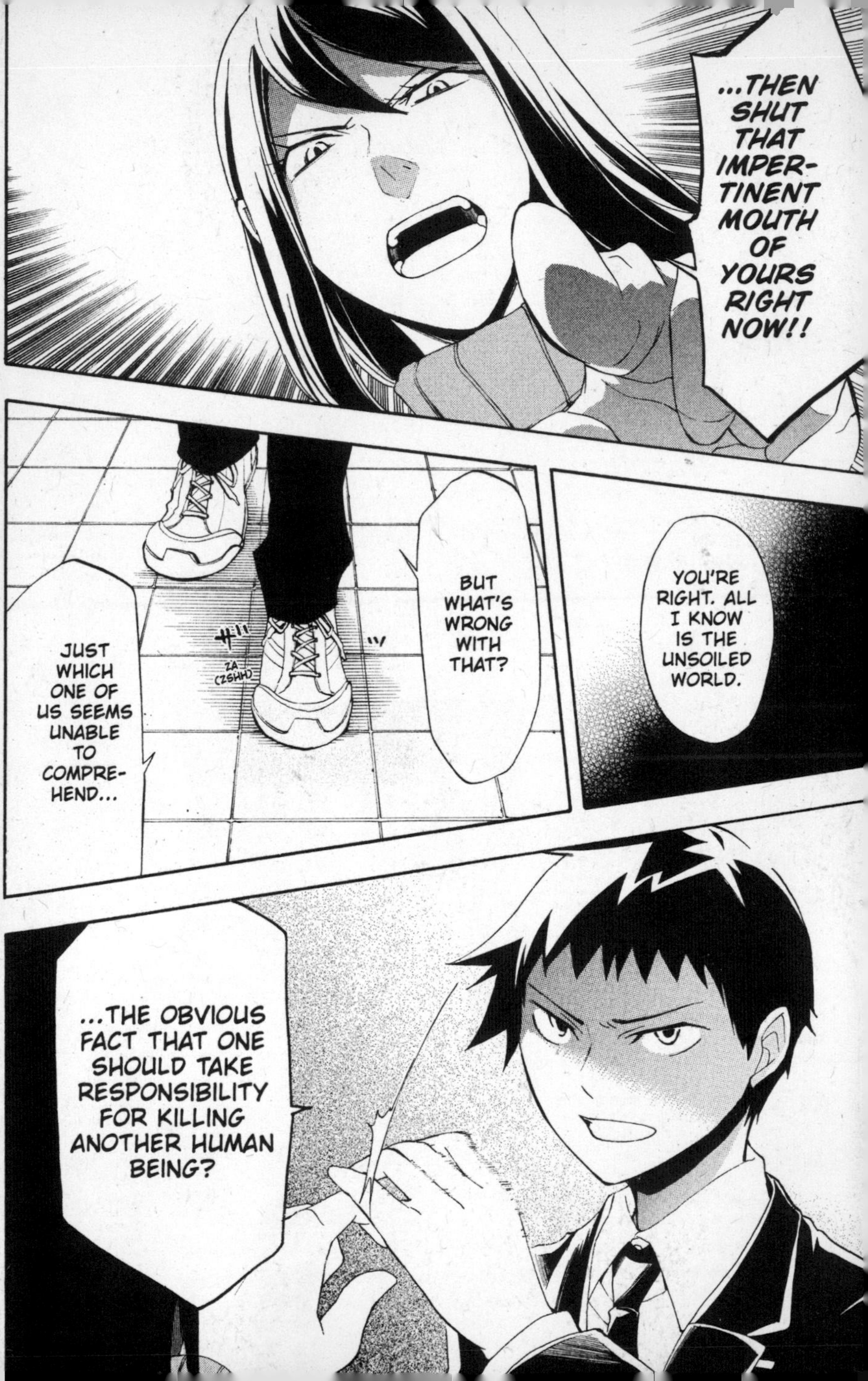
...THEN SHUT THAT IMPER-TINENT MOUTH OF YOURS RIGHT NOW!!
YOU'RE RIGHT. ALL I KNOW IS THE UNSOILED WORLD.
BUT WHAT'S WRONG WITH THAT?
ZA (ZSHH)
JUST WHICH ONE OF US SEEMS UNABLE TO COMPRE-HEND...
...THE OBVIOUS FACT THAT ONE SHOULD TAKE RESPONSIBILITY FOR KILLING ANOTHER HUMAN BEING?

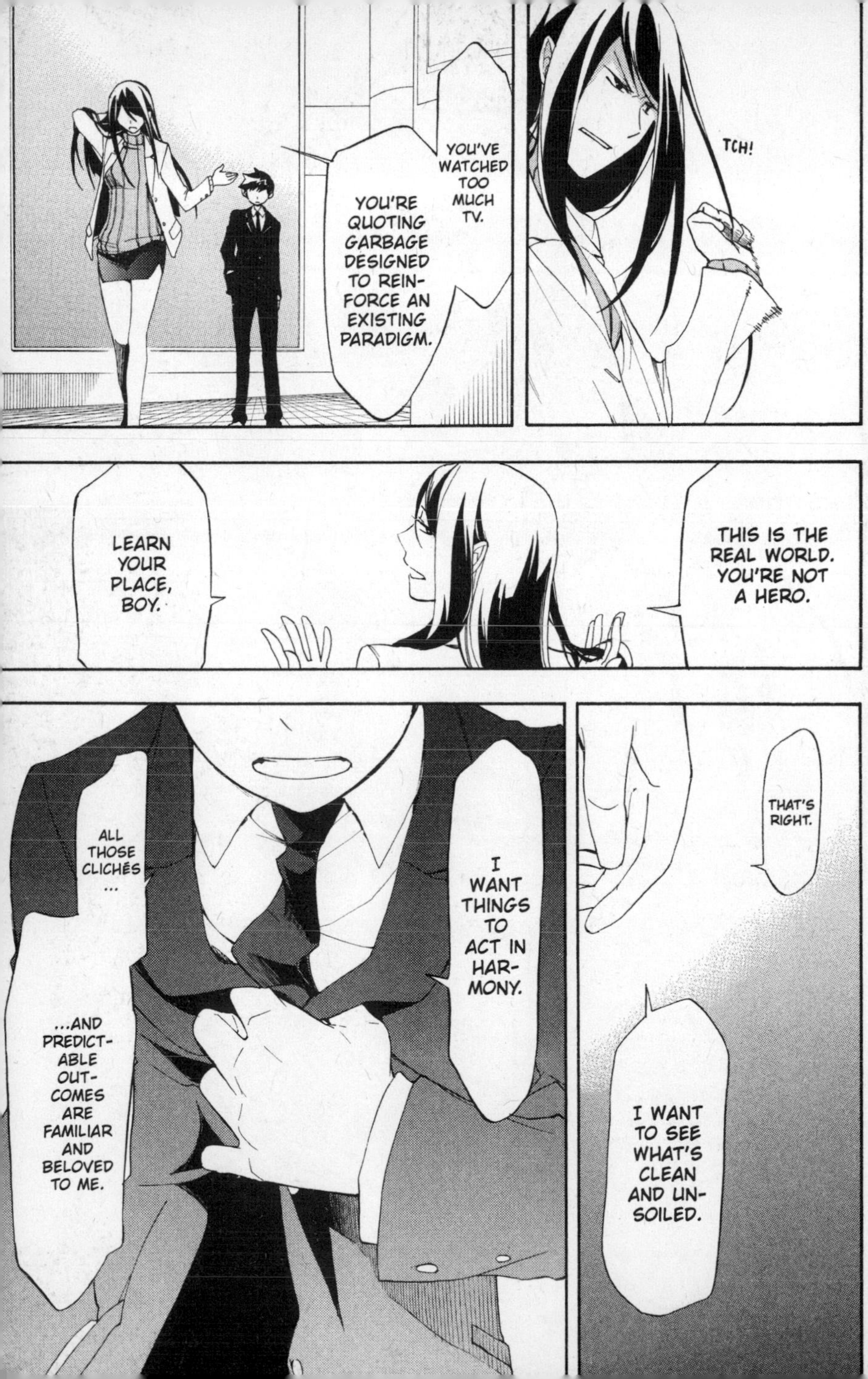
TCH!
YOU'VE WATCHED TOO MUCH TV.
YOU'RE QUOTING GARBAGE DESIGNED TO REINFORCE AN EXISTING PARADIGM.
THIS IS THE REAL WORLD. YOU'RE NOT A HERO.
LEARN YOUR PLACE, BOY.
THAT'S RIGHT.
I WANT TO SEE WHAT'S CLEAN AND UNSOILED.
I WANT THINGS TO ACT IN HARMONY.
ALL THOSE CLICHÉS...
...AND PREDICTABLE OUTCOMES ARE FAMILIAR AND BELOVED TO ME.

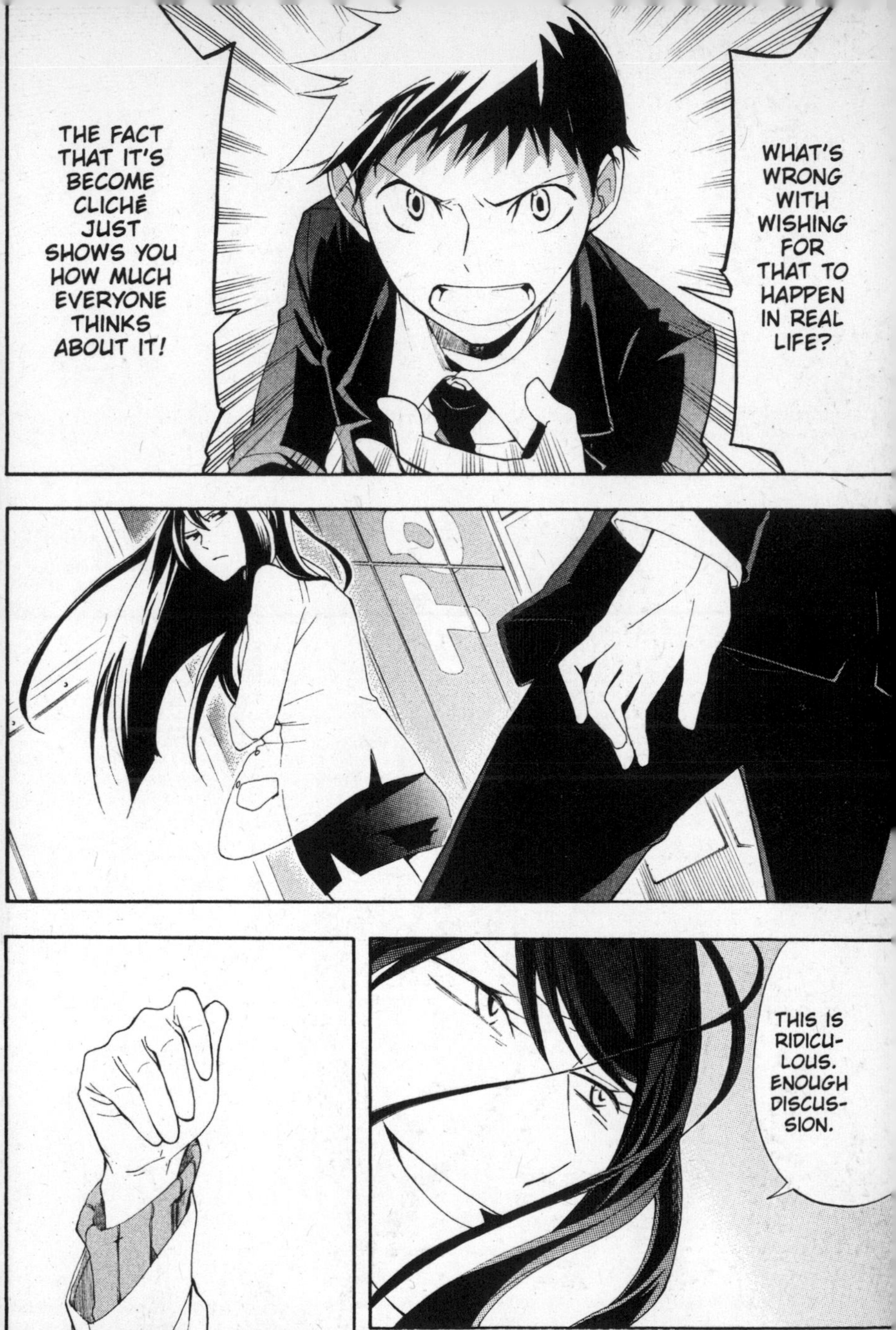
WHAT'S WRONG WITH WISHING FOR THAT TO HAPPEN IN REAL LIFE?
THE FACT THAT IT'S BECOME CLICHÉ JUST SHOWS YOU HOW MUCH EVERYONE THINKS ABOUT IT!
THIS IS RIDICU-LOUS. ENOUGH DISCUS-SION.

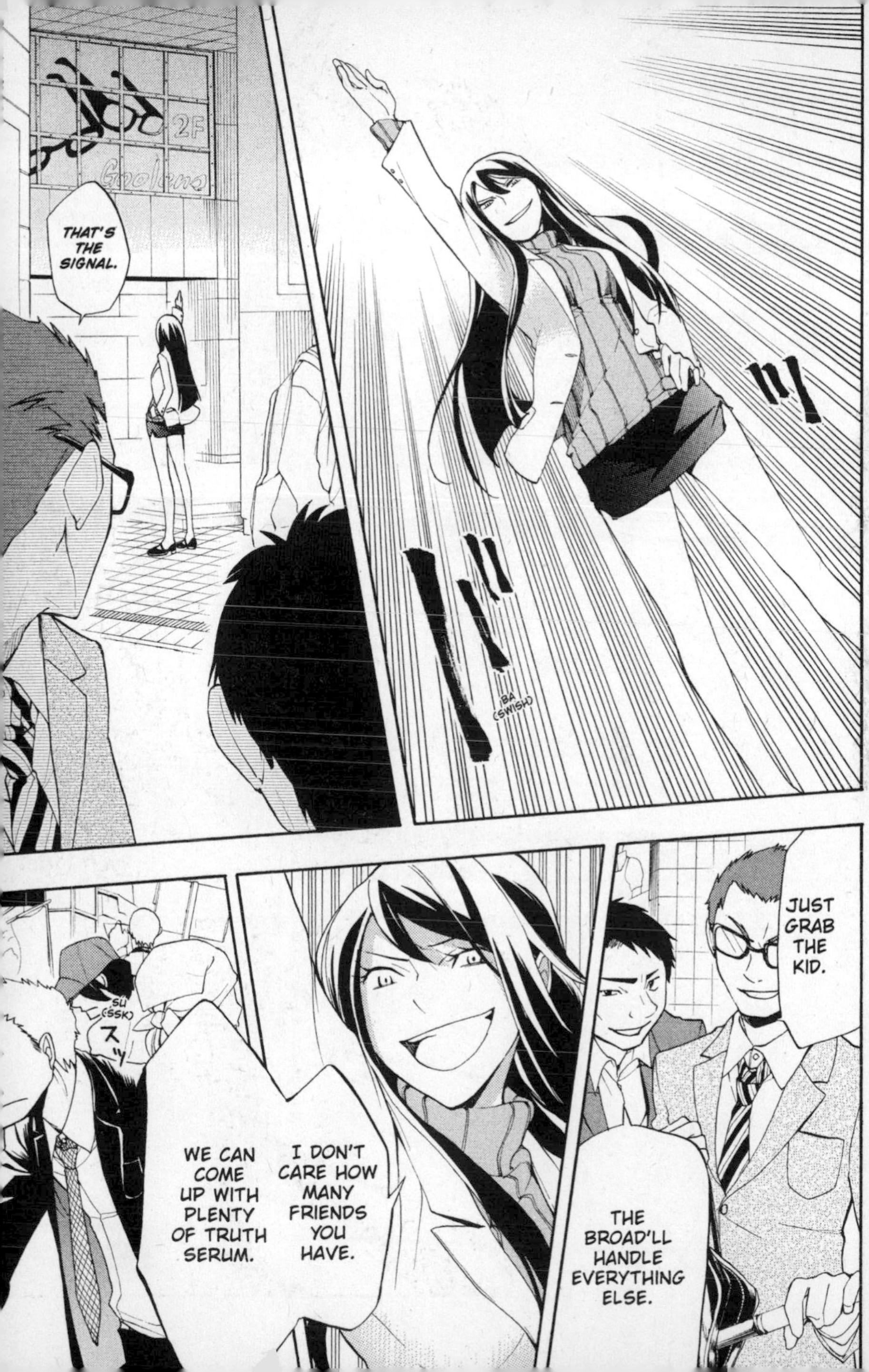
BA (SWISH)
THAT'S THE SIGNAL.
2F
JUST GRAB THE KID.
THE BROAD'LL HANDLE EVERYTHING ELSE.
I DON'T CARE HOW MANY FRIENDS YOU HAVE.
WE CAN COME UP WITH PLENTY OF TRUTH SERUM.
SU (SSK)
スッ

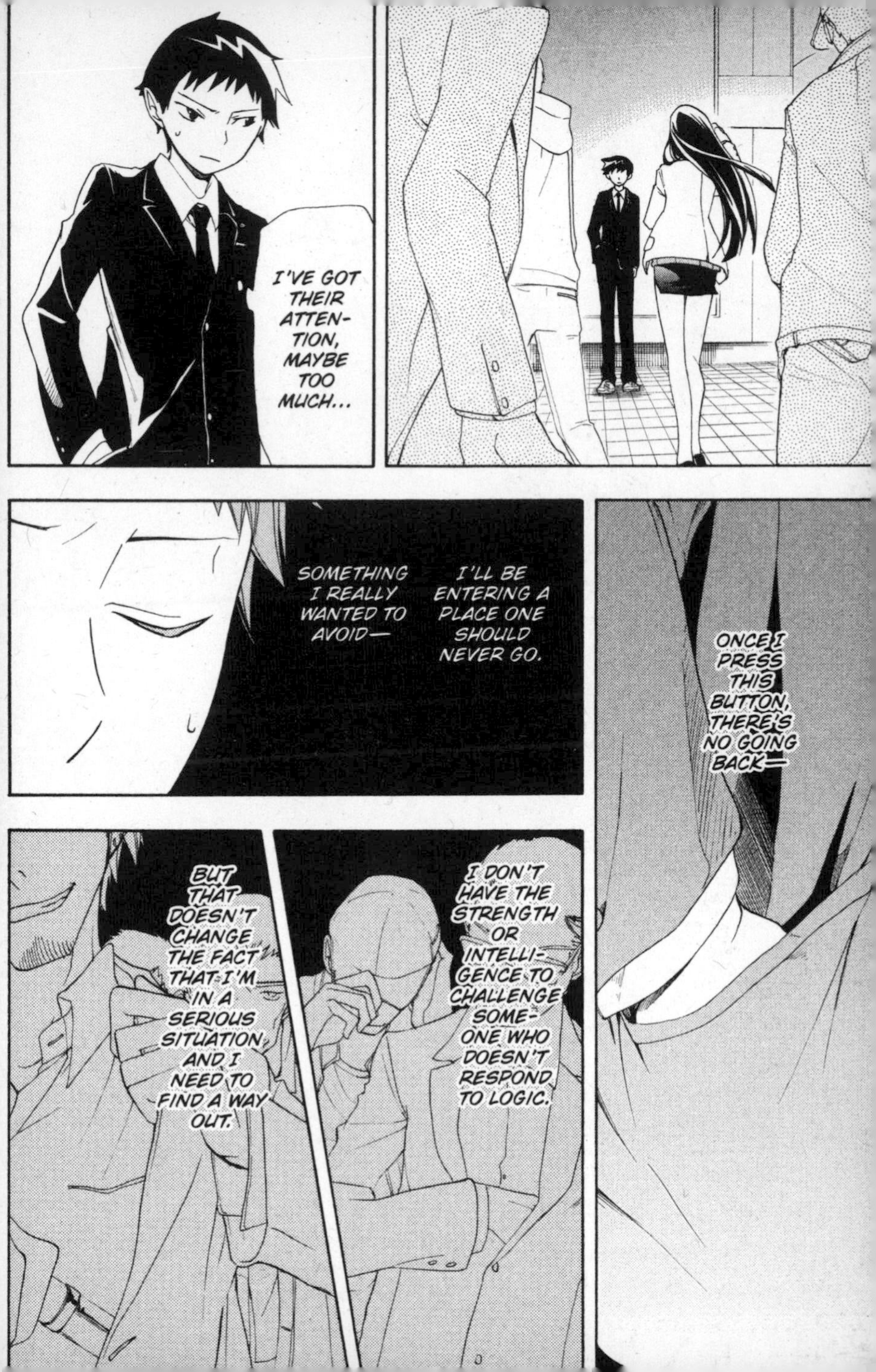
I'VE GOT THEIR ATTENTION, MAYBE TOO MUCH...
ONCE I PRESS THIS BUTTON, THERE'S NO GOING BACK—
I'LL BE ENTERING A PLACE ONE SHOULD NEVER GO.
SOMETHING I REALLY WANTED TO AVOID—
I DON'T HAVE THE STRENGTH OR INTELLIGENCE TO CHALLENGE SOMEONE WHO DOESN'T RESPOND TO LOGIC.
BUT THAT DOESN'T CHANGE THE FACT THAT I'M IN A SERIOUS SITUATION AND I NEED TO FIND A WAY OUT.

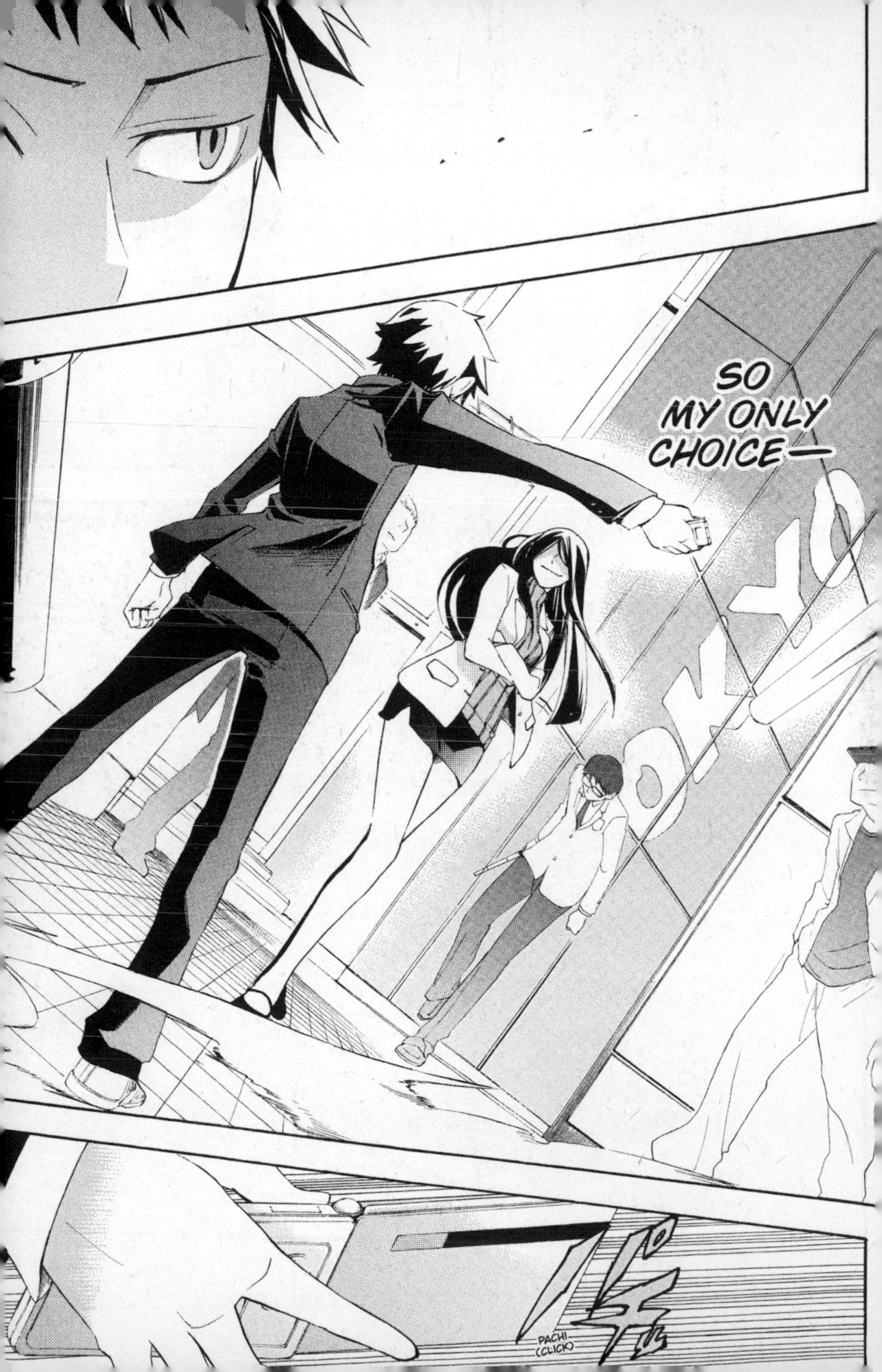
SO MY ONLY CHOICE—
PACHI (CLICK)

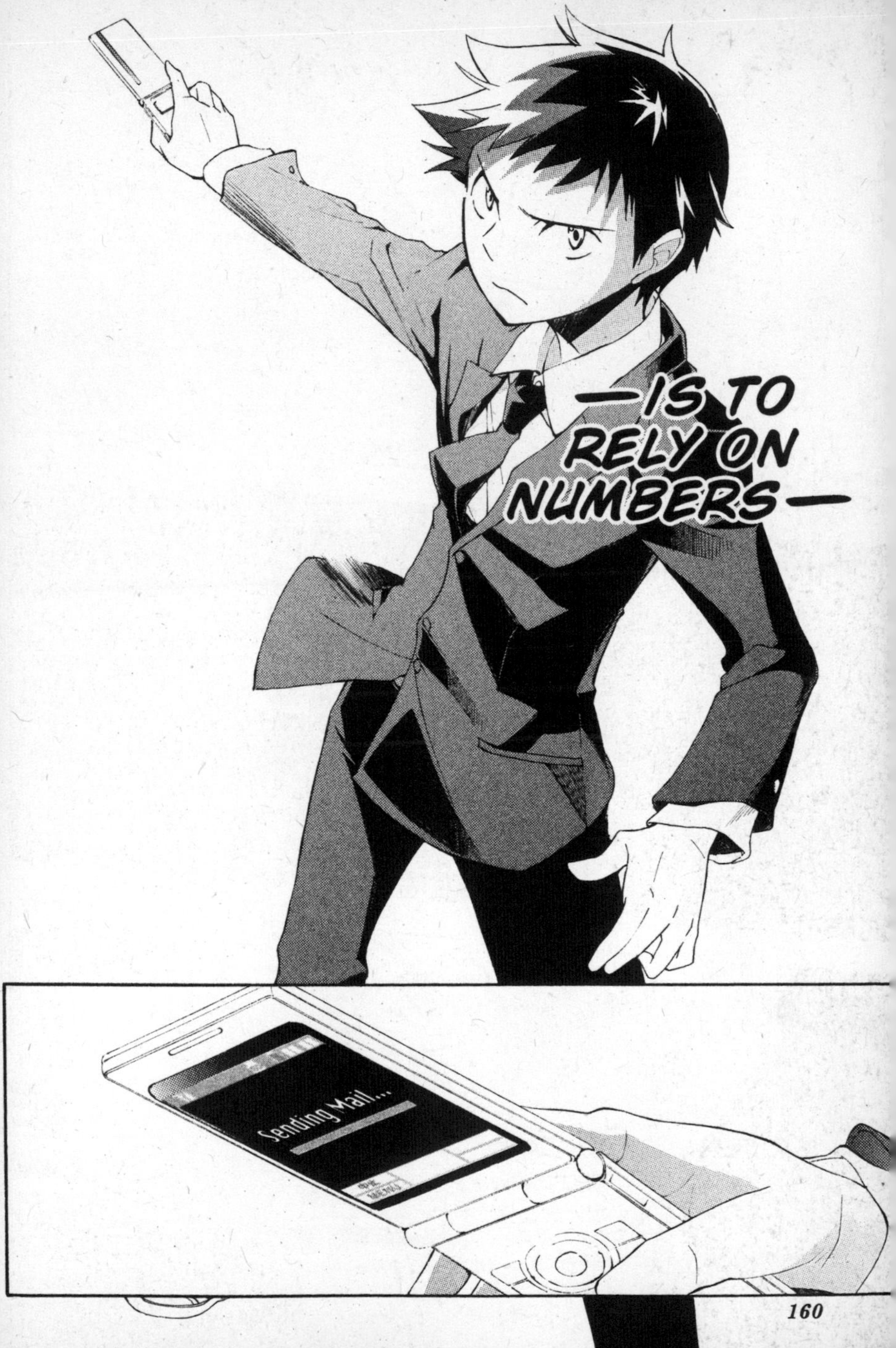
—IS TO RELY ON NUMBERS—
Sending Mail...

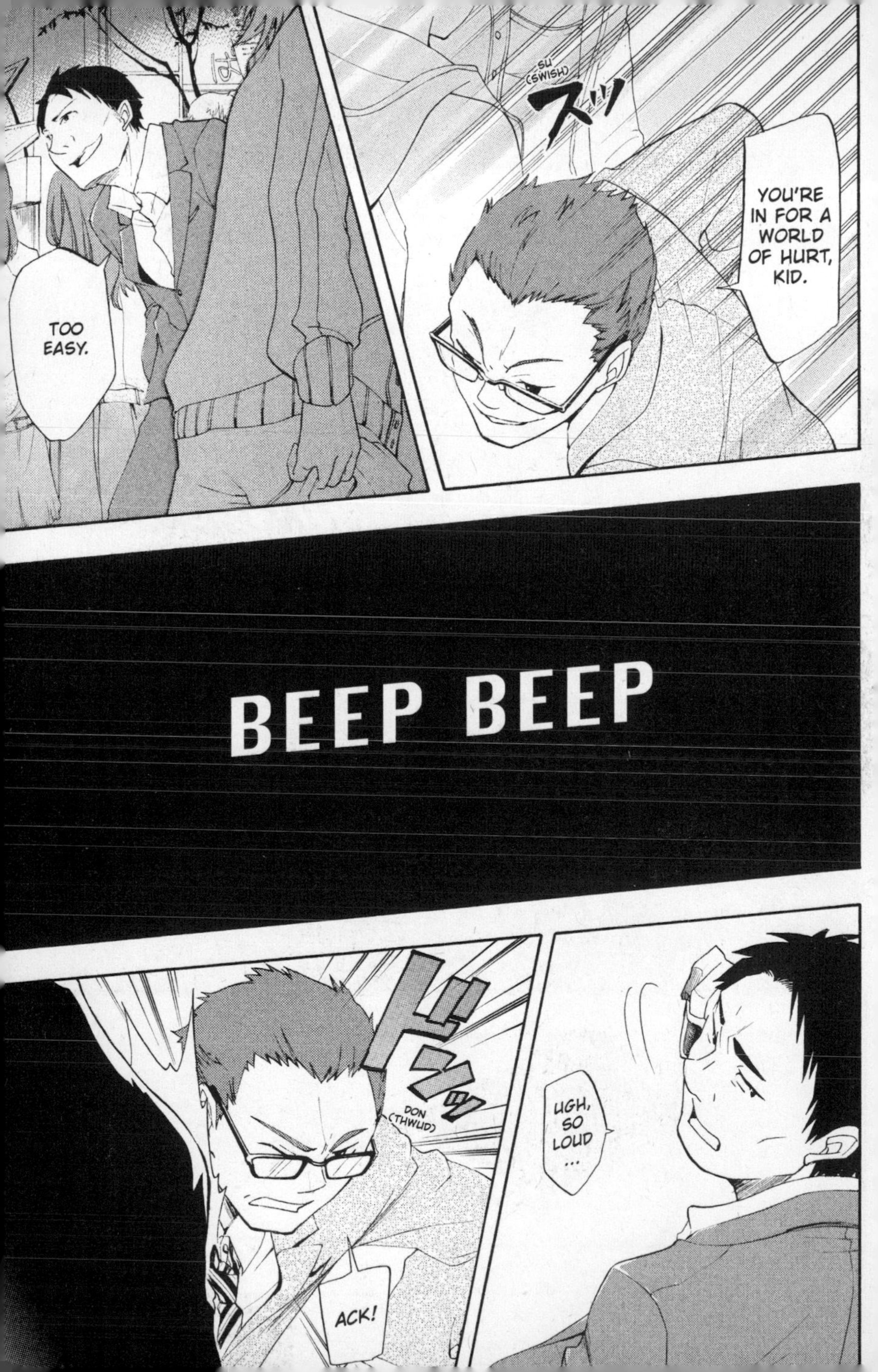
SU (SWISH)
YOU'RE IN FOR A WORLD OF HURT, KID.
TOO EASY.
BEEP BEEP
UGH, SO LOUD ...
DON (THWUD)
ACK!

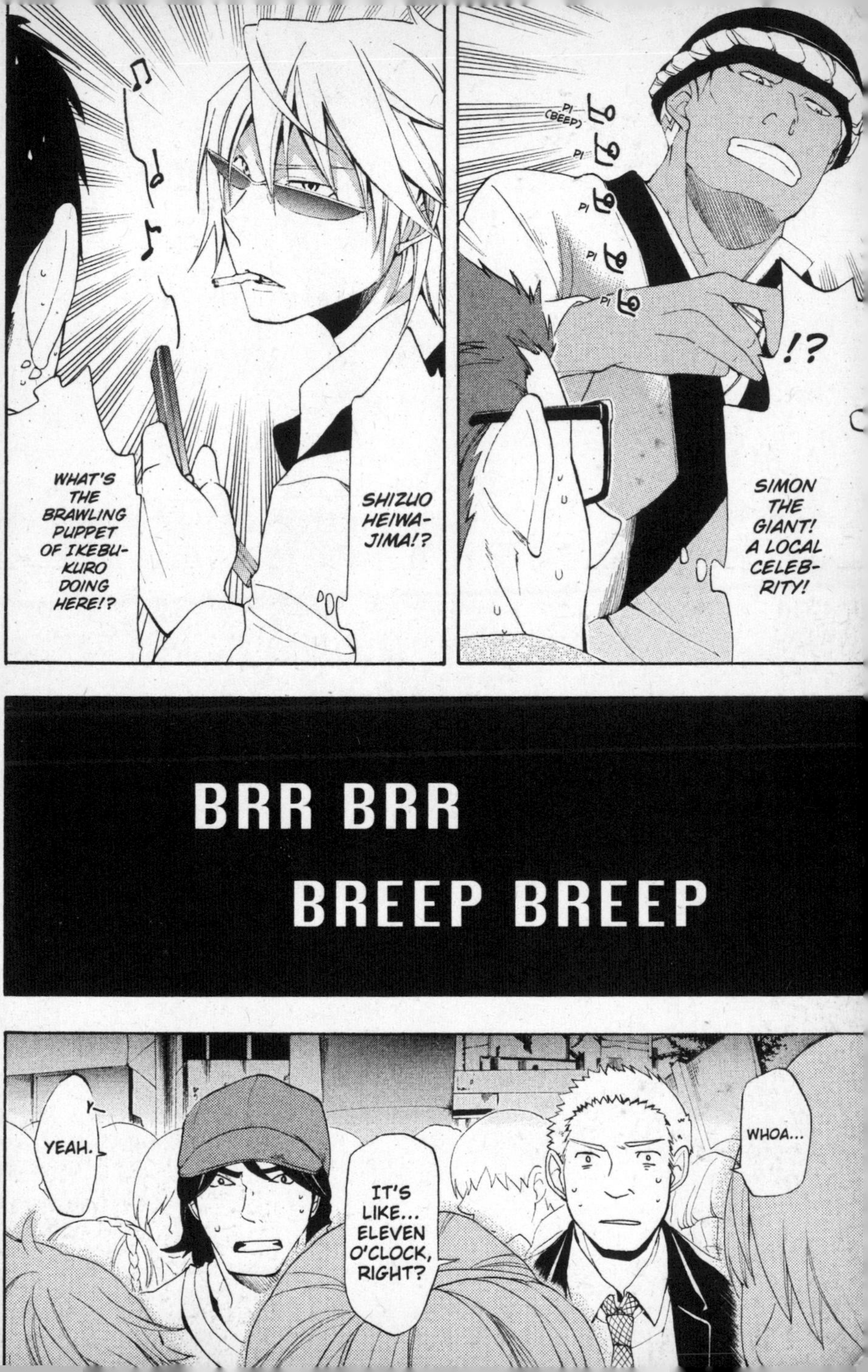
PI (BEEP)
PI
PI
PI
PI
!?
SIMON THE GIANT! A LOCAL CELEB-RITY!
SHIZUO HEIWA-JIMA!?
WHAT'S THE BRAWLING PUPPET OF IKEBU-KURO DOING HERE!?
BRR BRR
BREEP BREEP
WHOA...
IT'S LIKE... ELEVEN O'CLOCK, RIGHT?
Y— YEAH.

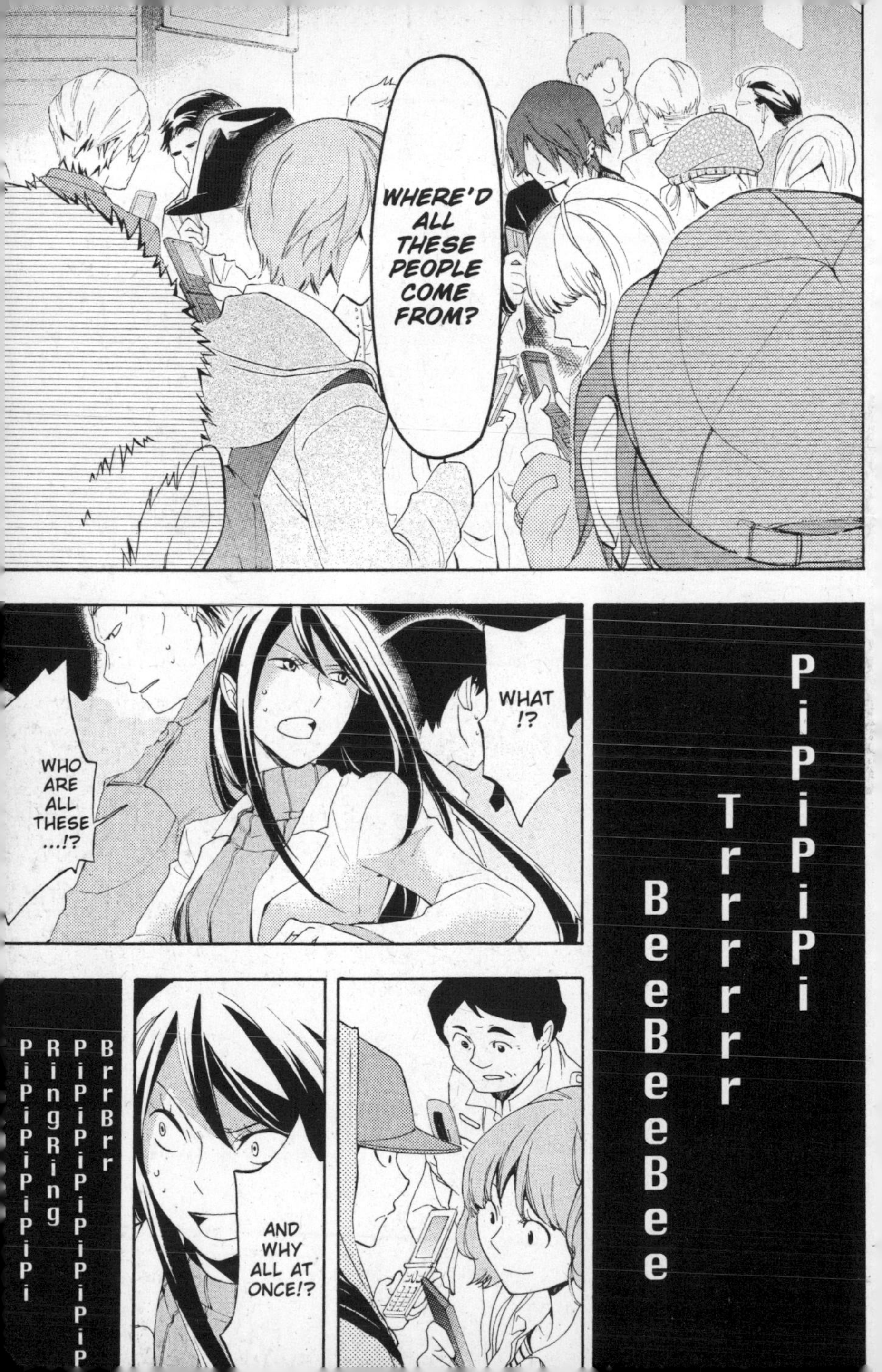
WHERE'D ALL THESE PEOPLE COME FROM?
PiPiPiPi
Trrrrr
BeeBeeBee
WHAT!?
WHO ARE ALL THESE...!?
AND WHY ALL AT ONCE!?
BrrBrr
PiPiPiPiPiPiPiP
RingRing
PiPiPiPiPiPi

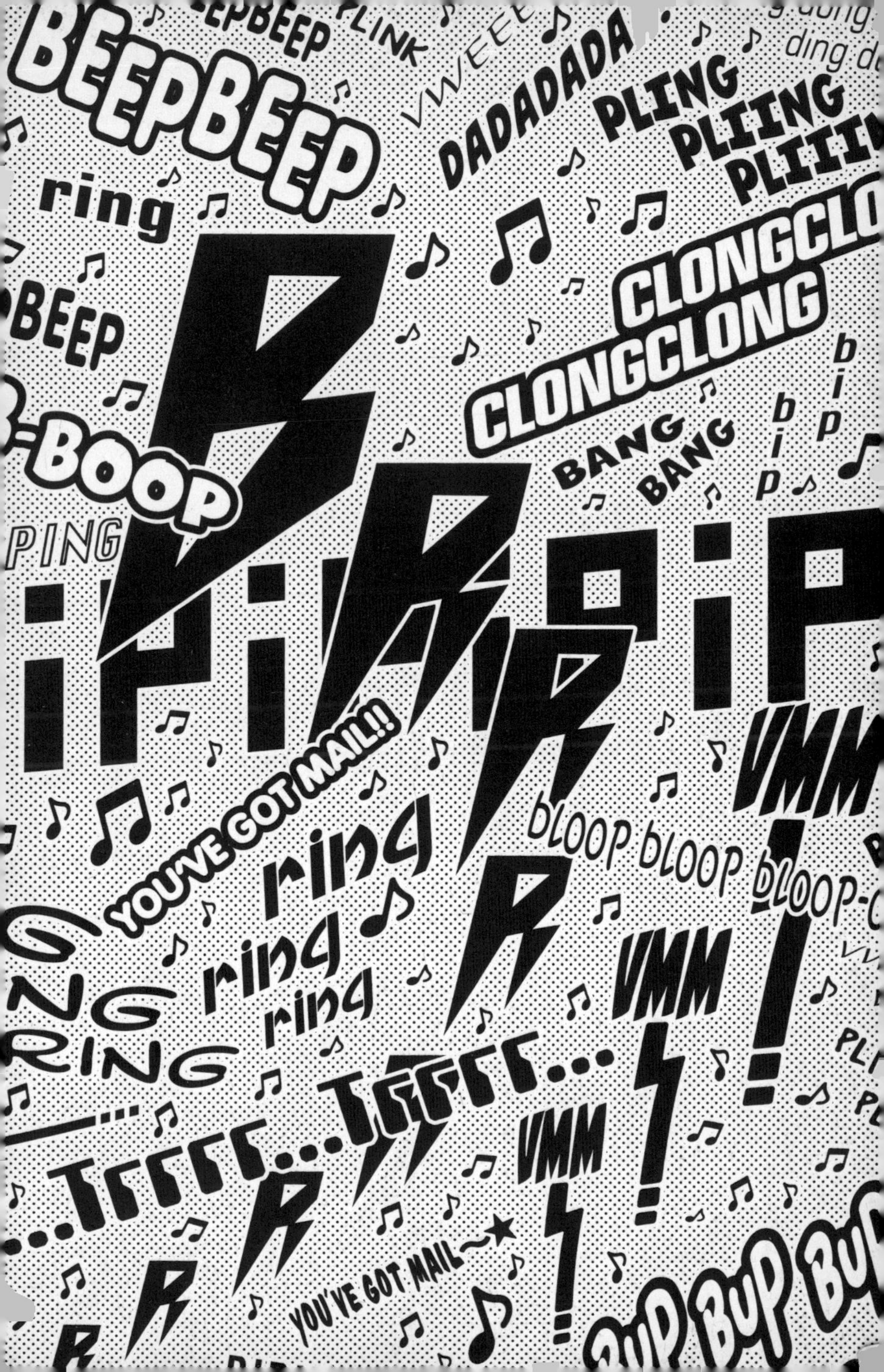

PLING
PLIING
DADADADA
PLINK
BEEPBEEP
ring
CLONGCLONG
BEEP
BOOP
bip
bip
BANG
BANG
PING
VMM
bloop bloop
YOU'VE GOT MAIL!!
ring
ring
ring
RING
VMM
VMM
YOU'VE GOT MAIL~★
BUP BUP

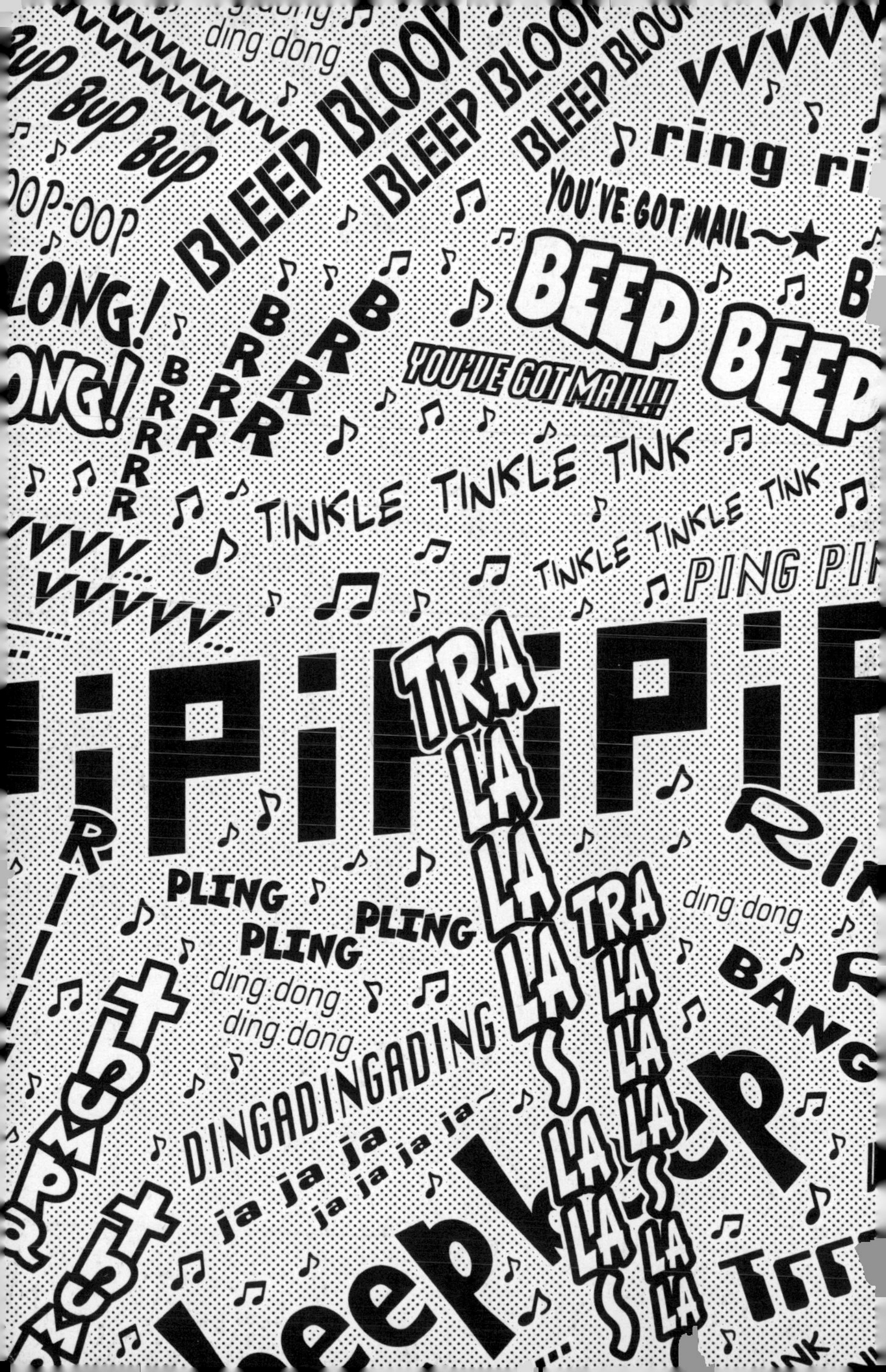
ding dong
BUP BUP BUP
BLEEP BLOOP
BLEEP BLOOP
BLEEP BLOOP
ring ri
YOU'VE GOT MAIL~★
BEEP BEEP
YOU'VE GOT MAIL!!
TINKLE TINKLE TINK
TINKLE TINKLE TINK
PING PI
TRA LA LA LA LA
TRA LA LA LA LA LA
PLING
PLING
PLING
ding dong
ding dong
ding dong
DINGADINGADING
BANG
ja ja ja ja~
ja ja ja ja~

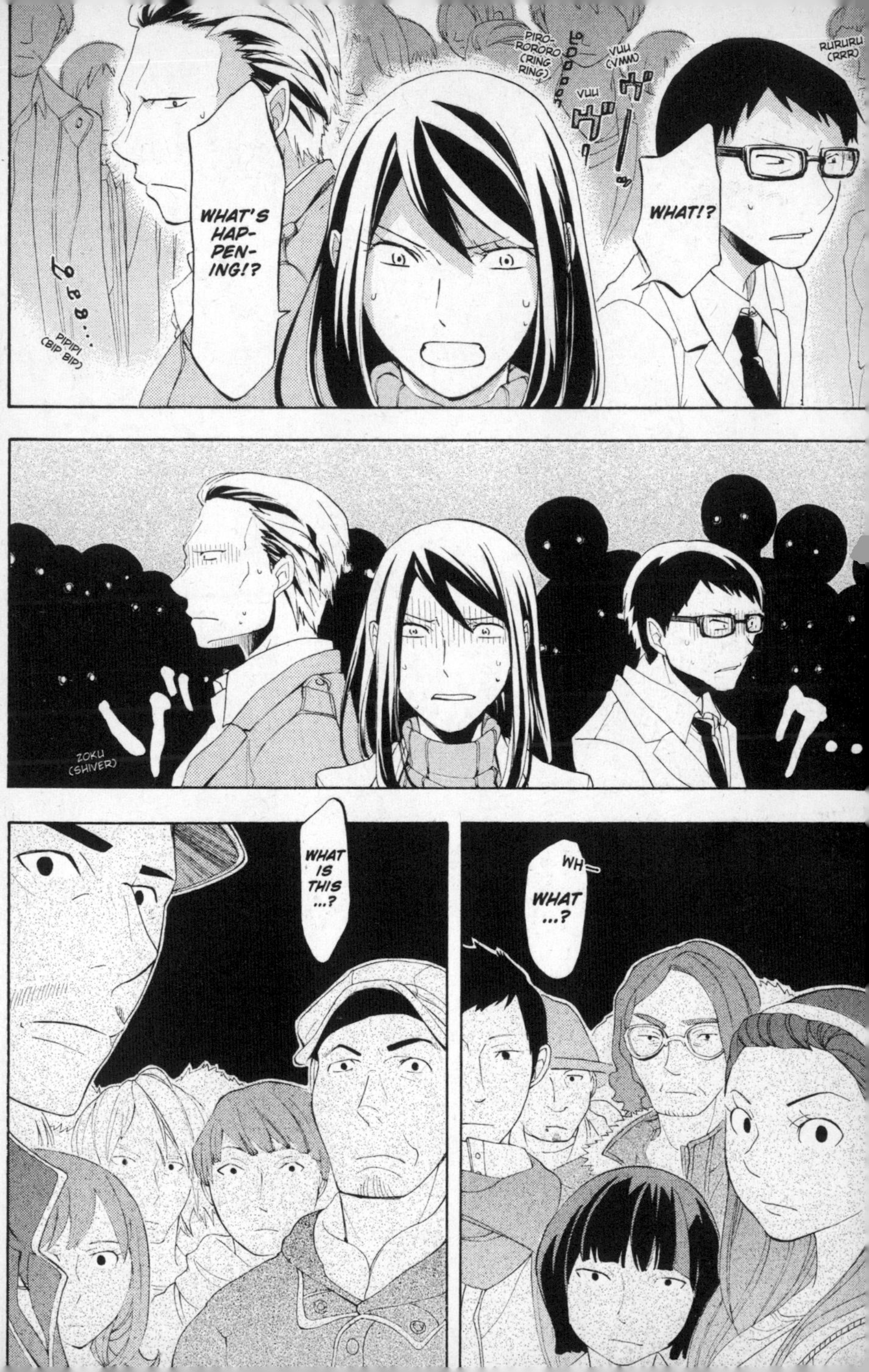
RURURU (RRR)
WHAT!?
VUU (VMM)
VUU
PIRO-ROROR (RING RING)
WHAT'S HAP-PEN-ING!?
PIPIPI (BIP BIP)
ZOKU (SHIVER)
WH— WHAT ...?
WHAT IS THIS ...?

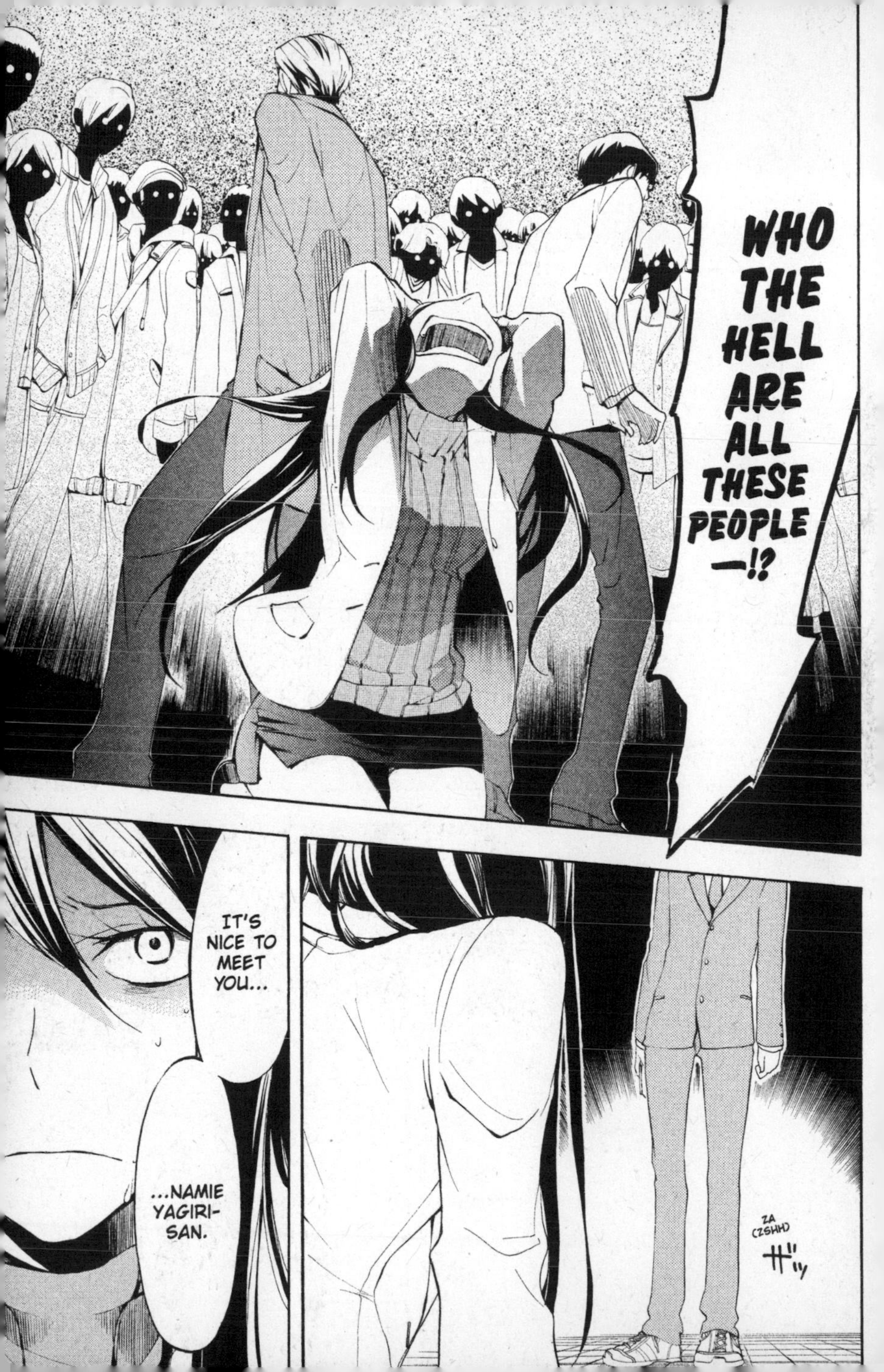
WHO THE HELL ARE ALL THESE PEOPLE—!?
ZA (ZSHH)
IT'S NICE TO MEET YOU...
...NAMIE YAGIRI-SAN.

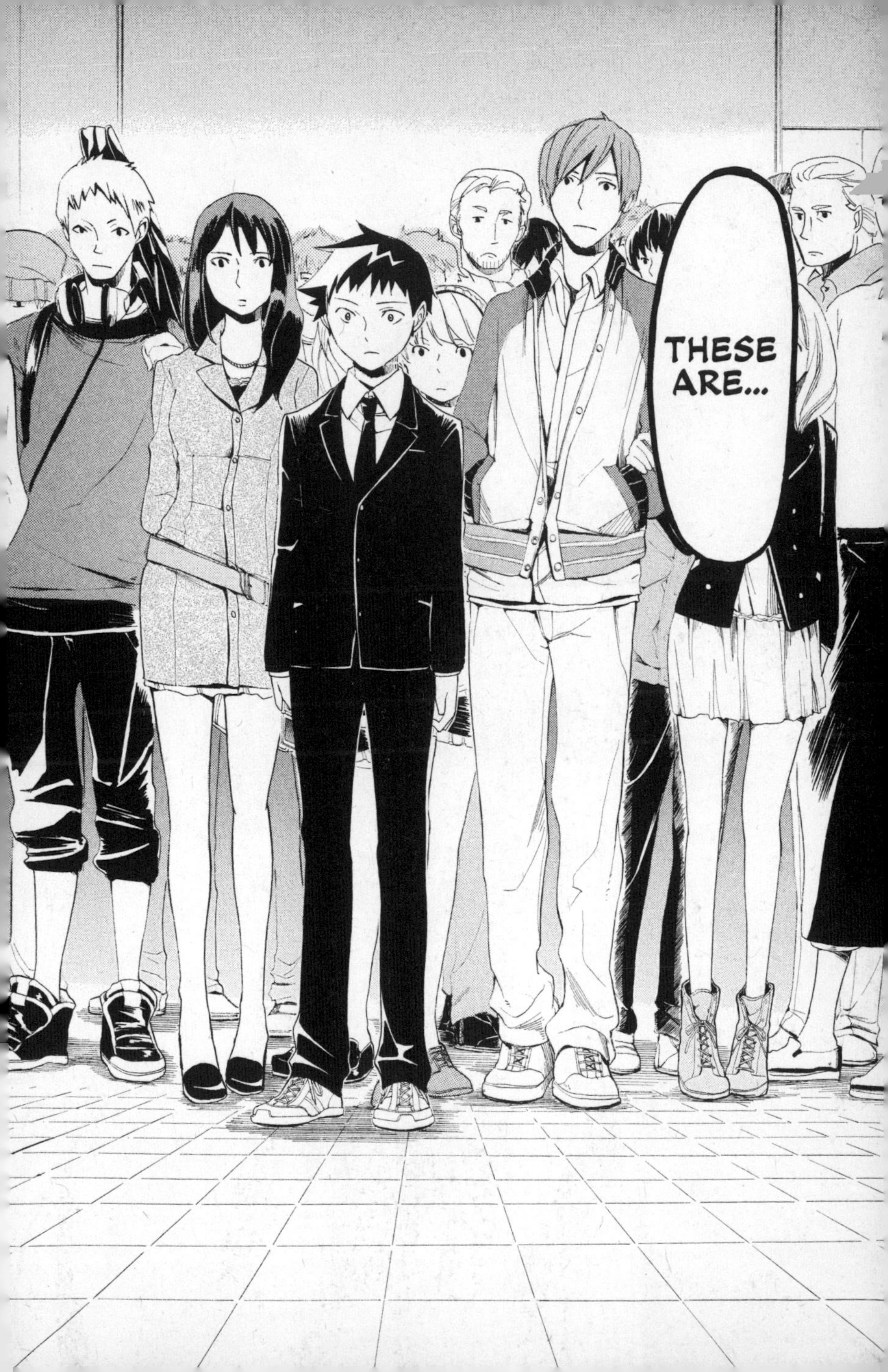
THESE ARE...

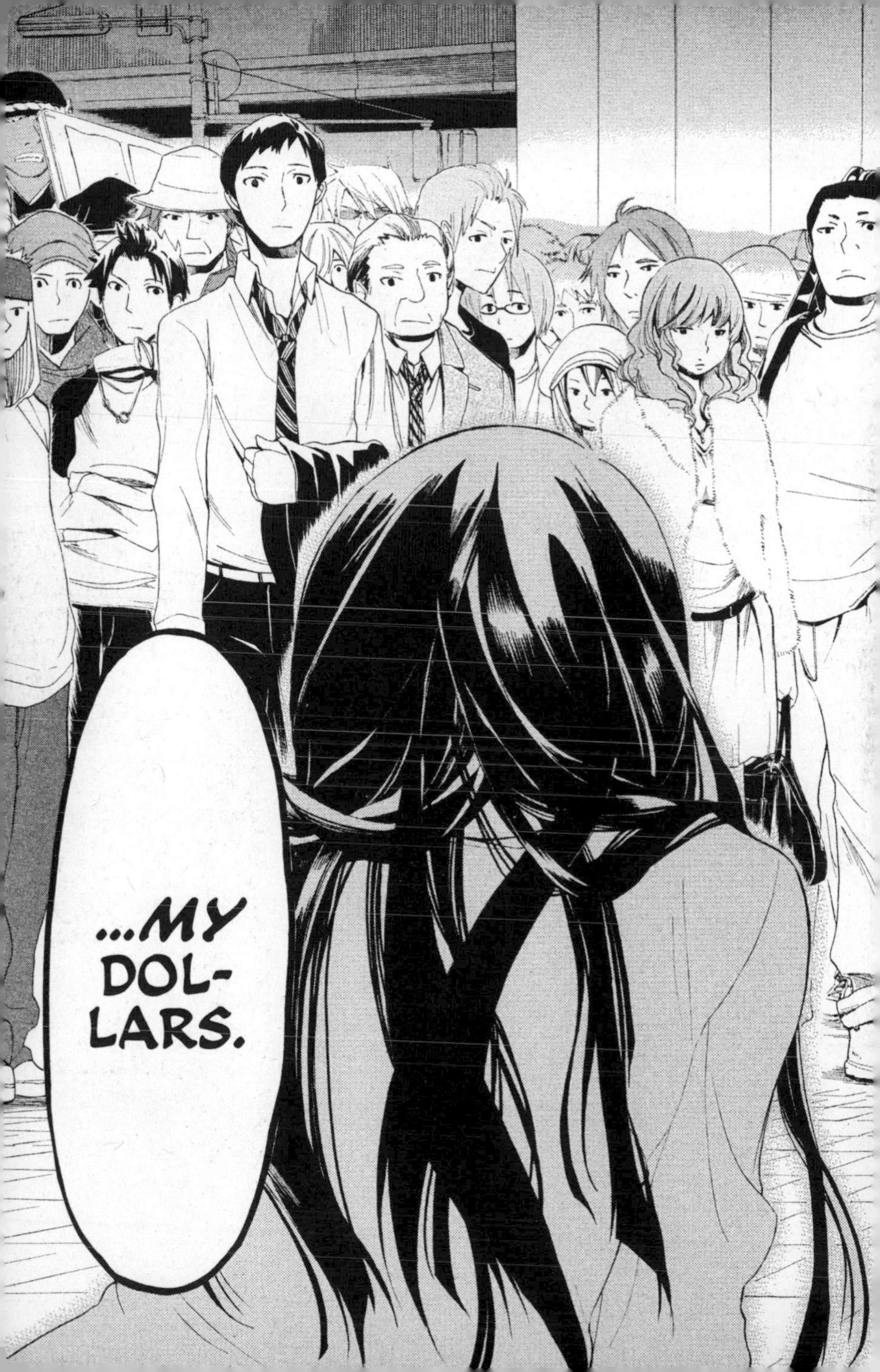
...MY DOL-LARS.

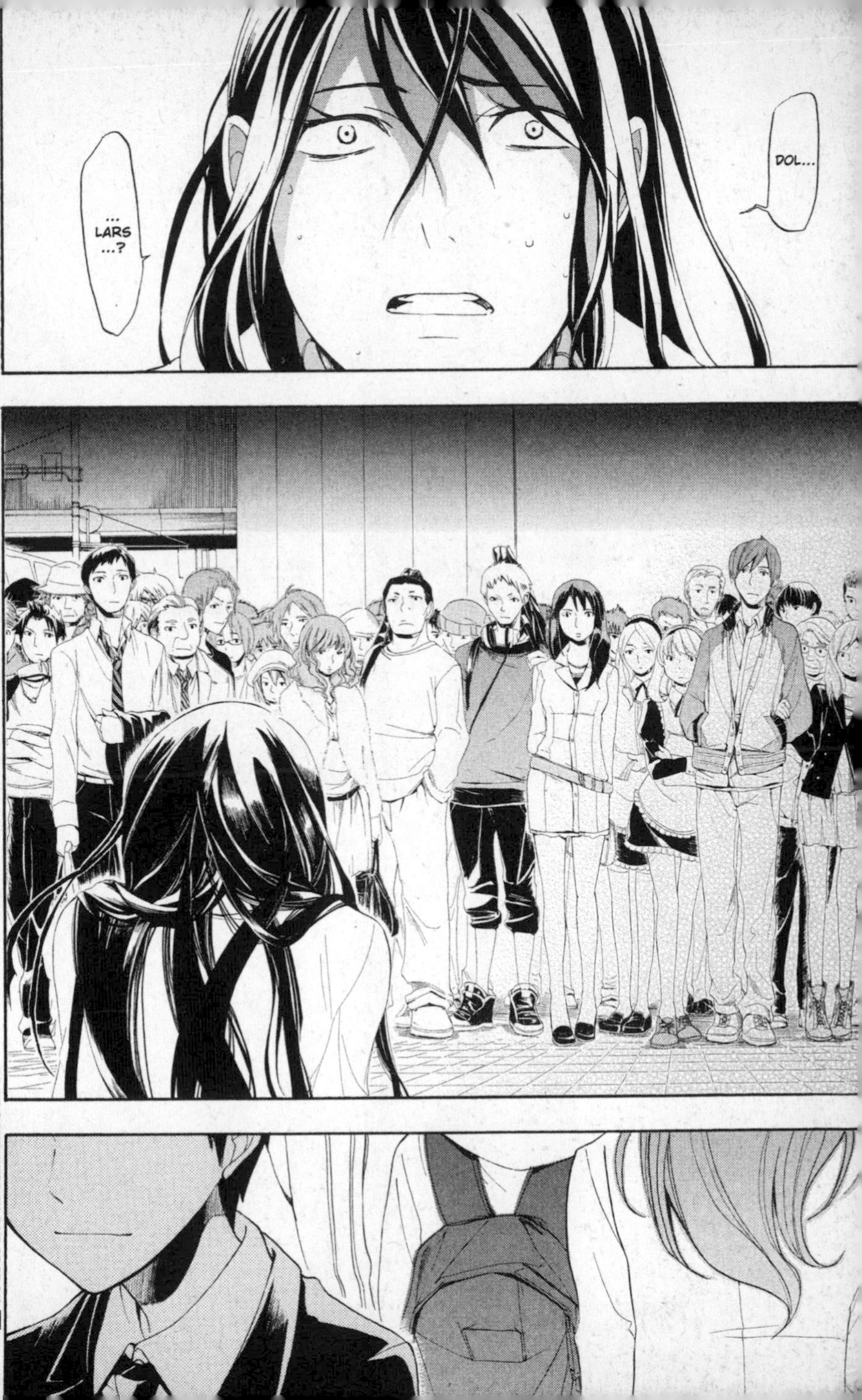
DOL...
...LARS ...?

TO BE CONTINUED IN DURARARA!! 4

TRANSLATION NOTES

PAGE 8
The guy who least lives up to his name in town:
Shizuo Heiwajima's given name means "peaceful hero," and his family name means "tranquil island." It's ironic, given Shizuo's violent tendencies.

PAGE 41
Razzie Award: The Golden Raspberry Awards, or "Razzies," are a tongue-in-cheek counterpart to the Academy Awards designed to highlight the worst films of the year rather than the best. Though many "winners" avoid the ignominy of the actual awards show, some directors and actors have proudly appeared in person to accept their trophies.

PAGE 53
There's no accounting for taste: The original saying in Japanese that corresponds to this English idiom literally reads, "Some insects actually like to eat water pepper." The plant known as water pepper (*tade* in Japanese) is a waterside plant with an acidic, bitter taste generally unsuited for people or livestock. Celty's original objection to the line was due to her being compared to an unpleasant weed.

PAGE 60
Miss Tery Girl: The name on the imaginary blackboard (representing the scene of the new student introducing herself to the class) reads "Nazono Bijo," spelled with characters that resemble common Japanese surnames. However, with different characters the name would mean "Mysterious Beauty."

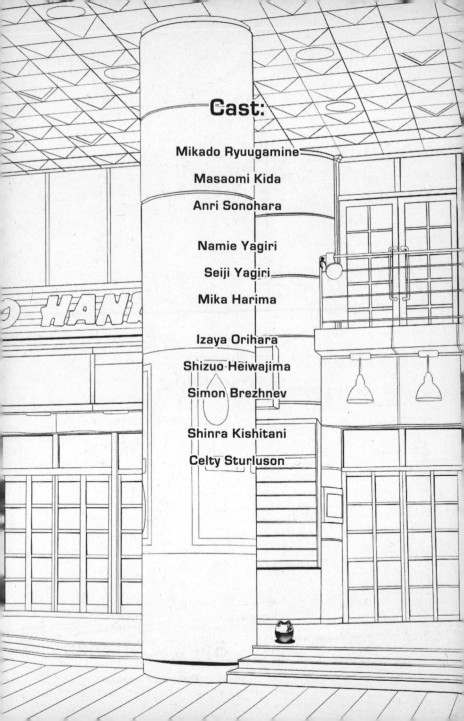

Cast:

Mikado Ryuugamine

Masaomi Kida

Anri Sonohara

Namie Yagiri

Seiji Yagiri

Mika Harima

Izaya Orihara

Shizuo Heiwajima

Simon Brezhnev

Shinra Kishitani

Celty Sturluson

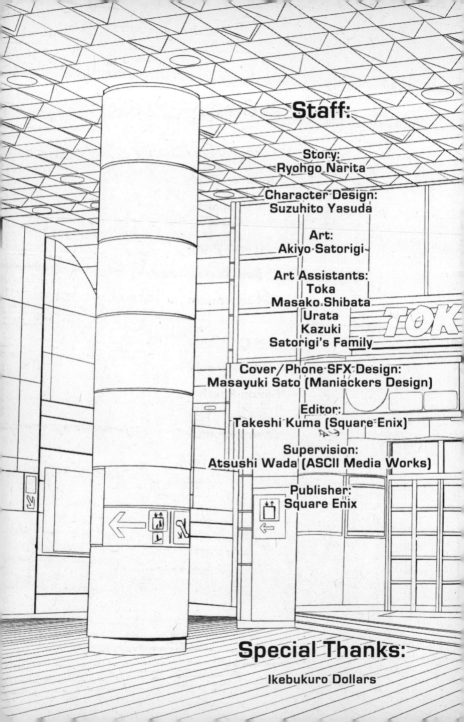

Staff:

Story:
Ryohgo Narita

Character Design:
Suzuhito Yasuda

Art:
Akiyo Satorigi

Art Assistants:
Toka
Masako Shibata
Urata
Kazuki
Satorigi's Family

Cover/Phone SFX Design:
Masayuki Sato (Maniackers Design)

Editor:
Takeshi Kuma (Square Enix)

Supervision:
Atsushi Wada (ASCII Media Works)

Publisher:
Square Enix

Special Thanks:

Ikebukuro Dollars

Illustration: Graphite Mon ster

Hello, nice to see you again! I am Ryohgo Narita, the so-called "creator" of this mixed-media project called *Durarara!!*

The fact that we've reached a third volume is thanks to Satorigi-san's fantastic art, the efforts of our editor Kuma-san and the rest of the *GFantasy* staff, and of course, the support of all you readers! Thank you so much!

The anime has finished its original run, but it's still showing on Tokyo MX and is available streaming on the PS3 and other platforms, so check those out and get the DVDs! (The complete *Durarara!!* anime series is now available on DVD from Aniplex in the US!)

...And now I'll lay off on the ads before I get yelled at for turning my afterword into a commercial...

The manga is currently leading up to the conclusion of the first novel, and as a reader, I can't wait to see how this will be presented! I think that novels, comics, and anime each have their own brand of direction. As you saw in this third volume, the scene in which Mikado describes running into the girl with the scar on her neck appears in a unique and comical style, and this blast of creativity was so funny, I nearly spit out my tea laughing. This is a good example of a piece of direction you cannot achieve with a novel.

Because of these differences, it's possible for me to enjoy my own story in manga and anime form as if it's a new experience, and likewise, people who first read the manga can find the novel version just as fresh and exciting a take from their perspective.

...On the other hand, there's also the unpleasant possibility that a manga reader could come to the novels and say, "How come such a beautiful manga has such a crappy, substandard novel?"—a thought that keeps me up at night, I assure you.

Of course, it's the quality of this mixed-media project that makes this thought so uneasy. In the afterword of Volume 1, I wrote that the three versions of novel, anime, and manga were a three-sided spiral drill. It was true, and now I'm terrified of the idea that the anime and manga are looking back, saying, "Hey, is the novel's engine even running?"

There are scenes original to the manga, such as the milk splashing Anri's face and the bathing scene with Seiji and his sister, that make me, the original author, curse myself—"Why the hell didn't I write that scene in the first place?" But the fact that these adaptations are good enough to elicit that emotion fills me with gratitude each and every month.

"Aaaargh, this is so much better than my novel! Damn you...damn you, Satorigi-san, and thank you! Wh...when's the next chapter!?"

So with that, I'll take my leave. I hope you continue to read Satorigi-san's take on *Durarara!!*

Ryohgo Narita

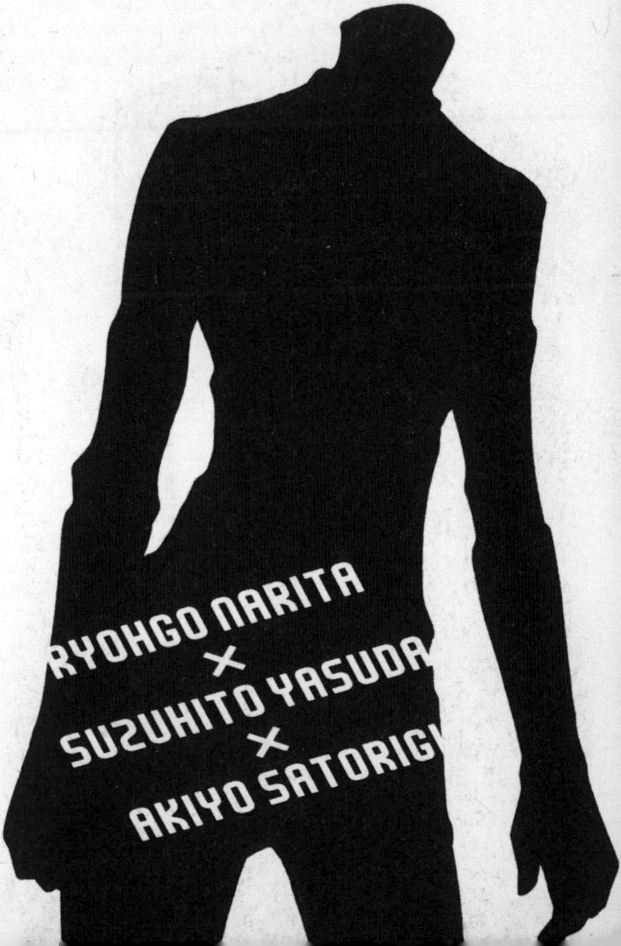
RYOHGO NARITA
×
SUZUHITO YASUDA
×
AKIYO SATORIGI

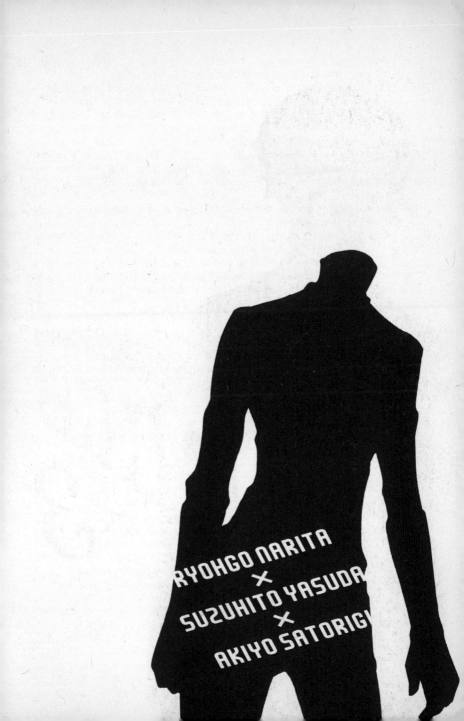

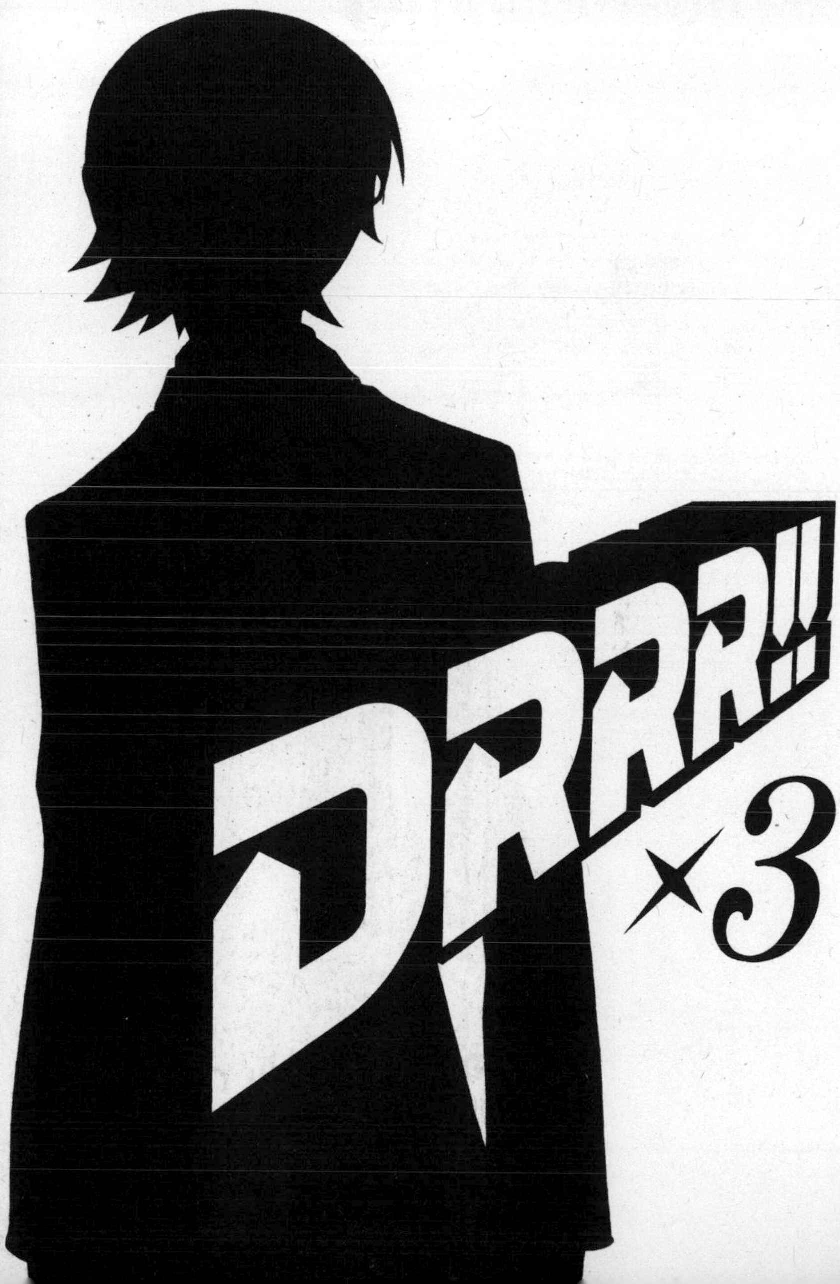
DRRR!!
×3

DURARAI

SUZUHITO YASUDA
AKIYO SATORIGI

Translation: Stephen Paul

Lettering: Lys Blakeslee

DURARARA!! Vol. 3 © Ryohgo Narita / ASCII MEDIA WORKS
© 2010 Akiyo Satorigi / SQUARE ENIX CO., LTD. All rights reserved. First published in Japan in 2010 by SQUARE ENIX CO., LTD. English translation rights arranged with SQUARE ENIX CO., LTD. and Hachette Book Group through Tuttle-Mori Agency, Inc.

Translation © 2012 by SQUARE ENIX CO., LTD.

Yen Press
Hachette Book Group
237 Park Avenue, New York, NY 10017

www.HachetteBookGroup.com
www.YenPress.com

Yen Press is an imprint of Hachette Book Group, Inc. The Yen Press name and logo are trademarks of Hachette Book Group, Inc.

First Yen Press Edition: July 2012

ISBN: 978-0-316-20932-8

10 9 8 7 6 5 4 3 2 1

BVG

Printed in the United States of America